LADY MARY WORTLEY MONTAGU

ESSAYS AND POEMS

AND

SIMPLICITY, A COMEDY

T H E
Nonfenfe of Common-Senfe.

To be Continued as long as the Author thinks fit, and the Publick likes it.

FRIDAY, DECEMBER 16, 1737.

PROVERBS i. 4.

To give Subtilty to the Simple, to the young Man Knowledge and Difcretion.

HE Title of this Paper would appear very abfurd, if thefe Words, *Common-Senfe*, were to be now underftood in the fame Manner they were left Chriftmas, when they were fuppofed to mean that low Degree of Underftanding, which directed a reafonable Man in the Conduct of his ordinary Affairs; for as to all Projectors and Reformers in Politicks, under whatever Shape they appeared, they were never believed to be under the Guidance of *Common-Senfe*. But thefe poor Words have fince been applied very differently; they now mean a certain Paper with many Flights and fenfible Reafon, that is handed about at Coffee-Houfes and Tea-Tables, for the Amufement of the Idle, the Entertainment of the Malicious, and the Aftonifhment of the Ignorant, who are very numerous in this Part of the World.

Out of a real Compaffion for thefe poor People, and being as fenfible as the Author himfelf,

June, and is fure to end in *September*. —— The other *nine* Months I would have them appear in a Habit that does Honour to their own Country, and would be an univerfal Benefit to the Nation.

—— The Gentry would feel it in the Payment of their Rents, and the Tenants in the Sale of their Wool. —— And, what fhould touch our pretty female Hearts, I can affure them it would be highly advantageous to their Complexions. —— Many cold Faces I have feen at an *Opera*, that in fpite of *Venus* and *Praxiteles*, and disfigured with Red Tips of Nofes, would have had an agreeable Glow of natural Heat, if their Bodies had been covered with the warm Produce of our native Sheep.

I do not doubt but the Encouragement of the Woollen Trade had fome Share in his Majefty's Confideration, together with the Refpect juftly due to the Memory of his beloved Confort. —— The Covering of the Coaches with Black Cloth will be a fenfible Benefit to the Clothiers, and the Expence only fall on thofe who can afford it. —— No Man is compelled to keep an Equipage; and if there be any Poor that cannot lowfully afford to pay for it, I think he may

it dropp'd, and the Sheriffs were left to do as they pleafed.

On Thurfday the 8th Inftant both Houfes of Parliament met at Weftminfter, purfuant to their laft Prorogation, and were (by Virtue of a Commiffion fign'd by his Majefty, directed to the Rt. Hon. the Lord Chancellor, the Right Hon. the Earl of Wilmington, Prefident of his Majefty's Council; his Grace the Duke of Dorfet, Lord Steward of his Majefty's Houfhold, and others) further prorogued to Tuefday the 24th of January next.

The fame Day two Writs pafs'd the Great Seal for the further Prorogation of the Convocations of Canterbury and York, which ftood prorogu'd to the 9th Inftant, to the 10th of February next.

The next Day in the Evening was iffued his Majefty's Royal Proclamation, for calling the Parliament to meet on Tuefday the 24th Day of January next at Weftminfter, then and there to fit for the Difpatch of divers weighty and important Affairs.

The Right Hon. the Earl of Ila, one of the Sixteen Peers of Scotland, is appointed Lord

Lady Mary Wortley Montagu

ESSAYS AND POEMS

AND

SIMPLICITY, A COMEDY

EDITED BY

ROBERT HALSBAND

AND

ISOBEL GRUNDY

CLARENDON PRESS · OXFORD

*This book has been printed digitally and produced in a standard specification
in order to ensure its continuing availability*

OXFORD
UNIVERSITY PRESS

Great Clarendon Street, Oxford OX2 6DP

Oxford University Press is a department of the University of Oxford.
It furthers the University's objective of excellence in research, scholarship,
and education by publishing world-wide in

Oxford New York

Auckland Bangkok Buenos Aires Cape Town Chennai
Dar es Salaam Delhi Hong Kong Istanbul Karachi Kolkata
Kuala Lumpur Madrid Melbourne Mexico City Mumbai Nairobi
São Paulo Shanghai Taipei Tokyo Toronto

Oxford is a registered trade mark of Oxford University Press
in the UK and in certain other countries

Published in the United States
by Oxford University Press Inc., New York

ISBN 0-19-812288-8

Antony Rowe Ltd., Eastbourne

PREFACE TO THE
PAPERBACK REPRINT

IT is fifteen years since the first edition of these *Essays and Poems* appeared, and therefore getting on for 300 years since Lady Mary Wortley Montagu first saw her writing in print (anonymously: readers of that *Spectator* essay of 1714 no doubt assumed it to be by Addison or Steele, or perhaps by one of their gentlemen associates). It is nearly 200 years since Lady Mary's descendants, the then Marquess of Bute and Earl of Wharncliffe, with several other interested parties, were deep in debate about a projected first edition of her *Works*. Like the *Spectator* regulars, these heirs and guardians of her reputation were all male; they planned a proper, family-sanctioned edition of her writings which was provoked by, and designed to nip in the bud, plans for more opportunistic and commercial publication. It is, alas, over three years since Robert Halsband died, who would have rejoiced to see a paperback edition extend her readership more widely.

Like others of her time, sex, and class, Lady Mary wrote firstly for her relations and intimate friends. But consistently, from her teens to the last year of her life, she sought a wider audience. Her first readership, a coterie of adolescent girls, spanned a surprising social range, from daughters of great dukes to daughters of provincial attorneys. She titled her manuscript volume of those days 'The Entire Works of Clarinda'; she annotated her critique of Addison's *Cato* (1712): 'Wrote at the Desire of Mr. Wortley, suppress'd at the desire of Mr. Adison'. Returning as a dying woman to England, she gave her own MS of her Embassy Letters to the Revd Mr Sowden. He was her last hope for making them public, in case the copyists she had already encouraged should fail to do so. She made no mistake in judging that her family would prefer them to remain unknown: her daughter was to treasure in secret her mother's lifelong diary, but eventually to burn it.

Today she belongs primarily to her readers. Very, very few of those readers share her class, and perhaps a minority share her nationality. Probably the greater number share her gender, and probably most of that majority share her feminism, or would at least like to believe that our own feminism can put us in touch with her writings and with her thought.

Lady Mary's thought, however, is less accessible than selected quotations might easily suggest. On the one hand it is highly idiosyncratic, delighting in paradox and the unexpected; on the other hand it is deeply coloured by her precise, and now fairly remote, socio-political position (as a noblewoman and an Old Whig, born in the first months of the Glorious Revolution), and by her extraordinary life-experience as courtier, traveller, and recluse, medical pioneer and political journalist, and by her equally extraordinary range of experiences as a woman (as runaway bride, disappointed mother, guardian sister; as victim and as demonized scapegoat; as headlong lover, separated wife, absent grandmother). She is a feminist with strong ties of reverence to patriarchal culture, an iconoclast with aristocratic prejudices, a figure in English literature who conducted much of her reading, writing, and friendship in languages other than English.

Even naming her presents a problem. The title 'Lady' (assigned to the daughters of earls or above) is of the kind which replaces the formal 'Miss' or 'Mrs', and makes it correct for strangers or social inferiors as well as friends to use the Christian-name. Lady Mary's surname from the date of her marriage was Wortley Montagu (sometimes shortened to Wortley, but not, in England, to Montagu), because her Montagu father-in-law had married the Wortley heiress. The socially correct 'Lady Mary' sounds right to eighteenth-century scholars, but to others it may sound either over-familiar or obsequious, suggesting a historical novel. In critical discourse 'Montagu' sounds right—although it violates eighteenth-century usage, encourages confusion of her with the bluestocking Elizabeth Montagu (with whom she had almost nothing in common except cousinship by marriage), and elides difference, concealing the gulf which divides her from the modern scholar, feminist, or professional writer. I shall try here, somewhat experimentally, to alternate these two less-than-satisfactory names according to context, using generally 'Lady Mary' for the woman and 'Montagu' for the author.

Formed as she is by her material circumstances, Montagu's works are not so much explained as rendered yet more extra-ordinary by a more detailed knowledge of her period and milieu. Her writing is consistent in no one thing but in challenging the assumptions around her. When I say her writing, I mean of course that which survives: the component of challenge is not likely to have been any less in what she or her heirs destroyed.

Like many authors, not all of them women, she wrote much which has not come down to us. Those texts which are *known* to be lost include the diary, burned for exposing its author's lack of Christian charity; her 'History of her Own Times', which—if her statement to her daughter can be believed—she destroyed as fast as she finished it, in a sustained, heroic act of self-censorship; and an unknown, unreckonable number of letters and short works. Many of these, probably not all in English, must have dated from her twenty-year sojourn in France and Italy: in 1758 she seems to take for granted her identity as a writer, yet also says: 'All my works are consecrated to the fire for fear of being put to more ignoble uses' (*Letters*, 3. 170, 173, 183). The appearance in 1980 of four previously unknown poems is a tantalizing reminder that new discoveries of her work always remain possible.

Because of her writing's close involvement with her life and with her changing milieu, I believe (despite the quantity which is undated and undatable) that a chronological approach to it is useful. This very brief survey of her achievement will follow the known stages of her writing, discussing the most salient general issues as they arise.

From the years before her marriage (at 23) there survives her largest coherent or homogenous body of poetry (dating from her mid-teens), her longest foray into prose fiction, and her longest, most ambitious translation. This work (none of it included here) favours genres particularly associated with women writers: the poems follow in the footsteps of Katherine Philips (as well as those of Abraham Cowley); the fiction (which is amatory and epistolary) in those of Aphra Behn. Whether or not Lady Mary knew of the achievements of such outstanding Renaissance translators as Ann Bacon, she would have known of the gendering of translation as a female—because ancillary—enterprise.

The family library where Lady Mary Pierrepont laboured at self-education was a remarkable one (the first private English library to achieve, fourteen years after her marriage and departure, a printed catalogue). Predictably, it was rich in texts, both original and translated, of the ancients like Homer, Virgil, Ovid, and Horace, the last of whom Lady Mary was to imitate and translate with *brio* herself (below, pp. 265–70, 302, 310–11). It offered an equally thorough grounding in the moderns, from More and Bacon to Dryden and Locke. It even included a few women writers, though in a skimpy and haphazard manner: nothing by Katherine Philips, but three volumes by Margaret Cavendish, Duchess of Newcastle. Madeleine de Scudéry is unlisted, though included: her works appear under her brother's name. Works by Marie-Catherine d'Aulnoy appear under three entirely different spellings of her name, and under the title of one of them. Aphra Behn appears under titles only.

Lady Mary's youthful network of scribbling friends included Mary (Molesworth) Monck, whose poems were soon to achieve print (and a place in the library)—but only through the combination of Monck's early death and her grieving father's pride in her. Since Lady Mary submitted her prose translation of Epictetus to Bishop Burnet, she may have been dreaming of publication, but she did not say this in her suitably demure and non-assertive covering letter about women's education. Her 'Indamora to Lindamira' (five letters from Indamora only) answers the anonymous *Adventures of Lindamira* (1702; letters from Lindamira only). It compares well in quality with its original, which went on being reprinted till 1751. Her early poetry is equally responsive and experimental. Writing sometimes as 'Strephon', sometimes as 'Clarinda', she employs a range of typical late seventeenth-century forms, praising friendship, the countryside, true love, and the renunciation of ambition. But she questions every convention she uses: friendship by poems of reproach to an inconstant friend, 'murmuring Groves' and civil shepherds by 'Bleak drowned plains' and 'awkard Swains', love and retirement by the recognition that neither a partner nor a path of life would be open for her to choose for herself.

When she snatched the choice from her father's hands by eloping with Edward Wortley Montagu, Lady Mary must surely have counted his friendship with Addison and Steele as one of his recommendations. It was not long before she followed up this link to the world of visible authorship, in the critique of Addison's *Cato* which, since she calls it suppressed, she surely wished to publish (below, pp. 62–8). Like her letter to Burnet three years before, it is a virtuoso piece, suggesting the work of the best graduate students in its determination to demonstrate wide and also esoteric consultation of respected authorities as context to its solid element of independent critical judgement.

In the early years of her marriage, especially the *annus mirabilis* (twenty months, in fact) that she spent in London between Queen Anne's death and her first departure from England, her intellectual and literary development was rapid. It is easy to read this development as extending critique as well as technique, ideology as well as skill. In verse she advanced from polished work in slightly old-fashioned styles to her town eclogues, whose brilliance and incisiveness justifies their continuing position as her best-known poems. In prose she advanced from her analysis of *Cato*, which keeps within approved generic guide-lines, to her startlingly original and outrageous *Spectator* essay (below, pp. 69–74), which ignores all the models on offer for writing about women (prescription, condemnation, or sentimental sympathy; feminine ideal, satiric butt, or candidate for reform), to present a first-person narrative of female progress from victim to successful player of the system, a forerunner of Jane Austen's Lady Susan without the malice.

Other *Spectator* papers approach marriage as a topic in morality; this one approaches it as a topic in business. It is out of step with its surroundings, ill-geared to its readership. One might imagine its ideal readers to be the lively circle of Lady Mary Pierrepont: girls looking at prospective marriage transactions from the sharp end, who had found the *Tatler* dull but enjoyed the scandal-fiction of Delarivier Manley. Montagu's authorship remained unguessed years later, when intimates of Samuel Johnson looked back at the considerable reputation once conferred by having written a single *Spectator* number;[1] but in debating the brilliance of particular essays, these readers would never have considered the tale of a woman playing the marriage market and winning. The topic, like the author, had low visibility.

At some unknown date, Montagu matched her *Spectator* essay's narrative authority, moral *laissez-faire*, and psychological acuity in writing of another arena of power: court politics. Her 'Account of the Court of George I' (below, pp. 82–94) has had more attention, because of its contribution to historical knowledge. But (like the

---

[1] Arthur Murphy, quoted in James Boswell, *Life of Samuel Johnson*, ed. G. B. Hill and L. F. Powell (Oxford: Clarendon, 1934), iii. 33.

essay, though for different reasons) it was a piece whose potential
for appreciative contemporary reception was limited: to be known
as its author would have put an end to Lady Mary's successful
career as a courtier. Her way of life in the years 1714–16 offered
more opportunities for becoming known as a poet than as a writer
of the kinds of prose she seems to have been attempting.

Her dateable poetry from this period begins with the ideologically impeccable 'Written . . . in a Glass Window the first year I was
marry'd' (below, p. 179). This reads like a distillation of her future
husband's reiterated advice to her during courtship: female vanity
and 'loose Advance[s]' are to blame for male amatory conquests,
and a properly virtuous woman effortlessly forestalls not only
scandal but also occasion for scandal; in woman lies the power to
control male sexuality.

Within a couple of years Lady Mary was deep in literary activity
with her socially inferior contemporaries Alexander Pope and John
Gay. Pope's *Rape of the Lock*, in its first version (1712), had
launched the new mock form in which the modern, the advanced,
the self-conscious, urban, and courtly related itself to the ancient,
the revered, the bucolically or martially primitive. Town eclogues
by Montagu and Gay retain this balance, while Gay's longer
works give it a significant nudge towards either the bucolic or the
urban.

Montagu seems to have begun writing her eclogues (below, pp.
182–204) with 'Monday'. In this she made the mistake of overstep-
ping her audience's irony threshold (like Defoe in *The Shortest
Way with the Dissenters*), and was read as satirizing Princess
Caroline when her actual butt was the Princess's uncomprehend-
ing and morally disapproving attendant. 'Friday' too presents a
slightly blurred focus in Montagu's version (in H MS 256, the
volume which she annotated, 'wrote by me, without the assistance
of one Line from any other'). Gay's different but overlapping
version is clearer, but presents a less complex subjectivity. (Forty-
three lines—slightly less than half of hers, slightly more than half
of his—are common to both versions, and were presumably jointly
composed.) Gay presents the straightforward pathos of an older
woman robbed by a younger of the sweets of love. Montagu looks
sceptically on those sweets. Her ageing beauty, dropped by her
lover, lashes out on the one hand against his equally ageing wife,
and on the other against the servitude of marriage: but the single

state and marital state as she depicts them are so much each other's mirror-image as to be almost indistinguishable.[2]

'Wednesday' too is ideologically opaque, though its structure is simple enough. A protestation in defence of chaste and purely sentimental love is unmasked at its end as spoken not by a virgin but by a married woman. Is Montagu's target the disproportion between the woman's sentimental words and the man's lewd intentions? This is the case in two separate alternative endings (one transcribed in Pope's copy), in which the man finally brings the woman round to his point of view. But Montagu rejected both of these. Is she then satirizing the fiction of feminine sexlessness, or the idea that infidelity is unexceptionable if it remains 'in the head'? Or is the delicate, even moving plea for sentiment rather than appetite (which she was to reformulate years later in non-ironical contexts) perhaps *not* wholly undercut by coming from the lips of a woman who is deceiving her husband? Or has Dancinda's predicament no detachable moral at all?

The remaining eclogues, those added to the series after the drama and trauma of unauthorized exposure of the earlier ones in print, avoid this kind of uncertainty. 'Tuesday' and 'Thursday' take the traditional form of the competitively boasting dialogue: in the former, two gentlemen compare amatory conquests; in the latter, two ladies compare, as objects of desire, the pastime of love (not competitive score-counting, but physical as well as emotional thrill) with that of gambling. 'Satturday', whose autobiographical basis Lady Mary later admitted (both in conversation and by quoting from it in a poem of personal feeling), stands in the place of the traditional closing eclogue on somebody's death. But the loss it laments is not that of life but that of beauty, which, it implies, means social and emotional death for a woman. Here the equipoise between earnestness and irony is a fine one; yet the poem is hardly open to misreading. The mock-heroine with her arms (a mirror) reversed, as if for a funeral, has lost a Circean ability to change the statesman into a wooer, the wit into a fool. The loss is real and grievous, though the power (like the drawing power Pope gives Belinda's 'single hair') was 'mock' or ambiguous. Montagu's Flavia greets this loss of power with a passionate outcry which expresses her subjectivity in a way that Belinda's outcries do not;

[2] See Ann Messenger, 'Town Eclogues', *His and Hers: Essays in Restoration and Eighteenth-Century Literature* (Kentucky 1986), 84–107.

'Satturday' contains no Clarissa to dismiss such loss with the throwaway: 'Curl'd or uncurl'd, since locks *will* turn to grey' (*Rape*, 1717, ii. 28; v. 26).

My purpose in calling attention to difference here is to suggest that Lady Mary's eclogues have suffered critically from being classified as among her collaborations. Published attention to them has tended to focus on her intellectual and artistic exchange with (or discipleship to) Pope and Gay. Undoubtedly these men, and the sense of literary community which they provided, were crucial in the production of these six poems. But the evidence suggests that, during the time of composing them, Lady Mary was moving rapidly away from the other poets. The ambitions, dilemmas, and moral failings of the court circle engage her closely; her characters, female and male, are always criticized yet are never wholly contemptible or wholly ridiculous.

The next three years, spent by Lady Mary in travel through Europe and residence in Turkey, turned her powers of observation outwards and produced, in the 'Embassy Letters', her nearest approach to a published book. She remains a divided voice, taking time off from her extrovert letters for a poem, 'Constantinople' (written in the final weeks of pregnancy), which turns aside from rehearsing the splendours of geography, history, and politics to end with a prayer for retreat and sanctuary from the threatening world (below, pp. 206–10). The Turkish climate, flowers, landscape, the 'Frantic Derviche' and 'Vizier proud', offer the spectator pure pleasures of the imagination; they cannot touch or hurt her. The evils which this refuge excludes (mobs, flattery, 'Party rage', and personal slander) are obviously drawn from memories of England.

It is fitting that her first return from abroad should be marked by her 'Epitaph' (below, pp. 215–16) on the lovers struck by lightning, with which she replied to Pope's demand for a tribute of tears ('The finest minds . . . dissolve the easiest').[3] Her lines have been censured for heartlessness; but they deal in ideas, not feelings. Rebuke to received ideas is here, as often, her driving force. Poetic tributes, the tears of sensibility, the institution of marriage, and the belief in providence are her targets (rather than, as has been suggested, any aggrandisement of the lower orders).

---

[3] Pope, *Correspondence*, ed. George Sherburn (1956), i. 493–6.

The woman who wrote this poem was not one to live comfortably with early Georgian pieties and assumptions.

Probably the experience of registering and describing a society as Other as that of the Islamic empire fed Lady Mary's critique of English institutions. Apart from the 'Account of the Court of George I', she wrote such a critique in many forms during the 1720s: glittering, alienated letters to her exiled sister; personal and critical squibs stemming from her friendship with Pope (of which many, no doubt, remain unknown or unidentified); contentious political discourse which trespasses on masculine territory (like her smallpox essay); and poems on women's issues.

On these issues, which preoccupied her during this decade, her writings range from luminous and forceful exposition of feminist positions to two poems on an attempted rape (below, pp. 216–24), which are guaranteed to embarrass her feminist admirers. In the extraordinary 'Epistle From Arthur G[ra]y', the would-be rapist, a servant, is made to voice a plea for liberation of sexuality from social trammels; in 'Virtue in Danger' (a ballad which Montagu *probably* wrote), the whole affair is reduced to helter-skelter slapstick. It may be that biographical facts, now lost, might help to explain the poems. Griselda Murray, victim of the rape attempt, was separated from her husband, living with her parents, and known to have a lover. She was, or had been, a friend of Lady Mary; perhaps some other factors besides the poems contributed to their estrangement.

The ballad form as Montagu uses it was the preserve of party propagandists and street hawkers, not of minstrels or peasants. It lends itself to derogatory similes and *doubles entendres*: in later examples by her, opposition supporters become screech-owls and bats, and the Prince of Wales with his mistress becomes a puppy with a bottle tied on its tail. In 'Virtue in Danger' the most shocking image is one the lady uses to her menial would-be ravisher: ''Tis not for scoundrell Scrubs to wish | To tast their Master's Meat.' For her, it seems, rank is the only issue; she is content to be meat, so long as it is for a gentleman. She also postpones crying for help till after the footman has fled, and thinks more highly of him for his attempt. The ballad light-heartedly assumes the truth of a damaging 'rape myth': that rape is what women really want. Jovial, irresponsible, irresistibly funny, it is a fine example of the sort of writing which makes enemies.

The high-flown, romantic 'Epistle' endorses another rape myth: that women's powerful beauty is to blame for male violence, which occurs as 'The cruel Consequence of Furious Love'. Montagu's speaker is 'Tender, Faithfull, Ardent, and sincere'; he lacks only rank to make him acceptable. His address to Mrs Murray centres on his devoted, self-suppressive service, his jealousy of rich and powerful rivals, his despair (in the poem he acquires for suicide the weapons he then uses for threat), and his sense that his love *ought* to be reciprocated. The structure of this poem does not admit the female viewpoint which Montagu voices elsewhere, which questions the good faith of a man who 'ask[s] so boldly like a begging Theife' (below, p. 245). It is strange that this tale of force offered by manservant to lady should cause Lady Mary both to challenge the class barriers which she generally upholds, and to uphold the gender imbalance which she generally challenges.

Her choice of a persona so unlike herself is typical as well as extraordinary. Though she also wrote self-revealingly in both poetry and prose, she is fond of masquerading as her Other, from the shepherd 'Strephon' to the professional widow, from the eclogue courtiers to male practitioners of trades: Turkey merchant, Italian inventor, the poet Pope. She crosses and re-crosses gender barriers at a bound; even while speaking in a female voice, as in most of her poems about sex and marriage, she draws on ideas and language generally classed as 'masculine'.

The female speakers in these 1720s poems frequently venture into areas of feeling which social and literary convention sought to deny them, and which were to become wholly unacceptable a couple of generations later. Montagu's Mrs Yonge, a wife whose adultery has been searingly exposed by her equally unfaithful husband, demands: 'Are we not form'd with Passions like your own? . . . Our Minds as Haughty, and as warm our blood' (below, p. 231). Her fictionalized version of her fellow-poet Judith Cowper, later Madan, wavers between desiring and despising her unreciprocating suitor, and strives against the passion which makes her 'Contemn your Folly, yet adore your Eyes' (below, p. 229). Such passions had been voiced in poetry by a thousand male lovers, but never by a respectable, unmarried young lady, let alone one allegedly drawn from life.

These poems set out to explore multiple viewpoints rather than define a normative one; but complaint against men is a *leitmotif*. 'A

Man in Love' and 'The Lover', both fantasies of an impossible
ideal man, 'qui ne se trouve point, et ne se trouvera jamais' (below,
pp. 233–6), are addressed to Molly Skerrett, a confidential friend.
'The Lover', in which the speaker herself is a prominent character,
devotes some energy to contrasting her ideal with the uninspiring
candidates actually on offer. To one of these non-ideals, Sir Robert
Walpole, Skerrett was or would soon become mistress, a position
which was in itself an ironic comment on the poems' message.

On his own account Walpole was another in Lady Mary's circle
who offered her a stimulus for poetry. The occasional or the
opportunistic suited her talent, her capacity to create a new vision
by juxtaposition or switch of context. A girl's singing, deaths of the
loved or the famous, portraits, texts, chance encounters, were all
provocations to verse, as well as society's handling of sexual
feelings and gender relations. Mrs Yonge evokes protest; the
premature death of Mrs Bowes evokes a celebration (below,
p. 233) of the rapturous early months of marriage and an
excoriation of the painful succeeding years. (The message overlaps
with that of the 'Epitaph' on the lovers struck by lightning, but the
tone, vibrant with Mrs Bowes's presumed delight and evaded
misery, is quite different.) Fickleness in Lord Bathurst is handled
with urbane amusement; but this poem (below, pp. 242–4)
idealizes female constancy no less romantically than the 'Epistle
from Mrs. Y[onge]'.

Far from single- or simple-mindedly advocating gender reform,
Montagu writes poems, like letters, to reflect the flux and tran-
sience of responses in life. Her confusions emerge in her 'Epilogue
to a New Play of M[ary] Queen of Scots'. Traditionally, the
epilogue was a forum for cynicism and anti-idealism; traditionally,
stage villainesses gave voice to sexual passion. Montagu, whose
poems often attribute passion to respectable, sympathetic women,
and coldness to controlling, sexually exploiting men, here ascribes
masculine detachment to Queen Elizabeth, and pitiable female
passion to Queen Mary. But she admonishes Mary and other too-
feeling women to copy the monarch who denies her gender: 'Love
for Amusement like those Traitors, Men . . . Secure your Hearts,
then fool with who you will.'

Some points are oft-repeated in these poems, but consistency is
not sought. The poet whose 'The Lover' insists: 'I am not as cold
as a Virgin in lead', offers the fixity of her 'cold Marble Breast' as a

desirable converse to Bathurst's emotional flightiness. Only emotional susceptibility arouses her poetic response (whether in Arthur Gray or Mary Queen of Scots), yet she tends to advocate firm control of susceptibility. Her comment on the Queen of Scots might provide an epigraph for the whole group: 'What long Repentance to short Joys is due!' This is not moral advice but statement of fact: little is to be enjoyed, much endured. Even without this Johnsonian formulation, it is a very Augustan idea. What is unusual in Montagu's work is the intensity of the love opposed to reason, the pleasure opposed to repentance.

Outside the field of gender relations, writing of issues generally deemed to concern only men, she continued to divide the world into exploiters and idealists. The *Cato* critique shows her already seriously interested in party politics. Her earliest-known statement on public affairs, 'A Plain Account of Innoculating of the Small Pox' (below, pp. 95–7) is also her most daring. In writing as a 'Turkey Merchant' she anticipates Swift's *Drapier's Letters* technique of speaking from the middle ground socially; she deploys the authority of personal experience against medical learning (which at this date meant the theoretical rather than the practical); and she deliberately stresses those outlandish origins of inoculation (exotic, non-Christian, non-scientific, female) which had already given offence. Whereas Lady Mary in life devoted her efforts to persuading society to inoculate its children (rather than do nothing), Montagu in print urges right methods of inoculation rather than wrong. She writes against those dangerous practices which are English, medical, and male. 'The old Nurse who is the General surgeon upon this Occasion at Constantinople' (says the 'Plain Account') operates gently, rationally, and successfully; 'our Learned Physicians', who back their hugely increased dose of the virus with purges, bleeding, and alcohol, are murderers—not by inadvertence but in order to protect their revenue derived from smallpox cases. Recent medical opinion supports Lady Mary's conviction that the strong-arm methods of western doctors had put most of the risk into inoculation (below, p. 95).

The force, confidence and anger of this squib are striking. No longer did Montagu need to placate the guardians of the literary establishment by showing off her scholarship (the latest example of such display is her letter to the Abbé Conti about the 'classic shores' of the Mediterranean). Instead, she adopts the stock-in-trade of the new, ephemeral, topical media. The 'Plain Account' suggests radically decreased respect both for learning and for patriarchal rank and gender systems, even while its choice of a mouthpiece who differs from her in sex as well as rank suggests a freedom from animus against men as such.

The pressure-group fierceness of this essay is no preparation for the range of her political writing, from topical epigram and parody, historical fantasy ('Caesar', below, pp. 150–2), and ironical party propaganda ('An Expedient to put a stop to the spreading Vice of Corruption', below, pp. 100–4), to the sustained *Nonsense of Common-Sense* (below, pp. 105–49). This periodical is not only the first certainly identified as by a woman, but the only one by an eighteenth-century woman to specialize in mainstream politics. Its detailed, informed attention to such 'hard' issues as the national debt, the earnings of workers in woollen mills, and the level of interest rates, suggests that its author would have made a highly competent Member of Parliament. She brings her usual mix of complexity and incisiveness to these topics, as well as to stock periodical material like fashions, operas, levées, to matters of feminist concern like the property of wives and the education of middle-class women, and to existing special interests of her own like Grub-Street journalism, anti-feminism, and obscenity.

It is not surprising that this wholly original venture should derive its title and *raison d'être* from the need to confute the anti-governmental *Common Sense*. Confutation had become a leading imperative of Montagu's writing from May 1728, when Pope first attacked her in the *Dunciad*. His printed campaign against her provoked a series of quarrelling poems which are, naturally, just as interactive as *The Nonsense of Common-Sense* or as her poems on marriage. She is a leading practitioner of the 'answer' to male satirical attacks and amatory demands which has been, perforce, a genre much favoured by women. She answered (and contradicted) women as well, sometimes writing at different times on different sides of a question, as in the poems (juxtaposed below, pp. 257–9) of which one advises immersion in the social whirl, and another indignantly rejects this advice when given by another.

Montagu mobilized against Pope the efforts of herself and of two collaborators. Her two untitled mock-epic fragments (below, pp. 247–55) were written in confederation with her young cousin Henry Fielding (who contributed another nameless fragment and

two 'cantos' numbered '2d' and '3d'). Her first such joint enterprise since 'Friday', the epic drafts initiate a campaign of opposi-
tional and confrontational writing which includes the notorious
Verses to the Imitator of . . . Horace, written in confederation with
Hervey. (Her mock-epic fragments share a couplet with Fielding's
separate but related ones; internal evidence, contemporary comment, and two copies annotated by Hervey as if for a new printed
version, mark the *Verses* as jointly produced.)

The mock-epic depicts warfare between the heirs of the Renaissance, headed by Addison, and the minions of Dulness, both
personified and living (Prophanation, Obscenity, Pope, Swift,
Gay). Its doctrine marks Montagu as a woman of the Enlightenment, holding that learning sprang from Reformation, and is the
only guarantee of liberty. It has the gall to turn both Pope's
opinions and his *Dunciad* techniques (grand style, historic sweep,
topical detail, grotesque outrageousness) against himself.

These poems of defensive and offensive alliance, and the solo
composition 'Pope to Bolingbroke', have a dash and vigour, an
inventiveness and ingenuity, which suggest a fighter's challenge
rather than a victim's complaint. The ingenuity appears chiefly in
adapting the materials supplied by actual events and by the
adversary's style. Montagu echoes and mocks in turn the *Dunciad*
machinery, the weighty rebuke and the confidential intimacy of
Pope's Horatian poems, and the fluent octosyllabics of Swift.
Indeed, her 'Reasons that Induced Dr S[wift]' is itself a virtuoso
pattern-book of Swiftian technique: rapid narrative, ruminative
digression, pedantic analogies, scatological or titillating detail. But
one weapon of Pope she avoids; her rebukes to him, unlike her
rebuke to Bathurst, make no use of idealizing self-construction.

Her verbal self-portraits assume a sympathetic audience. As
well as 'Satturday', they consist of an untitled romance-style
account of her courtship, in English (below, pp. 77–81), and
'Carabosse', a fairy-tale in French (below, pp. 153–5). Each
involves refashioning an established genre: something at which,
both in direct imitation and in mockery, she is adept. As she
converts the eclogue, the epic, the Ovidian love-epistle for social
protest, and the Horatian friendship-epistle for controversy, so she
converts these fictional forms for personal statement. Romance
and fairy-tale heighten the experience related, and idealize the
heroine, not in beauty or moral worth so much as in intellectual

gifts. Each portrays the mismatch between those gifts and her environment as a disaster. The romance closes with the marriage contract, the fairy-tale with the end of infancy: neither, it seems, can hope to encompass the story of its author's maturity.

Idealism and combativeness, though generically distinct, not occurring in the same literary piece, seem to have run side by side at every stage of Montagu's writing career. Her most extended expressions of idealism are a courtship comedy and a vindication of the joys as well as the uses of marriage: 'Simplicity' (below, pp. 313–79), which adapts Marivaux, and 'Sur la Maxime de Mr de Rochefoucault' (below, pp. 157–64), which takes issue with La Rochefoucauld, that 'bel esprit si celebre'. 'Simplicity', which belongs to the new mode of sentiment, probably dates from about 1734; the La Rochefoucauld answer, which mingles Enlightenment with sentimental attitudes, pre-dates it, belonging either to the years when her feminist poems were attacking marriage, or to those when Pope was attacking her.

She chose comedy to paint a rosier picture of courtship than in her autobiographical romance. This heroine, manipulated by her father, terrified to find herself smitten with—apparently—degrading desire for a servant, wins through to a double reward: a sincere and generous lover, and the pleasure of exercising power over him. It is a pity Montagu did not further develop this talent for the drama, though she made at least one other use of it: some stray scenes she entitled 'Some People' (not included here).

For her La Rochefoucauld answer she apparently chose French as the language of her adversary, and of the system of thinking which sharply separates the idea of spouse from that of lover; it lends itself well to the fervent tone in which she sketches her ideal. Yet at her most eager she leavens her sentiment with scepticism. Her ideal of marriage demands renunciations similar to those she links with celibacy in poems like 'The Answer to the foregoing Elegy' (below, pp. 270–2). 'Sur la Maxime' closes (in English translation) by acknowledging that as things are 'it is necessary, in order to be happy, to despise the established maxims' (below, p. 392). The ideal marriage, like the ideal man, remains a distant goal, not a present reality.

The late 1730s saw an event which, like the *Dunciad*, produced work of a new and revolutionary style. Lady Mary fell in love with the much younger Francesco Algarotti. The poems she wrote under the influence of her love (below, pp. 286–91, 295, 304–6, 381 ff.) are extraordinary documents, some for their vehemence of expression, and others for the way their violence of feeling submits itself to and defends itself against the chilling, reasonable scepticism of her old collaborator Hervey. Even the most passionate lines (like 'Ye soft Ideas', below p. 295) tend to express a desire to escape or evade passion rather than to realize it. Lady Mary writes her own love rather as she had written Dancinda's or Judith Cowper's; it is an experience to flee, not to welcome. This viewpoint situates her firmly among her own contemporaries and her own sex. She is romantic, but not a Romantic; and whereas Romantic male poets like Coleridge and Wordsworth wrote famous poems lamenting the loss of feeling, the encroachment of apathy, literally dozens of female eighteenth-century poets wrote to deplore their own susceptibility to feeling: most famously Frances Greville (below, p. 382 note).

Montagu's poetic skill does not desert her under the stress of powerful emotions. Abstract values like Reason ('if once I offer'd at thy Shrine') acquire the force of living agents, as does the vacillating ego swayed back and forth in a theatre of the mind. This psychomachia is disrupted by the larger drama of 'He comes!' only to resume its sway when the interruption turns out to be merely imagined. Conventional imagery and physical symptoms—rebel wishes, throbbing pulse—generate a sudden, startling birth-image: 'While expectation rends my labouring mind.'

This particular poem seems to have been abandoned when the writer realized that she had slid into quoting Congreve. Though she said some sharp things about plagiarism by others, her own writing—prose, verse, and drama—often seems part of a conversation with her peers and predecessors, carried on by reshaping the words of others as well as by addressing them directly (for example, Anna Maria van Schurman, below, pp. 165–7). This conversation did not cease at her death, but was extended in the works of others who praised, quoted, or debated with her.

Many who admired her writings (as distinct from her personal or travel letters or her smallpox campaigning) were of her own sex. The poet Elizabeth Tollet celebrated her before 1724, as did 'Mary Seymour Montague' in 1771 (for answering Pope on the subject of women) and Anna Seward in 1789 (making her the sole female poet of the Augustan age). In novels she was quoted by the future Duchess of Devonshire and misquoted by Elizabeth Griffith.[4]

I have dwelt here on Montagu's relation to the developing tradition of women's writing, in which she herself was both knowledgeable and influential. It is a topic which needs attention after generations of scholarly neglect. In old age Lady Mary saw herself as persecuted for being a writer in the way that old women used to be persecuted on suspicion of being witches. But she was too good an Augustan not to see human nature as universal, and men and women as 'very like one another'. She had all of us in mind when she asked: 'Why are our views so extensive and our power so miserably limited?' (*Letters*, 2. 392; 3. 198). Her own extensive views did much to push back the limits faced by women writers in particular; since the first publication of her *Essays and Poems* those limits have receded just a little more.

ISOBEL GRUNDY

Edmonton
May 1992

[4] Tollet, *Poems* (1724), 56; 'Montague', *An Original Essay on Woman* (1771), 38; Seward, *Gentleman's Magazine* (1789), i. 292; [Georgiana Spencer, later Duchess of Devonshire], *Emma, or the Unfortunate Attachment. A Sentimental Novel* (1773), iii. 161; Griffith, *The Story of Lady Juliana Harley* (1776), i. 117.

CONTENTS

Contents

LIST OF PLATES

ABBREVIATIONS

1747   LM, *Six Town Eclogues. With some other Poems* [ed. Horace Walpole].
1748   *A Collection of Poems*, printed for R. Dodsley.
1768   LM, *Poetical Works* [ed. Isaac Reed].
1803   LM, *Works* [ed. James Dallaway].
1837   LM, *Letters and Works*, ed. Lord Wharncliffe.
1861   LM, *Letters and Works*, 3rd ed., ed. W. Moy Thomas.

BM   British Museum (now British Library).
Dryden, *Works*   *Dramatic Works*, ed. M. Summers, 1931–2.
Halsband, *Hervey*   Robert Halsband, *Lord Hervey, Eighteenth-Century Courtier*, 1973.
Halsband, *LM*   Robert Halsband, *The Life of Lady Mary Wortley Montagu*, 1956.
Hervey, *Memoirs*   *Some Materials Towards Memoirs of the Reign of King George II*, ed. R. Sedgwick, 1931.
H.M.C.   Historical Manuscripts Commission Reports.
H MSS.   Harrowby Manuscripts Trust, Sandon Hall, Stafford.
LM   Lady Mary Wortley Montagu.
Letters   *Complete Letters of Lady Mary Wortley Montagu*, ed. R. Halsband, 1965–7.
Osborn Collection   Yale University Library, New Haven, Conn.
Pope, *Corr.*   *Correspondence*, ed. G. Sherburn, 1956.
Pope, *Poems*   'Twickenham Edition', ed. J. Butt *et al.*, 1940–61.
Prior, *Works*   *Literary Works*, ed. H. B. Wright and M. K. Spears, 2nd ed., 1971.
W   Wortley (Edward Wortley Montagu).
Walpole, *Corr.*   *Correspondence*, ed. W. S. Lewis *et al.*, 1937– .

ESSAYS

INTRODUCTION

SINCE her own time Lady Mary Wortley Montagu's reputation as a great letter-writer and an accomplished poet has been secure; to this double distinction can now be added another, that of an essayist. She belatedly assumes this new role in the twentieth century, for her essays had either been published anonymously during her lifetime or have remained in manuscript among her family papers. With their wide range of subject-matter and style they display the vigorous versatility that characterizes her epistolary prose and her verse.

I have begun this volume with long extracts from the 'Biographical Anecdotes' written by her granddaughter Lady Louisa Stuart because they contain reliable material by and about Lady Mary that is nowhere else preserved. To these anecdotes, first printed in 1837 and not previously edited, I have been able to add Lady Louisa's valuable 'Supplement to the Anecdotes', which she intended to publish but then decided to suppress.

None of Lady Mary's essays printed in her day bears her name, for as a *bel esprit*, an aristocrat, and a woman she spurned the vulgarity and commercial taint of practising the trade of authorship. Her earliest appearance in print is in a humorous feminist essay for the *Spectator*. During the controversy over smallpox inoculation, an operation she had advocated since observing it in Turkey, she contributed a vigorous defence of it to a popular newspaper in 1722. Her most extensive foray into journalism is her periodical *The Nonsense of Common-Sense*, for which she wrote all nine essays in 1737–8. In these, while attacking the Opposition newspaper *Common Sense* and defending the ministry of Sir Robert Walpole, she expresses more personal ideas about social satire and feminism.

Among the essays that she did not put into print is a long treatise in French on the subject of marriage, in refutation of a cynical maxim by La Rochefoucauld; she insists that true, romantic love can and should exist between husband and wife. Her defence, sustained with reasonable arguments, rests on her feminist creed, which she again treats, though more directly, in a brief French essay in the form of a letter. Several of her other unpublished essays deal with literary topics. Before the publication of *Cato* (in

1713) her husband, who was a friend of Joseph Addison, let her read the play in manuscript and encouraged her to write a critique, which he showed to Addison. When he revised the tragedy Addison followed some of her suggestions but insisted that her essay should not be published. Many years later her friendship with Francesco Algarotti stimulated her to write a brief piece on Julius Caesar in the form of a dramatic monologue. Her enmity toward Alexander Pope led her to attack him for publishing his private letters (in 1737), but she apparently abandoned what would have been still another pamphlet in the endless Popean warfare, and only its fragmentary opening section survives. A few other brief essays by her, in English or in French, are clever *jeux d'esprit* inspired by old friends or new ideas.

The most important piece of miscellaneous prose is her account of the court of George I on his accession to the English throne. (It was first printed in 1837, but has never been edited.) Whether this is merely the fragment of a long memoir that is lost or a self-contained essay it shines with a sustained brilliance perhaps unmatched in any of her other writings. As though there were not enough novelties in her literary career, an altogether new and striking episode was her excursion into dramatic literature as the translator and adapter of Marivaux's well-known comedy *Le Jeu de l'amour et du hasard*. Her version, entitled *Simplicity*, was neither published nor staged. Her varied literary accomplishments, whether public or private, were boundless.

In printing from manuscript I have used this style of transcription: exact spelling and numerals are retained; abbreviations, including the ampersand, are expanded; raised letters are lowered; punctuation is adjusted when required, and capital letters are provided for persons, places, book-titles, and the first word of sentences; apostrophes are added for possessives and deleted in plurals; square brackets [ ] are inserted for editorial additions, and angle brackets ⟨ ⟩ for doubtful readings.

During the many years that I have been investigating Lady Mary's life, career, and writings I have had the help of many friends and strangers, scholars, librarians, and collectors; and I am grateful to all of them. Most recently, the Research Board of the University of Illinois has generously provided assistance for the preparation of this volume. The prose (including *Simplicity*) has been edited by me, and the verse by Dr. Grundy; we are individually responsible for each section, though we have offered editorial counsel to each other. What we fully share is our warm gratitude to the Earl of Harrowby, Lady Mary's descendant and the custodian of her papers; he has always been unstintingly generous to both of us.

R. H.

Urbana, Illinois
June 1975

Biographical Anecdotes of Lady M. W. Montagu

'Some of the lineal descendants of Lady Mary Wortley Montagu have thought it due to her literary fame, that a complete Edition of her Works should be published under their authority.' Thus began the preface to the 1837 edition—a far from complete one—by Lord Wharncliffe, a great-grandson of Lady Mary's. His aunt Lady Louisa Stuart (1757-1851) contributed Biographical [Introductory] Anecdotes, which were intended to correct and supplement James Dallaway's Memoir, reprinted from the 1803 edition. Although the anecdotes were published with no explicit attribution of authorship Lord Wharncliffe's preface coyly hinted at it; he would be greatly disappointed, he wrote, 'if the spirit and vigour with which these anecdotes are written do not satisfy the Reader that a ray of Lady Mary's talent has fallen upon one of her descendants'.

The anecdotes are valuable for several reasons. Born in 1757, Lady Louisa was the last and favourite child of Lady Mary's only daughter, Lady Bute; and, fateful as it seems in retrospect, Lady Mary, then living in Italy, was chosen to serve as her godmother. (Her proxy at the baptism was the eccentric Lady Mary Coke.) As a child Lady Louisa was snubbed and scolded for reading books too eagerly, and warned not to be like her grandmother (*Letters to Louisa Clinton*, ed. J. A. Home, 1901, 2. 21). She was the only one of Lady Mary's numerous grandchildren to show any literary interest or talent. Her anecdotes are generally reliable because as the only unmarried daughter she remained for many years her mother's companion and confidante, and she was the only one permitted by her mother to read Lady Mary's diary before it was destroyed and the correspondence before it was culled.

Since the anecdotes in full are discursive, sometimes dealing with topics unrelated to Lady Mary, they have been excerpted here to include only what concerns Lady Mary, particularly if their information comes from documents and family tradition no longer in existence.

Text   1837, 1. 1-95 *passim*. (A 'Second Edition, Revised', issued the same year, contained very few alterations, and these evidently by Lord Wharncliffe).

LADY MARY WORTLEY MONTAGU, we must remember, was born a hundred and forty-five years[1] ago, and has now been dead more than seventy. Considering this, and also that the incidents of her life were in no respect linked to those historical or political facts which fix in men's memories even trifles if connected with them, it cannot be expected that her descendants themselves should possess very ample means of giving or gaining information upon a subject

[1] 'a hundred and forty-seven years': 2nd ed. This too is inaccurate since LM was born in 1689.

borne almost beyond their reach by the lapse of time. The multitude of stories circulated about her—as about all people who were objects of note in their day—increase, instead of lessening the difficulty. Some of these may be confidently pronounced inventions, simply and purely false; some, if true, concerned a different person; some were grounded upon egregious blunders; and not a few upon jests, mistaken by the dull and literal for earnest. Others again, where a little truth and a great deal of falsehood were probably intermingled, nobody now living can pretend to confirm, or contradict, or unravel. Nothing is so readily believed, yet nothing is usually so unworthy of credit, as tales learned from report, or caught up in casual conversation. A circumstance carelessly told, carelessly listened to, half comprehended, and imperfectly remembered, has a poor chance of being repeated accurately by the first hearer; but when, after passing through the moulding of countless hands, it comes, with time, place, and person, gloriously confounded, into those of a book-maker ignorant of all its bearings, it will be lucky indeed if any trace of the original groundwork remain distinguishable ... the particulars offered here cannot be otherwise than scanty, and may appear uninteresting and frivolous; but authentic they must be, because either received directly from the late Countess of Bute,[1] or else gathered from documents formerly seen in Lady Mary Wortley's own hand-writing.

A tale of pedigree would be little to the purpose; yet, as Lady Mary's letters allude more than once to her family history, it may throw some light upon passages of this kind to say that, in the great Civil War, the second Earl of Kingston, created Marquis of Dorchester by Charles the First, espoused the royal cause; while his next brother, William Pierrepont of Thoresby, surnamed *Wise William*, Lady Mary Wortley's great-grandfather, adhered to the Parliament.[2] The currency of such an epithet speaks his reputation for sagacity and prudence; he had considerable weight with his own party, and, according to tradition, was much courted and consulted by Cromwell. His eldest son died in his life-time, having

---

[1] Mary Wortley Montagu (1718–94), LM's only daughter, m. (1736) 3rd Earl of Bute.

[2] Henry Pierrepont (1606–80), 2nd Earl of Kingston-upon-Hull, was created Marquess of Dorchester 1645. William Pierrepont (1607?–78) sat in the Long Parliament of 1640, and in 1647 was granted £7,467, the amount his brother (Dorchester) had been fined.

married a Wiltshire heiress, whose maiden name, Evelyn,[1] has ever since been a favourite Christian-name, for both men and women, in most of the families descended from her. Lord Dorchester leaving no male issue, the earldom of Kingston devolved successively upon the three sons of this marriage, grandsons of Wise William. The third, Evelyn, fifth Earl of Kingston, created Marquis of Dorchester by Queen Anne in 1706, and Duke of Kingston by George the First in 1715, had by his wife, Lady Mary Fielding, three daughters, Mary, born in 1690 [*sic*], Frances and Evelyn, and one son, William, whose birth she did not long survive.[2] Her mother, Mary, Countess Dowager of Denbigh and Desmond, was the grandmother of whom Lady Mary Wortley speaks so highly, as having had a superior understanding, and retained it unimpaired at an extraordinary age.[3]

Lady Kingston dying thus early, her husband continued a widower till all his children were grown up and married; though, if Lady Mary may be believed, not through any over-anxious concern for their welfare. Richardson, she affirms, drew his picture without knowing it in Sir Thomas Grandison, the gay father of his hero Sir Charles, which says a great deal to those who have read the book and observed the character—that of a man of pleasure, far too fine a gentleman to be a tender or even a considerate parent.[4] Such men, always selfish and commonly vain, begin to view their offspring as rivals the moment they are old enough to put beholders in mind that those to whom they owe their birth can hardly be much less than a score of years older. But playthings are cherished while new, seldom flung aside in the first hour of acquisition; and, besides

---

[1] Elizabeth (1639–99), da. and coheiress of Sir John Evelyn of West Dean, Wilts., m. (before 1660) Robert Pierrepont (d. 1669).

[2] Evelyn Pierrepont (*c.* 1665-1726), successively Earl of Kingston-upon-Hull, Marquess of Dorchester, and Duke of Kingston-upon-Hull, m. (1687) Lady Mary Feilding (*c.* 1668-92), da. of 3rd Earl of Denbigh. Their children: Mary (1689-1762), m. (1712) Edward Wortley Montagu (1678-1761); Frances (1690-1761), m. (1714) 6th Earl of Mar; Evelyn (1691-1727), m. (1712) 2nd Lord Gower; William (1692-1713), Earl of Kingston-upon-Hull.

[3] Mary Carey (*c.* 1623-1719), da. of 2nd Earl of Monmouth, was the second wife of William Feilding (1640-85), 3rd Earl of Denbigh. Since LM's mother was his daughter by his first wife, the Dowager was LM's step-grandmother. In 1753 LM recalled that 'She dy'd at 96, retaining to the last the vivacity and clearness of her understanding, which was very uncommon' (*Letters*, 3. 27).

[4] LM wrote: 'I find in the pictures of Sir Thomas Grandison and his Lady what I have heard of my Mother and seen of my Father' (1755, *Letters*, 3. 90). Samuel Richardson (1689-1761) published *Sir Charles Grandison* in 1753.

being an admirable plaything, a sprightly beautiful child, while it *is* a child, reflects lustre upon a young father, from whom it may be presumed to have partly inherited its charms. Accordingly, a trifling incident, which Lady Mary loved to recall, will prove how much she was the object of Lord Kingston's pride and fondness in her childhood. As a leader of the fashionable world, and a strenuous Whig in party, he of course belonged to the Kit-cat club. One day, at a meeting to choose toasts for the year, a whim seized him to nominate her, then not eight years old, a candidate; alleging that she was far prettier than any lady on their list. The other members demurred, because the rules of the club forbade them to elect a beauty whom they had never seen. 'Then you shall see her,' cried he; and in the gaiety of the moment sent orders home to have her finely dressed, and brought to him at the tavern; where she was received with acclamations, her claim unanimously allowed, her health drunk by every one present, and her name engraved in due form upon a drinking-glass. The company consisting of some of the most eminent men in England, she went from the lap of one poet, or patriot, or statesman, to the arms of another, was feasted with sweetmeats, overwhelmed with caresses, and, what perhaps already pleased her better than either, heard her wit and beauty loudly extolled on every side. Pleasure, she said, was too poor a word to express her sensations; they amounted to ecstasy: never again, throughout her whole future life, did she pass so happy a day. Nor indeed could she; for the love of admiration, which this scene was calculated to excite or increase, could never again be so fully gratified: there is always some allaying ingredient in the cup, some drawback upon the triumphs of grown people. Her father carried on the frolic, and, we may conclude, confirmed the taste, by having her picture painted for the club-room, that she might be enrolled a regular toast.[1]

There can be no dispute that Lady Mary showed early signs of more than ordinary abilities; but whether they induced Lord Kingston to have her bred up with her brother and taught Latin and Greek by his tutor, is not so well ascertained. The boy was two or three years younger than the girl, which makes against it. Lady Bute expressly said that her mother understood little or no Greek,

---

[1] Lady Louisa Stuart is apparently the only source for this frequently quoted anecdote. For an account of the Kit-Cat Club, see Robert J. Allen, *The Clubs of Augustan London*, 1933, pp. 35–54.

and by her own account had taught herself Latin. And besides, would she, while so earnestly recommending a learned education for women, have complained of her own as 'one of the worst in the world,' if it had had this classical foundation?[1] Most likely not; most likely her father, whose amusement in her ceased when she grew past the age of sitting on a knee and playing with a doll, consigned all his daughters alike to the care and custody of such a good home-spun governess as her letters describe;[2] and, having thus done his supposed duty towards them, held himself at liberty to pursue his own pleasures, which lay elsewhere than at home. One remnant of his illegitimate progeny, an old General Armytage,[3] was still living long after the accession of George the Third.

But, admitting that Lady Mary's talents were only self-cultivated, her literary progress might not be the less considerable. Where industry, inspirited by genius, toils from free choice, and there exists unchecked that eager devouring appetite for reading, seldom felt but in the first freshness of intelligent youth, it will take in more nourishment, and faster, than the most assiduous tuition can cram down. It is true, the habit of idly turning over an unconnected variety of books, forgotten as soon as read, may be prejudicial to the mind; but a bee wanders to better purpose than a butterfly, although the one will sometimes seem just to touch the flower-bed and flit away as lightly as the other. Lady Mary read everything, but it was without forgetting anything,[4] and the mass of matter, whencesoever collected, gradually formed its own arrangement in her head. She probably had some assistance from Mr. William Fielding, her mother's brother,[5] a man of parts, who perceived her capacity, corresponded with her, and encouraged her pursuit of information. And she herself acknowledges her obligations to Bishop Burnet[6] for 'condescending to direct the studies of a girl.' Nevertheless, though labouring to acquire what may be termed

---

[1] For LM's education, see Halsband, *LM*, pp. 5–7. The quoted phrase comes from LM's letter (1753, *Letters*, 3. 25).

[2] LM described her governess thus: 'She took so much pains from my Infancy to fill my Head with superstitious Tales and false notions, it was none of her Fault I am not at this day afraid of Witches and Hobgoblins, or turn'd Methodist' (1753, *Letters*, 3. 26).

[3] Unidentified.

[4] In one of her notebooks (now H MS. 250) LM listed the characters in a prodigious number of plays and romances that she read as a girl.

[5] William Feilding (*c.* 1669–1723), M.P. 1705–23, 2nd son of 3rd Earl of Denbigh.

[6] Gilbert Burnet (1643–1715), Bishop of Salisbury (1689).

masculine knowledge, and translating under the Bishop's eye the
Latin version of Epictetus,[1] she was by no means disposed to
neglect works of fancy and fiction, but got by heart all the poetry
that came in her way, and indulged herself in the luxury of reading
every romance as yet invented. For she possessed, and left after her,
the whole library of Mrs. Lennox's Female Quixote[2]—Cleopatra,
Cassandra, Clelia, Cyrus, Pharamond, Ibrahim, &c. &c.—all, like
the Lady Arabella's collection, '*Englished*,' mostly by '*persons of
honour*.' The chief favourite appeared to have been a translation of
Monsieur Honoré d'Urfé's Astrea, once the delight of Henri
Quatre and his court, and still admired and quoted by the *savans*
who flourished under Louis XIV. In a blank page of this massive
volume (which might have counterbalanced a pig of lead of the same
size) Lady Mary had written in her fairest youthful hand the names
and characteristic qualities of the chief personages thus:—the
beautiful Diana, the volatile Climene, the melancholy Doris,
Celadon the faithful, Adamas the wise, and so on; forming two long
columns.[3] . . .

Some particulars, in themselves too insignificant to be worth
recording, may yet interest the curious, by setting before them the
manners of our ancestors. Lord Dorchester, having no wife to do
the honours of his table at Thoresby,[4] imposed that task upon his
eldest daughter, as soon as she had bodily strength for the office:
which in those days required no small share. For the mistress of a
country mansion was not only to invite—that is, urge and tease—
her company to eat more than human throats could conveniently
swallow, but to carve every dish, when chosen, with her own hands.
The greater the lady, the more indispensable the duty. Each joint
was carried up in its turn, to be operated upon by her, and her
alone;—since the peers and knights on either hand were so far from
being bound to offer their assistance, that the very master of the
house, posted opposite to her, might not act as her croupier; his
department was to push the bottle after dinner. As for the crowd of

---

[1] For her letter to Burnet about her translation (in 1710) see *Letters*, 1. 43–6; she
refers to it again in 1758 (*Letters*, 3. 158). Her translation, with Burnet's corrections,
is now H MS. 252.

[2] Charlotte Lennox, *The Female Quixote; or, The Adventures of Arabella*, 1752. In
the first volume of her copy LM wrote 'pretty plan, ill executed' (Sotheby Catalogue,
1 Aug. 1928, p. 94).

[3] For LM's allusion to this romance, see p. 159, n. 2 below.

[4] Thoresby House, near Nottingham, built *c*. 1683 (*Letters*, 1. 3).

guests, the most inconsiderable among them,—the curate, or subaltern, or squire's younger brother,—if suffered through her neglect to help himself to a slice of the mutton placed before him, would have chewed it in bitterness, and gone home an affronted man, half inclined to give a wrong vote at the next election. There were then professed carving-masters, who taught young ladies the art scientifically; from one of whom Lady Mary said she took lessons three times a week, that she might be perfect on her father's public days; when, in order to perform her functions without interruption, she was forced to eat her own dinner alone an hour or two beforehand.

Most of the intimacies formed by Lady Mary in her youth having died away before her daughter began to know what was passing, only a few of her early companions can be mentioned: viz. Mrs. Smith, maid of honour to Queen Anne, and daughter of the Whig Speaker Smith;[1] the beautiful Dolly Walpole, Sir Robert's sister, afterwards the second wife of Lord Townshend;[2] Lady Anne Vaughan, only child of Lord Carbery, the last of a family noted for having given Jeremy Taylor an asylum at Golden Grove.[3] This young lady was precisely in the situation which Lady Mary always maintained to be the most perilous and pitiable incident to womankind; that of a great heiress at her own free disposal. And truly her fate justified the paradox. She bestowed herself and her wealth upon Lord Winchester (third Duke of Bolton), a handsome agreeable libertine, who, much worse than indifferent to the first half of the gift, cast her off without any long delay, and, when her melancholy life at last came to an end, married the famous actress, Miss Fenton, best known by her stage-title of Polly Peachem.[4]

The name of another young friend will excite more attention—Mrs. Anne Wortley. *Mrs.* Anne has a most mature sound to our modern ears; but, in the phraseology of those days, *Miss*, which had

---

[1] Jane (d. 1730), da. of John Smith, Speaker of the House of Commons 1705–8.

[2] Dorothy Walpole (1686–1726), m. (1713) Lord Townshend (see p. 24, n. 1 below), who was a political ally of Robert Walpole (1676–1745).

[3] Lady Anne Vaughan (c. 1689–1751), da. of 3rd Earl of Carbery, m. (1713) Charles Paulet or Powlett (1685–1754), 3rd Duke of Bolton. During the Commonwealth, Jeremy Taylor (1613–67), the Anglican divine, took refuge at Golden Grove, the estate in Wales owned by Richard Vaughan (1600?–86), 2nd Earl of Carbery.

[4] Lavinia Fenton (1708–60), famous as the original Polly Peachum of *The Beggar's Opera* in 1728, by which time the Duke of Bolton had taken her into keeping. He married her in 1751, a month after his first wife's death. See LM, *Letters*, 3. 75.

hardly yet ceased to be a term of reproach, still denoted childishness, flippancy, or some other contemptible quality, and was rarely applied to young ladies of a respectable class. In Steele's Guardian, the youngest of Nestor Ironside's wards, aged fifteen, is Mrs. Mary Lizard.[1] Nay, Lady Bute herself could remember having been styled Mrs. Wortley, when a child, by two or three elderly visitors, as tenacious of their ancient modes of speech as of other old fashions. Mrs. Anne, then, was the second daughter of Mr. Sidney Wortley Montagu,[2] and the favourite sister of his son Edward.[3] She died in the bloom of youth, unmarried.[4] Lady Mary, in common with others who had known her, represented her as eminently pretty and agreeable; and her brother so cherished her memory, that, in after times, his little girl knew it to be the highest mark of his favour, when, pointing at herself, he said to her mother, 'Don't you think she grows like my poor sister Anne?'

Mrs. Wortley, the mother of the family, from whom it derived both estate and name, died before Lady Mary Pierrepont became acquainted with any branch of it: therefore all she could tell concerning her was, that she had been forced to demand a separation from her husband, and that her son always spoke of his father's conduct towards her with resentment and indignation. For Mr. Sidney Montagu had not breathed in the atmosphere of Charles the Second's reign during his best years without inhaling some of its poison. This old gentleman, and the scene surrounding him, were distinctly recollected by his grand-daughter. She described him as a large rough-looking man with a huge flapped hat, seated magisterially in his elbow-chair, talking very loud, and swearing boisterously at his servants. While beside him sate a venerable figure, meek and benign in aspect, with silver locks overshadowed by a black velvet cap. This was his brother, the pious Dean Montagu,[5] who every now and then fetched a deep sigh, and cast his eyes upwards, as if silently beseeching Heaven to pardon the

[1] The *Guardian* (12 Mar.–1 Oct. 1713) mentions Mrs. Mary Lizard in its fifth number (17 Mar. 1713).

[2] Sidney Montagu (1650–1727), 2nd son of 1st Earl of Sandwich, m. (*c*. 1676) Anne Newcomen (b. 1659), natural da. of Sir Francis Wortley, by the terms of whose will her husband had to assume the name of Wortley.

[3] Edward Wortley Montagu (1678–1761).

[4] Anne Wortley (d. Feb. 1710) 'died of grief for the follys and imprudences of the younger sister [Catherine]' (Anne Clavering in Sir James Clavering, *Corr.*, ed. H. T. Dickinson, Surtees Society, 178, 1967, pp. 69–70).

[5] John Montagu, D.D. (*c*. 1655–1728), Dean of Durham from 1699.

profane language which he condemned, but durst not reprove. Unlike as they were in their habits and their morals, the two brothers commonly lived together.

___

It is hard to divine why, or on what authority, Mr. Edward Wortley has been represented by late writers as a dull phlegmatic country gentleman—'of a tame genius and moderate capacity,' or 'of parts more solid than brilliant,'[1]—which in common parlance is a civil way of saying the same thing. He had, on the contrary, one of those strong characters that are little influenced by the world's opinion, and for that reason little understood by the unthinking part of it. All who really knew him while living held him a man distinguished for soundness of judgment and clearness of understanding, qualities nowise akin to dullness; they allowed him also to be a first-rate scholar; and as he had travelled more than most young men of his time,[2] a proof will presently appear that he surpassed them in the knowledge of modern languages. Polite literature was his passion; and though our having a taste for wit and talents may not certainly imply that we are gifted with them ourselves, yet it would be strange if the alderman-like mortal depicted above had sought out such companions as Steele, Garth, Congreve, Mainwaring, &c. or chosen Addison for his bosom friend.[3] The only picture of Mr. Wortley in existence belonged to Addison, from whose daughter Lady Bute obtained it through her (Miss Addison's) half-sister, Lady Charlotte Rich.[4] It is now in the possession of Lord Wharncliffe. The face seems very young, and, in spite of wig, cravat, and other deforming appendages, very handsome.[5]

Miss, or Mrs. Addison, Addison's daughter by Lady Warwick, and his only child, far from having sufficient endowments to keep up the credit of her great name, was one of those singular beings in whom nature seems to have left the mind half finished; not raised

[1] The first quotation is untraced; the second is adapted from the 'Memoir' by James Dallaway, printed 1803 and reprinted in 1837 (I. xi).

[2] He had taken the Grand Tour from 1700 to 1703.

[3] Richard Steele (1672–1729), Samuel Garth (1661–1719), William Congreve (1670–1729), Arthur Maynwaring (1668–1712), Joseph Addison (1672–1719).

[4] Addison's daughter was Charlotte Addison (1719–97). His wife Lady Warwick (1679–1728) had only a son by her first husband, the 6th Earl of Warwick. Lady Louisa is thus mistaken. Lady Charlotte Rich (1713–91) was the daughter of the 8th Earl, hence unrelated to Addison's daughter.

[5] The portrait, by an unknown artist, was among the Wharncliffe pictures sold at Christie's in 1958, when it was acquired by Robert A. Cecil. It is reproduced in Halsband, *LM*, facing p. 16.

to the average height of human intellect, yet not absolutely imbecile, nor so devoid of judgment in common every-day concerns as to need the guardianship of the law. With this imperfect understanding she possessed a gift, which, it is said, may sometimes be found where there is no great power of thinking,—such an astonishing memory that she could repeat the longest sermon word for word after hearing it once, or get by heart the contents of a whole dictionary. As she inherited all her father had to leave, her circumstances were affluent; but, by the advice of her friends, she lived in retirement at a country-seat, and never attempted to enter the world.

Mr. Wortley's chief intimates have been already named. His society was principally male; the wits and politicians of that day forming a class quite distinct from the 'white-gloved beaus' attendant upon ladies. Indeed, as the education of women had then reached its very lowest ebb, and if not coquettes, or gossips, or diligent card-players, their best praise was to be notable housewives, Mr. Wortley, however fond of his sister, could have no particular motive to seek the acquaintance of her companions. His surprise and delight were the greater, when one afternoon, having by chance loitered in her apartment till visitors arrived, he saw Lady Mary Pierrepont for the first time, and, on entering into conversation with her, found, in addition to beauty that charmed him, not only brilliant wit, but a thinking and cultivated mind. He was especially struck with the discovery that she understood Latin and could relish his beloved classics. Something that passed led to the mention of Quintus Curtius, which she said she had never read. This was a fair handle for a piece of gallantry; in a few days she received a superb edition of the author, with these lines facing the title-page:

> Beauty like this had vanquished Persia shown,
> The Macedon had laid his empire down,
> And polished Greece obeyed a barb'rous throne.
> Had wit so bright adorned a Grecian dame,
> The am'rous youth had lost his thirst for fame,
> Nor distant India sought through Syria's plain;
> But to the Muses' stream with her had run,
> And thought her lover more than Ammon's son.[1]

---

[1] LM copied the verse into one of her albums (H MS. 255) and headed it 'Written in a Lady's Quintus Curtius / By E. W. to the Lady M. Pierrepont.'

How soon this declaration of love in verse was followed by one in prose does not appear; but Mrs. Anne Wortley grew more eloquent in Lady Mary's praise, and more eagerly desirous of her correspondence. No wonder; since the rough draught of a letter in her brother's hand, indorsed 'For my sister to Lady M. P.' betrays that he was the writer, and she only the transcriber of professions and encomiums that sound extravagant as addressed by one woman to another.[1] But she did not live to be long the medium through which they passed; a more direct correspondence soon began, and was continued after her decease. When married, Mr. Wortley and Lady Mary agreed to put by and preserve as memorials of the days of courtship all their letters; a curious collection, and very different from what a romance-writer would have framed; on his side, no longer complimentary, but strikingly expressive of a real strong passion, combated in vain by a mind equally strong, which yielded to it against its conviction and against its will. '*Celui qui aime plus qu'il ne voudroit,*' as a French author somewhere says, is, after all, the person in whom love has taken the fastest hold. They were perpetually on the point of breaking altogether: he felt and knew that they suited each other very ill; he saw, or thought he saw, his rivals encouraged if not preferred; he was more affronted than satisfied with her assurances of a *sober* esteem and regard; and yet every struggle to get free did but end where it set out, leaving him still a captive, galled by his chain, but unable to sever one link of it effectually.

After some time thus spent in fluctuations, disputes, and lovers' quarrels, he at length made his proposals to Lord Dorchester, who received them favourably, and was very gracious to him, till the *Grim-gribber*[2] part of the business—the portion and settlements—came under consideration; but then broke off the match in great anger, on account of a disagreement which subsequent events have rendered memorable. We see how the practice of a man's entailing his estate upon his eldest son while as yet an unborn child, an unknown being, is ridiculed in the Tatler and Spectator; whose authors, it may be observed, had not estates to entail. Mr. Wortley, who *had*, entertained the same opinions. Possibly they were originally his own, and promulgated by Addison and Steele at his suggestion, for, as he always liked to think for himself, many of his

---

[1] Several of Anne's letters were transcribed from W's drafts (*Letters*, 1. 4–14 *passim*).
[2] Richard Steele, *The Conscious Lovers*, 1723, Act III.

notions were singular and speculative.[1] However this might be, he upheld the system, and acted upon it, offering to make the best provision in his power for Lady Mary, but steadily refusing to settle his landed property upon a son who, for aught he knew, might prove unworthy to possess it—might be a spendthrift, an idiot, or a villain.

Lord Dorchester, on the other hand, said that these philosophic theories were very fine, but *his* grandchildren should not run the risk of being left beggars; and, as he had to do with a person of no common firmness, the treaty ended there.

The secret correspondence and intercourse went on as before; and shortly Lady Mary acquainted her lover that she was peremptorily commanded to accept the offers of another suitor,[2] ready to close with all her father's terms, to settle handsome pin-money, jointure, provision for heirs, and so forth; and, moreover, concede the point most agreeable to herself, that of giving her a fixed establishment in London, which, by-the-bye, Mr. Wortley had always protested against. Lord Dorchester seems to have asked no questions touching her inclination in either instance. A man who is now about to sell an estate, seldom thinks of inquiring whether it will please or displease his tenantry to be transferred to a new landlord; and just as little then did parents in disposing of a daughter conceive it necessary to consult her will and pleasure. For a young lady to interfere, or claim a right of choice, was almost thought, as it is in France, a species of indelicacy. Lady Mary nevertheless declared, though timidly, her utter antipathy to the person proposed to her. Upon this, her father summoned her to his awful presence, and, after expressing surprise at her presumption in questioning his judgment, assured her he would not give her a single sixpence if she married anybody else. She sought the usual resource of poor damsels in the like case, begging permission to split the difference (if we may so say) by not marrying at all; but he answered that then she should be immediately sent to a remote place in the country, reside there during his life, and at his death

[1] W did provide the notes for Steele's *Tatler* papers Nos. 199 and 223 on marriage settlements and entail (Halsband, *LM*, pp. 13, 15; Richmond P. Bond, 'Mr. Bickerstaff and Mr. Wortley', in *Classical, Mediaeval and Renaissance Studies in Honor of Berthold Louis Ullman*, ed. C. Henderson, Jr., 1964, 2. 491–504). The subject of entail is also discussed in the *Spectator* Nos. 282 and 522.

[2] Clotworthy Skeffington (*c.* 1681–1739), son and heir of 3rd Viscount Massereene, an Irish peer.

have no portion save a moderate annuity. Relying upon the effect of these threats, he proceeded as if she had given her fullest and freest consent; settlements were drawn, wedding-clothes bought, the day was appointed, and everything made ready, when she left the house to marry Mr. Wortley.

The father's rage may be imagined; Lady Frances Pierrepont, afraid it should lead him to examine her sister's papers, and apprehending that he might there find matter to exasperate him still further, hastily burned all she could find, and amongst them a diary which Lady Mary had already kept for some years, and was not very well pleased to lose.

Soon after her marriage she resumed the practice of writing a journal, and persisted in it as long as she lived; communicating what she wrote to no person whatever. The diary of course became voluminous. Lady Bute, who knew nothing of it till it came into her possession a few days before her mother's death, always kept it under lock and key; and though she often looked over it herself, and would sometimes read passages from it aloud to her daughters and friends, yet she never trusted any part out of her own hands, excepting the five or six first copy-books, which, at a late period, she permitted one of her family to peruse alone,[1] upon condition that nothing should be transcribed. All that she thus in any way imparted related to distant days, to transactions long since past, and people of a former generation. Meanwhile she constantly declared it was her determined resolution to destroy the whole, as a sacred duty owing to the deceased, whose having forgotten or neglected to leave express orders for the purpose, made it only the more incumbent upon her survivors. The journal was accordingly burned, although with evident reluctance, and not till Lady Bute felt the close of her life drawing near; when the act itself sounded too solemn a note of preparation for those who loved her as she deserved to think of opposing it, or indeed to care at all about a matter which would then have seemed totally indifferent had it concerned the finest work in the world.

Lady Bute so admired her mother's writings, and took such pleasure in reading her letters to persons whom she thought endowed with taste enough to relish them, that it might have been held sufficiently certain she had the most cogent reasons for making

[1] No doubt Lady Louisa herself, who as a girl had literary interests and ambitions.

what clearly appeared a sacrifice. Yet, as youth is inconsiderate, and the fragments she did allow to be seen or heard were not a little amusing, she was very often assailed with intreaties to forego her design. When pressed on this head, she would ask whether, supposing the case one's own, one could bear the thought of having every crude opinion, every transient wish, every angry feeling that had flitted across one's mind, exposed to the world after one was no more? And though she always spoke of Lady Mary with great respect, yet it might be perceived that she knew it had been too much her custom to note down and enlarge upon all the scandalous rumours of the day, without weighing their truth or even their probability; to record as certain facts stories that perhaps sprang up like mushrooms from the dirt, and had as brief an existence, but tended to defame persons of the most spotless character. In this age, she said, everything got into print sooner or later; the name of Lady Mary Wortley would be sure to attract curiosity; and, were such details ever made public, they would neither edify the world, nor do honour to her memory. These were Lady Bute's arguments; and what could any one who had a sense of rectitude urge in reply? especially since it must be acknowledged, that in the volumes which she did communicate, the earliest written, and (one may be confident) the least exceptionable, there occasionally appeared traits of satire that showed what might ensue when the vexations and cares of advancing life should have soured the mind, given objects a darker shade of colour, and made farther demands upon a Christian charity not at 'all likely to have increased in the mean time.

These volumes comprised the years immediately succeeding Lady Mary's marriage, 1713, 1714, 1715; and also the time of Mr. Wortley's embassy. What passed every day was set down; often only in a line, or half a line, as thus: 'Stayed at home alone—went to such a place—saw such a person:' so that frequently three or four weeks took up but a single page. Sometimes, again, an occurrence or a conversation would be given at very great length; sometimes dispatched with one sharp sentence, like the following humorous application of a speech in Dryden's Spanish Friar: 'Lady Hinchinbroke has a dead daughter—it were unchristian not to be sorry for my cousin's misfortune; but if she has no live son, Mr. Wortley is heir—so there's comfort for a Christian.'[1]

---

[1] John Dryden, *The Spanish Fryar*, 1681 (*Works*, 5. 135). Lady Hinchingbrooke was

The three years previous to the embassy were passed by Lady Mary in various abodes, and occasionally apart from Mr. Wortley, while he attended parliament. She was sometimes, however, though seldom, in London; sometimes at Hinchinbroke, the seat of Lord Sandwich; sometimes near it, in the town of Huntingdon, for which Mr. Wortley was member;[1] but more often at hired houses in Yorkshire. About the time of Queen Anne's death, she dates her letters from Middlethorpe, in the neighbourhood of Bishopthorpe and of York. It is a mistake that she ever resided permanently at Wharncliffe Lodge.[2] Mr. Sidney Wortley Montagu chiefly inhabited that himself; and with him his daughter Mrs. Katherine Wortley, his youngest son Mr. John Montagu,[3] his brother the Dean of Durham, and the Dean's chaplain. How so many people, together with their servants, could be packed into so small a space will appear sufficiently wonderful to those who have seen the little dwelling; but a couple more could hardly have been stowed in by any human contrivance.

The first mention of Wharncliffe in Lady Mary's journal, after calling there to visit her father-in-law when on her road to some other place, was very remarkable; considering that she had hitherto known only the midland counties and the environs of London, and probably had never before seen anything like picturesque or romantic scenery. One would have supposed the first sight of so wild and beautiful a prospect as that eagle's nest commands, very sure to occasion surprise, if not excite transport, in a mind gifted with the least imagination. But no; nothing could be colder or more slight than the notice she took of it, almost making an excuse for saying thus much in its favour—'that it was a sequestered rural spot, quite of a rude nature; yet had something in it which she owned she did not dislike, odd as her fancy might appear.' In after days, her letters to Mr. Wortley do it more justice, possibly to please him;[4] but the journal gave the original impression. . . .

Elizabeth Popham (d. 1761), who m. (1707) the son and heir of 3rd Earl of Sandwich, W's cousin; hence W was still heir presumptive. A son later born to Hinchingbrooke (in 1718) became 4th Earl.

[1] From 1705 to 1713 W was M.P. for Huntingdon.

[2] At Wortley, about ten miles from Sheffield.

[3] Catherine Wortley (d. 1761), m. (1728) John Orme, later a naval captain. John Montagu died unmarried.

[4] Many years later: that Wharncliffe Lodge was 'the most beautifull land prospect' she had ever seen (1743, *Letters*, 2. 315).

To resume the journal. In the year 1713, Lady Frances Pierrepont married the Earl of Mar, then Secretary of State for Scotland[1]:—a match of which Lady Mary seems to have augured ill, having but an indifferent opinion of him, detesting the party he belonged to, and believing that her sister was drawn in by the persuasion of an officious female friend,—his relation. These sentiments, however, were expressed without any great warmth, and not as if the event interested her deeply. But the death of her brother, Lord Kingston, which soon followed it, does seem to have really touched her heart. It gave her the greater shock, because she knew nothing of the poor young man's illness until he was past all hope of recovery; for, as Lord Dorchester had not yet entirely forgiven her stolen marriage, he did not allow her to have much intercourse with the rest of his family. Lord Kingston, who died of the small-pox under age, though already a husband and a father, was of a most amiable disposition, and so affectionate to her, that he would have taken her part openly, and have done every thing in his power to facilitate her marriage, if the temper of Lord Dorchester had not been such as to render his endeavouring to oppose him more dangerous to himself than useful to his sister. Her reflections on his fate were consequently very bitter as well as very sorrowful; accusing her father of having blighted his youth, and destroyed all the peace and happiness of his short life, by marrying him to a silly, childish girl, for the sake of securing her fortune, before he could judge for himself or make a choice of his own.[2] In him she appeared to think she had lost her best, if not her only, natural friend.

Whenever Lady Mary's attention was much attracted by any report spread concerning one of her acquaintance, or any incident that happened in her society, a piece of good or ill fortune, a death or a marriage, her journal would often branch off into a kind of memoir while the subject was fresh in her mind. She certainly dwelt with most complacency upon whatever afforded the groundwork of a love-story, and as certainly did not spare her censures where the occasion called for them. The composition cost her no pains; she had the gift of writing freely in the first words that

[1] John Erskine (1675–1732), 6th Earl of Mar, Secretary of State for Scotland, 1705–9 and 1713–14, remarried in *1714*. A Jacobite, he fled abroad after the 1715 uprising.

[2] Lord Kingston m. (1711) Rachel Baynton (1695–1722), natural da. of John Hall of Bradford, Wilts., whose vast estates she inherited. He d. 1 July 1713 at the age of twenty.

presented themselves; so that the fair pages of the diary seldom betrayed a blot or an erasure. Both her daughter and the old servant, who had often seen her at her writing-desk, bore witness to this extraordinary facility.

The most interesting of the narratives was a history of her early companion Dolly Walpole, (as she always called her,)—according to her description a beautiful, innocent, well-meaning girl, but endowed with only a moderate portion of sense; giddy, thoughtless, vain, open to flattery, utterly ignorant of the world; in short, though not capable of acting wrong designedly, just the person, if we may use the vulgar tongue, *to get often into scrapes.* Her eldest brother, then Mr. Walpole, had brought her to London in hopes that her beauty, the pride of his county, might captivate something superior to a Norfolk squire. But being immersed in politics, and careless of what passed at home, he left her to the guidance of his wife, an empty, coquettish, affected woman,[1] anything rather than correct in her own conduct, or spotless in her fame; greedy of admiration, and extremely dissatisfied at having to share it with this younger fairer inmate. In spite of her envious machinations, lovers soon crowded round Dolly; and one of the number presently obtained the preference he languished for. He had all manner of good qualities, was handsome, pleasing, as passionately in love as romance could have required, and heir to a competent fortune; but not altogether his own master: he depended upon his friends. A young man's *friends*, in this sense, meaning parents, guardians, old uncles, and the like, are rarely propitious to love. As no second sight revealed to them the long glories of Sir Robert Walpole's reign, they looked solely to a matter nearer at hand—Dolly's portion; and finding that *null*, entered their protest in a determined manner. Mrs. Walpole triumphed; she told tales, made mischief, incited Dolly to flirt with other admirers, and then lamented her fickleness and coquetry to the very people who, she knew, would be sure to speed the lament onward with no favourable comments. Lady Mary took to herself the credit of having been all this while her simple friend's protecting genius; of having often counteracted Mrs. Walpole, and sometimes unmasked her; given Dolly the best advice, and cleared up the misunderstandings between her and her lover that continually arose from jealousy on one side and indiscretion on the other. The story proceeded like its fellows in the

[1] Catherine Shorter (*c.* 1682–1737), m. (1700) Robert Walpole.

Scudery folios,[1] with *ins and outs*, and *ups and downs*, more than can be remembered; but the sequel was, that the suitor, either inconstant or disgusted, finally withdrew from the chase, and the nymph remained disappointed and forsaken. Just at this unlucky moment, Lady Mary Pierrepont being absent at Thoresby, poor Dolly's evil star prevailed, and, while her mind was in that depressed, mortified state which makes us thankful to anybody who will give us so much as a kind look, led her into acquaintance with Lady Wharton, the very worst protectress she could acquire—a woman equally unfeeling and unprincipled;[2] flattering, fawning, canting, affecting prudery and even sanctity, yet in reality as abandoned and unscrupulous as her husband himself.—So said the journal.

It is worth noting that Lady Mary Wortley, who abhorred the very name of Dean Swift, should yet have spoken of both Lord and Lady Wharton precisely as he did.[3] The portraits were so alike that one might have been believed a copy of the other. To be sure, she was (in Doctor Johnson's phrase) almost as 'good a hater' as the dean himself,[4] and the diary proved it by certain passages relating to Queen Anne, Mrs. Masham,[5] and also to persons obnoxious to her for private reasons: but neither private nor public operated against Lord Wharton, with whom she had had no quarrel, who was intimate with her family and on the same side with her in party; therefore she probably only echoed the general voice in pronouncing him 'the most profligate, impious, and shameless of men.' Dolly Walpole, however, knowing nothing of any one's character, felt elated at being caressed and courted by so great and good a lady as the Countess of Wharton, told her all her secrets, and complained to her of all her grievances. The result was, that after one of these confidential conversations, when Mrs. Walpole had done something particularly spiteful, and Mr. Walpole happened to be out of town, Lady Wharton pressed the poor girl to leave his house for a few days and pass them in hers, where she should enjoy comfort and

---

[1] The voluminous prose romances by Madeleine de Scudéry (1607–1701).

[2] Lucy Loftus (1670–1717), m. (1692) Thomas, Earl, and later Marquess, of Wharton.

[3] Swift concentrated his attack on them in *A Short Character of his Excellency Thomas Earl of Wharton, Lord Lieutenant of Ireland* (1711), *Prose Works*, ed. H. Davis, 1939–68, 3. 175–84.

[4] Adapted from Dr. Johnson's comment on Dr. Richard Bathurst: 'he was a very good *hater*' (Mrs. Piozzi, *Anecdotes*, 1786, in *Johnsonian Miscellanies*, ed. G. B. Hill, 1897, 1. 204).

[5] Abigail Hill (d. 1734), m. (1707) Samuel, later Lord Masham; a cousin of the Duchess of Marlborough, whom she supplanted as Queen Anne's favourite.

tranquillity. Dolly consented with joy, not in the least aware that there could be any objection; and Mrs. Walpole made none, because perfectly well aware, and secretly exulting in what she knew likely to follow.

Now, as Lady Mary proceeded to state, Lord Wharton's character was so infamous, and his lady's complaisant subserviency so notorious, that no young woman could be four-and-twenty hours under their roof with safety to her reputation. Dean Swift says nothing much stronger than this. Upon Mr. Walpole's return home, enraged at finding whither his sister had betaken herself, he flew to Lord Wharton's, and, thundering for admittance, demanded her aloud, regardless who might hear him. My lord, not at all inclined to face him in this temper, thought it safest to abscond; so, crept privately out of his own house by a back-door, leaving my lady to bide the pelting of the storm, pitiless as it threatened to prove. Sir Robert, it is well known, was at no time apt to be over delicate or ceremonious: he accosted her ladyship in the plainest English, bestowed upon her some significant epithets, and, without listening to a word of explanation, forced away his weeping sister, with whom he set out for Norfolk the next morning.

Thus ended the first chapter of Dolly's adventures; but she was not doomed to be finally unfortunate. After doing penance for two or three years in a very dull retirement, she had the good luck to light upon a more capital prize in the country than she had ever aimed at in London, the person being Lord Townshend, one of the most unblemished statesmen and respectable gentlemen of that age. Foreign employments had kept him abroad until Queen Anne's change of ministry, and since that he had been a long and sincere mourner for his first wife, the sister of Lord Pelham. Dolly was to him therefore a new beauty, no tattle concerning whom had ever reached his ears. Falling in love at once, he proposed, she accepted, and the news of the match prompted Lady Mary to sit down and write her history.[1]

This brief memoir, it is observable, furnishes a clew to the origin

[1] Charles Townshend (1675–1738), 2nd Viscount, Joint Ambassador Extraordinary and Plenipotentiary at The Hague, 1709–11, m. 1st (1698) Elizabeth Pelham, and 2nd (1713) Dorothy Walpole. When Lady Strafford, a Tory, reported Dolly Walpole's marriage, she added: 'I can't tell whethere you know her Carrecter, but she is won Lord Wharton Keept. I am for having the Whiggs have all such wives' (*Wentworth Papers*, ed. J. J. Cartwright, 1883, p. 321). See also pp. 83–4 below.

of Horace Walpole's excessive dislike of Lady Mary Wortley.[1] His mother and she had been antagonists and enemies before he was born; '*car tout est reciproque*,' says La Bruyere. We see how Lady Mary represented Lady Walpole, and may take it for granted that Lady Walpole did not love or spare Lady Mary; and if they continued to keep up the outward forms of acquaintanceship, which of course brought them often into contact, they would naturally hate each other all the more.

Mr. Walpole's affection for his mother was so much the most amiable point in his character, and his expressions whenever he names or alludes to her are so touching, come so directly and evidently from the heart, that one would very fain think of her as he did, and believe she had every perfection his partiality assigns to her. But, in truth, there was a contrary version of the matter, not resting solely, nor yet principally, upon the authority of Lady Mary Wortley. It filled so prominent a place in the scandalous history of the time, that the world knew as well which way Captain Lemuel Gulliver was glancing when gravely vindicating the reputation of my Lord *Treasurer* Flimnap's excellent lady, as what he meant by the red, green, and blue girdles of the Lilliputian grandees, or the said Flimnap's feats of agility on the tight-rope.[2] Those ironical lines also, where Pope says that Sir Robert Walpole

> 'Had never made a friend in private life,
> And was besides *a tyrant to his wife*,'[3]

are equally well understood as conveying a sly allusion to his good-humoured unconcern about some things which more strait-laced husbands do not take so coolly. Openly laughing at their nicety, he professed it his method 'to go his own way, and let madam go hers.' In a word, Horace Walpole himself was generally supposed to be the son of Carr Lord Hervey,[4] and Sir Robert not to be ignorant of it. One striking circumstance was visible to the naked eye; no beings in human shape could resemble each other less than the two passing for father and son; and, while their *reverse* of personal

---

[1] The relationship between LM and Horace Walpole (1717–97), later Lord Orford, is treated in Halsband, 'Walpole *versus* Lady Mary', *Horace Walpole: Writer, Politician, and Connoisseur*, ed. W. H. Smith, 1967, pp. 215–26.

[2] In chapters 6, 3, and 3, respectively, of *Gulliver's Travels*, Part I.

[3] 'Epilogue to the Satires. Written in 1738. Dialogue II', in *Poems*, 4. 321.

[4] Carr, Lord Hervey (1691–1723), eldest son of 1st Earl of Bristol; at his death his courtesy title went to his half-brother John (1696–1743), the famous Lord Hervey.

likeness provoked a malicious whisper, Sir Robert's marked neglect of Horace in his infancy tended to confirm it. A number of children, young Walpole one, were accustomed to meet and play together. Such of them as, like himself, lived to grow old, all united in declaring that no other boy within their knowledge was left so entirely in the hands of his mother, or seemed to have so little acquaintance with his father; the fact being, that Sir Robert Walpole took scarcely any notice of him, till his proficiency at Eton school, when a lad of some standing, drew his attention, and proved that, whether he had, or had not, a right to the name he went by, he was likely to do it honour.

Though in all probability Lord Orford never suspected that any doubt hung over his own birth, yet the mortifications of his youth on his mother's account could not but be severe; for, as she lived till he reached manhood, he must have known how completely she was overlooked and disregarded, though not ill treated, by her husband; and, before his tears for her loss were dried, he had the pang of seeing Miss Skerritt, the rival she hated, installed in her place.[1] That Lady Mary Wortley had been the chief friend and protectress of his stepmother, was alone enough to make him bitter against her. In another instance, we must allow, he showed true generosity of mind. When Sir Robert Walpole, not content with publicly owning his natural daughter by Miss Skerritt, stretched his credit with the crown to the extent of obtaining for her a rank and title till then never conferred on the illegitimate offspring of any man but a prince,[2] his son Horace, instead of murmuring at it, or viewing her with an evil eye, frankly opened his arms to her as a sister, and so called and considered her the rest of his life.[3]

The daughter was not brought forward in this manner till after the death of the mother, who enjoyed her married situation a very few months. But the tale the recognition told could hardly be new to any one. Lady Bute never adverted to it without pain and regret, having a tenderness for Miss Skerritt's memory, which the recollec-

---

[1] Maria Skerrett (1702-38) became Walpole's mistress in the early 1720s. He married her in March 1738, seven months after the death of his first wife (and only three months before her own death).

[2] 'This morning Sir Robert Walpole kissed hands at Court for being created Earl of Orford, and his bastard daughter [Maria, c. 1725-1801] did the same on having a patent passed to her, to take place as an Earl's daughter, which cannot please the female sex' (8 Feb. 1742, H.M.C., *Egmont Diary*, 1920-3, 3. 248).

[3] Cf. Wilmarth Sheldon Lewis, *Horace Walpole*, 1960, p. 17.

tion of her many agreeable qualities, her sweetness of temper, and fondness of herself as a child, rendered it difficult to overcome.

Upon the death of Queen Anne, Mr. Wortley's friends coming into power, he was appointed a Lord of the Treasury.[1] He had long been an active, efficient member of parliament, and when he first obtained this office, people expected that he would have a considerable sway in the new King's counsels: for a reason which will now seem rather surprising,—he was the only man at the board (excepting perhaps Lord Halifax) who could converse with his Majesty, because the only one who spoke French; consequently, much of the business must have gone through his hands, if the sovereign, like his predecessors, William and Anne, had assisted in person at the meetings of the commissioners. But George the First leaving finance-affairs and all others to be managed as his ministers pleased, Mr. Wortley had no more personal intercourse with him than the rest. Lady Mary frequently[2] attracted his notice, and likewise that of the Prince of Wales (George the Second.) By her journal, indeed, it might have been imagined that the latter admired her rather more than the Princess[3] (though usually far from jealous) could quite approve. For once, in a rapture, he called her royal highness from the card-table to look how becomingly Lady Mary was dressed! 'Lady Mary always dresses well,' said the Princess drily, and returned to her cards. However, his favour was soon withdrawn, and hers regained. The father and son were already, almost at their first setting out, upon such hostile terms, that, the moment the Prince heard of Lady Mary's having been at one of the King's select parties, he grew not only cool but resentful, taunting her as a deserter gone over to the enemy's camp; and thenceforward she dressed becomingly in vain. An increase of graciousness on the part of the Princess made her amends.

A former edition tells us, 'that the court of George the First was modelled upon that of Louis the Fifteenth.'[4] A whimsical model! Since Louis was about seven years old when George, a man of sixty, ascended the British throne. One would think Louis the *Fourteenth* must have been the person meant, but that the retired

---

[1] On 13 Oct. 1714 he accepted the appointment from his relation Lord Halifax (see p. 83 below).   [2] Altered to 'presently' in 2nd edition.

[3] Caroline of Anspach (1683-1737).

[4] In James Dallaway's 'Memoir', 1803, reprinted without correction in 1837, along with these Biographical Anecdotes.

habits of the English monarch accorded no better with the stately
ceremonial of the elder French one, than with the amusements and
regulations of his great-grandson's nursery. George the First went
to the play or opera in a sedan-chair, and sate, like another gentleman, in the corner of a lady's (a German lady's) box, with a couple
of Turks[1] in waiting instead of lords and grooms of the bedchamber.
In one respect his court, if court it could be called, bore some
resemblance to the old establishment of Versailles. There was a
Madame de Maintenon. Of the three favourite ladies who had
accompanied him from Hanover, viz. Mademoiselle de Schulen-
berg, the Countess Platen, and Madame Kilmansegg,[2] the first
alone, whom he created Duchess of Kendal, was lodged in St.
James's Palace, and had such respect paid her as very much confirmed the rumour of a left-hand marriage. She presided at the
King's evening-parties, consisting of the Germans who formed his
familiar society, a few English ladies, and fewer English men:
among them Mr. Craggs, the Secretary of State,[3] who had been at
Hanover in the Queen's time, and by thus having the *entrée* in private,
passed for a sort of favourite.

Lady Mary's journal related a ridiculous adventure of her own
at one of these royal parties; which, by-the-bye, stood in great need
of some laughing-matter to enliven them, for they seem to have
been even more dull than it was reasonable to expect they should be.
She had on one evening a particular engagement that made her
wish to be dismissed unusually early; she explained her reasons to
the Duchess of Kendal, and the Duchess informed the King, who,
after a few complimentary remonstrances, appeared to acquiesce.
But when he saw her about to take her leave, he began battling the
point afresh, declaring it was unfair and perfidious to cheat him in
such a manner, and saying many other fine things, in spite of which
she at last contrived to escape. At the foot of the great stairs she ran
against Secretary Craggs just coming in, who stopped her to inquire
what was the matter? were the company put off? She told him why

---

[1] Mehemet and Mustapha had served George I in Hanover for over twenty-five years
(John M. Beattie, *The English Court in the Reign of George I*, 1967, p. 55).

[2] Lady Louisa bases her description of the courtiers on LM's 'Account of the Court
of George I' (see pp. 84–93 below). But LM writes that only two of these ladies came
to England; and after Lady Louisa's error was pointed out in John Wilson Croker's
review (see p. 55 below), it was silently corrected in the 2nd edition by omitting the
Countess Platen.

[3] James Craggs, the younger (1686–1721), was Secretary of State from Mar. 1718
until his death.

she went away, and how urgently the King had pressed her to stay longer; possibly dwelling on that head with some small complacency. Mr. Craggs made no remark; but, when he had heard all, snatching her up in his arms as a nurse carries a child, he ran full speed with her up-stairs, deposited her within the ante-chamber, kissed both her hands respectfully, (still not saying a word,) and vanished. The pages seeing her returned, they knew not how, hastily threw open the inner doors, and, before she had recovered her breath, she found herself again in the King's presence. '*Ah! la re-voilà!*' cried he and the Duchess, extremely pleased, and began thanking her for her obliging change of mind. The motto on all palace-gates is 'HUSH!' as Lady Mary very well knew. She had not to learn that mystery and caution ever spread their awful wings over the precincts of a court; where nobody knows what dire mischief may ensue from one unlucky syllable blabbed about anything, or about *nothing*, at a wrong time. But she was bewildered, fluttered, and entirely off her guard; so, beginning giddily with 'Oh Lord, sir! I have been so frightened!' she told his Majesty the whole story exactly as she would have told it to any one else. He had not done exclaiming, nor his Germans wondering, when again the door flew open, and the attendants announced Mr. Secretary Craggs, who, but that moment arrived, it should seem, entered with the usual obeisance, and as composed an air as if nothing had happened. '*Mais comment donc, Monsieur Craggs,*' said the King, going up to him, '*est-ce que c'est l'usage de ce pays de porter des belles dames comme un sac de froment?*' 'Is it the custom of this country to carry about fair ladies like a sack of wheat?' The minister, struck dumb by this unexpected attack, stood a minute or two not knowing which way to look; then, recovering his self-possession, answered with a low bow, 'There is nothing I would not do for your Majesty's satisfaction.' This was coming off tolerably well; but he did not forgive the tell-tale culprit, in whose ear, watching his opportunity when the King turned from them, he muttered a bitter reproach, with a round oath to enforce it; 'which I durst not resent,' continued she, 'for I had drawn it upon myself; and indeed I was heartily vexed at my own imprudence.'

The name of George the First recalls a remarkable anecdote of his mother, the Princess Sophia,[1] which Mr. Wortley and Lady

---

[1] Sophia (1630-1714), da. of King of Bohemia, m. (1658) Ernst August, later Elector of Hanover. Her mother was a daughter of James I.

Mary heard from Lord Halifax. When he and Lord Dorset were dispatched by the Whig administration upon the welcome errand of announcing to her the act of parliament that secured the Hanover succession,[1] at the same time carrying the garter to the Electoral Prince, her grandson, they were received, as may be supposed, with every mark of distinction. At their first formal audience, as they commenced a set speech, after delivering their credentials, the old Electress, who was standing, gave a kind of start, and almost *ran* to one corner of the room, where, fixing her back against the wall, she remained stiff and erect as if glued to it, till the ceremony ended, and they withdrew. Her behaviour being in all other respects very dignified and decorous, they were at a loss to divine what could have occasioned this extraordinary *move*, and very curious to discover the meaning of it; a secret which Lord Halifax at length got at, by dint of sifting and cross-questioning her courtiers. She had suddenly recollected that there hung in that room a picture of her cousin, the PRETENDER, and, in a fright lest it should catch their eyes, could hit upon no expedient to hide it but by screening it with her own person. The good Princess, however, was not in the least disloyal to herself; she harboured no dislike to the prospect of a crown, nor any scruples about accepting it; but, nevertheless, valuing her Stuart-descent, she had a family feeling for the young man, whom she firmly believed to be as much James the Second's son as George the First was her own. That is to say, she was what at the time all England would have styled '*a rank Jacobite.*'

The only event particularly interesting to Lady Mary that seems to have taken place between the King's accession and her journey to Constantinople was the marriage of her father, now Duke of Kingston, to 'the fair Isabella,' as she is called in the journal; in common speech, Lady Belle Bentinck, the youngest daughter of the late Earl of Portland, King William's favourite.[2] She was one of the most admired beauties in London, and had long been the object of his grace's pursuit. Her previous history supplied the diary with a romantic tale, but Lady Mary did not pretend that it had come

----

[1] In 1706 Charles Montagu (1661–1715), 1st Lord Halifax, and Lionel Cranfield (1688–1725), 7th Earl, later 1st Duke, of Dorset, presented Sophia with copies of the Regency and Naturalization Acts, which reinforced her family's claim to the throne.

[2] The Duke of Kingston, after being a widower for twenty-two years, m. (1714) Lady Isabella Bentinck (1688–1728), da. of 1st Earl of Portland. She was only one year older than LM.

under her own cognisance, like Dolly Walpole's, or say from what authority she gave it. The heads of it were, a passion for a younger lover,[1] and the combats and conflicts of love on one side, with interest and ambition on the other; until these latter, gaining a complete victory, made the offers of a man who had three married daughters older than the lady herself appear too tempting to be refused. It is needless to add that Lady Mary was free from any partial feeling towards a mother-in-law who, as she supposed, aimed straight at· becoming a rich widow. If so, she had not the happiness of being one long; for, notwithstanding the disparity of their ages, she survived her husband but two years. He died in 1726: Lady Bute remembered having seen him once only, but that in a manner likely to leave some impression on the mind of a child. Her mother was dressing, and she playing about the room, when there entered an elderly stranger (of dignified appearance, and still handsome) with the authoritative air of a person entitled to admittance at all times; upon which, to her great surprise, Lady Mary instantly starting up from the toilet-table, dishevelled as she was, fell on her knees to ask his blessing. A proof that even in the great and gay world this primitive custom was still universal.

Lady Bute witnessed the observance of another, now obsolete, in the ceremony that her grandfather's widow had to go through soon after his funeral was over. It behoved *to see company;* that is, to receive in person the compliments of condolence which every lady on her grace's visiting list was bound to tender, in person likewise. And this was the established form: the apartments, the staircase, and all that could be seen of the house, were hung with black cloth; the Duchess, closely veiled with crape, sate upright in her state-bed under a high black canopy; and at the foot of the bed stood ranged, like a row of mutes in a tragedy, the grandchildren of the deceased Duke—Lady Frances Pierrepont, Miss Wortley herself, and Lady Gower's daughters.[2] Profound silence reigned: the room had no light but from a single wax-taper; and the condoling visiters, who curtseyed in and out of it, approached the bed on tiptoe; if relations, all, down to the hundredth cousin, in black-glove-mourning for the occasion.

[1] Evidently Lady Isabella's 'younger lover' was Conyers Darcy (*c.* 1685–1758), a member of a prominent Whig family of Yorkshire (Walpole, *Corr.* 14. 243).

[2] Lady Frances Pierrepont was the orphaned daughter of LM's brother; Miss Wortley was LM's daughter; and Lady Gower, LM's sister, had six daughters living. Another grandchild, LM's son, attended Westminster School.

We may perceive from this that Sir Richard Steele's comedy of the 'Funeral' contained no exaggeration.[1] Nor was the custom of putting houses into mourning for their defunct owners confined to the great. In the supposed letter of Partridge the astrologer, the undertaker, concluding that 'the doctor must needs have died rich,' sets about measuring the wainscot, and says, 'Let's see: the passage and these two rooms hung in close mourning, with a stripe of black baize round the others, will be sufficient.'[2] How a miser must have grudged the expense of dying!

. . . During Lady Mary's travels[3] she copied into her diary the letters of Pope and Congreve as she received them; and it contained the whole substance of her own, meaning of those printed in 1763. The descriptions of her journey, of the court and society of Vienna, of inoculation, of Fatima, of the Sultana Hafiten[4], of the antiquities, baths, mosques, janissaries, effendis, &c. &c. were all there; sometimes more diffusedly given, but oftener in the very same words. It seemed her custom to note everything down without a moment's delay; and then, when she wrote a letter, to transcribe from the journal the passages she thought fittest to be communicated to her friends, or, one may say, to the world. For, although she did not design the correspondence for publication while she was living, she had it copied, and allowed many people to read it. The diary of course contained farther details; but the cream having been skimmed for the letters, the rest was not very interesting or important.[5] No Valida ever was named, therefore the princess represented by Voltaire as so active in befriending Charles the Twelfth had probably died before Mr. Wortley's arrival at her son's court.[6] Upon the whole, Lady Mary led a retired life most of the time she passed in that country.

It is known that when on her way to die, as it proved, in her own,

---

[1] *The Funeral: Or, Grief A-La-Mode*, 1701.

[2] In the Partridge hoax, begun by Swift in 1708, other writers contributed; this quotation is adapted from a pamphlet by Nicholas Rowe (Swift, *Prose Works*, ed. H. Davis, 1939–68, 2. 219).

[3] To Constantinople, from 1 Aug. 1716 to 2 Oct. 1718.

[4] Correctly: Hafise (LM, *Letters*, 1. 380 n.).

[5] The composition of the Embassy Letters is discussed in *Letters*, 1. xiv–xvii.

[6] Râbia Gülnûs (1642–1715), known as Valide Sultan, mother of the Sultan (Ahmed III), had been dead for two years when LM arrived in Turkey. Her friendship with the Swedish king is described in Book V of Voltaire's *Histoire de Charles XII*, 1731.

she gave a copy of the letters to Mr. Sowden, minister of the English church at Rotterdam,[1] attesting the gift by her signature. This showed it was her wish that they should eventually be published; but Lady Bute, hearing only that a number of her mother's letters were in a stranger's hands, and having no certainty what they might be, to whom addressed, or how little of a private nature, could not but earnestly desire to obtain them, and readily paid the price demanded,—five hundred pounds. In a few months she saw them appear in print. Such was the fact; and how it came about, nobody at this time of day need either care or inquire.

The first editor of these letters—a Mr. Cleland[2] as it is supposed, or whoever else he might be,—ascribes the preface, dated in 1724, and signed M.A., to a lady of quality, whom he terms 'the fair and elegant prefacer:'[3] epithets most unluckily chosen, unless the lovers of *fine style* hold them as inseparably annexed to a petticoat, as, in parliamentary language, 'honourable' is to an M.P. This fair and elegant lady of quality was no less a person than Mistress Mary Astell, of learned memory, the Madonella of the Tatler, a very pious, exemplary woman, and a profound scholar,[4] but as far from fair and elegant as any old schoolmaster of her time: in outward form, indeed, rather ill-favoured and forbidding, and of a humour to have repulsed the compliment roughly, had it been paid her while she lived. For she regarded such commonplace phrases as insults in disguise, impertinently offered by men through a secret persuasion that all women were fools. She may be thought to have dealt in wholesale praise herself, but her encomiums, though excessive, were sincere; she was an enthusiast, not a flatterer, and felt for Lady Mary Wortley that fond partiality which old people of ardent tempers sometimes entertain for a rising genius in their own line. Literature had been hers; and she triumphed in Lady Mary's talents as proofs of what it was her first wish to demonstrate, namely, the mental equality of the sexes; if not the superiority of woman to man. Many a tract have the worms long ago eaten, or the pastry-

---

[1] Benjamin Sowden (d. 1796); the letters are H MSS. 253, 254.
[2] John Cleland, more famous for his novel *Memoirs of a Woman of Pleasure*, 1748.
[3] The publication of LM's Embassy Letters is discussed in Halsband, *LM*, pp. 278–9, 287–9, and *Letters*, I. xvii–xviii. See also William Epstein, *John Cleland* [1709–89]: *A Biography*, 1974, pp. 142–5.
[4] Mary Astell (1668–1731), the feminist writer, was satirized in *Tatler* No. 32 (23 June 1709) and No. 63 (3 Sept. 1709).

cooks demolished, in which she laid down this doctrine; exposing the injustice and tyranny of one sex, and maintaining the capacity of the other, if allowed fair play, for the highest attainments. But, like most people who are bent upon establishing a theory which they know others will controvert, and suspect they may laugh at, she often wrote herself into a passion as she went on, and made more free with the words jackanapes, puppy, booby, and block-head, than we should think becoming in a fair and elegant authoress at present.

Among Lady Mary Wortley's books there was one of these treatises, splendidly bound, and inscribed 'From the Author.'[1] The language of it was coarse but forcible, Mrs. Astell's wrath and zeal and spite against saucy mankind comically bitter, and her indignation excessive at the eagerness of foolish womankind to get husbands; but for which unaccountable weakness, she felt assured that a new leaf might be turned over and the tyrants be brought to confusion. This sentence is recollected: 'If a young fellow do but know enough to keep himself clean, you shall have him thinking forsooth that he may pretend to a woman of the best quality and understanding.'[2] And when by chance the clean men succeeded better with the high and wise women than their presumption deserved—an accident which will now and then happen—it was matter of positive pain and grief to her righteous spirit. . . . Whatever were her foibles and prejudices, her piety was genuine, fervent, and humble: cordially loving as well as admiring Lady Mary Wortley, she had nothing so much at heart as to promote her spiritual welfare, and turn her attention from the vanities of this world to the chief concern of accountable beings.

One day, after a serious discussion of some religious subject, very eagerly pursued on Mrs. Astell's side, she paused, and, gazing at Lady Mary with melancholy earnestness, said impressively, 'My days are numbered: I am old; that you know; but I now tell you in confidence, I have a mortal disease which must soon bring me to the grave. I go hence, I humbly trust in Christ, to a state of happiness; and if departed spirits be permitted to re-visit those whom

[1] The treatise is *A Serious Proposal to the Ladies, For the Advancement of their True and Greatest Interest*, 1694; the copy inscribed to LM is now in the BM.

[2] Mrs. Astell's actual words are 'A Husband indeed is thought by both Sexes so very valuable, that scarce a Man who can keep himself clean and make a Bow, but thinks he is good enough to pretend to any Woman, no matter for the Difference of Birth or Fortune . . .' (*Some Reflections upon Marriage*, 2nd ed., 1703, pp. 66–7).

they have loved on earth, remember I make you a solemn promise that mine shall appear to you, and confirm the truth of all I have been saying.'—Surely a most affecting proof of true and tender friendship, whether the forming such an intention be thought presumptuous or pardonable. A few weeks afterwards she died (of a cancer); but Lady Mary said the awful apparition never came. . . .

Lady Mary's introduction of inoculation on her return from the East, is a subject of far greater importance.[1] The small-pox was a disorder which she had sufficient reason to dread: it carried off her only brother, and had visited her so severely that she always said she meant the Flavia of her sixth Town-Eclogue for herself, having expressed in that poem what her own sensations were while slowly recovering under the apprehension of being totally disfigured.[2] Although this did not happen, yet the disease left tokens of its passage, for it deprived her of very fine eye-lashes; which gave a fierceness to her eyes that impaired their beauty. Former sufferings and mortifications therefore, she acknowledged, led her to observe the Turkish invention with particular interest; but only the higher motive of hoping to save numberless lives could have given her courage to resolve upon bringing home the discovery. For what an arduous, what a fearful, and, we may add, what a thankless enterprise it was, nobody is now in the least aware. Those who have heard her applauded for it ever since they were born, and have also seen how joyfully vaccination was welcomed in their own days, may naturally conclude that when once the experiment had been made, and had proved successful, she could have nothing to do but to sit down triumphant, . . . Lady Mary protested that in the four or five years immediately succeeding her arrival at home, she seldom passed a day without repenting of her patriotic undertaking; and she vowed that she never would have attempted it if she had foreseen the vexation, the persecution, and even the obloquy it brought upon her. The clamours raised against the practice, and of course against her, were beyond belief. The faculty all rose in arms to a man, foretelling failure and the most disastrous consequences; the clergy descanted from their pulpits on the impiety of thus seeking to take events out of the hand of Providence; the common people were taught to hoot at her as an unnatural mother, who had risked the

---

[1] LM wrote an Embassy Letter on inoculation (*Letters*, 1. 338–40) as well as a newspaper essay (printed on pp. 95–7 below).
[2] See her poem on pp. 201–4 below.

lives of her own children. And notwithstanding that she soon gained many supporters amongst the higher and more enlightened classes, headed by the Princess of Wales (Queen Caroline), who stood by her firmly, some even of her acquaintance were weak enough to join in the outcry.

We now read in grave medical biography that the discovery was instantly hailed, and the method adopted, by the principal members of that profession. Very likely they left this recorded; for, whenever an invention or a project—and the same may be said of persons—has made its way so well by itself as to establish a certain reputation, most people are sure to find out that they always patronized it from the beginning; and a happy gift of forgetfulness enables many to believe their own assertion. But what said Lady Mary of the actual fact and actual time? Why that the four great physicians deputed by government to watch the progress of her daughter's inoculation, betrayed not only such incredulity as to its success, but such an unwillingness to have it succeed, such an evident spirit of rancour and malignity, that she never cared to leave the child alone with them one second, lest it should in some secret way suffer from their interference.

Lady Bute herself could partly confirm her mother's account by her own testimony, for afterwards the battle was often fought in her presence. As inoculation gained ground, all who could make or claim the slightest acquaintance with Lady Mary Wortley used to beg for her advice and superintendence while it was going on in their families; and she constantly carried her little daughter along with her to the house, and into the sick-room, to prove her security from infection.

A child, especially a solitary child, if intelligent, attends to what passes before it, much earlier and more heedfully than people imagine. From six years old upwards, Lady Bute could see the significant shrugs of the nurses and servants, and observe the looks of dislike they cast at her mother. She also overheard anxious parents repeating to Lady Mary the arguments that had been used to deter them from venturing upon the trial; and aunts and grandmothers, in the warmth of their zeal against it, quoting the opinion of this doctor or that apothecary. All which, well remembered, enabled her to conceive how strong were the prejudices it originally had to encounter. . . .

———————

1. Lady Louisa Stuart. From a chalk drawing by John Hayter

a Letter to A P in answer to y^e preface
of His Letters.

I agree wth P. in all that he says of y^e
Indecency, & immorality of publishing
private Letters but what then must be
said of himselfe, who is now become y^e
Publisher of dead Mens letters, from whom
he could have no previous leave of
publication, several of which I do not
doubt are wrote by himselfe & falsly
ascrib'd to them, particularly that from
Dr A. dated Feb 26 1721-2., for I cannot
beleive (tho' I have no extrodinary high
Opinion of ye Bishops morals) that he
would applaud his unjust satyr on m^r
Addison, or encourage him to abuse Hers

13

2. First page of 'A Letter to A[lexander] P[ope]', in Lady Mary's autograph. *See page 98*

The next point of much consequence in Lady Mary Wortley's history is her quarrel with Pope. If this had made less noise and been less canvassed, it would be desirable to pass it by unnoticed; for when two persons of distinguished ability misemploy their talents and degrade themselves by striving to vilify each other, the honest part of their admirers must feel more inclination to avert their eyes from the conflict than to engage in it as partisans of either. Her own statement, however, was this; that at some ill-chosen time, when she least expected what romances call a *declaration*, he made such passionate love to her, as, in spite of her utmost endeavours to be angry and look grave, provoked an immoderate fit of laughter; from which moment he became her implacable enemy.[1]

When we see how a personal defect, comparatively trifling, weighed upon Lord Byron's mind, and, by his own avowal, warped his character, we cannot wonder that a temper so irritable as Pope's should have winced at being reminded of his extreme deformity more forcibly than by a thousand words. Doubtless, too, his vanity had taken as encouragement her permitting him to write her love-letters—*i.e.* letters commonly so called, expressive neither of passion, nor affection, nor any natural feeling whatsoever; tissues of far-fetched conceits and extravagant compliments; the prose counterparts of those love-verses which Dr. Johnson christened metaphysical.[2] But let it be observed, in justice to Lady Mary's taste, that her answers treat this kind of language with tacit contempt. Viewing it probably, with the widow in Hudibras, as only 'high-heroic fustian,'[3] she returns him a recital of some plain matter of fact, and never takes the smallest notice of protestation or panegyric.

Pope certainly thought that ladies could not be addressed without these flourishes, or in any simpler style than that of Balzac and Voiture, then the received models of letter-writing.[4] To men he wrote differently; yet surely his letters, even to them, to his intimate friends, smell of the lamp, and bear the marks of study and composition as visibly as his most finished poems.

ALAS!—is all that can be said about the warfare that followed. It

---

[1] Lady Louisa is generally used as the source for this anecdote; it also appears in a contemporary satire, *Mr. Taste, the Poetical Fop*, 1732.

[2] Samuel Johnson in his life of Cowley (*Lives of the English Poets*, 1779–81, ed. G. B. Hill, 1905, I. 24–34).

[3] Samuel Butler, *Hudibras*, 1663–78, ed. A. R. Waller, 1905, p. 120.

[4] Jean-Louis Guez de Balzac (1594–1654) and Vincent Voiture (1598–1648) were both noted for their highly ornate prose.

is to be hoped that Lady Mary had little share in the 'Verses to the Imitator of Horace,' and some others which shall not be reprinted in this edition.[1] If they were chiefly Lord Hervey's, they have no business here; and, at any rate, are better forgotten than remembered.

The readers of Dr. Johnson will recollect this passage in his Life of Pope: 'The table (Lord Oxford's) was infested by Lady Mary Wortley, who was the friend of Lady Oxford, and who, knowing his peevishness, could by no intreaties be restrained from contradicting him, till their disputes were sharpened to such asperity that the one or the other quitted the house.'[2] When Lady Bute read the Lives of the Poets on their first publication, she pointed out this paragraph to one of her daughters, observing, 'How ill Johnson must have been informed! My mother's intimacy with Lady Oxford was by no means of an early date; their acquaintance first began within my own memory,[3] long after the quarrel with Pope had risen to such a height, and become so public, that it would have been insulting her grossly to admit him into any house where she was one of the guests expected. I am confident they never met at Lord Oxford's table in their lives.'

Upon her mentioning the subject to her friend, the dowager Duchess of Portland, Lord Oxford's only child,[4] the Duchess, who, being her elder by three years, could go those three years farther back, and speak to the point so much more positively, said she was *certain* that no such meeting had ever taken place beneath her father's roof. 'If *he* could have dreamed of inviting them at the same time, (said she,) which his good breeding and sense of propriety made impossible, my mother, who adored Lady Mary and hated Pope, would no more have consented to it than she would have put her hand in the fire.' That great poet, it was clear from many expressions that escaped the Duchess, had not won the good-will of Lord Oxford's family in the same degree as Matthew Prior; of whom she always spoke with affection, and said he made himself beloved by every living thing in the house,—master, child, and servant, human creature or animal.[5]

---

[1] The 'Verses' are printed on pp. 265–70 below.

[2] *Lives of the English Poets*, ed. G. B. Hill, 1905, 3. 202.

[3] Lady Henrietta Cavendish Holles (1694–1755), only da. of 1st Duke of Newcastle, m. (1713) Edward, Lord Harley (1689–1741), later 2nd Earl of Oxford. Lady Oxford had actually been a childhood friend of LM's (*Letters*, 1. 114).

[4] Margaret Cavendish Harley (1715–85) m. (1734) 2nd Duke of Portland.

[5] According to Samuel Johnson, Matthew Prior (1664–1721) 'seems to have adhered,

It is a common remark, that people of brilliant parts often have no objection to relax, or *rest*, their understandings in the society of those whose intellects are a little more obtuse. Here was an instance: the gods never made anybody less poetical than Lady Oxford; and yet Lady Mary Wortley, though in general not over tolerant to her inferiors in capacity, appears upon the whole to have loved nobody so well. And there was an exception equally striking in her favour, for Lady Oxford, heartily detesting most of the wits who surrounded her husband, yet admired Lady Mary with all her might; pretty much as the parish-clerk reverences the rector for his Greek and Hebrew. Lady Bute confessed that she sometimes got into sad disgrace by exclaiming, 'Dear mama! how can you be so fond of that stupid woman?' which never failed to bring upon her a sharp reprimand, and a lecture against rash judgments, ending with, 'Lady Oxford is not shining, but she has much more in her than such giddy things as you and your companions can discern.' Her daughter, the Duchess, perhaps from being at that unripe season giddy too, was suspected of having penetrated no farther into the hidden treasures of her mother's mind than any of her young friends. Dullness assuredly had no share in her own composition.

Another of Lady Mary's friends, the famous Lord Hervey, however blackened or extolled, must have been anything but stupid. Their intimacy did not always prevent her from laughing at him, as is proved by the well-known sentence, almost a proverb, 'that this world consisted of men, women, and Herveys,' which was originally hers. And so might be a chance-epigram or ballad besides, yet no great harm done. For as there are some people who must be handled seriously or not meddled with, and a few whom it would be sacrilege and profanation to laugh at, there are others with whom their friends take that liberty every day; nay, who invite it by laughing at themselves. This is very commonly the case with those who, being conscious of some whimsical peculiarity, and withal no fools, think that humorously exaggerating their own foible, gives them a privilege to indulge it. The exaggeration then gets abroad, and by that the character is stamped. For 'half the strange stories you hear in the world' (said one who knew it well) 'come from people's not understanding a joke.' Accordingly, it has been handed down as a proof of the extreme to which Lord Hervey carried his

not only by concurrence of political designs but by peculiar affection, to the earl of Oxford and his family' (*Lives of the Poets*, 2. 197–8).

effeminate nicety, that, when asked at dinner whether he would have some beef, he answered, 'Beef?—Oh, no!—Faugh! Don't you know I never eat beef, nor *horse*, nor any of those things?'—Could any mortal have said this in earnest?[1]

Lord Hervey dying a few years after Lady Mary Wortley settled abroad, his eldest son[2] sealed up and sent her her letters, with an assurance that none of them had been read or opened. The late Lord Orford affirmed that Sir Robert Walpole did the same with regard to those she had written to his second wife; but she probably destroyed both collections, for no traces of them appeared among her papers. To Lord Hervey's heir she wrote a letter of thanks for his honourable conduct, adding, that she could almost regret he had not glanced his eye over a correspondence which would have shown him what so young a man might perhaps be inclined to doubt,—the possibility of a long and steady friendship subsisting between two persons of different sexes without the least mixture of love. Much pleased with this letter, he preserved it; and, when Lady Mary came to England, showed it to Lady Bute, desiring she would ask leave for him to visit her mother.

His own mother, Lady Hervey, made no such request; for she had partaken neither of the correspondence nor the friendship.[3] That *dessous des cartes*, which Madame de Sevigné[4] advises us to peep at, would here have betrayed that Lord and Lady Hervey had lived together upon very amicable terms, 'as well-bred as if not married at all,' according to the demands of Mrs. Millamant in the play; but without any strong sympathies, and more like a French couple than an English one.[5] It might be from suspecting this state of things, that his avowed enemies, Pope for one, went out of their

---

[1] As a disciple of Dr. George Cheyne, Hervey was a confirmed vegetarian (Halsband, *Hervey*, pp. 56–7).

[2] George William Hervey (1721–75) succeeded his grandfather (in 1751) as 2nd Earl of Bristol.

[3] Mary Lepell (1700–68) m. (1720) John, later Lord Hervey.

[4] Marie de Rabutin-Chantal (1626–96), marquise de Sévigné.

[5] Lady Louisa quotes William Congreve's *The Way of the World*, 1700, Act IV. Although it is true that Hervey and his wife were frequently apart and that he travelled abroad for one and a half years with Stephen Fox, their relationship remained connubial, and she became a warm friend of Fox's. But in his will Hervey treated her very unkindly (Halsband, *Hervey*, pp. 149, 304–6).

way to compliment and eulogise her.[1] However, their praises were
not unmerited: by the attractions she retained in age, she must have
been singularly captivating when young, gay, and handsome; and
never was there so perfect a model of the finely-polished, highly-
bred, genuine woman of fashion. Her manners had a foreign tinge,
which some called affected; but they were gentle, easy, dignified,
and altogether exquisitely pleasing. One circumstance will excite
surprise; notwithstanding her constant close connexion with the
old court, she was, at heart and in opinion, a zealous Jacobite;
hardly, perhaps, to the pitch of wishing the Pretender's enterprise
success, yet enough so to take fire in defence of James the Second
if ever she heard any blame laid to his charge.[2]

At the time of Lady Mary Wortley's return home, Lady Hervey
was living in great intimacy with Lady Bute, for whom she professed, and it is believed really felt, the highest esteem and admiration. On hearing of her mother's arrival, she came to her, owning
herself embarrassed by the fear of giving her pain or offence, but
yet compelled to declare, that formerly something had passed
between her and Lady Mary which made any renewal of their
acquaintance impossible; therefore, if she forbore visiting her, she
threw herself upon Lady Bute's friendship and candour for pardon.
No explanation followed. Lady Bute, who must have early seen the
necessity of taking care not to be entangled in her mother's quarrels,
which, to speak truth, were seldom few in number, only knew that
there had been an old feud between her, Lady Hervey, and Lady
Hervey's friend, Mrs. (or Lady) Murray[3]; the particulars of which,
forgotten even then by every lady but themselves, may well be now
beyond recall. Those treble-refined sets of company who occupy
the pinnacle of fashion, are at all times subject to such intestine
jars as only the French word *tracasseries* can fitly express. Lady
Mary's letters to Lady Mar betray how much of this sort of work
was continually going on in their society.

Mrs. Murray, whom she so often mentions, was the daughter of
Mr. Baillie, of Jerviswood, Bishop Burnet's near relation, a leading

---

[1] Pope had praised Lady Hervey before her marriage (*Poems*, 6. 180). But see Chesterfield, *Letters*, ed. B. Dobrée, 1932, 4. 1594; Walpole, *Corr.* 23. 58–9.

[2] Her own son noted that she 'had acted a most shameful part by my youngest sisters,
that she had made them rank Jacobites and taught them to reverence the Pretender . . .'
(*Augustus Hervey's Journal*, ed. D. Erskine, 1953, p. 105).

[3] Griselda Baillie (1692–1759) m. (1710) Alexander, later Sir Alexander, Murray of
Stanhope, from whom she was legally separated in 1714.

man in Parliament, of most respectable character.[1] Though married, she resided with her father, as did also the rest of his family. Lady Hervey's Letters, published in 1821, contain a warm panegyric upon her;[2] and Lady Mary Wortley herself could not deny her the praise of being very pretty, very agreeable, and very generally admired: all which rendered only the more grating a strange adventure that befell her in the midst of her brilliant career. One of her father's footmen, probably either mad or drunk, entered her room at midnight armed with a pistol, and declared a passion for her, which he swore he would gratify, or take her life. Her cries brought assistance: he was seized, tried, and transported; she forced to give evidence against him at the Old Bailey. How such a story, and such a public appearance, must have wounded the feelings of a gentlewoman, it is easy to conceive. Any allusion to it must have been galling; and one cannot wonder if she took unkindly even Lady Mary's 'Epistle from Arthur Grey in Newgate,' although complimentary to her charms, and containing nothing injurious to her character. But she accused Lady Mary of having also made her the subject of a very offensive ballad; and this Lady Mary positively denied.[3] Various bickerings took place; peace seems to have been sometimes patched up, but war to have quickly broken out afresh, and, like all other wars, to have left marks of its footsteps long visible on the soil.

In these old days, people's brains being more active and ingenious than their fingers, ballads swarmed as abundantly as caricatures are swarming at present, and were struck off almost as hastily, whenever wit and humour, or malice and scurrility, found a theme to fasten upon. A ballad was sure to follow every incident that had in it a ludicrous corner, from

> 'The woeful christening late there did
> In James's house befall,'

and the King's turning his son and daughter out of doors after it,[4]

---

[1] George Baillie (1664–1738), M.P. 1708–34; Burnet's first cousin.

[2] *Letters of Mary Lepel, Lady Hervey* [ed. J. W. Croker], pp. 254–6.

[3] This entire controversy is investigated by Robert Halsband in '*Virtue in Danger*, or The Case of Griselda Murray', *History Today*, Oct. 1967, pp. 692–700. See also pp. 216–24 below.

[4] The anonymous ballad 'The Christening' (W. W. Wilkins, *Political Ballads of the Seventeenth and Eighteenth Centuries*, 1860, 2. 186–90) followed George I's expulsion of his son's family from St. James's Palace in 1717.

down to a lady's dropping her shoe in the Park. Though printed on the coarsest paper, sung about the streets, and sold for half-pence, they often came from no mean quarter. That just now quoted was ascribed to Arbuthnot;[1] Lord Binning wrote an admirable one, describing the Duke of Argyll's levee;[2] Mr. Pulteney, Lord Chesterfield,[3] Lord Hervey, had the credit of others; and Lady Mary Wortley was a person who often fell under suspicion in matters of the kind, because known to have talents which the world would not believe she left unemployed. But, as she said herself, it attributed to her a great deal of trash that she never wrote—never even saw; and thus made her an object of ill-will to people whose adventures she was so far from having celebrated, that she hardly knew their names.

The impression these unjust imputations made upon her mind will now be shown. When Lady Bute was nearly grown up, some of her young friends wanted to bring about an acquaintance between her and Miss Furnese, an heiress of their own age.[4] Miss Wortley had no objection; but Miss Furnese held off, and so resolutely, that they insisted upon knowing the reason. 'Why, then,' said she, at last, 'I will honestly own your praises of Miss Wortley make me sure I shall dislike her. You tell me she is lively and clever, now I know I am very dull; so, of course, she will despise me, and turn me into ridicule, and I am resolved to keep out of her way.' The young set laughed most heartily at this avowal; and Lady Bute, laughing too when told of it, ran to divert her mother with the story. But, instead of amusing Lady Mary, it made her unusually serious. 'Now, child,' she began, after a moment's reflection, 'you see nothing in this but a good joke, an absurdity to laugh at; and are not aware what an important lesson you have received; one which you ought to remember as long as you live. What that poor girl in her simplicity has uttered aloud, is no more than what passes in the mind of every dull person you will meet with. Those who cannot but feel that they are deficient in ability always look with a mixture of fear and aversion on people cleverer than themselves; regarding

---

[1] John Arbuthnot (1667-1735), physician and wit.

[2] 'The Duke of Argyle's Levee', although assigned to Lord Binning (Charles Hamilton, 1697-1732), was written by Joseph Mitchell (1684-1738).

[3] William Pulteney (1684-1764), 1st Earl of Bath; Philip Stanhope (1694-1773), 4th Earl of Chesterfield.

[4] Katherine Furnese (d. 1766) m. 1st (1736) Lewis Watson (c. 1714-45), 2nd Earl of Rockingham; m. 2nd (1751) Francis North (1704-90), 1st Earl of Guilford.

them as born their natural enemies. If ever then you feel yourself flattered by the reputation of superiority, remember that to be the object of suspicion, jealousy, and a secret dislike, is the sure price you must pay for it.'

No one who has seen much of the world will think this assertion altogether unfounded. But the lurking grudge (supposing it always alive) may be lulled into slumber, or it may be stirred up and provoked to show its teeth in the guise of open animosity; and Lady Mary Wortley took the latter course with it too often. She was not ill-tempered; for our men and maids are the best judges of us in that particular, and the old servant fostered under her roof used to talk of her indulgence and familiarity, was fond of repeating her sayings, and almost seemed to have tasted her wit. But mankind is so made, that reproaches, invectives, nay, veritable injuries, are not half so sharply felt, or bitterly resented, as the stings of ridicule; therefore a quick perception of the ridiculous must ever be a dangerous quality, although in some few persons it wears a playful, harmless shape, and is quite distinct from the spirit of satire. Lady Mary, one cannot deny, united both qualities, instantly seized the comical point, saw the matter of mirth wherever it was to be found; but had as keen an eye to detect matter of censure, and rarely forbore a cutting sarcasm out of tenderness to the feelings of others. In short, a professed wit, flushed with success and bent on shining in society, bears too much resemblance to a staunch foxhunter eager in the chase, who takes a leap over his fallen companion, whether friend or foe, without stopping to examine how he came down, or what bone he has broken.

The truth is, that affectation and folly must be borne with, or at least let alone, if one would go peaceably through this motley world; which Lady Mary could not expect to do, because she had not Christian patience with either, but attacked and exposed them when they were guiltless of hurting anybody but their owner; and thus made mortal enemies of the vain tribe who would have plumed themselves upon her acquaintance if they could have hoped to escape her animadversions. For example, her former friend, or correspondent, Lady Rich,[1] when become that melancholy thing—a decayed beauty, strove to keep up the appearance of youth by affecting a girlish simplicity, which suited her age much worse than

---

[1] Elizabeth Griffith (1692–1773) m. (*c.* 1710) Sir Robert Rich. Several of LM's Embassy Letters are addressed to her.

rose-coloured ribbands, and served as a constant whetstone to Lady Mary's raillery. The Master of the Rolls happened to be mentioned; the same old Sir Joseph Jekyll 'who never changed his principles or wig,' and who had held the office so long that he was identified with it in every one's mind.[1] 'Pray who is Master of the Rolls?' asked Lady Rich in an innocent tone. 'Sir Humphrey Monneux, madam,' answered Lady Mary, naming off-hand the most unlikely person she could think of.[2] The company laughed, and the lady looked disconcerted; but, not daring to betray her better knowledge by disputing the fact, went on in desperation to be more simple still. 'Well! I am vastly ashamed of being so prodigiously ignorant. I dare say I ask a mighty silly question; but, pray now, what is it to be Master of the Rolls? What does he do? for I really don't know.' 'Why, madam, he superintends all the French rolls that are baked in London; and without him you would have no bread and butter for your breakfast.' There was no parrying this: Lady Rich coloured, flirted her fan, and professed herself unable to cope with Lady Mary Wortley's wit—*she* had no *wit*. 'Nay; but look you, my dear madam, I grant it a very fine thing to continue always fifteen,—*that* every body must approve of; it is quite fair: but, indeed, indeed, one need not be five years old.'

Yet there was one very conspicuous, very assailable, and very irritable person, whom Lady Mary, let her say what she would, in jest or in earnest, could never affront or offend; and this was no other than Sarah Duchess of Marlborough,[3] so celebrated for quarrelling with all the rest of human kind. She would take in good part the most home truths if spoken by Lady Mary, who seemed to be out of the hurricane-latitude, securely stationed beyond the scope of those capricious fits of anger which she continually saw bursting like waterspouts on the heads of her acquaintance. The Duchess also grew partial to Lady Mary's daughter: both of them were privileged to visit her at any hour and be always welcome. Lady Bute often sate by her while she dined, or watched her in the curious process of casting up her accounts. Curious, because her

---

[1] Sir Joseph Jekyll (*c.* 1662–1738), M.P. 1696–1738, had been Master of the Rolls, the third member of the Supreme Court of Judicature, since 1717. The quotation is from Pope's 'Epilogue to the Satires, Dialogue I' (*Poems*, 4. 301).

[2] Sir Humphrey Monoux (1702?–57), Baronet, M.P. 1728–41, was generally regarded as disreputable and a Jacobite.

[3] Sarah Jennings (1660–1744) m. John Churchill, later 1st Duke of Marlborough.

grace, well versed as she was in all matters relating to money, such as getting it, hoarding it, and turning it to the best advantage, knew nothing of common arithmetic. But her sound clear head could devise an arithmetic of its own; to lookers-on it appeared as if a child had scrabbled over the paper, setting down figures here and there at random; and yet every sum came right to a fraction at last, in defiance of Cocker.[1]

She was extremely communicative, and, it need not be added, proportionably entertaining; thus far too very fair and candid—she laboured at no self-vindication, but told facts just as they were, or as she believed them to be, with an openness and honesty that almost redeemed her faults; though this might partly proceed from never thinking herself in the wrong, or caring what was thought of her by others. She had still, at a great age, considerable remains of beauty, most expressive eyes, and the finest fair hair imaginable; the colour of which she said she had preserved unchanged by the constant use of honey-water,—hardly such as perfumers now sell, for that has an unlucky aptitude to turn the hair grey. By this superb head of hair hung a tale, an instance of her waywardness and violence, which (strange to say) she took particular pleasure in telling. None of her charms, when they were at their proudest height, had been so fondly prized by the poor Duke her husband. Therefore, one day, upon his offending her by some act of disobedience to her '*strong sovereign will*,'[2] the bright thought occurred, as she sate considering how she could plague him most, that it would be a hearty vexation to see his favourite tresses cut off. Instantly the deed was done; she cropped them short, and laid them in an ante-chamber he must pass through to enter her apartment. But, to her cruel disappointment, he passed, entered, and re-passed, calm enough to provoke a saint; neither angry nor sorrowful; seemingly quite unconscious both of his crime and his punishment. Concluding he must have overlooked the hair, she ran to secure it. Lo! it had vanished,—and she remained in great perplexity the rest of the day. The next, as he continued silent, and her looking-glass spoke the change a rueful one, she began for once to think she had done rather a foolish thing. Nothing more ever transpired upon the subject until after the Duke's death, when she found her beautiful ringlets carefully laid

---

[1] Edward Cocker (1631–75), arithmetician, presumed author of Cocker's *Arithmetick*.
[2] Thomas Parnell, 'Hesiod; Or, The Rise of Woman', *Poetical Works*, ed. G. A. Aitken, 1894, p. 7.

by in a cabinet where he kept whatever he held most precious: and at this point of the story she regularly fell a crying.[1]

The only topic upon which she seemed guarded was what concerned Queen Anne, whom she never mentioned disrespectfully, but in general avoided speaking of; while she liked to dilate upon the first arrival of the present royal family, and would describe with great glee many little circumstances of their ways and manners which were new and somewhat uncouth to English eyes. She had had a nearer view of them than perhaps it was prudent to give her; for, at their outset, wishing to conciliate the Marlborough party, they invited her to a degree of intimacy sure to end in proving the truth of that wise saying about *familiarity* which we can all remember to have indited in round hand. The second or third time she had the honour of being admitted, she said she found the Princess (Queen Caroline) maintaining discipline in her nursery, where one of the children, having been naughty, had just undergone wholesome correction, and was roaring piteously in consequence. The Duchess tried to hush and console it. 'Ay! see there,' cried the Prince with an air of triumph; 'you English are none of you well-bred, because you was not whipt when you was young.' 'Humph!' quoth her grace, 'I thought to myself, I am sure you could not have been whipt when you were young, but I choked it in.' Not being at all accustomed either to choke her thoughts in, or to stand in awe of royalty, she soon made her attendance more formidable than agreeable, and gladly returned to her natural vocation of governing others, instead of reverencing the powers entitled to rule over her
. . . .

Many other people remarkable in different ways must have been known to Lady Mary Wortley; many authors appear to have courted her approbation, but only those persons are mentioned here of whom Lady Bute could speak from her own recollection or her mother's report. Both had made her well informed of every particular that concerned her relation Henry Fielding; nor was she a stranger to that beloved first wife whose picture he drew in his Amelia,[2] where, as she said, even the glowing language he knew how to employ did not do more than justice to the amiable qualities of

---

[1] Lady Louisa Stuart is apparently the only source for this anecdote.

[2] Henry Fielding (1707–54) and LM had the same great-grandfather, George Feilding (*c.* 1614–66), 1st Earl of Desmond. Fielding's first wife, Charlotte Cradock, whom he married in 1734, died ten years later. He published *Amelia* in 1751.

the original, or to her beauty, although this had suffered a little
from the accident related in the novel,—a frightful overturn, which
destroyed the gristle of her nose. He loved her passionately, and
she returned his affection; yet led no happy life, for they were
almost always miserably poor, and seldom in a state of quiet and
safety. All the world knows what was his imprudence; if ever he
possessed a score of pounds, nothing could keep him from lavishing
it idly, or make him think of tomorrow. Sometimes they were living
in decent lodgings with tolerable comfort; sometimes in a wretched
garret without necessaries; not to speak of the spunging-houses and
hiding-places where he was occasionally to be found. His elastic
gaiety of spirit carried him through it all; but, meanwhile, care and
anxiety were preying upon her more delicate mind, and undermining her constitution. She gradually declined, caught a fever, and
died in his arms.

His biographers seem to have been shy of disclosing that after
the death of this charming woman he married her maid.[1] And yet
the act was not so discreditable to his character as it may sound. The
maid had few personal charms, but was an excellent creature,
devotedly attached to her mistress, and almost broken-hearted for
her loss. In the first agonies of his own grief, which approached to
frenzy, he found no relief but from weeping along with her; nor
solace, when a degree calmer, but in talking to her of the angel they
mutually regretted. This made her his habitual confidential associate,
and in process of time he began to think he could not give his children a tenderer mother, or secure for himself a more faithful house-
keeper and nurse. At least this was what he told his friends; and it is
certain that her conduct as his wife confirmed it, and fully justified
his good opinion.

Lady Mary Wortley had a great regard for Fielding; she pitied
his misfortunes, excused his failings, and warmly admired his best
writings; above all Tom Jones, in her own copy of which she wrote
Ne plus ultra.[2] Nevertheless, she frankly said she was sorry he did
not himself perceive that he had made Tom Jones a scoundrel;
alluding to the adventure with Lady Bellaston. She would indeed

---

[1] Fielding married his housekeeper Mary Daniel (d. 1802) in Nov. 1747, when she
was six months pregnant.

[2] LM may have owned more than one copy, for in the one that survives she had
written 'agreeable' on the flyleaf of the last volume (Sotheby Catalogue, 1 Aug. 1928,
p. 85). For LM's further opinion of *Amelia* and of *Tom Jones, A Foundling* (1749), see
Letters, 3. 66 and n. 3.

have seldom passed a wrong judgment on what she read, if her natural good taste had taken its way unbiassed; but where personal enmity or party-prejudice stepped in, they too frequently drove it blinded before them. A book is a book, no matter who wrote it; in fair criticism it has a right to stand upon its own proper ground, and should no more be condemned for the sins of its author, than commended for his virtues. This, to be sure, was not her way of handling any contemporary performance. Most people will now admit that Pope betrayed unmanly and mean malevolence in his attacks upon her; yet when she pronounced his verses to be 'all sound and no sense,'[1] she was aiming a pointless arrow at a poet who, wherever he judged it expedient, could compress more meaning into fewer words than almost any other in our language. Not Pope alone however, but the larger half of that noble band of authors that rendered the literary age of Anne illustrious, lay for her under an interdict, a species of *taboo*, obnoxious both as Tories and as his confederates. She forbade herself to relish the wit and humour of Swift and Arbuthnot; and could not, or would not, be sensible that the former, Bolingbroke, and Atterbury, ranked with her own friend Addison, as the standard writers of English prose.[2]

With regard to later works, though her remarks upon Richardson have incensed his zealous admirers beyond measure and past forgiveness, yet, while making them, she has involuntarily borne a more convincing, unquestionable testimony to his chief merits than if she had been ever so eloquent in his praise. She acknowledges having sobbed over his volumes;—she could not lay them down, she sate up all night to finish them.[3] What greater triumph could an author who wrote to the feelings desire? But then it seems she was guilty of saying that, never having lived in the society of real gentlemen and ladies, he had given his fictitious ones a language and manners as different from theirs as could be devised.[4] So was it

---

[1] The phrase is attributed to LM by James Dallaway (1803, 1. 74; 1837, 1. xli). LM's own phrase, as recorded by Joseph Spence, is 'all tune and no meaning' (*Anecdotes*, ed. J. M. Osborn, 1966, 1. 306).

[2] Henry St. John (1678–1751), 1st Viscount Bolingbroke; Francis Atterbury (1662–1732), Bishop of Rochester (1713–23). LM herself wrote that Bolingbroke was 'far below either Tillotson or Addison even in style, thô the latter was sometimes more diffuse than his Judgment approv'd . . .' (1754, *Letters*, 3. 62–3). For her further criticism of Bolingbroke's style, see *Letters*, 2. 433; 3. 76–7, 220.

[3] Lady Louisa Stuart combines LM's sobbing over Richardson's works in 1755 (*Letters*, 3. 90) and staying up all night to read Fielding's in 1749 (*Letters*, 2. 443).

[4] LM says this of characters in *Clarissa* (1755, *Letters*, 3. 97).

also said of Garrick, the first and finest of actors, that, performing every other part in exquisite perfection, he never could succeed in that of a mere ordinary *gentleman*.[1] Both assertions were strictly true, and they amount to nothing more than a proof of the old trite position 'that every one must fail in something.' If Richardson's inelegancies disturb us less than they did Lady Mary Wortley, it is because we take for old-fashioned much that our fathers and mothers knew to be vulgar, or even ridiculous. A man's living friends will have the presumption to find fault with his portrait when their eyes tell them it has no likeness to *him*, though it may not be at all the worse picture a hundred years hence; and this was exactly the case with Lady Mary, who thought no otherwise than her neighbours at the time. Mrs. Donellan, an accomplished woman,[2] whom the readers of Swift may recollect to have been one of his correspondents, told the late Mr. Edward Hamilton,[3] her godson, that Richardson once brought her a manuscript volume of Sir Charles Grandison, begging her to examine it, and point out any errors she perceived in this very particular. He was conscious, he said, of his own ignorance touching the manners of people of distinction; and, knowing that she had passed her life in the best company, he could depend upon her judgment. Mrs. Donellan, who both admired his genius and respected his character, undertook the task with good faith as well as good will; but no sooner did she begin criticising, than she found she had to deal with an Archbishop of Grenada.[4] Richardson changed colour, shut up the book, and muttering sullenly, that if there were so many faults, he supposed his best way would be to throw it into the fire at once, walked off in the mood vulgarly, but expressively, yclept *dudgeon*. It was long ere he troubled her with another visit.[5]

---

[1] Lady Louisa is citing Dr. Johnson: 'Garrick's great distinction is his universality. He can represent all modes of life, but that of an easy fine-bred gentleman' (James Boswell, *The Journal of a Tour to the Hebrides with Samuel Johnson*, in Boswell, *Life of Johnson*, ed. G. B. Hill and L. F. Powell, 1934–50, 5. 126). David Garrick (1717–79) was the leading actor and manager of his day.

[2] Ann Donellan (d. 1762), da. of Nehemiah Donellan, Lord Chief Baron of the Exchequer in Ireland.   [3] Unidentified.

[4] In Le Sage's *Gil Blas* (1715–35) the Bishop, incensed at Gil's gentle criticism of his deplorable sermon, dismisses him forthwith (Book VII, Chapter iv).

[5] In 1752 Richardson asked both Mary Delany and Ann Donellan to supply him with scenes from 'upper life' for use in *Grandison* (*Corr.*, ed. A. L. Barbauld, 1804, 4. 61). Although Ann Donellan offered criticism of *Grandison* there is no evidence that Richardson was irritated to the extent that Lady Louisa reports.

After all, Lady Mary Wortley's insensibility to the excellence, or, let us say, the charm of Madame de Sevigné's Letters,[1] is the thing most surprising in her observations on literary subjects; and it can only be accounted for by a marked opposition of character between the two women. The head was the governing power with the one, the heart with the other. If they had lived at the same time, and in the same country and society, they would not have accorded well together. Madame de Sevigné would have respected Lady Mary's talents, but rather dreaded than coveted her acquaintance. Lady Mary, in lieu of prizing that simplicity of mind which Madame de Sevigné so wonderfully preserved in the midst of such a world as surrounded her, might have been apt to confound it with weakness; and to hold in contempt not only her foible for court favour, but her passionate devotion to her daughter.

As writers also they were dissimilar: Lady Mary wrote admirable letters; *letters*—not dissertations, nor sentimental *effusions*, nor strings of witticisms, but real letters; such as any person of plain sense would be glad to receive. Her style, though correct and perspicuous, was unstudied, natural, flowing, spirited; she never used an unnecessary word, nor a phrase savouring of affectation; but still she meant to write well, and was conscious of having succeeded. Madame de Sevigné had no such consciousness; she did not so much *write*, as talk and think upon paper, with no other aim than to make Madame de Grignan[2] present at every incident, and partaker of every feeling, throughout the twenty-four hours of her day. By this means she makes us present likewise; as we read, we see her, hear her, feel with her, enter into all her concerns. Not that she ever dreamt of pleasing us. 'If the post knew what it carried,' says she, 'it would leave these packets by the way-side.' 'Keep my letters,' said Lady Mary, on the contrary; 'they will be as good as Madame de Sevigné's forty years hence.'[3] And in some measure she said true. What she terms the tittle-tattle of a fine lady would have lost nothing in her hands. She could relate passing events, and satirise fashionable follies with as much vivacity and more wit than Madame de Sevigné herself; and there was more depth in her reflections, for she had the superiority in strength of understanding. But all that she sought to

[1] First published in 1726.
[2] Mme de Sévigné's daughter, Françoise-Marguerite (1646–1705), comtesse de Grignan.
[3] 1726, *Letters*, 2. 66. For her severe opinion of Mme de Sévigné's letters, see *Letters*, 3. 62, 215.

degrade by the epithet 'tittle-tattle of an old nurse,' including, as it does, so many touches of truth and nature; all the little traits that bring before our eyes the persons spoken of; all the details which render Les Rochers and Livry as interesting to us as Versailles[1]; all this part, it must be confessed, lay out of Lady Mary's province; and she proved it did so by viewing it with disdain.[2]

From the books Lady Mary Wortley died possessed of, which were but few, she appears to have been particularly fond of that ancient English drama lately revived among us; for she had several volumes of differently sized and wretchedly printed plays bound up together, such as the Duke of Roxburghe would have bought at any price[3]; the works of Shirley, Ford, Marston, Heywood, Webster, and the rest, as far back as Gammer Gurton's Needle, and coming down to the trash of Durfey.[4] But Lillo's domestic tragedies were what she most admired; for 'My lady used to declare,' said the old servant so often quoted, 'that whoever did not cry at George Barnwell must deserve to be hanged.'[5] And she passed the same sentence on people who could see unmoved the fine scene between Dorax and Sebastian in Dryden, who was also one of her favourite authors.[6] She had his plays, his fables, and his Virgil, in folio, as they were first published; Theobald's edition of Shakspeare, manifestly much read;[7] and Tonson's quarto Milton.[8] Besides Cowley, Waller,

[1] Most of Mme de Sévigné's letters were sent from her house, Les Rochers in Brittany, and her uncle's at Livry, near Paris.

[2] Voltaire praised LM's letters as greatly superior to his countrywoman's (*Œuvres complètes*, ed. L. Moland, 1883-4, 25. 163).

[3] John Ker (1740-1804), 3rd Duke of Roxburgh, was a book collector whose library contained over two thousand volumes devoted to drama (*Catalogue of the Library of the Late John Duke of Roxburghe*, ed. G. and W. Nicol, 1812).

[4] *Gammer Gurton's Needle*, of uncertain authorship, was published in 1575; Thomas D'Urfey (1653-1723) was a playwright and popular poet. Actually LM's large library (listed in Wharncliffe MS. 135, Sheffield Central Library) was brought back to England. The early drama, retained by the 1st Marquess of Bute, is now in the National Library of Scotland (described by Marion Linton in *TLS* of 21 Dec. 1956). At least 300 volumes had evidently accompanied the Marquess's daughter after she married (in 1823) the 2nd Earl of Harrowby, and are now in that family's collection at Sandon Hall, Stafford (Sotheby Catalogue of 1 Aug. 1928). See also *Sale Catalogues of Libraries of Eminent Persons*, ed. A. N. L. Munby, vol. 7, ed. H. Amory, 1973.

[5] George Lillo, *The London Merchant: or The History of George Barnwell*, 1731.

[6] The 'fine scene' is undoubtedly that in the fourth act of *Don Sebastian King of Portugal*, 1690 (Dryden, *Works*, 6. 103-13).

[7] Theobald's edition was published in 1734. For LM's use of other editions, see *Letters*, 2. 27.

[8] Jacob Tonson's quarto edition, published in 1695 and again in 1720.

Denham, &c. there were some less known poets, and some of an earlier age, such as Suckling and Drayton. Nothing further can be called to mind, excepting the outward shape of three ultra-sized volumes, the works of Margaret Duchess of Newcastle.[1]

. . .

As for the particulars of Lady Mary's history, society, and way of life, during her residence on the Continent, they must be gathered from her own letters. . . . Those of latest date, written after she finally established herself at Venice, seem to turn very much upon the annoyances she suffered from the behaviour of Mr. Murray, then the British minister there;[2] between whom and her reigned, or rather raged, the utmost animosity. But none of the letters explain, nor are there now any means of discovering, whence the quarrel first sprung, or which of the parties was the most to blame. It certainly tells against *him* that his enmity extended to so respectable a man as her friend, Sir James Steuart of Coltness,[3] whose situation as an exile soliciting recall must have made him more cautious of giving any real cause of offence than a free unfettered person, even if he had not been too much engrossed by his literary labours to meddle with diplomatic intrigues.

She survived her return home too short a time to afford much more matter for anecdotes. Those who could remember her arrival, spoke with delight of the clearness, vivacity, and raciness of her conversation, and the youthful vigour which seemed to animate her mind. She did not appear displeased at the general curiosity to see her, nor void of curiosity herself concerning the new things and people that her native country presented to her view after so long an absence: yet, had her life lasted half as many years as it did months, the probability is that she would have gone abroad again;[4] for her habits had become completely foreign in all those little circumstances, the sum of which must constitute the comfort or discomfort of every passing day. She was accustomed to foreign

---

[1] Margaret Cavendish (1624?–74), Duchess of Newcastle, was a prolific writer. LM's library sent abroad in 1739 contained her plays in two volumes (Wharncliffe MS. 135).

[2] John Murray (*c.* 1715–75), British Resident in Venice 1754–66.

[3] Sir James Steuart (1713–80), political economist, formerly a Jacobite.

[4] A few weeks after her return to London LM wrote to Mme Michiel, her friend in Venice, '. . . plût a Dieu que j'ai la force de retourner a Venise, et me sauver dans vostre aimable Maison' (*Letters*, 3. 287).

servants and to the spaciousness of a foreign dwelling. Her description of the harpsichord-shaped house she inhabited in one of the streets bordering upon Hanover Square[1] grew into a proverbial phrase: 'I am most handsomely lodged,' said she; 'I have two very decent closets and a cupboard on each floor.' This served to laugh at, but could not be a pleasant exchange for the Italian palazzo. However, all earthly good and evil were very soon terminated by a fatal malady, the growth of which she had long concealed.[2] The fatigues she underwent in her journey to England tended to exasperate its symptoms; it increased rapidly, and before ten months were over she died in the seventy-third year of her age.

[1] On Great George Street (now St. George Street).

[2] As reported by Horace Walpole: 'she brought over a cancer in her breast' (*Corr.* 22. 56). She died on 21 Aug. 1762.

Supplement to the Anecdotes

The 1837 edition of Lady Mary's *Letters and Works* was reviewed at great length by John Wilson Croker in the Feb. 1837 issue of the *Quarterly Review*. His criticism was neither kind nor tactful. But what infuriated Lady Louisa was his statement that the Biographical Anecdotes and frequent explanatory notes came 'from the pen of Lady Louisa Stuart, the daughter of Lord and Lady Bute—the grandchild of Lady Mary'. She wrote to a friend: 'Yes truly, in my opinion Croker has outdone even himself in impertinence. I confess my fingers itch to give him a suitable reply; he has laid himself open to it repeatedly. What provoked *me*—me personally—the most, is his naming me outright, which as Lord Wharncliffe had not done, nobody else had a right to do; and only a blackguard like him would have done' (to Lady Louisa Bromley, 9 Mar. [1837], MS. formerly owned by W. D. Clark, Esq.). Two days later she wrote to Wharncliffe about Croker's review, saying that 'it would be easy to give him a stinging retort', and she then continued, in her 'immensely long letter', to provide detailed comments (11 Mar. [1837], Wharncliffe MS., Sheffield Central Library).

Not content with this private expostulation she intended a public defence, perhaps to be added to the second edition of Lady Mary's *Letters and Works*. She entitled it 'Supplement to the Anecdotes' and sent it to Wharncliffe for his opinion, promising that if he disapproved of it she would put it in the fire. She was provoked, she tells him in the accompanying letter, by Croker's 'extreme impertinence of using my name outright so often and so flippantly . . . he has thus dragged me out of the quiet hole in which I have hitherto passed my days and wished to end them. I do long for revenge, that is the truth of it; for it has made me desperate' (Ditton Park, Monday [March 1837], Wharncliffe MS.). But she promised: 'if you disapprove there is an end of it'. Evidently Wharncliffe disapproved, yet Lady Louisa did not put it in the fire. A few weeks later she told her friend that she had subsided and given up the thought of 'directly clawing Croker', and instead that she would try to persuade Wharncliffe to contradict him factually and politely (8 Apr. [1837], Clark MS.). A few minor changes in the 'Second Edition, Revised': this was Wharncliffe's reply to Croker.

Text Wharncliffe MS. 439, Sheffield Central Library; printed with the kind permission of the Earl of Wharncliffe.

IN case any indistinct phrase in the Anecdotes should have occasioned their being misunderstood, it is repeated afresh that Lady Mary Wortley's diary—meaning always the only part of it which Lady Bute thought fit to communicate—ended with her return to England in July 1718. Consequently nothing subsequent to that period could have been contained in it or quoted from it. About two years afterwards she made an intimacy with Miss Skerritt at Twicken-ham—[1] 'the thing on earth (she tells Lady Pomfret) the most remote from power and politics'[2]—Miss Skerritt being then a stranger to Sir Robert Walpole. Lady Mary's memoir of his sister, dated 1713, certainly described his wife as a woman of the lightest character and conduct, but generally, giving no particulars.[3] We never heard any thing repeated that she *said* of her, good or bad; nor was she any farther mentioned in the journal. A journal which no one saw while Lady Mary lived, and which therefore, if it told scandalous tales, told them to herself alone. The reader is requested to bear all this in mind, especially the dates. Because, if he should suppose every thing else the Anecdotes say of Lady Walpole to have been taken from the diary, the mistake would involve in it some rather extra-ordinary positions. For instance,—that Sir Robert's intrigue with Miss Skerritt, a scandalous injury to his wife, was inflicted upon her by—Lady Mary Wortley!—That—as the injurer never forgives, and as

—'coming events cast their shadows before'—[4]

her guilty consciousness of having inflicted this injury, in or about the year *1725*, cast so very long a shadow as to have made her traduce her future victim in *1713*. And last, not least, that the same cause induced her and Miss Skerritt, long before they were ac-quainted, to invent together a calumnious story touching Horace Walpole's parentage, four years before he was born.[5]

It would have been unfair to rely either solely or principally upon the authority of the above passage in Lady M[ary] W[ortley]'s journal; but it was confirmed, or in strictness we should say it had been *preceded*, by the uniform concurrent testimony of all the old people, men and women, heard to descant upon the events of their own time. They spoke of Lady Walpole's amours, of Sir Robert's indifference, and of Pope's sly allusion to it,[6] not as things whispered in corners, but as common talk, familiar to all the world. To name one among them (because a remarkable person) Mrs. Anne Pitt,

---

[1] See pp. 26–7 above.
[2] *Letters*, 2. 182–3. Lady Pomfret: Henrietta Louisa (1698–1761), da. of 2nd Baron Jeffreys, wife of 1st Earl of Pomfret.
[3] See pp. 22, 25 above.
[4] Thomas Campbell, *Lochiel's Warning* (1803), line 56.
[5] Here Lady Louisa is replying to Croker's review, *Quarterly Review*, 58 (1837), 181–4.
[6] See p. 25 above.

Lord Chatham's sister, formerly maid of honour to Queen Caroline.[1] The circumstance that led her to the subject was this: she had been viewing Westminster Abbey with a party of foreign friends, and had there seen for the first time Horace Walpole's inscription on his mother's monument,[2] at which she expressed her amazement with uplifted eyes and hands. How wonderful, she said, that a man of his sense and knowledge of the world should venture to set forth such a panygeric on a woman whose gallantries were so notorious!— And if it were possible that they could have altogether escaped his own knowledge, that was more wonderful still—She added much besides, concluding with—'Why who ever believed Horace himself to be Sir Robert Walpole's son?'—Nothing she told or alluded to seemed new or strange to the elderly part of the company present, though such as knew Mr. Walpole best inclined to think him happily unconscious of any blot on his mother's fame. This conversation passed several years before the writer of the Anecdotes ever saw Lady M[ary] W[ortley]'s journal.[3]

It is surely needless to say that the Duchess of Marlborough's quarrels with her grandchildren could not be noticed in a diary written while they were unborn or in their cradles. As for the blackened picture,[4] its present unstained condition would furnish

---

[1] Anne Pitt (1721–81), sister of William Pitt, the younger (1708–78), cr. (1766) Earl of Chatham.

[2] The inscription is printed in Walpole, *Works*, 1798, I. 131.

[3] In a private letter to Lord Wharncliffe, Lady Louisa amplifies her account of Anne Pitt's testimony: 'I remember her coming to us once just after she had been viewing the newer monuments in Westminster Abbey, and expressing the utmost astonishment that a man of Horace Walpole's cleverness and knowledge of the world should have ventured to put up that inscription to his mother's memory which we have all read—"Good Heavens!" said she, "her gallantries were so *very* notorious!—Can it be possible that no whisper concerning them ever reached his ears? Why who ever thought either him or Sir Edward [Sir Robert's second son (1706–84)] Sir Robert's children? Who has not heard the story of General Churchill [Charles Churchill (*c.* 1679–1745)]?" This I afterwards found to be, that Sir Robert, upon making a discovery needless to specify, shook hands with the general and said "Dear Charles, only tell nobody and I'll befriend you as long as I live." And but two or three years ago, as Miss Fox [probably Holland's daughter] and I were one day talking of Lord Orford, she told me Lord Holland *had always heard* he was Lord Hervey's son, though their ages did not confirm it. On her mentioning to him that I had named an elder Lord Hervey, he said, "Oh that explained it perfectly." You may ask him whether he recollects it' (letter of 11 March [1837]). Lord Holland was Henry Richard Fox (1773–1840), 3rd Baron, whose grandfather, Henry Fox, had been an intimate friend of John, Lord Hervey. The 'elder Lord Hervey', Carr (see p. 25 above), was five years older than the famous John, Lord Hervey.

[4] Lady Louisa had related (1837, I. 79) that the Duchess of Marlborough, after quarrelling with her granddaughter the Duchess of Bedford, had taken a portrait of the young woman, blackened its face, and inscribed on the frame, '*She is much blacker*

an unanswerable proof that the face was not smeared with soot or lamp-black by the angry duchess a hundred years ago—*if* pictures never could be cleaned. But as they can, and as the original of the portrait was alive to see it when it came into the possession of her brother, Lord Spencer's ancestor,[1] nothing appears more natural than that he should have had her grace's handywork effaced with a spunge and warm water before he hung the piece up at Althorpe. His widow, Lady Cowper,[2] whom Mr. Walpole knew very well, must have been able to vouch for the story.

Though Lord Orford's [Walpole's] feelings of dislike were intense, yet he did not *intail* them upon successive generations. He was Lady Bute's old acquaintance and frequent visitor; and as they lived very much in the same set of company her family, beside hearing constantly of whatever he said or did, had sufficient opportunities of listening to his conversation, and conversing with him themselves, to form some notion of his character: and we may add, to be often much amused, in later days, with the peremptory judgements passed upon it by writers who never saw him in their lives. Particularly with the avarice and parsimony discovered to have been a part of it: vices from which no man ever was more free. But he was not equally so from extreme bitterness of spirit when either offended or strongly prejudiced. Nor was it his foible, any more than Lady Mary Wortley's, to think too indulgently of his fellow-creatures.

Lord Dover says with truth that 'Mr Walpole's* hostility was unvarying and unbounded towards any of his contemporaries who had been adverse to the person and administration of Sir Robert Walpole'—and accordingly Mr Wortley, one of Sir Robert's most steady opponents, is never named by him without some expression of the hostile feeling Lord Dover indicates. Nothing but such a

---

* Letters to Sir Horace Mann Preface Volume 1 page 9. [*Letters of Horace Walpole to Horace Mann*, ed. Lord Dover (George Ellis (1795-1833), cr. Baron Dover, 1831), 1833, 1. ix.]

---

within'. Citing Horace Walpole's version of this anecdote ('Reminiscences', *Works*, 1798, 4. 314-15), Croker, in his review (p. 186), correctly identifies the granddaughter as Lady Bateman, and describes the anecdote as exaggerated. Lady Louisa, tacitly accepting his identification of the granddaughter, now replies.

[1] Hon. John Spencer (1708-46), father of 1st Earl Spencer of Althorpe, Northampton-shire, and ancestor of Lady Louisa's contemporary, John Charles (1782-1845), 3rd Earl Spencer.

[2] Lady Georgiana Carolina (d. 1780), da. of John Carteret, 2nd Earl Granville; as a widow she m. (1750) William, 2nd Earl Cowper.

feeling would have made him listen one moment to the ridiculous story of Mr Wortley's having amassed thirteen hundred and fifty thousand pounds (equivalent to five or six millions now).[1] He gives to be sure the idle report of the day as we all do in a careless letter, and probably laughed at it himself next week; but its vulgar absurdity was so glaring that he would have paused to add—what nonsense!—if it had not concerned a person he looked upon as Sir Robert Walpole's enemy, and wished to believe a miser.

If thus sensitive for Sir Robert, who, as Lord Dover farther observes*—'appears to have been rather a harsh father to his youngest son'—more the object of his respect and pride than his tenderness, what must he have been where *She* was concerned, of whom he says in a beautiful letter to General Conway—'If I ever felt much for any thing it was for my mother. I look on you as her nearest relation, and think I never can do enough to show my gratitude and affection for her.'[2]—Angry feelings might be reverenced and even malevolence itself forgiven when springing from such a source, which we are convinced was the case with his inveterate hatred to Lady Mary Wortley. That the grudge he bore her had an origin connected with his mother we believe the more firmly because it never led to an open breach or even avoidance. For Lady Mary expressly says—'Mr. Walpole was very civil to me at Florence'[3] —the place whence he wrote of her the most abusively: therefore he had some private motive for keeping outwardly on good terms with the person he described as so detestable. Whether he did hate her or did not, let the common sense of the reader decide, after considering every passage in his letters relating to her. Let it say whether Pope might not be full as fitly called to her character (in legal phrase) as Walpole, and whether it would not be unjust to reprobate the one if we receive as valid the evidence of the other?

Another question remains. Did the world at large agree with either? Was Lady Mary generally thought not only as worthless but as ridiculous as Horace Walpole represents her?—If so, we know the inevitable consequence. With her wit and talents, backed by a high situation, she might have kept her ground, have shone and

* Note on the Letters to Sir Horace Mann Volume 1 page 168.

---

[1] Walpole, *Corr.* 9. 338; mentioned by Croker, p. 168.
[2] To Henry Seymour Conway (1719–95), 20 July 1744, *Corr.* 37. 170.
[3] *Letters*, 3. 184. Lady Louisa's quotation is slightly inaccurate.

triumphed, in public promiscuous assemblies; but would she not have been banished from all really respectable society? Would not the virtuous part of her sex have kept coldly aloof, and the decorous of the other wished their wives and daughters to avoid her acquaintance? If women who had any character to lose associated with her, were they not mean enough in mind as well as in class to think a title covered all defects? She might have toadeaters among these, but could she have friends among her equals?—We need merely subjoin the list: The Duchess of Marlborough, who with all her faults and all her enemies never was nor could be assailed by the breath of scandal; the duke and dutchess of Montagu;[1] Lady Stafford;[2] the unfortunate duchess of Bolton;[3] Sir [   ][4] and Lady Knatchbull, Lord and Lady Oxford,[5] Lord and Lady Pomfret, Sir James and Lady Frances Steuart.[6] On which of these was a blemish to be found?[7] We grant Miss Skerritt an exception—the only one—and Miss Skerritt was young and innocent when Lady Mary first became partial to her.

But at the very time when Horace Walpole was painting her in such odious colours to his correspondents, and telling them that every body laughed at her,[8] she somehow inspired another young Englishman, of as good sense as himself and quite as much a man of the world, with sentiments of admiration and respect which he retained to the end of a long life. We mean Mr Mackenzie,[9] who travelled through Italy in the selfsame year; was at Venice, at Florence, at Rome—was intimate with Sir Horace Mann,[10] Sir Francis Dashwood,[11] the Pomfret family, Mr (or Lord) Coke,[12]

---

[1] John Montagu (1690–1749), 2nd Duke of Montagu, m. (1705) Mary Churchill (1689–1751), da. of 1st Duke of Marlborough.

[2] Claude-Charlotte de Gramont (d. 1739), da. of Comte de Gramont, m. (1694) Henry, 1st Earl of Stafford, and separated from him after a year.

[3] See p. 12 above.

[4] Blank in MS. Sir Wyndham Knatchbull-Wyndham (d. 1749) m. (1730) Catherine Harris (d. 1741) of Salisbury (*Letters*, 3. 158–9).   [5] See p. 38 above.

[6] For Sir James, see p. 53 above. He m. (1743) Lady Frances Wemyss (1723–89), da. of 5th Earl of Wemyss.

[7] The Duchess of Montagu's reputation was not unblemished (see e.g. Halsband, *Hervey*, p. 9).

[8] Croker (p. 188) quotes this letter of 25 Sept. 1740 from Walpole to Conway (Walpole, *Corr.* 37. 78).

[9] James Stuart (1719?–1800), Lord Bute's only brother, assumed the name Mackenzie on inheriting (in 1723) the estates of his great-grandfather.

[10] (1701–86), appointed (1740) British Resident in Florence.

[11] (1708–81), later Baron Le Despencer, famous as a rake.

[12] Edward (1719–53), styled Viscount Coke, had been on the Grand Tour during the

Lord Strafford,[1] in short all the people Walpole's letters name. His connection with Lady Mary, as the mother in·law of his elder brother, was far too slight to make other young men scrupulous about what they said of her in his presence. As he had eyes, he could not but see whatever Walpole saw, and we may be sure he could not fail of hearing whatever Walpole heard; only his organs were clear of prejudice; and we have stated the result. Before Lady Mary left Italy, he again visited it as Envoy to the Court of Turin;[2] and then again must have heard any stories that were current concerning her; but his opinion never varied, his regard for her never abated, and his praise of her was always re-ecchoed by his wife.[3] Both delighted to talk of her in their old age as the person they were most pleased and proud to have known in those earlier days of enjoyment which age loves to recall and dwell upon with melancholy gratification.

We imagine it is unnecessary to say more.

same years as Walpole; LM had known him in Venice (*Letters*, 2. 385). In 1747 he m. Lady Mary Campbell, da. of 2nd Duke of Argyll.

[1] William Wentworth (1722–91), 2nd Earl of Strafford.
[2] From 1758 to 1761.
[3] Lady Betty Campbell (d. 1799), sister of Lord Coke's wife, m. (1749) Mackenzie.

[Critique of *Cato*]
Wrote at the Desire of Mr. Wortley,
suppress'd at the desire of Mr. Adison

At the beginning of 1713, probably, Lady Mary composed this critique of *Cato*, the verse tragedy that became the most famous of the century. Her husband, Edward Wortley Montagu, whom she had married the previous summer, was a close friend of Joseph Addison; and (as the heading indicates) he gave her the manuscript of the play, which was not staged or published until April 1713, with the request that she send him her opinion of it. She performed her task with a firm confidence that is surprising in a young woman whose literary ambition had as yet expressed itself only in omnivorous reading and in private writings. Evidently Wortley showed her paper to Addison, who then altered his play in several ways to conform to her suggestions. (See Halsband, 'Addison's *Cato* and Lady Mary Wortley Montagu', *PMLA*, 65 (1950), 1122–9; Halsband, *LM*, pp. 32–3; Peter Smithers, *The Life of Joseph Addison*, 2nd ed., 1968, pp. 261–4, 271–5.) A year later Addison accepted an essay by Lady Mary for *The Spectator*.

Text H MS. 80. 388–98. *Printed* (in part) in George Paston [Emily Morse Symonds], *Lady Mary Wortley Montagu and Her Times*, 1907, pp. 169–73.

To speak in the first place of the Plot, or Fable: if I may beleive the Translations of Aristotle,[1] or rely on the Opinions of all the French critics,[2] or Horace in his Art of Poetry,[3] or of Mr. Addison him selfe,[4] it ought to be entire, I mean to admit of no Episodes that do not naturally arise from the Principal Fable: this is, as I remember, the first Law of dramatic poetry, which I am afraid is very much violated in this Tragedy of Cato. The death of Cato is certainly the Principal action, as he was perhaps the greatest character amongst the Romans; a Greater subject cannot be chosen for Tragedy. But what relation to the carry[ing] on of that action, there is to be found in the Loves of Juba, Marcus, or Portia, I can't

---

[1] *Poetics*, II. viii.

[2] Pierre Corneille, for example, in his 'Discours des trois unités' (*Œuvres*, ed. C. Marty-Laveaux, 1862–1922, I. 99).

[3] *Ars Poetica*, line 23.

[4] In *Spectator* No. 409, 19 June 1712, Addison writes that in poetry it is 'absolutely necessary that the Unities of Time, Place and Action . . . should be thoroughly explained and understood . . .' (ed. D. F. Bond, 1965, 3. 530).

discover, or indeed, why Marcus is represented in Love at all.[1]
The Passion he talks with, the fine Lines that are put in his mouth,
and the Fire of his character, prepares us for some very extrodinary
Event. I expected something very surprising in his discovering his
belov'd Brother to be the belov'd Lover of his Mistresse. I confesse
I was yet more surpris'd at his death in the 4th Act, which might
have happen'd without his being in Love at all. I attended a Scene
between the Brothers to excell that of Brutus and Cassius by
Shakespeare,[2] or Troilus and Hector by Mr. Dryden,[3] or even that
of Menelaus and Agamemnon by Euripides.[4] The Passion of the
Gentleman puts me in mind of Mr. Bayes' petticoat and the Belly
ach, who being ask'd 'What happen'd upon it,' reply'd, 'Nothing at
all, no earthly thing igad—.'[5]

I am not going to speak of the Andromaque of Mr. Racine as the
best Tragedy in the World.[6] But it has been gennerally esteem'd a
good one; his Conduct is very different. The death of Pyrrhus is his
principal Action. Hermione is represented loving him, with the
utmost rage of a Woman's Love; Orestes doated on her with the
blindest Fondnesse; Pyrrhus appears agitated by a violent passion
for Andromache without being able to make any Impression on her
heart: all these Passions were necessary to the carrying on the
principal design. The death of Pyrrhus was caus'd by the rage of
Hermione, who had no other way of putting that rage in Execution
but by imposing on Orestes in so grosse a manner as would have
pass'd on none but a doating Lover. Pyrrhus himselfe carrys on the
same design; his ill usage of Hermione, in every part of it, was
necessary to heighten her Resentment to so cruel a degree. The
disdain of Andromache made the irregularity of his proceeding with
her more provoking; every Passion and almost every Line in that
Play Leads to the Principal design of it. The Love of Marcus, the
rivalry of his Brother, etc have no relation to the death of Cato; he
appears ignorant of it from one end to tother, nor can I perceive one
considerable Event it produces. I think this hinders the Play from
being one Action and in my opinion Shakespear's manner of Trans-

[1] Both Pope and Young thought the love plot had been inserted by Addison only to
win popularity (Joseph Spence, *Anecdotes*, ed. J. M. Osborn, 1966, I. 65, 332).
[2] *Julius Caesar*, I. ii or IV. iii.
[3] *Troilus and Cressida: Or Truth Found Too Late*, 1679, III. ii.
[4] *Iphegenia at Aulis*, lines 317–542.
[5] Adapted from Duke of Buckingham, *The Rehearsal*, 1672, III. v.
[6] Jean Racine (1639–99), *Andromaque*, 1667.

gression is more pardonable. He makes his Play of Julius Caesar a series of Actions; he begins with the death of Caesar and concludes with that of Brutus. He offends in point of Time. But he does not introduce Mark Anthony makeing Love to a Roman Lady, who has nothing to do with the Plot of the Play, tho' he describes him a man adicted to his Pleasures. Caesar's death was his design and we hear of no Episodes not relateing to that. Marcus being son to Cato is no Excuse for our hearing so much of his Affairs; the Loves of his sons are improperly represented in the play, except they some way occassion'd his death.

I don't think Mr. Addison could have chose a greater subject. But tis too Barren for a Tragedy, which I allways thought impossible to be made of it, without intermixing things foreign to the Principal Action, and I am more than ever perswaded so, since Mr. Adison could not do it. The subject of a Tragedy should be neither too full of Events, nor too Plain. On the One, tis impossible to avoid confusion, and crouding many things in so short a compasse must make it obscure to the Audience. I hate to see a Plot thicken when manny Characters appear on the stage; none can be carry'd on as they ought to be; any thing intricate tires, and grows Dull. On the other hand a Barren subject will not aford 5 Acts without introduceing Persons and things foreign to it.

The Characters in this tragedy are all well carry'd on; above all I admire that of Cato. The Figure that Great Man makes in History is so noble and at the same time so Simple, I hardly beleivd it possible to shew him on our stage. He appears here in all his Beauty; his Sentiments are great, and express'd without affectation; his Language is Sublime without Fustian, and smooth without a misbecoming softnesse. I think I hear a Roman with all the Plain Greatnesse of Ancient Rome. Marcus appears impetuous and in nothing he says deviates from himselfe; I am only sorry his character is form'd to no purpose. I cannot forget a considerable Beauty in these characters. Marcia is represented a copy of her Father; the greatnesse of his Spirit and degree of his Fortitude is express'd in the Powr she shews over her Passions in reproaching Juba for neglecting the common cause of Liberty and Rome, tho by an Effect of his Love; she overcomes her tendernesse when she sends him out to danger with the same Greatnesse of Mind that Cato commands his, when he sees his son brought in dead before him. Lucia is shewn to us, with all the melting softnesse of a Woman.

Her compassion even for a Man she did not Love breaks out into
sighs and tears; she terrifys her selfe with her own Fear, and shews
irresolution and tendernesse at the complaint of her Lover. She can
not disguise her Heart from him, and discovers all its weakness in
her sorrow. This difference of Behaviour in Minds equally Virtuous
makes us reflect on the difference of their Birth and Education.
Cato is intrepid, and austerely good. We see Lucius more enclin'd
to mildnesse and compassion; he is capable of Fear, and less strong
in his Resolves. These Ladys seem to pertake of their Fathers'
different Tempers; we are warm'd by the great spirit of Marcia, and
soften'd by the gentlenesse of Lucia. Juba is a perfect character of
a Virtuous Young Man; even his Mistakes, and the Impositions of
Syphax on his credulity, the Beautifull sorrow he expresses on the
remembrance of his Father, and his confusion at having (as he
fear'd) lessen'd his Esteem with Cato, exalt the sweetnesse of his
temper, and set in a full Light the Modesty, the Diffidences, and
good nature which renders Youth more Lovely. The craft of
Syphax shews a Life Lead in dissimulation; his caution and desire
of safety tho purchas'd by Treason, the Fondnesse old Men have
for Life, the seeming coolnesse with which he hears the rages of
Juba, and the Artfull concealment of his Resentment is a finish'd
character of an old designing Statesman. Sempronius is younger,
and owes his Ruin to his Passions. Yet the Art with which he
flatters Cato, and endeavors to make Lucius suspected, is well
drawn to represent an Ambitious, Envious Man, who Aims at
Glory and is too impetuous to pursue it in the calm Paths of Virtu.
Portius is a character of Resolution and steddy virtu.

I cannot omit, that I do not observe throughout the whole
Tragedy one thought improper for the person that speaks it tho'
I think in some few instances Mr. Addison descends from the stile
proper for Tragedy and has made use of a few low Expressions.
'Beleive me' is repeated in the mouth of every person in the Play.[1]
The Phrase is so common in ordinary conversation, it should not
have a place, at least, not above onçe. 'In troth', in the 8th page, is
more proper for Farce, than Tragedy.[2] Lucia when she calls Juba
'good natur'd', gives him a praise we hear so often attributed to

[1] In the play as printed 'believe me' occurs seven times, spoken by three of the
characters. It was a favourite phrase of Addison in real life (Smithers, p. 328 n.).
[2] Addison retained this phrase (I. iii. 43). The edition of *Cato* cited is in *Misc. Works*,
ed. A. C. Guthkelch, 1914, I. 335–420.

people of lesse Figure I wish that Expression could be chang'd
for something that might signify the same in a higher stile.[1] For
the same reason I would have Syphax expresse the Heats of Lybia
(which I think might be easily done) otherwise than by 'dog days'.[2]
'Boy' would expresse his Resentment in the 29th page, as much as
'Brat', without so mean a sound.[3] 'Hold my tongue' ibid. is Liable
to the same Exception, and 'rarely well' in the 45th Page.[4] I can not
recollect one obscure Expression throughout the whole Tragedy.
In

> Tis not in Mortals to command Successe
> But we'll do more Sempronius we'll deserve it

is a fine Thought,[5] But I have read it too often. Breneralt says something very like it, speaking of his Mistresse,

> I will deserve her tho I never gain her.[6]

I am mistaken if I have not read in some other Play, something yet
nearer, tho I cannot just now remember it. Syphax giving his Love
of Juba to the Winds, page 31, looks too like a copy of Othello when
he speaks of his Wife,[7] and Torismond says

> Begone my cares I give you to the Winds.[8]

I know nothing more that seems borrow'd, and on the Whole I know
no Play that has so few Exceptionable Expressions, and in which
the Sublime never rises into Fustian or obscurity.

Tho I do not think Cato's children properly introduc'd into the
Story of his death, I cannot Forbear takeing notice of that Beautiful
scene in the 4th Act, where the double Mistake and the pleasing
Unfolding of it, gives the Audience all the Pleasures of tendernesse,
and shews the Author not inferior to Otway in the power of moving
the passions.[9] I confesse I could not read it without tears, and I
think it cannot fail of that Effect, when heightend by just Action.

---

[1] Addison retained this expression (I. vi. 2).

[2] Addison retained it (II. v. 16).

[3] Addison followed LM's suggestion (II. v. 69).

[4] Addison retained 'Hold my tongue' (II. v. 85), but deleted 'rarely well'.

[5] *Cato*, I. ii. 44–5.

[6] The exact words are 'I will deserve her, though I have her not' (John Suckling,
The Discontented Colonel, ?1640, in his *Works*, 1696, p. 348).

[7] *Cato*, II. v. 139, and *Othello*, III. iii. 264–7.

[8] Adapted from Dryden's *The Spanish Fryar*, 1681, II. i, concluding couplet.

[9] In *Spectator* No. 39, 14 Apr. 1711, Addison praised Thomas Otway for this quality.
The Orphan, 1680, was a very popular tragedy of the day. A pamphleteer in 1713 wrote
that Addison's tragedy had 'excited the Curiosity of the Town, more than any one since
the Orphan' (*Mr. Addison turn'd Tory: or, The Scene Inverted*, 1713, p. 21).

Tho We know the Mistake we cannot help sharing with Marcia in a sorrow so well Express'd, and feeling part of the Lovers when she finds him alive, and he discovers her Love. The distresse of Cato, and the greatnesse of Mind which he shews at the veiw of his dead son moves us more than any Griefe he could expresse on that occassion and we are more sensible of his Smothered Sorrow than we could be of any Expressions of it. The last scene has something in it wonderfully touching; I could only wish the soliloquy of Cato had been longer; the subject affords manny Beautifull Reflections. I know a Long Speech is not easily sufer'd on Our stage, but when it is printed I wish he would Enlarge on the Immortality of the Soul.[1] I would have some stronger Lines on Liberty scatter'd through the Play,[2] and I beleive it would have a very good Effect on the Minds of the People, for whose sake I think Mr. Addison in some degree obligd to publish it on the stage.[3] His Reputation will give a force to what he says, and This Tragedy may renew in the Minds of the Audience the Lost Love of Liberty, and contempt of servitude.

It would be too tedious to point out all the fine Lines in the Play; the Language is every where smooth, The Refflections just, and the sentiments noble and proper for the Persons that speak them. I am particularly pleas'd with that of Cato on his first knowledge of the Treachery of his professed Freind, and the Loudest of his Party, which seems to come from a Mind collected, and prepar'd for all Events. The Blemishes of the Play will escape the observation of the croud of Hearers and Readers, and the Beautys are conspicuous, and obvious, to every one. We have no Patterns of Perfect Tragedy, and the common Taste is so far vitiated by Custom, I don't doubt the Faults will find great Applause on our stage. If every Act ended with halfe a dozen Rhimes, which would be done with little trouble, it would inflame the sucesse, and there are manny Plays owe their good Fortune to Sounding Lines.[4]

[1] Addison probably followed LM's suggestion since Cato's speech extends to forty lines (v. i).

[2] Again, Addison probably concurred, since lines on liberty are declaimed by Cato in every one of his scenes, and by Juba, Marcia, and Cato's sons.

[3] A similar sentiment was voiced by Dr. George Smalridge in a letter to Addison after the staging of the play: 'I gave mySelf the pleasure of seeing Cato acted, and heartily wish all Discourses from the Pulpit were as instructive and edifying, as pathetical and affecting, as that which the Audience was then entertain'd with from the Stage' (2 Aug. 1713, Harvard University Library, MS. Eng. 4).

[4] LM's precept had been recommended by Addison himself in *Spectator* No. 39,

I have now gone through the Task you enjoyn'd me, in as short a manner as I could, which I cannot excuse undertakeing (being so much above my skill) but by remembering you, that it was by your Command.

14 Apr. 1711, where, after voicing disapproval of rhyme or rhyme mixed with blank verse in tragedy, he continues: 'I would not however debar the Poet from concluding his Tragedy, or, if he pleases, every Act of it, with two or three Couplets' (ed. D. F. Bond, 1965, 1. 165). In its printed version each act of *Cato* ended with three or four couplets.

Essay in *The Spectator*

The *Spectator* essay No. 561 (30 June 1714), written by Addison, was a satiric letter about a club of nine widows headed by Mrs. President, who is thinking of taking her seventh husband. Addison printed a reply by Lady Mary as Mrs. President. For the financial issues at stake here see Susan Staves, *Married Women's Separate Property in England, 1660–1833*, 1990.

Text   original printed folio.

The SPECTATOR, No. 573[1]
Castigata remordent. Juv.[2]
Wednesday, July 28, 1714

MY Paper on the Club of Widows, has brought me in several Letters; and, among the rest, a long one from Mrs. President, as follows.

Smart SIR,

'You are pleased to be very Merry, as you imagine, with us Widows: And you seem to ground your Satyr on our receiving Consolation so soon after the Death of our Dears, and the Number we are pleased to admit for our Companions; but you never reflect what Husbands we have bury'd, and how short a Sorrow the loss of them was capable of occasioning. For my own Part, Mrs. President as you call me, my First Husband I was Marry'd to at Fourteen, by my Uncle and Guardian, (as I afterwards discovered) by way of Sale, for the Third part of my Fortune. This Fellow looked upon me as a meer Child, he might breed up after his own Fancy; if he kissed my Chamber-Maid before my Face, I was supposed so ignorant, how could I think there was any hurt in it? When he came home Roaring Drunk at five in the Morning, 'twas the Custom of all Men that live in the World. I was not to see a Penny of Mony, for, poor Thing, how could I manage it? He took a handsome Cousin of his into the House, (as he said) to be my House-keeper, and to govern my Servants; for how should I know how to rule a Family? and while she had what Money she pleased, which was but reason-

---

[1] For proof of her authorship, see Halsband, *LM*, p. 37.
[2] Juvenal, *Satires*, 2. 35: 'being reproved they bite back'.

able for the Trouble she was at for my good, I was not to be so Censorious as to dislike Familiarity and Kindness between near Relations. I was too great a Coward to contend, but not so ignorant a Child to be thus impos'd upon. I resented his Contempt as I ought to do, and as most poor passive blinded Wives do, till it pleased Heaven to take away my Tyrant, who left me free possession of my own Land, and a large Jointure. My Youth and Money brought me many Lovers, and several endeavour'd to Establish an Interest in my Heart while my Husband was in his last Sickness; the Honourable *Edward Waitfort*[1] was one of the First who Addressed to me, advised to it by a Cousin of his that was my intimate Friend, and knew to a Penny what I was worth. Mr. *Waitfort* is a very agreeable Man, and every Body would like him as well as he does himself, if they did not plainly see that his Esteem and Love is all taken up, and by such an Object as 'tis impossible to get the better of, I mean himself. He made no doubt of marrying me within Four or Five Months, and begun to proceed with such an assured easie Air, that piqued my Pride not to banish him; quite contrary, out of pure Malice, I heard his first Declaration with so much innocent Surprise, and blushed so prettily, I perceived it touched his very Heart, and he thought me the best-natured Silly poor thing upon Earth. When a Man has such a Notion of a Woman, he loves her better than he thinks he does. I was overjoyed to be thus revenged on him, for designing on my Fortune; and finding 'twas in my Power to make his Heart ake, I resolved to compleat my Conquest, and entertained several other Pretenders. The first Impression of my undesigning Innocence was so strong in his Head, he attributed all my Followers to the inevitable force of my Charms, and from several Blushes, and side Glances, concluded himself the Favourite; and when I used him like a Dog for my Diversion, he thought it was all Prudence and Fear, and pitied the Violence I did my own Inclinations, to comply with my Friends, when I married Sir *Nicholas Fribble* of sixty Years of Age. You know Sir, the Case of Mrs. *Medlar*,[2] I hope you would not have had me cry out my

[1] Suggesting the name of LM's husband (whose courtship was protracted over more than two years) and that of Lady Wishfort in Congreve's *The Way of the World*, 1700.

[2] The third of the nine widows in the Widow-Club. After two husbands and a gallant, Mrs. Medlar has been married for a week to a gentleman of sixty; but since their marriage has apparently not been consummated she is permitted to resume her status as a widow. The medlar is a fruit which becomes a delicacy in decay.

Eyes for such a Husband. I shed Tears enough for my Widowhood
a Week after my Marriage, and when he was put in his Grave,
reckoning he had been two Years Dead, and my self a Widow of that
standing, I married three Weeks afterwards *John Sturdy* Esq; his
next Heir. I had indeed some Thoughts of taking Mr. *Waitfort*,
but I found he could stay, and besides he thought it Indecent to ask
me to Marry again till my Year was out; so privately resolving him
for my Fourth, I took Mr. *Sturdy* for the Present. Would you
believe it Sir, Mr. *Sturdy* was just Five and Twenty, about six
Foot high, and the stoutest Fox-hunter in the County, and I believe
I wished Ten thousand times for my Old *Fribble* again; he was
following his Dogs all the Day, and all the Night keeping them up
at Table with him and his Companions; however I think my self
obliged to them for leading him a Chase in which he broke his Neck.
Mr. *Waitfort* begun his Addresses anew, and I verily believe I had
Married him now, but there was a young Officer in the Guards, that
had Debauched two or three of my Acquaintance, and I could not
forbear being a little Vain of his Courtship. Mr. *Waitfort* heard of it,
and read me such an insolent Lecture upon the Conduct of Women,
I Married the Officer that very Day, out of pure Spite to him. Half
an Hour after I was Married I received a Penitential Letter from
the Honourable Mr. *Edward Waitfort*, in which he begged Pardon
for his Passion, as proceeding from the violence of his Love: I
triumphed when I Read it, and could not help, out of the pride of
my Heart, shewing it to my new Spouse; and we were very merry
together upon it. Alas! my Mirth lasted a short time; my young
Husband was very much in Debt when I marryed him, and his first
Action afterwards was to set up a gilt Chariot and Six, in fine
Trappings before and behind. I had married so hastily, I had not
the Prudence to reserve my Estate in my own Hands; my ready
Mony was lost in two Nights at the Groom Porters;[1] and my
Diamond Necklace, which was Stole I did not know how, I met in
the Street upon *Jenny Wheadle*'s Neck. My Plate[2] vanished piece by
piece, and I had been reduced to downright Pewter, if my Officer
had not been deliciously killed in a Duel, by a Fellow that had
cheated him of Five hundred Pounds, and afterwards, at his own
Request, satisfied him and me too, by running him through the
Body. Mr. *Waitfort* was still in Love, and told me so again; to

---

[1] An officer of the English Royal Household, whose principal function was to regulate
all matters connected with gaming at court, and who maintained his own gaming-house.
[2] Silver plate.

prevent all Fears of ill Usage, he desired me to reserve every thing in my own Hands; but now my Acquaintance begun to wish me Joy of his Constancy, my Charms were declining, and I could not resist the Delight I took in shewing the young Flirts about Town, it was yet in my Power to give pain to a Man of Sense: This and some private hopes he would hang himself, and what a Glory would it be for me, and how I should be envy'd, made me accept of being third Wife to my Lord *Friday*. I proposed, from my Rank and his Estate,[1] to live in all the Joys of Pride, but how was I mistaken? He was neither extravagant, nor ill-natured, nor debauched; I suffered however more with him than with all my others. He was splenatick. I was forced to sit whole Days harkening to his imaginary Ails; it was impossible to tell what would please him; what he liked when the Sun shined, made him sick when it rained; he had no Distemper, but lived in constant Fear of them all; my good Genius dictated to me to bring him acquainted with Doctor *Gruel*; from that Day he was always contented, because he had Names for all his Complaints; the good Doctor furnished him with Reasons for all his Pains, and Prescriptions for every Fancy that troubled him; in hot Weather he lived upon Juleps,[2] and let Blood to prevent Feavers; when it grew cloudy, he generally apprehended a Consumption; to shorten the History of this wretched part of my Life, he ruined a good Constitution by endeavouring to mend it, and took several Medicines, which ended in taking the grand Remedy, which cured both him and me of all our Uneasinesses. After his Death, I did not expect to hear any more of Mr. *Waitfort*, I knew he had renounced me to all his Friends, and been very witty upon my Choice, which he affected to talk of with great Indifferency; I gave over thinking of him, being told that he was engaging with a pretty Woman and a great Fortune; it vexed me a little, but not enough to make me neglect the Advice of my Cousin *Wishwell*, that came to see me, the Day my Lord went into the Country with *Russel*;[3] she told me experimentally, nothing put an unfaithful Lover and a dead

---

[1] Although D. F. Bond calls this phrase a slip for 'his Rank and my Estate' (4. 559 n. 1) the phrase as printed can be justified. Mrs President proposes to enjoy being Lady Friday, and to spend her new husband's wealth rather than her own. The phrase was left unaltered in the 1714 collected (and corrected) edition of the *Spectator*.

[2] An 'extemporaneous form of medicine' (first quotation in Johnson's *Dictionary*).

[3] This may be an elaborate way of referring to Lord Friday's death. William, Lord Russell (1639–83), was a member of the 'country party' in opposition to Charles II's court party. He was executed for treason.

Husband so soon out of ones Head, as a new one,[1] and, at the same
time proposed to me a Kinsman of hers; you understand enough
of the World (said she) to know Mony is the most valuable Consideration, he is very rich, and I'm sure, cannot live long; he has
a Cough that must carry him off soon. I knew afterwards she had
given the self same Character of me to him; but however I was so
much persuaded by her, I hastened on the Match, for fear he should
die before the time came; he had the same Fears, and was so pressing, I married him in a Fortnight, resolving to keep it private a
Fortnight longer. During this Fortnight Mr. *Waitfort* came to
make me a Visit, he told me he had waited on me sooner, but had
that Respect for me, he would not interrupt me in the first Day of
my Affliction for my dead Lord; that as soon as he heard I was at
Liberty to make another Choice, he had broke off a Match very
advantagious for his Fortune just upon the Point of Conclusion,
and was forty times more in Love with me than ever. I never
received more Pleasure in my Life than from this Declaration, but
I composed my Face to a grave Air, and said the News of his Engagement had touched me to the Heart, that in a rash jealous Fit,
I had married a Man I could never have thought on if I had not lost
all Hopes of him. Good-natured Mr. *Waitfort* had like to have
dropped down dead at hearing this, but went from me with such
an Air as plainly shewed me he laid all the Blame upon himself,
and hated those Friends that had advised him to the fatal Application; he seemed as much touched by my Misfortune as his own, for
he had not the least Doubt I was still passionately in Love with him.
The truth of the Story is, my new Husband gave me reason to
repent I had not staid for him; he had married me for my Mony,
and I soon found he lov'd Mony to Distraction; there was nothing
he would not do to get it, nothing he would not suffer to preserve
it; the smallest Expence kept him awake whole Nights, and when
he paid a Bill, 'twas with as many Sighs, and after as many Delays,
as a Man that endures the loss of a Limb. I heard nothing but
Reproofs for Extravagancy, whatever I did. I saw very well that he
would have starved me, but for losing my Jointures; and he suffered
Agonies between the Grief of seeing me have so good a Stomach,
and the Fear that if he made me fast it might prejudice my Health.
I did not doubt he would have broke my Heart, if I did not break

---

[1] A similar sentiment appears in LM's song addressed to the widowed Lady Irwin
(pp. 257–8 below), and in lines to her by Hervey (p. 288 below).

his, which was allowable by the Law of Self-defence; the way was very easie. I resolved to spend as much Mony as I could, and before he was aware of the Stroke, appeared before him in a two thousand Pound Diamond Necklace; he said nothing, but went quietly to his Chamber, and, as it is thought, composed himself with a Dose of Opium. I behaved my self so well upon the Occasion, that to this Day I believe he died of an Apoplexy.[1] Mr. *Waitfort* was resolved not to be too late this time, and I heard from him in two Days. I am almost out of my Weed[2] at this present Writing, and very doubtful whether I'll marry him or no; I do not think of a Seventh, for the Ridiculous Reason you mention,[3] but out of pure Morality that I think so much Constancy should be rewarded, tho' I may not do it after all perhaps. I do not believe all the unreasonable Malice of Mankind can give a Pretence why I should have been constant to the Memory of any of the deceased, or have spent much time in grieving for an insolent, insignificant, negligent, extravagant, splenatick, or covetous Husband; my first insulted me, my second was nothing to me, my third disgusted me, the fourth would have ruined me, the fifth tormented me, and the sixth would have starved me. If the other Ladies you name would thus give in their Husbands Pictures, at length, you would see, they have had as little Reason as my self to lose their Hours in weeping and wailing.'

[1] Mrs. President's good behaviour extends to correct thinking.
[2] The 'deep mourning worn by a widow' (*OED*).
[3] The reason mentioned in No. 561 was 'that there is as much Vertue in the Touch of a seventh Husband as of a seventh Son'. The touch of a seventh son purportedly could cure the King's Evil (*The Spectator*, 1965, 4. 516).

[A Letter from the other world to a Lady from her former Husband][1]

This brief essay, written after 1723, probably after 1728, is derived from a venerable genre, the dialogue of the dead and its epistolary offshoot. LM would have known Tom Brown's *Letters from the Dead to the Living*, 1702, and Elizabeth (Singer) Rowe's very popular *Friendship in Death, in . . . Letters from the Dead to the Living*, 1728, besides French examples. She probably had in mind an actual, unidentified twice-married woman. That she was herself accustomed to think of the form in her everyday life can be seen in her remark to a friend in 1709: 'I believe you will expect this letter to be dated from the other world, for sure I am you never heard an inhabitant of this talk so before' (*Letters*, 1.7).

Text H MS. 79. 291–2. *Printed* 1803.

THIS Letter will surprize you less than it would any other of your Sex; and therefore I think I need no Apology in breaking through a rule of good breeding which has been observ'd so strictly by all Husbands for so many Ages, who, however troublesome while they liv'd, have never frighten'd their Wives by the least notice of 'em after their Deaths. But your Reverend Doctor will inform you that there is nothing supernatural in this Correspondance, and that the Existence of Immortal Spirits includes a tender Concern for ⟨the⟩ poor militant mortals of your World. I own I was a little puzzled how to convey this Epistle, and thought it best to assume a material form for some few moments and put it my selfe into the penny post.[2] In my hurry (being very impatient to let you hear from me) I unluckily forgot my little finger, which produc'd an odd accident, for the Wench at the post office would have taken me up for one of the Incendiarys. Allready the mob assembled round the door, and nothing but disolving into air could have sav'd me from Newgate.[3] Several run down the allys in persuit of me, and particular care was taken of my Letter in hopes of reading it in the news paper.

You may imagine I would not have expos'd my selfe to this adventure but out of the sincerest regard to the Happyness of the dear Partner of my worldly Cares. Without the least uneasyness I have seen you dispose of your selfe into the Arms of Another; and I would

---

[1] Title in the hand of Lady Louisa Stuart.
[2] The London penny post was instituted in 1680.
[3] Provisions against threatening letters were made in the 'Black Act', effectual 1 June 1723.

never disturb you while you were seeking pleasure in forgetting me, but I cannot bear you should constrain your selfe out of respect to me. ⟨I⟩ see every motion of your mind now much clearer than I did in my Life (thô then I guess'd pretty shrewdly sometimes). I know the real content that you find in pink colour'd Riband, and am sensible how much you sacrifice to Imaginary decency every time you put on that odious rusty black, which is halfe worn out.

Alas, my dear Eliza, in these seats of perfect Love and Beauty the veriest scrub of a cherubim (some of which have rak'd cinders behind Mountague House,[1] as they often tell me) is more charming than you were on your first Wedding day. Judge then whither I can have any satisfaction in looking at your crape hood when I am in this bright Company. You know that in my terrestial state, 3 bottles would sometimes raise me to that pitch of Philosophy, I utterly forgot you when you were but some few Inches from me. Do not fancy me grown so Impertinent here as to observe so nicely whither you obey the Forms of Widowhood, and do not think to cajole me with such instances of your affection when you are giving the most substantial proofe of it to another Man. I have allready assur'd you I am exalted above Jealousy. If I could have been sensible of it, You have provok'd me by a second Cho⟨ice⟩ so absolutely opposite to your First. He is often talking of certain fellows he calls Classic Authors, who I never trouble'd my Head with; and I know this Letter will meet with more regard from him than from you, for he is better skill'd in the Language of the Dead than the Living.

---

[1] In Bloomsbury, the London residence of the Duke of Montagu; now the site of the British Museum.

[Autobiographical romance: fragment]

This autobiographical fragment—apparently all that Lady Mary composed—sketches her life until the summer of 1710, when her suitor, Edward Wortley Montagu, formally applied to her father for her hand. Exactly when she wrote it is uncertain—probably after 1715, for in that year her father became Duke of Kingston, whose name she literally translates as Regiavilla, the heroine's father. In plot the fragment follows the outline of Lady Mary's life except that she makes herself precociously young (fourteen) at her first meeting with Wortley; she was closer to nineteen.

Text H MS. 80. 196–9. *Printed* in part in George Paston [Emily Morse Symonds], *Lady Mary Wortley Montagu and Her Times*, 1907, pp. 4–5, 7–8, 21–2, 28–30.

I AM going to write a History so uncommon that in how plain a manner so ever I relate it, It will have the Air of a Romance, thô there shall not be a sillable feign'd in it except those of the Names, which I cannot resolve to set down at length.

I need say nothing of the Pedigree of the unfortunate Lady whose Life I have undertaken to write. Tis enough to say she was Daughter to the Duke of Regiavilla to inform my reader there is no Nobler descent in Portugal. Her first misfortune happen'd in a time of Life when she could not be sensible of it, thô she was sufficiently so in the course of it, I mean the Death of a Noble Mother,[1] whose virtue and good sense might have supported and instructed her Youth, which was now left to the Care of a Young Father, who thô naturally an honest Man, was abandonn'd to his pleasures, and (like most of those of his Quality) did not think himselfe oblig'd to be very attentive to his children's Education. Thus was the unfortunate left to the care of an old Governess, who thô perfectly good and pious wanted a capacity for so great a Trust.

Læticia had naturally the strongest Inclination for Reading, and finding in her Father's house a well furnish'd Library,[2] instead of the usual diversions of children, made that the seat of her Pleasures, and had very soon run through the English part of it. Her Appetite for

---

[1] In 1692, when LM was three years old. For her mother, see p. 8 above.
[2] For the magnificence of LM's father's library, see the *Catalogus Bibliothecae Kingstonianae* [?1726] (in BM); and the Abbé Le Blanc's description (Hélène Monod-Cassidy, *Un Voyageur-philosophe au XVIIIe siècle*, 1941, pp. 266–7).

knowledge encreasing with her years, without considering the
toilsome task she undertook she begun to learn her selfe the Latin
Grammar, and with the help of an uncommon memory and inde-
fatigable Labour made her selfe so far mistrisse of that Language as
to be able to understand allmost any Author. This extrodinary
attachment to study became the Theme of Public discourse. Her
Father, thô no Scholar himself, was flatter'd with a pleasure in the
progress she made; and this Reputation, which she did not seek
(having no end in view but her own Amusements), gave her Enviers
and consequently Enemys amongst the Girls of her own Age. One
of these was Mlle ——. She had a large fortune, which was enough
to draw after her a croud of those that otherwaies would never have
thought of her. She fancy'd she triumph'd over Lætitia when she
related to her the Number of her Conquests, and amongst others
nam'd to her Sebastian[1] as he that was most passionatly her servant
and had made most Impression on her Heart. Lætitia, who saw
through the little vanity that agitated her, and had a very mean
Idea of a Man that could be captivated with such charms, laugh'd
at her Panegyric, and the other, who insisted on the merit of her
imagin'd Lover, would make her a Wittness both of his agreableness
and passion. A party for this purpose was very easily contriv'd, and
Lætitia invited to play where he was to tailly at Bassette. She was
then but newly enter'd into her teens, but never being tall had
allready attain'd the height she allways had, and her person was in
all the Childish bloom of that Age.

Sebastian who seriously design'd upon the Fortune of Mlle ——,
who was 3 year older, propos'd nothing by coming there but an
Occasion of obliging her, and being at that time near 30 did not
expect much Conversation amongst a set of Romps. Tea came in
before Cards; and a new play being then acted, it was the first thing
mention'd on which Lætitia took occasion to criticise in a manner
so just and so knowing, he was as much amaz'd as if he had heard
a piece of Waxwork talk on that subject. This led them into a
discourse of Poetry; he was still more astonish'd to find her not only
well read in the moderns, but that there was hardly any beautifull
passage in the Classics she did not remember. This was striking him
in the most sensible manner. He was a throrough [*sic*] Scholar, and
rather an Adorer than an Admirer of Learning. The conversation
grew so eager on both sides, neither Cards nor Mlle were thought

[1] Edward Wortley Montagu.

upon; and she was force'd to call to him several times before she could prevail on him to go towards the Table. When he did, it was only to continue his Discourse with Lætitia, and she had the full pleasure of triumphing over Mlle, who was force'd to be silent while they talk'd what she could not understand.

This Day put an end to his Inclination ever to see her [Mlle] again, and his admiration [for Lætitia] was so visible that his Sisters[1] (who are generally ready to make court to an Elder Brother) made all sort of Advances of Freindship to Lætitia, who receiv'd them very obligingly, and the⟨ir⟩ Acquaintance was very soon made. Several visits succeeded, and without his makeing any public declaration of it Lætitia easily saw the conquest she had made of his heart; but that Merit which was so powerfull with Mlle made very small Impression on her. She had a way of thinking very different from that of other Girls, and instead of looking on a Husband as the ultimate aim of her wishes she never thought of marriage but as a Bond that was to subject her to a Master, and she dreaded an Engagement of that sort. The little plan she had form'd to her selfe was retirement and study,[2] and if she found any Pleasure in Sebastian's Company it was only when he directed her in the Choice of her Books or explain'd some passages to her in Virgil and Horace.

He never spoke of his Passion, perhaps thinking her too young for a Declaration of that Nature; and as long as he kept himselfe within those limits she did not think she err'd in seeing him as often as she could. It was allways in his Sisters' Company, and her Youth hinder'd much observation being made on it. The whole Winter pass'd in this manner; and when she went into the Country,[3] his Sisters begg'd the Honour of her Correspondance, which she very readily granted them. She easily saw the Letters were such as they could not write, thô they came in their hands, and she was very regular in answer[ing] them, which was fresh subject of surprize to Sebastian, ⟨who⟩ had no notion that a Girl of 14 could write as good English as his Freind Mr. Addison. After the Summer Correspondance, the Winter conversations renew'd. His Applications seem'd more serious, but were allways receiv'd by her in such a manner, he never mention'd his Love for fear of loseing the little compliances she seem'd to have for him. The Duke had a seat very near the

---

[1] Anne and Catherine Wortley.
[2] In her old age LM reflected on her studious disposition (*Letters*, 3. 97).
[3] Thoresby House, Notts. (*Letters*, 1. 3 n. 1).

Town,[1] and as he never consulted the pleasure of his Daughters
when his own were in question, the matches at N[ewmarket] giveing
him an occasion of leaving the Town he resolv'd to send them to his
Villa very early in the Spring, which was a great mortification, particularly having there no Library, which would have been in leiu of
every thing to Lætitia.

The night before her departure she went ⟨to⟩ the Park.[2] Sebastian was there and endeavor'd, by his looks and messages that he
sent her by the orange Women, to shew her that this sudden remove
made him very miserable. One of these Jades, who make it their
Busyness to find out people's Inclinations in order to find their
account in serving them, seeing an unfeign'd melancholy in his Air
and behaviour, told him after the farewell Bow of Lætitia that she
gave him permission to write to her, and her selfe orders to convey
the Letter. Nothing could be more improbable than this message in
every light, but he was so far transported with this surprizing favor,
he wrote a very passionate declaration of Love, which he put into
that Woman's hands next morning, to which she brought him a
very kind Answer of her own Invention. He too well knew the stile
and character of Lætitia to take it for hers, but the contents were
so agreable (however express'd) that he would beleive it was wrote
by her order by her chambermaid. But having very little Opinion
of the discretion of this Messenger he intrusted a faithfull servant of
his own with the Answer, in which after an Acknowledgment full of
Transport for the happyness she gave him, he gently represented
to her the danger to her Reputation in employing a Woman of that
sort, that he was even glad she had not trusted her with a letter under
her own Hand, but he begg'd she would contrive some other method
that might make their correspondance less hazardous to her.

This Letter was carry'd to the Duke's villa, where the servant
ask'd for Lætitia and deliver'd it to her own hand. I cannot describe
the astonishment with which she read it. She had been educated
with a strictness that made her look on a Love letter as a mortal
Crime, and to be accus'd of writeing one to a Man she never had
a tender thought for, made it doubly provoking. She look'd upon
it as unpardonable vanity in him, and a want of Esteem for her to
suppose her capable of it, and in the present Hurry of her Resent-

---

[1] The Duke's suburban seat was at Acton; his Newmarket pleasures were horse-
racing.
[2] Green Park, no doubt, adjoining Arlington Street, where LM's father's house stood.

ment wrote him a few lines in which she express'd it in the severest manner, which she gave to his Messenger.

But this was not the whole Consequence. It was a new thing in that regular Family to have an unknown person enquire for Lætitia, deliver her a Letter, and receive an Answer, and her Governess was too attentive to let it pass without examination. She said nothing at that time, but searching her pocket at night found Sebastian's letter. The sight of a Man's hand alarm'd her. She sent it immediately to the Duke as an affair of the last Consequence, and he made haste to his daughter, who for the first time of his Life he severely reprimanded in so much Fury that he would [not] hear her Justification and treated her as if she had been surpriz'd in the most criminal Correspondance.

Poor Lætitia retir'd to her Closet, drown'd in tears, and could think of no Expedient to set her Innocence in a clear light, but to employ Sebastian, who she did not doubt had too much Generosity to let her suffer for his sake. She wrote to tell him, her Father had surpriz'd his Letter, that he was in the utmost rage against her for receiving it; and as he had occasion'd this mischeife, she left it to his conduct to justify her. She got this convey'd by a maid servant by the help of a guinea, but it had a very different Effect from what she propos'd. Sebastian had so far flatter'd himselfe with her Love, he did not doubt she had her selfe carry'd his letter to her Father, and it was an Artifice to bring this affair to a proper Conclusion.[1] He was delighted with the Wit of this Contrivance, which was very far from her thoughts, and full of the most charming hopes went next morning to her Father with a formal Proposal of marriage, accompany'd with the particulars of his Estate, which was too considerable to be refus'd. The Duke gave him as favourable an Answer as he could expect, and the Lawyers were appointed to meet on both Sides, according to Custom.

[1] This episode of the letters occurred in Apr.–May 1710 (*Letters*, 1. 27–40 *passim*).

[Account of the Court of George I]

The account of George I's court, although some of its assertions are questionable, is valuable as a historical document because so little remains for this period of British history. The King and his court circle had undoubtedly been a subject of interest and gossip long before they arrived in England, for the Act of Settlement (in 1701) firmly directed that the Hanoverians should succeed to the throne on Queen Anne's death. In the autumn of 1714, when the new monarch and his court arrived, Lady Mary was living in the country, but after she moved to London (in Jan. 1715) she could attend the court to meet and converse with those she had heard about. Her husband, a prominent Whig even during the Tory years of Queen Anne, had been appointed to the Treasury Board a month after the King's accession.

Exactly when Lady Mary wrote her 'Account' she does not say. It is tempting to see it as a fragment of what she called 'the History of my own time' that she was writing in 1752 while living in Italy. It was her chief amusement, she confessed to her daughter: 'It has been my Fortune to have a more exact knowledge both of the Persons and Facts that have made the greatest figure in England in this Age than is common, and I take pleasure in putting together what I know, with an Impartialty that is altogether unusual. . . . I can assure you I regularly burn every Quire as soon as it is finish'd, and mean nothing more than to divert my solitary hours' (*Letters*, 3. 18–19). She strikes a similar verbal posture in the 'Account': 'as I write only for my selfe I shall allways think I am at Liberty to make what digression I think fit.' Lady Louisa Stuart assumed that this fragment had escaped the flames, but John Wilson Croker disagreed. Calling it 'a curious piece of court gossip', he thought that from internal evidence it was probably written early in the reign of George I (*Quarterly Review*, 58 (1837), 175, 181).

One specific bit of evidence suggests that Lady Mary wrote her 'Account' in the spring of 1715. In referring to Thomas Wharton she calls him the 'Earl of Wharton (now Marquis)': *now* must refer to the very brief period between his elevation to the marquessate, on 15 Feb. 1715, and his death, on 12 Apr. 1715. Further corroboration of a more general nature is that the 'Account' contains no fact that can unequivocally be dated after the spring of 1715. ('Collonel Stanhope' received an earldom in 1718.) Lady Mary would have been a remarkably disciplined artist to have written in 1752 a memoir which so rigorously excludes anything that happened after 1715.

If true that she wrote the 'Account' in 1715 it is also remarkable that in the brief span of a few months she should have been able to compose a memoir so brilliant and incisive. Its tone is so firmly confident that the 'Account' has been used as a reliable historical source by at least two eminent German historians: Eduard Vehse in his *Geschichte der deutschen Höfe seit der Reformation* (vol. 18, 1853) and Wolfgang Michael in the first volume of his *Englische Geschichte im achtzehnten Jahrhundert*, 1896.

Text H MS. 80. 188–95. *Printed* 1837.

I WAS then in Yorkshire;¹ Mr. W[ortley] (who had at that time that sort of Passion for me, that would have made me invisible to all but himselfe, had it been in his power) had sent me thither. He staid in Town on the account of some busyness, and the Queen's death detain'd him there.² Lord Halifax, his near Relation, was put at the Head of [the] Treasury,³ and willing to have the rest of the commissioners such as he thought he could depend on, name'd him for one of them. It will be surprizing to add that he hesitated to accept of it at a time when his Father was alive and his present income very small; but he had that Opinion of his own Merit as made him think any offer below that of Secretary of State not worth his acceptance, and had certainly refus'd it if he had not been persuaded to the contrary by a rich old Uncle of Mine, Lord Pierrepont, whose fondness for me gave him expectations of a large Legacy.⁴

The new Court with all their Train was arriv'd before I left the Country. The Duke of Marlbrô was return'd in a sort of Triumph with the apparent merit of having suffer'd for his Fidelity to the succession, and was reinstated in his office of General etc.⁵ In short, all people who had suffer'd any hardship or disgrace during the late ministry would have it beleiv'd that it was occasion'd by their attachment to the House of Hanover. Even Mr. Walpole, who had been sent to the Tower for a piece of Bribery prov'd upon him, was call'd a Confessor to the Cause.⁶ But he had another piece of good Luck that yet more contributed to his Advancement; he had a very handsome Sister, whose Folly had lost her Reputation in London,

¹ At Middlethorpe, near York. LM moved to London about 9 Jan. 1715, after having lived mainly in the country since her marriage in 1712.

² Queen Anne died 1 Aug. 1714.

³ W was related to Halifax by descent from Sir Edward Montagu of Boughton (1532–1602) and by marriage. On his accession George I, instead of appointing a Lord Treasurer, set up a Treasury Board headed by Halifax, who appointed W a junior commissioner on 13 Oct. 1714 at a salary of £1,600 p.a. (*Calendar of Treasury Books*, vol. 29, 1957, ed. W. S. Shaw, p. 16). For Halifax, see p. 30 above.

⁴ Gervase Pierrepont (*c.* 1656–1715), 1st Baron, was uncle to LM's father. In his will he completely disregarded LM. W confirms her explanation, for in a letter to Addison from Constantinople on 18 July 1717 O.S. he writes: 'I think I had not cared for going into the Treasury, but from my Lord Pierrepont's persuasion, from whom you know I had great expectations and on very good grounds' (Tickell MS.). Sidney Wortley died in 1727.

⁵ The Duke, who had arrived in England six weeks before the King, was received by him on 18 Sept. 1714 and reinstated to his military appointments (Winston Churchill, *Marlborough: His Life and Times*, 1933–8, 4. 627).

⁶ In 1711 Walpole was accused of corruption as Secretary-at-War, and although blameless of bribery was found guilty in Jan. 1712. He was clearly the victim of Tory revenge (J. H. Plumb, *Sir Robert Walpole*, 1956, 1961, 1. 178–81).

but the yet greater Folly of Lord Townshend who happen'd to be a Neighbour in Norfolk to Mr. Walpole had occasion'd his being drawn in to marry her some months before the Queen dy'd.[1]

Lord Townshend had that sort of understanding which commonly makes men honest in the first part of their Lives; they follow the instruction of their Tutor, and till somebody thinks it worth their while to shew them a new path, go regularly on in the Road where they are set. Lord Townshend had then been many years an excellent Husband to a sober wife,[2] a kind Master to all his servants and dependants, a serviceable Relation where ever it was in his power, and follow'd the Instinct of Nature in being fond of his Children. Such a sort of behaviour, without any glareing absurdity either in prodigality or Avarice, allways gains a Man the Reputation of reasonable and Honest; and this was his character when the Earl of Godolphin sent him envoy to the States,[3] not doubting but he would be faithfull to his orders, without giving himselfe the trouble of criticiseing on them, which is what all Ministers wish in an Envoy. Robotun, a French refugee (secretary to Bernstaff,[4] one of the Elector of Hannover's ministers) happen'd then to be at the Hague, and was civilly receiv'd at Lord Townshend's, who treated him at his table with the English Hospitality, and he was charm'd with a reception which his Birth and Education did not entitle him to. Lord Townshend was recall'd when the Queen chang'd her Ministry. His Wife dy'd, and he retir'd into the Country where (as I have said before) Walpole had art enough to make him marry his sister Dolly. At that time I beleive he did not propose much more advantage by the match than to get rid of a Girl that lay heavy on his hands.

When King George ascended the Throne, he was surrounded by all his German Ministers and playfellows male and female. Baron Goretz[5] was the most considerable amongst them both for Birth and Fortune. He had mannag'd the King's Treasury 30

---

[1] The marriage took place on 25 July 1713. See p. 24 above.

[2] Elizabeth Pelham (1681–1711), da. of 1st Lord Pelham, m. (1698) Townshend.

[3] Sidney Godolphin (1645–1712), 1st Earl, was Lord High Treasurer 1702-10. Townshend was envoy at The Hague 1709-11.

[4] Jean de Robethon (d. 1722) was at The Hague in 1709 as Bernstorff's secretary for the signing of the Barrier Treaty. Andreas Gottlieb von Bernstorff (1649-1726) had entered the service of the Elector of Hanover (later George I) in 1705.

[5] Friedrich Wilhelm von Schlitz, called von Görtz (1647-1728), entered the service of Hanover in 1686. He accompanied George I to England but stayed only a short while.

year with the utmost fidelity and Oeconomy, and had the true German honesty, being a plain, sincere and unambitious Man. Bernstaff, the Secretary, was of a different turn; he was avaritious, artfull and designing, and had got his share in the King's Councils by bribeing his Women. Robotun was employ'd in these matters, and had the sanguine Ambition of a Frenchman. He resolv'd there should be an English Ministry of his chuseing; and knowing none of them personally but Townshend he had not fail'd to recommend him to his Master, and his Master to the King as the only proper Man for the Important post of Secretary of State; and he enter'd upon that office with universal applause, having at that time a very popular Character, which he might possibly have retain'd for ever if he had not been entirely govern'd by his wife and her Brother R. Walpole, who he immediately advance'd to be pay Master,[1] esteem'd a post of exceeding profit, and very necessary for his indebted Estate.

But he had yet higher views, or rather, he found it necessary to move higher, least he should not be able to keep that. The Earl of Wharton (now Marquis) both hated and despise'd him. His large estate, the whole income of which was spent in the service of the party, and his own parts, made him considerable, thô his profligate Life lessen'd the weight that a more regular Conduct would have given him.

Lord Halifax, who was now advance'd to the dignity of Earl, grac'd with the Garter, and first commissioner of the Treasury, treated him with contempt. The Earl of Nottingham, who had the real merit of haveing renounce'd the Ministry in Queen Anne's reign, when he thought they were going to alter the succession,[2] was not to be reconcile'd to Walpole, who he look'd upon as stigmatiz'd for corruption.

The Duke of Marlbrô who in his old age was makeing allmost the same figure at Court that he did when he first came into it, I mean bowing and smileing in the antichamber while Townshend was in the closet, was not however pleas'd with Walpole, who begun to behave to him with the insolence of new favour; and his Dutchess, who never restrain'd her tongue in her Life, us'd to make public

[1] Paymaster to the Forces.

[2] Daniel Finch (1647–1730), 2nd Earl of Nottingham, a staunch anti-Jacobite Tory, had offended Queen Anne (in 1705) by persuading some of his Tory friends to join him in an address to the crown begging that the Electress Sophia be invited to reside in England. His final rupture with the court occurred in 1711.

jokes of the beggary she first knew him in, when her Caprice gave him a considerable place[1] against the Opinion of Lord Godolphin and the Duke of Marlbrô.

To ballance these he had introduce'd some freinds of his own, by his reccommendation to Lord Townshend (who did nothing but by his instigation). Collonel Stanhope was made the other Secretary of State. He had been unfortunate in Spain, and there did not want those who attributed it to ill conduct, but he was call'd generous, Brave, true to his Freinds,[2] and had an air of probity that prejudice'd the world in his Favour.[3]

The King's character may be compriz'd in very few words. In private Life, he would have been call'd an Honest Blockhead; and Fortune that made him a King added nothing to his happyness, only prejudice'd his Honesty and shorten'd his days. No man was ever more free from Ambition; he lov'd Money, but lov'd to keep his own without being rapacious of other men's. He would have grown rich by saveing, but was incapable of laying schemes for getting. He was more properly Dull than Lazy, and would have been so well contented to have remain'd in his little Town of Hanover that if the Ambition of those about him had not been greater than his own, we should never have seen him in England; and the natural honesty of his temper joyn'd with the narrow notions of a low Education made him look upon his acceptance of the crown as an Act of usurpation, which was allways uneasy to him. But he was carry'd by the stream of the people about him in that, as in every other Action of his Life. He could speak no English and was past the Age of learning it. Our Customs and Laws were all mysterys to him, which he neither try'd to understand, or was capable of understanding, if he had endeavor'd it. He was passively good natur'd, and wish'd all Mankind enjoy'd Quiet, if they would let him do so.

The Mistriss [Schulenburg] that follow'd him hither[4] was so

---

[1] As Treasurer of the Navy in 1710.

[2] James Stanhope (1673–1721), 1st Earl (1718). In the Spanish campaign of 1707 he was blamed for the defeat at Almanza (the House of Lords inquiry later sustained the censure); and early in 1711, having been taken prisoner, he was kept at Saragossa for one and a half years. Horace Walpole records a somewhat different reputation: that Stanhope was 'a man of strong and violent passions' ('Reminiscences', *Works*, 1798, 4. 287).

[3] In 1753 LM recalled his telling her that he imposed on foreign ministers by simply telling them the truth (*Letters*, 3. 26).

[4] Ehrengard Melusine von der Schulenburg (1667–1743), later Duchess of Kendal. She was probably his morganatic wife, and is described by George I's recent bio-

much of his own temper that I do not wonder at the Engagement between them. She was duller than himselfe and consequently did not find out that he was so, and had liv'd in that figure at Hannover allmost 40 year (for she came hither at threescore) without meddling in any affairs of the Electorate, content with the small pension he allow'd her and the Honor of his visits when he had nothing else to do, which happen'd very often. She even refus'd comeing hither at first, fearing that the people of England (who she thought were accustom'd to use their Kings barbarously) might chop off his Head in the first Fortnight, and [she] had not Love or Gratitude enough to venture being involv'd in his Ruin; and the poor Man was in peril of comeing hither without knowing where to pass his Evenings, which he was accustom'd to do in the apartments of Women, free from busyness. But Madame Kilmansegg sav'd him from this misfortune.[1] She was told that Mlle Schulenburge scrupul'd this terrible Journey, and took that opertunity of offering her service to his Majesty, who willingly accepted of it, thô he did not offer to facillitate it to her by the payments of her debts, which made it very difficult for her to leave Hanover without the permission of her Creditors. But she was a Woman of Wit and Spirit, and knew very well of what Importance this step was to her fortune. She got out of the Town in disguise, and made the best of her way in a post chaise to Holland,[2] from whence she embark'd with the King and arriv'd at the same time with him in England, which was enough to make her call'd his Mistriss, or at least so great a favourite that the whole court begun to pay her uncommon Respect.[3]

This Lady deserves I should be a little particular in her character, there being something in it worth speaking of. She was past 40, she had never been a Beauty, but certainly very agreable in her

grapher as 'pliant and patient', and as not clever but intelligent and well educated (R. M. Hatton, *George I Elector and King*, 1976, Ch. 2).

[1] Sophie Charlotte von Platen (1675–1725) m. (1701) Johann Adolf, Freiherr von Kielmansegg (1668–1718); later Countess of Darlington. She was George I's half-sister, her mother having been mistress to his father.

[2] The Kielmansegg family historian denies that she fled to avoid her debts (Erich, Graf von Kielmansegg, *Familien-Chronik der Herren, Freiherren und Grafen von Kielmansegg*, 1910, p. 453 n.).

[3] Horace Walpole, on the other hand, unequivocally calls Mme Kielmansegg 'another acknowledged mistress' by whom the King was 'indisputably' father of her daughter, who later married Viscount Howe ('Reminiscences', p. 284). The Kielmansegg *Familien-Chronik* firmly consigns this daughter and her five brothers and sisters to their lawful father.

person when adorn'd by Youth, and had once appear'd so charming to the King that it was said the divorce and Ruin of his beautifull Princesse, the Duke of Zell's daughter,[1] was owing to the Hopes her mother (who was declar'd mistrisse to the King's Father and all powerfull in his Court)[2] had of setting her daughter in her place, and that the project did not succeed, by the passion that Madame Kilmansegge took for Mr. Kilmansegg, who was son of a Merchant of Hamburgh;[3] and after having a child by him there was nothing left for her but to marry him. Her Ambitious Mother ran Mad with the Disapointment and dy'd in that deplorable manner,[4] leaving £40,000 which she had heap'd by the Favor of the Elector, to this Daughter, which was very easily squander'd by one of her temper. She was both Luxurious and Generous, devoted to her Pleasures, and seem'd to have taken Lord Rochester's resolution of avoiding all sorts of selfe denial.[5] She had a greater vivacity in Conversation than ever I knew in a German of either Sex. She lov'd Reading, and had a taste of all polite learning. Her Humour was easy and sociable; her constitution enclin'd her to Galantry; she was well bred and amuseing in Company; she knew how both to please and be pleas'd, and had experience enough to know it was hard to do either without money. Her unlimited expences had left her very little remaining, and she made what haste she could to make advantages of the Opinion the English had of her power with the King, by receiving the presents that were made her from all Quarters and which she knew very well must cease when it was known that the King's Idleness carry'd him to her Lodgings, without either regard for her Advice or affection for her Person, which time and very bad Paint

---

[1] Sophie Dorothea (1666–1726), da. of George William (1624–1705), Duke of Celle, m. (1682) George Lewis, later Elector of Hanover. In 1694, when she was detected in a liaison with a Swedish nobleman, she was divorced and sequestered for the rest of her life in a castle in Celle.

[2] Mme Kielmansegg's mother, official mistress to the Elector Ernst August (1629–98), was Clara Elisabeth de Meysebug-Züschen, wife of his chamberlain Franz-Ernst, Graf von Platen (1631–1709).

[3] Kielmansegg's father was Friedrich Christian, Freiherr von Kielmansegg (1639–1714), who had been a diplomatist for Schleswig-Holstein; he lived near Hamburg, where he died and was buried (Kielmansegg, *Familien-Chronik*, pp. 402–7).

[4] Here LM's gossip seems to be wildly inaccurate. While Sophie Charlotte's marriage was being planned her mother died (in 1700) and so it was postponed until June 1701. Her first child was born ten months later.

[5] John Wilmot (1647–80), 2nd Earl of Rochester. He 'thought that all pleasure . . . was to be indulged as the gratification of our natural Appetites' (Gilbert Burnet, *Some Passages of the Life and Death of John Earl of Rochester*, 1680, p. 38).

had left without any of the Charms that had once attracted him. His best beloved Mistrisse remain'd still at Hanover, which was the Beautifull Countesse of Platen.[1]

Perhaps it will be thought a digression in this place to tell the story of his amour with her, but as I write only for my selfe I shall allways think I am at Liberty to make what digression I think fit, proper or improper, beside that in my Opinion nothing can set the King's character in a clearer Light. That Lady was marry'd to Madame Kilmanseg's Brother, the most considerable Man in Hannover for Birth and Fortune, and her Beauty was as far beyond that of any of the other Women that appear'd. However, the King saw her every day without takeing notice of it, and contented himselfe with his Habitual commerce with Mlle Schulenburge.

In those little Courts there is no distinction of much value but what arises from the Favor of the Prince, and Madame Platen saw with great Indignation that all her charms was pass'd over unregarded, and she took a method to get over this misfortune, which would never have enter'd into the Head of a Woman of Sense, and yet which met with wonderfull Success. She ask'd an audience of his Highness, who granted it without guessing what she meant by it; and she told him that as nobody could refuse her the first Rank in that Place, it was very mortifying to see his Highness not shew her any Mark of Favor; and as no person could be more attach'd to his person than her selfe, she begg'd with tears in her fine eyes that he would alter his behavior to her. The Elector, very much astonish'd at this complaint, answer'd that he did not know any reason he had given her to beleive he was wanting in his Respect for her, and that he thought her not only the greatest Lady, but the greatest Beauty of the Court. 'If that be true, Sir' (reply'd she, sobbing) 'why do you pass all your time with Schulenburge, while I hardly receive the Honor of a visit from you?' His Highness promis'd to mend his manners and from that time was very assiduous in waiting on her. This ended in a Fondness, which her Husband dislik'd so much that he parted with her; and she had the Glory of possessing the Heart and person of her Master, and to turn the whole stream of courtiers that us'd to attend Mlle Schulenburg to her side. However, he did not break with his first Love, and often went to her apartment to cut paper, which was his cheife employment there, which the Countesse of Platen easily permitted him, haveing often occasion

[1] Sophie-Caroline d'Uffeln m. (1697) Ernst August, Graf von Platen.

for his Absence. She was naturally Galant, and after having thus satisfy'd her ambition persu'd her warmer Inclinations.

Young Craggs[1] came about this time to Hannover, where his Father sent him to take a view of that Court in his tour of Travelling. He was in his First bloom of Youth and Vigour, and had so strong an appearance of that perfection that it was call'd Beauty by the Generallity of Women, thô in my Opinion there was a Coarseness in his Face and shape that had more the Air of a Porter than a Gentleman; and if Fortune had not interpos'd her allmighty power, he might by his Birth have appear'd in that figure, his Father being nothing more considerable at his first appearance in the World than Footman to Lady Mary Mordant, the Galant Dutchesse of Norfolk,[2] who had allways halfe a dozen intreigues to mannage.

Some servant must allways be trusted in affairs of that kind, and James Craggs [the elder] had the good Fortune to be chose for that purpose. She found him both faithfull and discreet, and he was soon advanc'd to the dignity of Valet de chambre. King James 2nd had an Amour with her after he was on the throne, and respected the Queen enough to endeavor to keep it entirely from her knowledge.[3] James Craggs was the Messenger between the King and the Dutchess, and did not fail to make the best use of so important a Trust. He scrap'd a great deal of Money from the Bounty of this Royal Lover, and was too inconsiderable to be hurt by his Ruin, nor did not concern himselfe much for that of his mistriss, which (by lower intreigues) happen'd soon after. This fellow from the report of all partys, and even from that of his profess'd enemys, had a very uncommon Genius, a Head well turn'd for calculation, great Industry, and so just an Observer of the World, that the meaness of his Education never appear'd in his conversation.

The Duke of Marlbrô, who was sensible how well he was qualify'd for affairs that requir'd secrecy, employ'd him as his [pimp *struck out*] procurer both for Women and Money, and he acquitted himselfe so well of these trusts as to please his Master, and yet raise

---

¹ See p. 28 above.

² The early career of James Craggs the elder (1657–1721) is obscure, but he evidently came from a landed family in Durham. In 1684 he was steward to the Duke of Norfolk. Mary Mordaunt (*c.* 1659–1705), da. of 2nd Earl of Peterborough, m. (1677) Lord Mowbray, later 7th Duke of Norfolk. In 1684 she was separated from her husband for misconduct, and in 1700 divorced.

³ The Duchess of Norfolk's gallantry as James II's mistress would have been between 1686 and 1688, but is nowhere else recorded. The widowed James had married Mary of Modena (1658–1718) in 1673.

a considerable Fortune by turning his Money in the public Funds, the secret of which came often to his knowledge, by the Duke's employing him.[1] He had this only Son, who he look'd on with the partiality of a Parent, and resolv'd to spare nothing in his Education that could add to his Figure.

Young Craggs had great Vivacity, a happy memory and flowing Elocution; he was brave and Generous, and had an appearance of Open heartedness in his manner, that gain'd him a universal good Will, if not a universal Esteem. It is true, there appear'd a Heat and want of Judgment in all his words and actions, which did not make him very valuable in the Eyes of cool Judges,[2] but Madam Platen was not of that Number. His Youth and Fire made him appear a Conquest worthy her charms, and her charms made her appear very well worthy his passionate addresses. Two people so well dispos'd towards one another were very soon in the closest engagement; and the first proofe Madam Platen gave him of her affection was introduceing him to the Favour of the Elector, who took it on her Word that he was a young Man of extrodinary Merit, and he nam'd him for Cofferer at his first accession to the Crown of England,[3] and I beleive it was the only place that he then dispos'd of, from any Inclination of his own. This proofe of Madam Platen's power hinder'd her comeing hither. Bernstaff was afraid she might meddle in the disposition of Places that he was willing to keep in his own hands, and he represented to the King that the Roman Catholic Religion that she profess'd was an insuperable bar to her appearance in the Court of England, at least so early; but he gave her private hopes that things might be so mannag'd as to make her admittance easy when the King was settle'd in his new Dominions; and with this hope she consented without much concern to let him go without her, not refflecting that weak minds lose all impressions by even short Absences. But as her own understanding did not furnish her with very great refinements she was troubled with none of the Fears that would have affected a stronger head, and had too

---

[1] After having served as steward to the Duke of Norfolk, Craggs was attached to the household of the Duke of Marlborough, whom he served as financial agent and indispensable confidant. He later won a seat in Parliament through the Duchess of Marlborough's patronage.

[2] Horace Walpole characterized him as 'a showy vapouring man' ('Reminiscences', p. 288).

[3] Craggs was appointed cofferer not to the King (the Earl of Godolphin won that appointment) but to the Prince of Wales.

good an Opinion of her own Beauty to beleive any thing in England could Efface it, while Madam Kilmansegg attach'd her selfe to the one thing necessary, getting what money she could by the sale of places and the credulity of those who thought themselves very politic in secureing her Favor.

Lord Halifax was one of this Number; his Ambition was unbounded and he aim'd at no less than the Treasurer's staff, and thought himselfe in a fine road to it by Furnishing Madam Kilmansegg both with money and a Lover. Mr. Methuen was the Man he pick'd out for that purpose.[1] He was one of the Lords of the Treasury; he was handsome and well made; he had wit enough to be able to affect any part he pleas'd, and a Romantic turn in his conversation that could entertain a Lady with as many adventures as Othello and it is no ill way of gaining Desdemonas. Women are very apt to take their Lovers' characters from their own Mouths; and if you will believe Mr. Methuen's account of himselfe, neither Artamenes or Oroondates[2] ever had more Valour, Honnour, Constancy, and discretion. Halfe of these bright Qualitys were enough to charm Madam Kilmansegg; and they were very soon in the strictest familiarity, which continu'd (for different Reasons) to the pleasure of both partys[3] till the arrival of Mlle Schulenburge, which was hasten'd by the German Ministers, who envy'd the money accumulated by Madam Kilmansegg, which they long'd to turn into another channel, which they thought would be more easily drawn into their own hands. They took care to inform Mlle Schulenburg of the fond reception all the Germans met in England, and gave her a view of the immense Fortune that waited for her here. This was enough to cure her Fears, and she arriv'd accompany'd with a young Niece, who had allready made some Noise at Hanover.[4] She had projected the Conquest of the Prince of Wales, and had so

---

[1] Paul Methuen (1672–1757), diplomatist, knighted 1725. At a supper party in 1714 Lady Cowper noted that 'Mr. *Methuen* . . . makes sweet Eyes at Madame *K*.' (Mary, Lady Cowper, *Diary*, ed. S. Cowper, 2nd ed., 1865, p. 29).

[2] The heroes of, respectively, *Le Grand Cyrus* by Madeleine de Scudéry and *Cassandre* by La Calprenède.

[3] Methuen's biographer quotes this anecdote of his alliance with Mme Kielmansegg (A. D. Francis, *The Methuens and Portugal 1691–1708*, 1966, pp. 347–8).

[4] Mme von der Schulenburg bore George I three daughters—in 1692, 1693, and 1701—who were presented to the world as her nieces. Since the eldest was already married in 1714, the second 'niece' must be the one mentioned here: Petronella Melusine (1693–1778), who m. (1733) Lord Chesterfield (R. M. Hatton, 'George I as an English and a European Figure', *The Triumph of Culture: 18th Century Perspectives*, 1972, pp. 195–6).

far succeeded as to obtain his Favors for some few months; but the Princesse, who dreaded a Rival to her power, soon put an end to the Correspondance, and she was no longer possess'd of his good Graces when he came hither.

I have not yet given the Character of the Prince. The fire of his temper appear'd in every look and Gesture, which being unhappily under the Direction of a small understanding was every day throwing him upon some Indiscretion. He was naturally sincere, and his Pride told him that he was place'd above constraint, not refflecting that a high Rank carrys along with it a necessity of a more decent and regular behaviour than is expected from those who are not set in so conspicuous a light. He was so far from being of that Opinion that he look'd on all the Men and Women he saw as Creatures he might kick or kiss for his diversion, and whenever he met with any Oposition in those designs he thought his Opposers impudent Rebells to the Will of God who created them for his use, and judg'd of the merit of all people by their ready Submission to his orders, or the Relation they had to his person. And in this view he look'd upon the Princesse as the most meritorious of her Sex, and she took care to keep him in that sentiment by all the Art she was mistrisse of. He had marry'd her by Inclination; his good natur'd Father had been so complaisant to let him a choose a Wife for himselfe. She was of the House of Anspach and brought him no great addition either of Money or Alliance, but was at that time esteem'd a German Beauty, and had that Genius which qualify'd her for the Government of a Fool and made her despicable in the Eyes of all Men of Sense; I mean a Low Cunning which gave her an Inclination to cheat all the people she convers'd with and often cheated her selfe in the first place, by shewing the wrong side of her Interest, not haveing understanding enough to observe that falsehood in Conversation, like red on the Face, should be us'd very seldom and very spareingly or they destroy that Interest and Beauty they are design'd to heighten.

Her first thought on her marriage was to secure to her selfe the sole and whole direction of her Spouse, and to that purpose counterfeited the most extravagant fondness for his person, yet at the same time so devoted to his pleasures (which she often told him were the rule of all her thoughts and Actions) that whenever he thought proper to find them with other Women she even lov'd who ever was instrumental to his Entertainment, and never resented any thing but what appear'd to her a want of Respect to him, and in this light she really could not help takeing notice that the presents made to her on her wedding were not worthy of his Bride, and at least she ought to have had all his mother's Jewells. This was enough to make him lose all Respect to his Indulgent Father. He downright abus'd his ministers, and talk'd impertinently to his old Grandmother, the Princesse Sophia, which ended in such a coldness towards all his Family, as left him entirely under the Government of his Wife. The Indolent Elector contented himselfe with shewing his Resentment by his Silence towards him; and this was the Situation the Family first appear'd in, when they came into England. This behaviour did not, however, hinder schemes being laid by various persons of gratifying their Ambition or makeing their fortune by particular attachment to each of the Royal Family.

A Plain Account of the Innoculating of the Small Pox by a Turkey Merchant

Lady Mary wrote this brief essay in the form of a letter during the controversy over smallpox inoculation that raged in England in the early 1720s. Although privately she was a vigorous champion of the operation this is her only identified public advocacy. It was published anonymously in *The Flying-Post: or, Post-Master* of 11–13 Sept. 1722. Before printing it the newspaper editor cautiously excised or toned down Lady Mary's sarcasm and passionate indignation against physicians. Recent historians confirm her view that 'heroic' measures by western doctors made the procedure more, not less, dangerous (Peter Razzell, *The Conquest of Smallpox: The Impact of Inoculation on Smallpox Mortality in Eighteenth Century Britain*, 1977). Within a fortnight of the essay's publication a pamphleteer called it 'a Sham Turkey Merchant's letter' but its actual authorship remained effectively hidden. For the background and a collation of the MS. with the printed text see Halsband, 'New Light on Lady Mary Wortley Montagu's Contribution to Inoculation', *Journal of the History of Medicine*, 8 (1953), 390–405; also Halsband, *LM*, pp. 109–12; and Genevieve Miller, *The Adoption of Inoculation for Smallpox in England and France*, 1957, pp. 70–80.

Text H MS. 80. 201–3.

OUT of compassion to the Numbers abus'd and deluded by the Knavery and Ignorance of Physicians, I am determin'd to give a true Account of the Manner of Innoculating the Small Pox, as it is practis'd at Constantinople with constant successe, and without any ill consequence whatever. I shall sell no drugs, nor take no Fees, could I persuade people of the safety and reasonableness of this easy operation. 'Tis no way my Interest (according to the common Acceptation of that word) to convince the World of their Errors, that is, I shall get nothing by it, but the private satisfaction of having done good to Mankind, and I know no body that reckons that satisfaction any part of their Interest.

The Matter ought to be taken from a Young Person, of a Sound Constitution, and the best sort of the Small Pox, when tis turn'd of the height. The old Nurse who is the General surgeon upon this Occasion at Constantinople, takes it in a Nut Shell, which holds enough to infect 50 people, contrary to the Infamous practise here, which is to fill the blood with such a Quantity of that Matter, as often endangers the Life, and never fails of making the distemper more violent than it need to be. She opens the Arms, and sometimes Legs, with a small rip of a Needle, and with the point of the same Needle takes as much of the matter as will lye upon it, and mixes it with that drop of blood that follows the little Incision. The wounds are bound up with a small nut still over them which is thrown off in 12 or 16 hours, and the Inflamation appears, more or less, as the blood is more or less dispos'd to receive the Infection. From that time the Patient is confin'd to a warm chamber and a low diet, being utterly forbid Wine or Flesh meat. The Erruption generally appears the 7 or 8th day afterwards. They give no Cordials to heighten the Fever, and leaving Nature to her selfe, never fail of the good successe which generally follows a rational Way of Acting, upon all Occasions. And the Murders that have been committed on two unfortunate Persons that have dy'd under this operation,[1] has been wholly occasion'd by the preparatives given by our Learned Physicians, of whom I have too good an Opinion not to suppose they knew what they did, by weakening Bodys that were to go through a distemper. I am confirm'd in this Opinion by the unfair Accounts that were given in the Public Papers of their deaths. I believe 'tis much to be doubted if Purges or any violent method ever brings the body into a moderate temper, which may allways be done by a cool diet, and regular hours; but as I am not of the College,[2] I will not pretend to dispute with those Gentlemen concerning their Genneral Practice in other distempers, but they must give me leave to tell them, from my own knowledge, wittness'd by every one of our Company[3] that has ever resided at Constantinople, and several Thousands of those there, that have happily undergone this operation, That their long preparations only serve to destroy the strength of Body, necessary to throw off the Infection. The miserable gashes, that they give people in the Arms, may endanger the loss of them, and the vast Quantity they throw in of that Infectious Matter, may possibly give them the worst kind of Small Pox, and the cordials that they pour down their Throats may encrease the Fever

---

[1] The Earl of Sunderland's son, two and a half years old, died in Apr. 1722, and a nineteen-year-old servant of Lord Bathurst in May (William Douglass, *A Practical Essay Concerning the Small Pox*, 1730, p. 68).

[2] Royal College of Physicians, founded in 1518.

[3] The Turkey (Levant) Company, chartered in the reign of James I.

to such a degree, as may put an end to their Lives; and after some few more Sacrifices of this kind it may be hop'd this terrible design against the Revenue of the College may be entirely defeated, and those Worthy members receive 2 guineas a day as before, of the wretches that send for them in that distemper.

Since I writ this, I have read some Querys publishd in the St. James' Evening Post, stated in a very unfair manner, most of the Facts there mention'd being utterly false.[1] However I never will deny but tis in the Power of a surgeon to make an ulcer with the help of Lancet and Plaister, and of a doctor to Kill by Prescriptions.[2]

[1] The only mention of inoculation in this newspaper during the previous weeks was on 11–13 Sept. 1722: that Lord Chesterfield's third son had been inoculated, that the 'Pustules were very large and distinct, but something more in Number than is usual in this Method', and that he was now perfectly recovered.

[2] In the printed newspaper text this is followed by the initials 'E. T.' But Emanuele Timoni, if in fact his name is meant, had died a suicide in 1718. He was a physician who as early as 1713 had publicized smallpox inoculation; in 1717 he had attended Wortley's family in Constantinople (Halsband, *LM*, p. 80; Miller, cited in headnote, pp. 55–8).

A Letter to A[lexander] P[ope] in answer to the preface of His Letters

Having arranged clandestinely for Edmund Curll to publish a volume of his letters (in 1735), Pope himself then prepared an edition of 'authentic' letters, which was issued on 19 May 1737. He introduced the volume with a preface justifying his action; and it is this that Lady Mary answers. She must have read it soon after publication. Only this brief fragment remains, evidently all she wrote. Many years later (1754), in a letter to her daughter, she again condemned Pope for publishing these letters (*Letters*, 3. 58). In pamphlet attacks on Pope by other satirists only two mentioned the publication of his letters: in Aug. 1737 and in Jan. 1743 (Joseph V. Guerinot, *Pamphlet Attacks on Alexander Pope, 1711–1744: a Descriptive Bibliography*, 1969, pp. 269, 309–10).

Text H MS. 78. 8. *Printed* in George Paston [Emily Morse Symonds], *Lady Mary Wortley Montagu and Her Times*, 1907, pp. 351–2.

I AGREE with P. in all that he says of the Indecency and immorality of publishing private Letters,[1] but what then must be said of himselfe, who is now become the Publisher of dead Men's letters, from whom he could have no previous leave of publication, several of which I do not doubt are wrote by himselfe and falsly ascrib'd to them, particularly that from Dr A[tterbury] dated Feb. 26, 1721/2.[2] For I cannot beleive (thô I have no extrodinary high Opinion of the Bishop's morals) that he would applaud his unjust satyr on Mr Addison,[3] or encourrage him to abuse others by telling him that he had at last found out what he could write upon, and had an excellent talent at railing etc.[4] As to his marginal note asserting his never

---

[1] 'To open Letters is esteem'd the greatest breach of honour; even to look into them already open'd or accidentally dropt, is held an ungenerous, if not an immoral act. What then can be thought of the procuring them merely by Fraud, and the printing them merely for Lucre?' (Preface, Pope, *Letters*, 1737.)

[2] This letter is genuine, having been only slightly altered by Pope (Pope, *Corr.* 2. 104–5).

[3] After requesting 'a compleat copy' of Pope's verses on Addison, the Bishop continues: 'No small piece of your writing has been ever sought after so much: it has pleased every man without exception, to whom it has been read' (p. 239). Pope's satiric 'Character' of Addison was drafted in 1715, and published anonymously in a newspaper in Dec. 1722, almost a year after Atterbury asked for it (Pope, *Poems*, 6. 144).

[4] 'Since you now therefore know where your real strength lies', Atterbury writes, 'I hope you will not suffer that talent to lye unemploy'd' (p. 239).

haveing shewn those verses,[1] it must make every one laugh that has thrown away so much time as to read his miscellanys[2] or his satyr on Women, publish'd by himselfe.[3]

I suppose the Letter said to be wrote by Mr. Wycherly, May 26, 1709,[4] comes from the same hand and I am the more enclin'd to this Beleife, knowing so many little mean Falsitys publish'd in this Monument of Freindship, as he calls it,[5] where he has imputed a Letter to poor dead Gay, which I have seen under his own [hand] address'd to another person,[6] and that Letter[7] which he pretends to have sent the late D[uke] of Buck[ingham] as a jest upon his description of his House in the park. . . .

¹ Pope's footnote reads: 'An imperfect Copy was got out, very much to the Author's surprize, who never would give any' (p. 239).

² Pope published a longer version of the 'Character' in his *Miscellanies. The Last Volume*, 1727 [1728].

³ By a slip of memory LM erroneously names *Of the Characters of Women* (Feb. 1735) instead of the *Epistle to Dr. Arbuthnot*, published one month earlier, which contained the final version of the 'Character' of Addison as Atticus. But she is being disingenuous in her comment on Pope's footnote; he refers to 1722, when Atterbury is writing to him, and not to 1728 or 1735.

⁴ *Letters*, 1737, pp. 24–5. Pope had reprinted it from Wycherley's posthumous works of 1729.

⁵ In the Preface Pope states that 'it is not to *Vanity* but to *Friendship* that he intends this Monument'.

⁶ The letter from John Gay (1685–1732) is on pp. 265–7. It contains an account of the death of two rustic lovers at Stanton Harcourt; Pope had sent the pathetic story to various friends, including Martha Blount, Lord Bathurst—and LM (Pope, *Corr.* i. 479–82, 488, 494–6). The editor of Gay's letters apparently accepts this one as authentic though he admits that its similarity to Pope's letter to Martha Blount is 'striking' (*Letters*, ed. C. F. Burgess, 1966, pp. 33–5).

⁷ pp. 215–20. This may be a revision of a letter sent by Pope to LM in mid-Sept. 1718 (Pope, *Corr.* i. 505–8).

An Expedient to put a stop to the spreading Vice of Corruption

In 1737 the Opposition to Walpole's ministry raised a hue and cry about corruption in the parliamentary election the previous year; in her essay Lady Mary ironically proposes to purify Parliament by eliminating it. In 1735 she had uttered a witticism to the same effect (Halsband, *LM*, pp. 163–4). The fact that she attacks the *Craftsman* by name rather than *Common Sense* suggests that she was writing before *Common Sense* began publication in Feb. 1737. Her essay, although of a length suitable for publication in a newspaper, could not have been printed, for its highly seditious expedient would certainly have put its printer—and author, if known—in danger of arrest. At the end of 1737, however, Lady Mary began to write political essays for publication—as the anonymous author of *The Nonsense of Common-Sense*.

Text H MS. 80. 253–7. *Printed* with *The Nonsense of Common-Sense* in 1947.

THERE is no occasion for Eloquent declamations to prove the daily Growth of this fashionable vice: every man's own memory will furnish him with all most as many instances of it as he has Neighbors or Acquaintances, and most men's own consciences present them with some certain knowledge of it. The Evil Effect of it in the public administration has long been the Theme of that Virtuous Patriot, the Craftsman,[1] but I wish with all my Heart it would stop there (with his leave). The Effect it has on private Life is much worse. The neglect of public Honour lessens and at length takes off all regard to the private. The Mind takes a turn of being Vain of Infamy, and every sort of baseness is not only avow'd but applauded if it appears profitable. All the sentiments of Humanity or Gratitude are look'd upon as childish prejudices, and people of the Highest rank in Life talk every day, over their Wine and Tea, Maxims one would only expect to hear in the holds of Newgate. They transfer the Praise that was once given to Generosity, Valour, and Integrity (obsolete words) to embroider'd Coats, Brussells Lace, Jewells, and Equipage; consequently the most Honourable Man is him that posesses these Virtues in the Highest degree, and most tenacious of them. For these a man may rob, poison, cheat, inform, nay on occasion be kick'd, spit upon, and publickly affronted. Nothing is mean that leads to the great End of acquiring Money, without which

[1] An Opposition paper begun by Bolingbroke in 1726 to attack Walpole's ministry.

there can be no fine Houses nor fine Equipages, and this seems so truly the Universal passion that all I can perceive by the politicks on both sides is the struggle who shall get most of it; and a sincere disertation upon Partys would shew you, the one cants and the other votes with the same ultimate view.

The Man that has sold his vote has taken the order of Roguery upon him, solemnly renounc'd shame, and from that moment gives himselfe no farther trouble either to be or appear Honest in any part of Life: so far Corruption influences our National Morality. As to Learning of what kind so ever, it is all most equally destructive to it. The Younger Brothers of Gentlemen's familys were certain recruits to Law, Divinity, the navy, the Army; and in order to their advancement in any of these professions they with Emulation endeavor'd to excell in those parts of knowledge that could distinguish them. Now, as soon as a ⟨Lad⟩ has reach'd one and twenty, if his views are a ship, a Regiment, or a solicitor's place in any of the offices, he and his Family for him use all their endeavors to squeeze him into Parliament, and a Campaign there shall set him nearer his wishes then 7 years' study in any of the Inns of Court or 7 years' service on board the Fleet or in the Army. This piece of skill is so notoriously known and most men are in such haste to get money that all Education will shortly be thought needless after 2 year old, when the gennerallity of children can say plainly, No and Yes, when they are bid. I have sufficiently set forth the Evil of Corruption, and it has been often most pompously perform'd by other pens. But How can we prevent this contagion after it has gain'd so strong a Head that it passes among Foreigners for a part of our Constitution?

I humbly propose we may have no more Parliaments, and that I may be heard impartially a few words in favour of this bold proposition before it be absolutly condemn'd. I entirely agree with our Patriots[1] that Parliaments are an Essential part of our Body Politic, and I believe no man alive will deny but that legs and arms are essential and usefull Parts of the Human Body. But when a Leg or an Arm is so far corrupted that there appears no possibillity of restoreing it to its primitive soundness, all wise Physicians advise the lopping it to stop the spreading Corruption, and no Man would be thought in his senses that would chuse to perish whole, rather than lose a part that no longer answer'd the end of its being.

[1] A synonym for the Opposition.

I perceive I have rais'd against me all the clamour of the Catos of the Age, and am concluded to be the most impudent of the minister's vermin, and one of the meanest that in the ingenious Dr. Swift's phrase (in the usual purity of his Language) are said to lick a Scoundrel Statesman spittle.[1] But I here solemnly declare in the Face of God and the Holy Angels that I nor any of my Freinds either enjoy or hope to enjoy any place in the Government. As to my Freinds, I think it is all most impossible, for I know none that I have. As to my selfe, I am sure it is impossible for a private reason that I have, which I do not think fit to show any Man alive.[2]

My proposal proceeds from a sincere Love to my poor Country-men, who to preserve the Shadow of a Liberty which they never had are enslav'd by the worst and basest methods. We have a King upon the Throne who both by Nature and Education has realy many excellent and Heroic Virtues. He is naturally sincere, which is the Foundation of all Honour, and incompatible with a base abject mind. His innate Bravery makes him despise a disguise, and when ever he is compell'd to wear it, it is visible that it sits heavily upon him, and he throws it off as soon as possible. Sir R[obert] W[alpole] is as Honest as his present post gives him leave to be; and when ever he acts contrary to his principles of Justice and good nature he thinks him selfe led into it by the temptations of Fear or Necessity. That the force of Temptation has a great weight on the Human mind, we are taught to believe even by our Saviour, who thought it a more proper prayer that we might not to be led into it than that we might resist it, which is all most asking a miracle to assist us.

Now if we Good People (I now speak to real Commons of England, not their pretended representatives) had the sense to make the K[ing] a present of our Nominal Liberty all at once, in a Handsome manner, we should leave him at Liberty to act the dictates of his own Royal mind without constraint; and his minister would not (as the poor man is now often forc'd to do) advance a known Block head or Scoundrel, which even he knows to be such, to a good place because he is cousin to the wive's brother of the wife of a Parliament man, nor would a man of real merit and learning dye unobserv'd in a little curacy or starve in a Garret in Lincoln's Inn

---

[1] For LM's dislike of Swift and of his works, see *Letters*, 2. 71-2; 3. 56-8; and pp. 273-6 below. The phrase itself appears in Swift's 'A Libel on D[r.] D[elany]', 1730, and in 'A Panegyric on Dean Swift', 1730 (*Poems*, ed. H. Williams, 1958, 2. 482, 495).

[2] The 'private reason' was, of course, that the writer of the essay was a woman.

for want of such Alliance. Merit would then [be] the road to prefer-ment. Emulation would be rais'd amongst the younger sort, and every one endeavor to shine in his profession when there was no other way to be distinguished in it. Sense, probity, and courage would be recommendations at Court, instead of the Influence over a county or the part play'd at the last Election, and Honour be no longer the jest of polite Company when it did not appear to them necessary to explode a Notion by which all [are] supposed Rascals that seek their vote.

People of Quality would then (at least their discourse) set a value upon Honesty when they had no opportunity of parting with it publickly, and this discourse would influence the minds of their inferiors that now in their turn openly avow a contempt for every-thing but Gain in order to imitate their Betters. The Clergy would by degrees regain a Veneration and Esteem that is now entirely lost by their venal voteing in the House of Lords, and people may begin to believe it possible that they themselves may be persuaded of the Truth of what they preach, when they do not know that they are a band of prostitute pensioners gapeing and (those that can talk) prateing for better Translations.[1] The Country Gentlemen would live in the Country, and their Ladys have no pretence to weary them out of their Lives till they get them to London in order to get a place. Their Estates would not be mortgag'd (as now above half of them are) by expensive Elections, not to reckon the quarrels, Lawsuits, and train of ills, occasion'd by contention of neighboring Squires. Hospitality, good nature, and all the social virtues might again flourish amongst us. Our Court might be Honnourable and our Country Happy.

I see no body that has any reason to oppose this Scheme but those who are conscious to themselves that they have nothing to recommend them but a certain profligacy of Principles that renders them proper tools in a mix'd Government, and would certainly be laid aside as useless in a plain one. 'How!' cry out the whole set of Patriots, 'would you introduce Arbitrary power?' Is not this as ridiculous as a child that will not bear the taste of Physic till it is call'd Sack Wine and then drink it down very greedily? What would you think of a Nation in the Indies where the King civilly desired to be absolute, upon which all the people as with one voice roar'd,

---

[1] The removal (promotion) of a bishop to a different diocese.

'Sir, you shall not be absolute, and we will sacrifice our Fortunes, Lives, wives, and children rather than suffer it. But here, if you please to accept of 900,000 per Annum (which we present you for that purpose) to distribute amongst 500 of the greatest scoundrels amongst us, you may then at your own will and pleasure dispose of our Lives, fortunes and all that belongs to us, but on any other terms we scorn to hear of it.'

Is not this the plain state of the Case? 'But,' say they, 'have you that implicite Faith in the K[ing], and minister to believe it impossible for them to be mistaken in the choice of those they prefer? May not they be blinded by Passion, prejudices, and false informations?' Doubtless as they have no supernatural gifts they may be liable to mistakes in the distribution of favours, but these mistakes would be rare. They would rather and oftner prefer men of sense and Honour than fools and Rascals; at least it would be no recommendation to have forsaken a man's freinds or renounced his principles. The K[ing], who is himselfe Honest, would take pleasure in preferring an Honest man; and Sir R[obert], who went formerly to school himselfe, would shew some value for a scholar.[1] And at worst, if our late posterity should see on the Throne a knavish King, and he should employ even a wicked minister, the greatest Villain upon Earth does not love another Villain. If they have no dirty work for them to do they will chuse to employ men of Reputation and Honour; and I am so well convinced of the universal benefit that would arise from this proposal, I heartily pray God could open the Eyes of the people to see it as plain as I do; and instead [of] bellowing about the excise and mobbing the Minister[2] the whole city would rise, and with a great deal of good manners surround the Parliament House the first day of their meeting, and telling them plainly they are a pernicious set of people who assume to themselves a power of defrauding poor Tradesmen of just debts,[3] turn them all out of Doors, distinguishing some few by some Gentle Kicks, and assure them they should meet there no more to cant Liberty and promote Slavery, talk pertly of the King and sell the Subject.

[1] Walpole, elected to King's College, Cambridge, on a scholarship from Eton, left after only two years when he became heir to his father's estate.

[2] In Apr. 1733, after the crucial debate on the Excise Bill, Walpole had to brave a noisy and dangerous mob as he left the House.

[3] Members of Parliament enjoyed immunity from lawsuits for debt.

The Nonsense of Common-Sense
1737-8

The Nonsense of Common-Sense was a weekly newspaper, of which nine issues survive—from 16 Dec. 1737 to 14 Mar. 1738—probably all that were published. (They were first identified and reprinted in 1947, ed. R. Halsband, Northwestern University Press.) Each paper was printed on a large folio sheet, the greater part containing a single essay. Of the nine essays Lady Mary's drafts of six survive among her manuscripts and provide the copy text here; the remaining three were undoubtedly by her as well.

The title of her paper could have been suggested by an essay in *Common Sense* (the Opposition paper) on 10 Dec. 1737: 'I am NONSENSE, a Terrestrial Goddess, your avow'd and irreconcileable Foe.... I have the Ladies, the Poetasters, and the M[inistry] on my Side.' One week later the first issue of *The Nonsense of Common-Sense* appeared. Although its anonymous author poses as an impartial commentator on manners, morals, and politics its purpose was clearly to defend Walpole and his ministry from the attacks of the Opposition press.

Text H MS. 80. 142–3.

Numb. I[1]

THE NONSENSE OF COMMON-SENSE
To be continued as long as the Author thinks fit, and the Publick likes it.
FRIDAY, December 16, 1737

Prov. Chap. 1. V. 4. *to give subtiltie to the Simple; to the young man knowledge and discretion*

THE title of this paper would appear very absurd if those words (common sense) were to be now understood in the same manner they were last Xmas[2] when they were suppos'd to mean, that plain degree of understanding which directed a reasonable Man in the

---

[1] Of the six MS. papers, LM supplied the title and motto for No. I, and the mottoes for Nos. II and VIII—all of them Biblical. The Author's witty promise about continuing the paper, which appears in every issue, must have been conveyed to the printer by LM in person. In the top margin of No. I in the Yale University Library is a note in LM's hand: 'all these wrote by me M.W.M. to serve an unhappy worthy man.' (His identity is unknown: perhaps the editor, who put together the newspaper, or even the Prime Minister himself.)

[2] The first issue of *Common Sense* was published 5 Feb. 1737.

course of his ordinary affairs; for as to all Refiners in politics, and projectors under what kind of shape whatever, they were never beleiv'd to ⟨be⟩ under the guidance of common sense. But these poor words have since been apply'd very differently; they now mean a certain paper, with many flights and small reason, that is handed about at coffee and tea tables, for the amusement of the Idle, the entertainment of the malicious, and the astonishment of the Ignorant, which are very numerous in this part of the World.

Out of a real compassion to these poor people, and being as sensible as the Author himselfe of the necessity of good Œconomy under the present pressure of national debts, I would exhort all his Gentlemen and Lady Readers seriously to consider the value of two pence before they bestow it on a paper not worth one farthing, which thô it may sometimes tickle the irascible particles in their constitution, there is nothing more dangerous than this indulging of Spleen, beside that it deprives them of that good humour to which they owe the most agreable moments of Life, puts many to great expence, some in drams, others in Hartshorn to raise their spirits after the fantoms that are presented to their imagination by this pernicious[1] paper.

I will therefore out of pure charity administer some comfort to them, amidst the dismal aprehensions they are weekly frighten'd with; and as this Author takes the Liberty of blameing whatever he dislikes, I will positively praise whatever I think right, thô I foresee that I shall be supported in this design by no party whatever. The usual way of answering one Satyr is by another, and the conclusion drawn from reading both sides, by any Indifferent Man, is, that there are Rogues on both sides, which is no very comfortable Refflection. Now I will leave *all* Rogues to the remorse of their own consciences, and the confusion that is the natural consequence of ill concerted Villainy without any mention of them at all, and proceed to the defence of any reasonable attempt I see, thô it should be attended with the most unreasonable Murmurs against it.

I begin by the Regulation of the present mourning,[2] which is so highly advantageous to the Woolen manufacture, the staple commodity of these Kingdoms, the natural growth of our own Lands, the

---

[1] The printer (or editor) changed this word to 'formidable'.

[2] For Queen Caroline, who had died on 20 Nov. 1737. On 4 Dec., a fortnight later, coaches and servants were ordered to observe mourning (*General Evening Post*, 22–4 Nov. 1737).

support of the poor, reduce'd now to a very low ebb by the Luxury and ill taste of the Rich, and the Fantastic mimicry of our Ladys, who are so accustom'd to shiver in silks, that they exclaim on the Hardships of Warmth and Decency. Notwithstanding the great Respect I bear to their Sex, I confess I do not only aplaud the present order that confines them to appear in stuff, but wish that the Winter court Dress was for ever oblig'd to be Cloath, which is capable of imbibeing the most beautifull Colours, and might be ornamented by Lace and Embroidery to the utmost Magnificence. I would indulge my fair Country Women in Lutestrings for the summer, which in this climate never begins earlier than June, and is sure to end in September. The other 9 months I would have them appear in a Habit that does honnour to their own Country, and would be a universal benefit to the Nation. The Gentry would feel it in the payment of their Rents, and the Tenants in the sale of their wool; and what should touch their pretty Hearts,[1] I can assure them it would be highly advantageous to their complexions. Many cold Faces that I have seen at the Opera, disfigur'd with red tips of Noses, dress'd in slight Tabbys and paduasois,[2] would have had an agreable glow of natural Heat if their Bodys had been cover'd with the warm product of our sheep.

And I do not doubt but the encourragment of the Woolen Trade had some share in his M—ty's consideration together with the Respect justly due to the memory of his belov'd consort. The covering of the Coaches with black cloath will be a sensible benefit to the Clothiers, and the expence only fall on those who can afford it.[3] No man is compell'd to keep an Equipage; and if there be any Peer that cannot honestly afford to pay for it, I think he may honnourably discharge it.[4] Footmen and Coaches never appear'd to me amongst the necessarys of Life, and I own I am a Freind even to every Tax that is, or can be laid on superfluitys; and I am so com-

---

[1] The printer, ignoring LM's pose as a male author, printed this to read: 'our pretty female Hearts'.

[2] LM refers to silk from Padua. The printed paper, however, reads peaudesoys (skin-of-silk), that is, thick silk with a dull satin finish. Johnson calls tabby a 'waved' silk.

[3] Several weeks before, black bombazine (a cloth containing no wool) rose in price from £6 to £15 a piece (*General Evening Post*, 26–9 Nov. 1737).

[4] Because the late Queen had been the ministry's most ardent supporter in the Royal Family, members of the Opposition begrudged her even posthumous homage. Lord Chesterfield, writing of the Order of Mourning to ¹Lyttelton, hoped that peers who were neither paid for voting nor mourning would have spirit enough not to comply (*Letters*, ed. B. Dobrée, 1932, 2. 314–15).

passionate to the Industrious poor as to see with Horror the oppressions of the whole sale Monopolizers over the miserable workers. This is particularly to be seen in the cloth Trade, where the utmost cruelty and oppressions are us'd against the helpless Labourer, who after being beaten down with the greatest Hardness in the price of his Labour, is forc'd to take his payments in commoditys of halfe value which he must sell as he can. I cannot help hopeing that truly noble Lord[1] who has shewn so uncommon and so generous a compassion in the releife of those wretches thus distress'd within his own view, will extend his charity yet farther, by getting a general Redress of the oppression groan'd under all over the nation, where the Master tradesmen without mercy grind the Faces of the Poor, who are vainly Industrious, and whose Familys suffer more real misery[2] in a free Country[3] than the slaves in Jamaica or Algiers.[4]

[1] Unidentified.

[2] This sympathy was not undeserved, and the most successful attempt to raise wages by combinations (unions) occurred in the woollen industry in 1738 (N. A. Brisco, *Economic Policy of Robert Walpole*, 1907, pp. 176–8).

[3] The phrase 'in a free Country' was omitted in the printed paper.

[4] Following this is a brief letter from LM to her printer, partly obliterated by her (*Letters*, 2. 114). The printed paper continues: '*N.B.* Numb. II. of this Paper will be published on *Tuesday* the 27th Instant, and from thenceforth the Paper is to be published every *Tuesday*.'

THE NONSENSE OF COMMON-SENSE

To be continued as long as the Author thinks fit, and the
Publick likes it.

TUESDAY, December 27, 1737

Nehemiah. Ch. 5. V. 5. We bring into Bondage our Sons, and our Daughters,
to be servants, and some of our Daughters are brought into Bondage already,
neither is it in our power to redeem them: for other men have our Lands.
V. 10—I pray you, let us leave off this Usury.

I HAVE allways been an Humble Admirer of the Fair Sex, nay, I
beleive I think of them with more tenderness than any Man in the
World. I do not only look upon them as Objects of pleasure, but
I compassionate the many Hardships both Nature and Custom has
subjected them to. I never expose the Foibles to which Education
has enclin'd them; and (contrary to all other Authors) I see with
a favourable Eye the little vanitys with which they amuse themselves,
and am glad they can find in the imaginary Empire of Beauty, a
consolation for being excluded every part of Government in the
State.[1] But with all this fondness for them, I am shock'd when I see
their Influence in opposition to Reason, Justice, and the common
Welfare of the Nation.

It is their Tongues that have so loudly exclaim'd against the real
patriot scheme of reduceing of Interest; and this united Tattle has
had force enough to put a stop to the most reasonable Design that
has appear'd in public for a long time.[2] For I do not beleive a word
of the Insinuations of those, who suppose great people so childishly
vain to reject a scheme for no other reason but because it did not
first come from themselves. I am persuaded that the Brittish
Mothers, sisters, and mistrisses (for Wives are out of the Question)

---

[1] LM repeats this feminist idea in her letters.

[2] In Mar. 1737 Sir John Barnard had introduced a bill to lower the interest on the
national sinking fund from four to three per cent; it had been defeated in Apr. In Nov.
the *Gentleman's Magazine* reported the debate (pp. 653–70). On 25 Feb. 1738 *Common
Sense* printed a long letter (dated 6 June 1737) from a 'constant Reader' advocating the
reduction, and refuted it by an editorial postscript.

have exerted their Authority on this occasion and have met with astonishing Success. I would therefore offer some plain Refflections to their consideration, which possibly they have not yet heard.

That we are a Tradeing Nation I suppose they may have been told, but how far the high Rate of Interest is detrimental to our Trade may not have come to their knowledge. Yet there is nothing more certain than that while our Interest is so high, it brings in more Money than the same summ would do employ'd in Trade (reckoning for the hazard and trouble attending commerce). Men who are naturally adicted to Pride and Lazyness will even chuse a less profit that leaves them their time to throw away, with the polite Accomplishment of being good for nothing, than venture their Money in Merchandizing with the Scandal of being Traders; and there is no way of making these drones serviceable to the public but by Forceing them to improve their money this way or renounce all their darling expences.

'Tis now a common thing even for shop keepers to employ only a small part of their stock in Trade; the rest goes into the Funds; and if they can leave each daughter £500 they are gentlewomen for Life. These projects would be destroy'd by a low Interest, and the aforesaid Daughters bound out to honest Trades might in their sphere contribute to the Wealth of their Country. I shall be answer'd that it is not the Interest of these mechanics that give them any pain, and tis very indifferent what becomes of them; but there are many Ladys of high Birth with the small Fortunes of 5 or £6000 and how can they live upon 2 or 3 per cent? Very easily, very agreably, if they can abandonn Quadrille and Fine cloaths. It is to be hop'd that they would substitute some more improveing amusement in the room of the first; and I can assure them that the second is of no manner of advantage to their persons, of which I do not doubt they will have a sensible demonstration this very Winter. All Ladys are now oblig'd to appear in Stuff and plain Linnen; and yet I do not question but they will make as glorious a Campaign as ever they did in their Lives, and have as many Conquests to boast of, as when they shin'd in silks and Laces.

But this Nation is overrun with an odd sort of Nuns, of I know not what wandering order, that declare against Marriage if they cannot marry very great, and in the mean time croud all the public places, and enjoy every Fashionable Folly. 'Tis true many of these grow weary of their Scheme about five and forty, and then bestow their Money to advance an Ensign, but alas! they are then past doing any service to their Country; and if a low Interest had put this system out of their Heads and they had accepted of an Honest Merchant at twenty, there had been so much more Money employ'd in Trade,[1] and perhaps 10 or 12 children that might have been usefull to the public in different stations of Life. However, if these virgins are so far enamour'd with the state of Celibacy to exclaim against the cruelty of being oblig'd to be Wives, it is but conforming to a plainer Habit, and they need submit to no such necessity.

If I must suppose there are great Numbers of Ladys in these narrow circumstances, I will suppose at least one in Twenty of them to be handsome enough to make the rest of their Sex desirous of looking like them. What a great Advantage then will they bring to their Country by the suppression of Luxury, when the plainest Dress will be thought the Genteelest! As to the Old Maids, I see no Calamity ariseing from it if they are driven by this Reduction to some more retir'd part of the Kingdom, from whence their prayers (which ought to be their cheif employment) will be as well heard as from this metropolis.

I hope I have now convince'd the Ornamental halfe of Mankind that the Lowering of Interest is not attended with such terrible consequences in Relation to them. As to the Men, I beleive the Generallity of them see plainly the profit ariseing from it, to the merchant in the encrease of Trade, to the LandLords in the value of their Estates, and to the King in his Customs. As to the silly objection of Foreigners drawing their money from hence when they are no longer tempted to let it lye, from the Interest being higher than in their own country, these Objectors should consider[2] that it is not Gold and Silver, but bills of Exchange[3] that are sent hither from Foreign countrys, and they eat us out with our own Money.[4] I tremble to think of the great summs due to strangers, and I know no expedient but this, to pay those Debts and preserve

---

[1] LM's arguments on trade echo those heard in the House of Commons when the bill had been debated (e.g. Richard Chandler, *History and Proceedings of the House of Commons*, 1742–4, 9. 419, 445). A quarter of upper-class women are estimated to have remained single, probably from their families' inability or unwillingness to raise an acceptable dowry.

[2] Here the printer inserted 'that the longer it stays, the more we pay'.

[3] Here the printer inserted 'perhaps without valuable Consideration'.

[4] Here the printer inserted a footnote: '*N.B.* The *Spaniards* and *Portuguese*, the only Nations from whence Gold and Silver is imported, have no Share in our Stocks.'

the Credit of the Nation. We have too long mistaken Paper for
Money, and I wish we are not at length undeceiv'd in as melancholy
a manner as the Farmer that bought a Horse of Dr. Faustus, and
found him a Bundle of Hay the first Water he came into.[1]

The Interest of Money in England was once 10 per cent. I beleive
there is no one now living who will not agree, if that exorbitant
Interest had gone on, we had long since been ruin'd. Yet I do not
doubt on the first reduction from 10 to 8 per cent there were Men
in those days that then made use of the same arguments that are
talk'd now against lowering of Interest. Yet the Patriots (I call every
Man so, in or out of Court, that acts for the real good of his Country)
persu'd their point; and we are sensible how much we are oblig'd
to them. A new benefit arose on sinking it to 6; and we gain'd yet
more advantage by reduceing it to 5. Why then should we stop?
Why should we not beleive we should yet thrive better, was it sunk
to 3 per cent?[2] We have experience'd the good effects of the manage-
ment of our Fathers. Let us leave our sons something to thank us
for, and despise weak Clamours whatever kindness we may have for
the Exclaimers, like a tender mother who forces necessary Physic
down the Throat of a beloved Infant, thô it squalls and struggles
with all its strength.[3]

P.S.

I shall be told perhaps that in order to keep up to the Title of
my paper I should offer some little Criticism on those[4] of last
Saturday; but I will take no notice of the stuff call'd Common
Sense when ever it is either dull or unintteligible, and therefore
I beleive I shall meddle with it very seldom. I think his last Libel
very cruel on a Drama so long forgotten,[5] particularly his barbarous
Refflections on Mr. H——l (the only person I can guess he means

---

[1] The horse dealer, thinking that Faustus's injunction to keep the horse away from
water is an attempt to prevent him from learning 'some hidden mystery', rides it into
the water. It turns to straw, and he almost drowns (Christopher Marlowe, *Doctor
Faustus*, 1601/4, IV. v).

[2] For an account of these reductions in interest and of the bills see Brisco, pp. 71–4,
and Eric Hargreaves, *The National Debt*, 1930 (repr. 1966), pp. 6 ff., especially 47–52.

[3] Here the printer added, 'or like a Lover that, &c.' For LM's objections see p. 127
below.

[4] The printer changed 'those' to 'the Papers'.

[5] *Common Sense* of 17 Dec. 1737 converts the plot of the opera *Camilla* into an
allegory attacking Walpole. *Camilla*, by Bononcini and Haym, was frequently performed
in London between 1706 and 1728, but not since then (*The London Stage: 1660–1800*,
Part 2, ed. E. L. Avery, 1960).

by P[rince] Prenesto, because he perform'd that part). That Gentleman is now retir'd, and not very prosperous, and should obtain Oblivion at least from every good natur'd man.[1] I intend to attack all vulgar Errors which now go under the name of Common Sense. I will preach against Mistaken Charity, False Honor, and ill Taste, where ever I think I see it.[2]

[1] The writer in *Common Sense* had been shocked at seeing King Latinus (not Prince Prenesto) played by 'old *Hall* the Cheesemonger'.

[2] The printed paper continues, '*N.B.* Numb. III. of this Paper to be published next Tuesday.'

THE NONSENSE OF COMMON-SENSE

To be continued as long as the Author thinks fit, and the Publick likes it.

TUESDAY, January 3, 1738.

To the AUTHOR.

SIR,

I fancy your Paper is not so much designed either to support the Measures of the Court, or to justify the Complaints of the Patriots, as to expose common Prejudices and vulgar Errors wherever you meet with them. It is on this Account I apply myself to you; for as I intend to get Money from both, I would not offend either; and we Foreigners are seldom, you know, great Zealots either in Politicks or Religion, our chief Principle of Action being, to serve those by whom we get most Money, which is the only End most of us have in sojourning amongst you.

As I have met with a most kind and generous Reception in this Country, I have taken a Liking to the Country and People, therefore would wish to pass the rest of my Days in the Country, and shall always be proud to serve the People.—I have observed with Regret the almost universal Prejudice, especially among your Quality, in favour of the *Singers of my Country:* I consider with Grief the vast Sums yearly sent out of the Nation for the Purchase of Creatures, most of whom may properly be said to be quite useless in their Generation.[1]

Now as I understand the Business of Statuary, Machinery, and Musick, as I have made myself famous in the two first Branches, I have thought of a Method by which the Curiosity of the Quality, and the Vanity of those that mimick them, may be satisfied without costing the Nation near so much Money.—Some of the latter will, I doubt not, upon Sight of this, exclaim and say, They wonder at my Impudence in imagining, that any of the polite Customs or Appetites of Persons of Quality like them, can be called common

[1] This, of course, is a pun on the sterility of *castrati*, most of whom were Italian.

Prejudices, or vulgar Errors.—I know the Prejudices of Persons of Quality are generally too costly to become common, and their Errors differ in this from the Vulgar, that a vulgar Fellow discovers his Error, and often gives it up, as soon as he finds it hurts him; but a Person of Quality is seldom made wiser by Experience, nay often hugs his Error after it has left him nothing else to hug. Therefore to please all Parties, I shall, if they think fit, call this melodious Phrenzy, a Quality Prejudice; and if I cannot remove it, I hope, I have hit upon a Way of allaying it, at a much less Expence to the Nation.[1]

By my Art, I have found out a Method of making a Statue imitate so exactly the Voice of any *Singer* that ever did, or ever can appear upon the Stage, that I'll defy the ravished Hearer to distinguish the one from the other. Nay, what is more, this Statue shall sing any *Opera* Air the Audience pleases to call for, and shall chant it over again and again, as long as they please to cry, *Ancora*, which is an Honour, I presume, they will as often confer upon my artificial Machines, as ever they did upon any of the natural Machines of *Italy*; and to add to the Astonishment of all Persons of polite Taste, it shall perform at first Sight any the most difficult Piece of Musick the learned Mr. *H——l* can compose.[2]—Then, Sir, by the Help of my wonderful Art in Machinery, I can make my Statue walk about, and tread the Stage with as good a Grace, and look upon the Pit with as much Contempt, as ever did the famous *Senesino*;[3] by which Means it will be able to perform its Part in the *Recitativo*, and shall rage with Fury, die away in Raptures, or stare with Amazement and Surprize, in as natural a Manner, and with as true a Taste, as any Actor that ever trod the Stage; for the great Advantage of my Actors will be in this, that when they come to the Performance, they will observe, with the nicest Exactness, the Instructions they received from the learned and ingenious *Criticks* at the *Rehearsal*, without confounding the Justness of Action with any fanciful and absurd Gesticulations of their own.

---

[1] The *castrati* were frequently attacked in the press and in Parliament (e.g. House of Commons, 5 Mar. 1735) for the vast sums paid to them (see Angus Heriot, *The Castrati in Opera*, 1956, pp. 67–8).

[2] George Frederick Handel (1685–1759), foremost composer in England, had declared himself a bankrupt in June 1737. Having begun a season again in Nov., only to be forced to close by the Queen's death, he resumed on 3 Jan. 1738.

[3] Francesco Bernardi (b. 1680?–c. 1750), called Senesino, a famous *castrato* of the day. After quarrelling with Handel (in 1733) he joined the newly founded 'Opera of Nobility'. Early in 1737 he had left England to return to Siena.

Beside this Advantage, with respect to the Action, I must take Notice, that this Project will be a great Ease to the ingenious *Superintendant of the* English *Diversions*, as his witty and facetious Countrymen are pleased to call him,[1] and to the Directors of the *Academy of Musick*, who have often been obliged to use all their Art, and all their Politicks, to pacify the domestick Feuds of the *Opera* Stage, and to reconcile the several Actors and Actresses to one another[2]—and to the Parts allotted them respectively; for which Purpose these worthy Patriots, to the high Emolument of their Country, and to their own immortal Renown, have often watch'd whilst others slept.[3] To this I must add, that it will likewise be an Advantage to all future Compositions of Musick; for every one knows, that the Justness and Beauty of the Composition, in *Operas* as well as *Plays*, has been often sacrificed to the Humour of a splenetick Actor, or vapourish Actress, who was to act the Part. Whereas I can undertake that my *Dramatis Personae* shall never have any Feuds, nor shall any of them find Fault with the Allotment of the several Parts. Both these Advantages are acknowledged by the aforesaid *Superintendant*, and also by Mr. *H——l*, and for this Reason both of them very much approve of my Project.

It would be endless to sum up all the Advantages of this Project, for I can give my Statues not only the Shape but the Air and Mien, the Gestures, and even the Queerness or Oddities of any Actor, Male, Female, or Neutral. I have already got one made so exactly resembling the famous *Farinelli*,[4] that it is impossible to distinguish the one from the other, either by seeing, hearing, or smelling, and neither of them, you know, are fit for being tasted or felt.—In this Production of my Art, I can assure you, I rejoice exceedingly; for I do not know but I may thereby be able to preserve the Tranquillity of *Europe*, and to prevent this Country, which I beg leave now to

[1] John James Heidegger (1659?–1749) managed the Haymarket opera house in partnership with Handel from 1728 to 1734; he and Handel joined in partnership again briefly in the autumn of 1737.

[2] The Royal Academy of Music, patronized by the King and directed by Handel, produced opera at the Haymarket Theatre from 1719 to 1728. Once during its last season, Faustina and Cuzzoni had amused the audience with a squabble on stage (Heriot, p. 92 n.).

[3] This jibe was directed at the Opposition 'Patriots', whose 'Opera of the Nobility', supported by the Prince of Wales, performed in rivalry to Handel's company, which was patronized by the King. Both companies had failed in June 1737.

[4] Carlo Broschi (1705–82)—called Farinelli—another *castrato* of great fame, came to England in 1734 to sing with the Opera of the Nobility. In June 1737 he had left to perform in Spain, where he remained for twenty-five years.

call my own, from being involved in a War with *Spain:* I am sure
I shall at least remove one of the Reasons we have for going to War,
and the principal one with all polite Ladies and Gentlemen, which
is that of their having rob'd us of that charming Singer, in whom we
certainly had an undoubted Property, by that very Title upon which
they lay claim to the whole Continent and Islands of *America,* I
mean the first Possession. I say I shall remove this chief Reason for
a War; because my Copy will serve our Purpose every bit as well
as the Original, and will cost us much less Money yearly; and
surely we are not become such *Don Quixots,* as to go to War meerly
for a Point of Honour, which, when obtained, would be a Prejudice
to the Nation.[1]

I have likewise got another Statue already made, so exactly
resembling *Senesino,* that the beautiful Lady who laments his
Absence in such moving and melancholy Lays, will again, I hope,
hold up her Head. Methinks I see her in the *Side-Box* just recovering from her mournful Posture, and a Ray of Joy brightening up her
Countenance, upon my *Senesino's* approaching from behind the
Scenes.[2] As I have always had a great Regard and Affection for the
fair Sex, as I sympathize with them in all their Sufferings, especially
such as proceed from Love, it will give me great Pleasure to find
I have relieved any one *British* Lady from Distress; and tho' the
Song be applicable but to one, I am told it is the Case of many of
the pretty Ladies of this Island, which makes me use all possible
Expedition. For this Purpose *Cutzoni* and *Faustina* are both now
in Hand,[3] and will be finished by the Time my Project is ripe for
Execution; with this Advantage, that I have taken Care to form.
them so as that they shall never fall out, or form any Parties in the
Kingdom, where, I think, if a Foreigner may be allowed to say it,
there are too many already; and for the Comfort of all old Misers
as well as jealous Ladies, I shall now assure them, that I can answer

---

[1] *Common Sense* of 10 Dec. 1737, censuring Spain's depredations on English shipping,
had humorously written that 'those Rapacious *Dons* have seiz'd the Charming *Farinelli*
as counterband Goods'. LM was sympathetic to the ministry's conciliatory attitude in
maintaining peace with Spain.

[2] 'The Ladies' Lamentation for ye Loss of Senesino', a satirical ballad of seven stanzas
(*Catalogue of Prints and Drawings in the British Museum,* Vol. 3, Part 1, ed. F. G. Stephens,
1877, No. 2147), was sung by Mrs. Clive at Drury Lane on 12 Mar. 1737.

[3] Francesca Cuzzoni (1700–70) had sung in London 1723–8, the last two years in
rivalry with Faustina Bordoni (1700–81); she again sang in London in 1734–5 with
Farinelli and Senesino. In a letter from Venice in 1740 LM again mentions these two
singers (*Letters,* 2. 180).

for the Chastity of all the Actresses I shall bring upon the Stage, which, I believe, is more than any Master of a Stage in *Europe* will undertake.

In short, I shall not only oblige the Publick with a Review of all the fine *Italian Singers* they have ever heard, or heard of; but I propose *like our Quality Cooks*, to travel, *not to study*, but in order that I may furnish this rich and flourishing Kingdom, with every new *Singer* that shall hereafter become famous in *Italy*, or any other Part of *Europe*. Nay, if any young Nobleman, upon his Return from his Travels, shall set our Quality agog after some new *Singer* just blazed out at *Venice, Naples,* or *Rome,* I shall presently take Post, and with the utmost Expedition, bring him over in Effigy, without costing the Nation any Thing but the Expences of my Journey. So that our Ladies who never were, nor ever desire to be out of the Sound of *Beau Bells*,[1] shall be as well acquainted with, and shall talk as politely and learn'dly of the Voice, the Manner, the Grace, the Action, &c. of all the fine *Singers* of *Italy*, as any young Heir, who has spent many *Thousands* in his Travels, without bringing his Country or Family any one other Piece of Knowledge or Advantage in return.

It is easy to see what a vast Sum of Money will be saved to the Nation yearly by this Project; nay, considering the great Collections we have already got of *Italian* Pictures, Statues, Busts, and Antiques, and the many *French* Valets, and Cooks we have amongst us, I do not know but it may cure our young Nobility and Gentry of that Fondness for gadding beyond Seas, which is at present so Epidemical in this Country; because there will then be nothing worth while to be seen or learnt either in *France* or *Italy*, but what may be had in our own Kingdom; in which Case Foreigners would not see near so much of our Money, nor near so much of our Foolishness, as they have done for many Years past. However, I do not propose to diminish the Price of an *Opera Ticket*, or that any of my *Singers* shall perform in private for *a less weighty Purse* than the proudest of our late Performers; for this, I know, would spoil all; nothing can be fit for Persons of an elegant Taste that can be had at a small Price. Yet I am not so avaritious as to propose to take all the Profits to myself: On the contrary, I shall be satisfied with my net Charges, and a very moderate Salary. As for the Residue of the Profits, which will certainly amount to a large Sum yearly, the

---

[1] A pun on the bells of the church of St. Mary-le-Bow in the City.

Disposal of it shall be left to the great Wisdom of the Directors of the *Academy of Musick;* in which Case I would humbly propose, it should be distributed yearly by Way of Charity, for the Subsistence of those antiquated *Beaus* and *Belles,* who in their younger Years had ruined themselves by attending *Operas, Masquerades,* &c.

This is a Proposition which almost convinces me of my being a deep Politician; for the highest Perfection of Politicks, they say, is, to make the Vices of the People contribute to the Welfare of the State.[1] In the common vulgar Way, a Man provides for old Age by the Industry and Frugality of his Youth; but by this you see, we shall make a Man provide for old Age by the Idleness and Extravagance of his Youth; which may very probably be hereafter of great Service to many Persons of Quality and Distinction; so that the present usual Exclamation in Fits of Extravagance or Debauchery, *I must go upon the* high Way *at last!* will soon, I hope, be turned into this more honest, and therefore, I humbly think, more honourable Exclamation, *I must come upon the* Opera *at last!*

I could shew many other publick Benefits which must necessarily accrue from this Project; and as to its Success, when once set on Foot, I do not in the least question it. No Nation, I find, is more fond than this of Novelty and Variety: As for Novelty, I am sure no such Thing was ever attempted before, or so much as imagined, not even by any of our *Travel-Writers*; and as for Variety, one may easily see we have an inexhaustible Source; for if new or living Voices should fail us, if the *Pope* should turn *Christian* and forbid *Mutilation prepense,*[2] I do not see what should hinder us from bringing *Orpheus,* and the other antient *Grecian* Musicians upon the Stage: I am sure no Man, no, not even any of the Members of our *Antiquarian Society,* so famous for their profound Skill in useful Learning, could say that either the Voice or the Person was not the same; and it is not the first Time *a modern Performance* has been put upon our best *Connoisseurs* for an *Antique.*

Your publishing of this, Sir, may contribute to the Success of my Project, and as it is calculated for saving to the Nation the

[1] Walpole's tax policy relied on the 'vices of the people'. He had tried in vain to apply the excise to wine and tobacco in 1733, and succeeded in applying it to spirits in 1736.

[2] *Castrati* were used in the Papal choir in Rome. Charles Burney (*General History of Music,* 1789, 4. 40–4) speaks also with detestation of this practice, but he admired the artistry of the singers.

Expence of a very odd Sort of common Prejudice, I hope you'll comply with my Desire. I am,

SIR, Your most humble Servant,
BALDUCCI.[1]

N.B. Numb. IV. of this Paper to be published next Tuesday.

---

[1] This fictitious name is unexplained.

THE NONSENSE OF COMMON-SENSE

To be continued as long as the Author thinks fit, and the Publick likes it.

TUESDAY, January 10, 1738.

THERE are in this Country, and in all Countries, some Customs which appear at first View so ridiculous, that one is apt to wonder how they came first to be established; yet if we enquire into the Origin of the most ridiculous Custom, we shall find it proceeded at first from Reason, and that it is nothing but a good Custom turned to a ridiculous Use by Vanity or Ostentation.—I must however except from this Rule many Customs which proceed from Superstition; for very few of such Customs can be impeached of having Reason either in their Foundation or Superstructure.

That of a great King or great Minister's having a Levee, was certainly a very reasonable Thing at first; for as such Men have always a vast Multiplicity of Business, they cannot spare a particular Hour for every Person who may want to speak with them, or to present a Petition to them; therefore the Hour of their Dressing was appointed for all those who had not very serious Business, or who could not get Access at any other Time; and as every Man had then free Access, it prevented Kings from being made the Tools of their Ministers, as well as Ministers from being made the Tools of their Favourites and Slaves.

But now every Creature that has got a great Title, or a great Estate, must have a Levee, whether he has any Business or no; and many who have *great* Titles with *small* Estates, have Levees, not because they have *Business*, but because they have *Creditors.*— Thus Levees are made ridiculous by many of those who now pretend to keep them; for nothing but Multiplicity of Business can intitle a Man to keep a Levee; no Title can, not even that of Royalty itself, unless where the King has Ears and Eyes of his own; nor can any Post intitle a Man to such a Privilege, if he is to be but *a Puppet in a Post,* and to move in it only by those Springs which are under the Direction of another.

Then with respect to those who are to be at Levees: These Assemblies were certainly at first entirely dedicated to Business, so that no Man came there to *shew* his *Face*, but to *shew* his *Business*; nor was that precious Hour to be taken up by great Favourites, or by those who had Matters of great Importance to communicate, which could not but take up a great deal of Time. As Favourites are always basking in the Sun of Power, they ought not, by their Inter-position, to prevent his Rays falling on those to whom he never appears but in those few and fleeting Moments; and as the whole Crew of Attendance at a Levee are always upon short Subsistence, those who have Business of Importance ought to open in the shortest Manner what they have to communicate, and desire a particular Hour for explaining themselves more fully, otherwise they may consume the Allowance of the whole Company, which is neither honest nor fair.

But the original Design of Levees seems now to be quite altered, for at our modern Levees few but Favourites appear, and most of them come there only to shew their Impudence and Assiduity. If a Stranger goes now to such an Assembly, especially if he be a modest Man, as Men of Merit generally are, he is hustled into some Corner, and so overshadowed by the Crowd of attending Slaves, that it is impossible for the most piercing Eye to dart thro' the thick Cloud, in order to pull him from Obscurity. Then as all Men are fond of making the World believe they have the Ear of a King or Minister, every impudent Fellow will whisper, tho' it be nothing but an impertinent Joke, as every Joke must be at a Time which a great Man sets a-part for Business only. By this Means the Levees even of our real great Men are become quite useless both to them and to their Country: Nay they are really become such a Farce, that I wonder the ingenious Mr. *H——th* has never thought of obliging the World with such a Piece as *a modern Levee*. I am convinced he would succeed as well as he has done in his *Modern Midnight's Conversation*; because I am sure the Cringes, the Grins, and the fawning Countenance of a thoroughbred Levee-haunter, would make as droll a Figure, as the Ideot-Face or Bedlamite Posture of a drunken Sot or frolicksome Debauchee; and to grace the Piece, a P——n will seldom be wanting in the one as well as in the other.[1]

---

[1] H——th: William Hogarth (1697–1764); P——n: Parson. *A Midnight Modern Conversation*, 1733, portrays a drunken debauch with a parson prominent in the group. In the text the first two words of Hogarth's title are transposed by LM or her printer.

These Reflections were occasioned by reading one of *Horace*'s Satires, where that admirable Poet describes his first Introduction to *Mecænas*, and where we may see the good Sense of the Ministers as well as the Modesty of the People of that Age, or at least of such as that Minister chose to be his Favourites: I do not find any Authority for saying that Ministers had then what we now call Levees; but let me suppose *Mecænas* had a Levee once or twice a Week as our Ministers now have, and that he had the same Method of picking up Favourites. If this had been the Case, the poor, good-natur'd, bashful *Horace* would never have been a Favourite with him or *Augustus*. *Horace* was introduced by *Virgil* and *Varius*, two of *Mecænas*'s most intimate Friends. According to the modern Custom, this would have been a sufficient Introduction for *Horace*, to have shewed his Face at that Minister's Levee for many Years after; and by great Assiduity and great Impudence, in cracking a Joke every now and then, he might at last have become a Favourite; but notwithstanding this powerful Introduction, *Horace* never went back again, so much as to shew his Face to this great Minister, till he was sent for, which was not till *nine Months* after.[1]—This is a sufficient Testimony that the Favour of Ministers was not then, as now, to be gained, like the Kingdom of Heaven, by Violence.

The great Men of this Age seem to think, no Man is fit to be imployed who does not sue for Imployment, nor any Man fit to be made their Friend, who does not impudently and assiduously court their Friendship; and this Mistake among the Great has produced a very troublesome Opinion, I am sorry I cannot now call it a Mistake, among the Small, That the only Way of gaining any Favour from the Great, is to be teasing and importunate. Whereas, if either judged rightly, the Great would consider, that those who are most capable of Imployment, are generally least fond of it, and never will sue for it, if it is to be obtained only by long Attendance and great Importunity; and the lower Rank of Men would consider, that good States-men have no Time to spare either for paying or receiving Visits, therefore no Man ought to go near them but when sent for, or when they have some real Business to communicate; for when a great Man has a Mind to have a Party of Pleasure, surely he ought to be allowed to chuse his Companions; and in this respect he ought to take particular Care to make choice of Men of Merit and Character; he ought to be so far from allowing Men to

[1] *Satires*, I. vi. 52–64.

force themselves upon him by Impudence and Assiduity, that he ought to be diligent in searching for and associating to himself those who are eminent for Virtue and Knowledge; because the World will form a Character of him from the Characters of those who are his Companions upon such Occasions.

Modesty, or even Bashfulness, seems to have been a Qualification necessary for recommending a Man to *Augustus* or *Mecænas*. *Virgil* was remarkable for his Bashfulness; and by the Account *Horace* gives in this Satire, of his first Introduction to *Mecænas*, he seems to have been none of those impudent familiar Coxcombs, who now make themselves the chief Companions of most of the Men of Rank and Quality in this as well as every other Country of *Europe*. The Custom of the *Augustan* Age was so far different from the present, that, I believe, the Reason for *Mecænas*'s being so long before he sent for *Horace*, after his first Introduction, was in order to put his Modesty to the Trial; and that if *Horace* had from that Introduction assumed to himself the Privilege of attending constantly afterwards at that great Man's Levee, which we now most ridiculously call, paying his Court, he would never have been chosen by that Minister as one of his Friends, nor would he ever have been made his Companion in any of his Parties of Pleasure.[1]

[1] Under the title 'Of Levees' part of this essay was reprinted in the *London Magazine* of Jan. 1738.

Text H MS. 80. 236-9.

THE NONSENSE OF COMMON-SENSE

To be continued as long as the Author thinks fit, and the Publick likes it.

TUESDAY, January 17, 1738

I HAVE seen the world in a great variety of Lights, but till very lately never saw it in the Light of an Author, nor was sensible what difficulties those poor Creatures are oblig'd to struggle with. I allways beleiv'd we enjoy'd at present the Liberty of the press, and I was confirm'd in this opinion by observeing that some people even abus'd that Liberty to a degree of Licentiousness, and without Respect to the Highest Characters or a due regard to moral Truth endeavor'd to raise laughter and get readers, by the severest and (sometimes) by the most unjust raillery.[1] This provok'd me to handle a Weapon very new to me, and take up my pen in defence of good nature and good breeding. I very well foresaw that so innocent a design would meet with but small applause; and (as I declar'd in my first paper) I did not expect to be supported by any party. I was not ignorant, if my ultimate intention had been the sale of my writeings, that I chose a very wrong plan. The Herd of readers only seek for gratifications of their own envy; and as Mr. Dryden has said some where

> The reader's malice helps the writer's out.

Tis very easy to be witty in marking out the Frailties of particular men, or at least to appear so to those who are willing to beleive the pleasure they receive from a Libel rather rises from the Author's wit than their own ill nature, when God knows a very small portion of the First with a large Quantity of the other will put off the coarsest stile, and the most trite conceits that were ever wrote by —— or ——. Thô I was sensible of this, yet I thought that an

---

[1] Liberty of the press and its suppression by Robert Walpole was a frequent topic of the Opposition. *Common Sense* of 7 Jan. 1738 had dealt with liberty of the press, alleging that it was being threatened by the ministry. The *Daily Gazetteer* on 6, 9, and 10 Jan. defended the ministry; and LM here adds her oblique defence (on the 17th). On 21 Jan. 1738 both *Common Sense* and the *Craftsman* spoke out more openly and strongly.

Honest indifferent subject of England might utter his own neutral sentiments without any molestation whatever, and that the worst misfortune would be the censure of being very dull, when he confin'd himselfe to antiquated morals without satyr, puns, or *double entendres.*

You shall hear by a plain story how much I was mistaken. I carry'd my paper with great Innocence to the first printer came into my Head, not enquireing what party or principle he was of, beleiveing it ought to be as indifferent to me as the religion of my shoemaker when I bespeak a pair of shoes, supposeing he would follow my orders upon being paid for his Labour. He read it over with great earnestness, and being charm'd with the novelty, gave me many thanks for chuseing him for the publisher, and assur'd me with very significant Gestures, it was lucky that I did not go to any of his Brethren who would have us'd me ill. I did not trouble my selfe with enquiring what he meant, but desir'd him to print away, and a few days after carry'd him my second paper. I then found him in a very different temper; he told me in a great fright, that he had not question'd I intended to write against the Ministry, that his Bread depended on that set of people, that he was told by some of my readers that I was on the other side, which he never could have suppos'd a Gentleman of my appearance to be, that the Court writers were a parcel of miserable hirelings; and he should be undone if he was thought to be employ'd by them. I could not help laughing at his scruples, and had the patience to read over my paper three times to him, and endeavor'd to make him comprehend that there was not one party stroke from one end to the other of it. He sigh'd, shook his head, and murmur'd several times to himselfe— 'This will never take'—and then turning short upon me, said, 'Sir, what if you clapp'd in a home refflection or two about Sir —— ——? I own tis very hard to find any thing new to say against him. A little Dash against 'Squire —— his competitor might sell too.'[1] When he found me not willing to comply with these projects, 'But Sir,' added he vehemently, 'Here is no waggery: if you are obstinately bent not to be read by the politicians on either side, you should try to please the Ladys and the fine Gentlemen of the age. A Joke now and then would be very acceptable; if you have none of your own (thô that's strange methinks) there are a great many of D'Urfey's plays and Tom Brown's epistles that you may steal from

---

[1] Probably 'Sir' Robert Walpole and 'Squire' William Pulteney.

safely, they being mostly out of print.[1] I have a collection by me at your service.'—I gave him thanks for this courteous offer, but utterly refus'd makeing use of it, and told him, my Intention was to write to those that could admit of plain reasoning without any touches of that kind, that I was not yet persuaded that there was not still a considerable number of Honest men and modest Women in the nation, and it was to them I dedicated my Labours. With some other persuasions and the money paid before hand, I prevail'd on him to promise to print my last paper, thô I saw he left me with a visible discontent in his Countenance and a great contempt for my Whimsical way of thinking.

However my paper appears the Tuesday following but to my great surprize my Ingenious[2] printer had thrown in a little Bawdy at the end of a Paragraph, that no way led to any Idea of that sort.[3] You may imagine how much I was provok'd. I blotted it out of the few Copys I sent to my Freinds, and immediately sent for the Fellow to expostulate with him, but found him as much out of Humour as my selfe. 'I'll assure you, Sir' (said he in a Heat) 'I have done all I could for the service of your paper; but 'tis a damn'd ministerial thing, and the Hawkers refuse to sell it, the coffee houses won't take it in, and if you will rail at no body, nor put in no feign'd names that every body may understand, all the Bawdy in the Dunciad[4] won't carry it off. Here's a paper!' (continu'd he, pulling the Common Sense of December 31. out of his pocket) 'I'll engage this shall be read all over the Kingdom. Do but observe how wittily this polite Author raillys Mr. Henly in his affliction! What a charming jest he makes of all sentiments of Freindship and conjugal affection! Then there is some thing very sly in the sneers upon the words, Piety, Affability, and Sincerity.—'[5] He had gone on much farther in his praise of this paper, with which he was quite

---

[1] Thomas D'Urfey published twenty-nine plays from 1676 to 1709, and in 1721 three plays, none of them acted. Tom Brown (1663-1704) contributed to *Letters from the Dead to the Living*, 1702, and published *Certamen Epistolare; or, VIII. Letters between an Attorney and a Dead Parson*, 1703, as well as other letters printed individually or in miscellanies.

[2] The printer omitted this sarcastic adjective.   [3] On p. 112 above.

[4] Published 1728/9; 'its chief fault is the grossness of its images' (Samuel Johnson, *Lives of the Poets*, ed. G. B. Hill, 1905, 3. 242).

[5] John Henley (1692-1756), sharply attacked in the *Dunciad*, was one of Walpole's journalistic supporters and pensioners; he is called 'my Chief Priest' in a letter from Nonsense to *Common Sense* on 10 Dec. 1737. The paper of 31 Dec. ridiculed the courtship, marriage, and mutual devotion of the 'Orator' and his recently deceased wife. Two months later the *Englishman's Journal* continued to question the motive of Henley's grief (Graham Midgley, *The Life of Orator Henley*, 1973, pp. 255-7).

delighted, but that finding my selfe beginning to be angry, I told him coldly that he should be no longer trouble'd with mine, and that I found my selfe entirely unqualify'd to be an Author according to his taste.

After he was gone I begun seriously to consider the Injustice and ill consequences of the paper he recommended. I look upon tenderness and Greife as the Excrescencies of Virtue. They are only to be found in the Humane and Honest mind, as only such a one is capable of the Impression of a sincere Freindship, divested of all interested views. The sincerity of such a Freindship never appears in so strong a light as by the marks of respect and the tears we pay to the ashes of a dead Freind from whom we can expect no return. Whatever services are done, or proffessions made to a living Freind, even those to one in distress (as rarely as they happen) may possibly be in a view of receiveing some pleasure or future advantage from them, since no body is thrown so low by Fortune, but some accident may make them usefull to those even in the highest Rank. But when the expressions of our Love can never reach their knowledge they can only proceed from a Heart truly touch'd, a real Gratitude for past Obligations, and are real effects of Love and Esteem.

How aimable appears to me a Heart capable of such an attachment! How rare is it to see a Freindship continu'd for a length of Years without decay! It is natural for weak minds to grow weary of any Engagement that lasts long, and tis beyond the power of any Merit to fix a light or engage a selfish Man. 'Tis in my Opinion the best measure we can take of any one's value to know how far they are capable of being a Freind. I could on this occasion quote the greatest Authors of Antiquity; few have ever been capable of such Freindships as they have describ'd, but hitherto all have seem'd (at least) to respect those who could feel such disinterested and delicate Sentiments. We are now in an Age that they are become the Objects of ridicule, and we are told we are to laugh at the most legitimate sorrow, and despise the noblest proofes of the noblest mind.

My Head being full of these thoughts I could not help throwing some of them together which I intended to publish, and carry'd them to a declar'd Printer on the Court side, not with any view of listing my selfe under him, but despairing of prevailing with any others to print for me. I confess I was us'd with more civility. My paper was courteously read over but return'd with, 'Sir, I can print nothing against the ministry.' 'This is not against any ministry'

(I answerd) 'either past, present, or future.' 'Why I own' (said he) 'it is very well couch'd, and I cannot directly point where the sting lyes, but it must be so, for I never heard of any volunteers in their service, and you are not recommended to me by any considerable person; but If it should be so, and that you desire to be taken notice of, in order to be taken in, let me tell you, Sir, 'tis takeing bread out of other men's mouths. Between you and I, Sir, all my writers are paid, and considering their number, there is not too much comes to every man's share.' I interrupted him by saying, this was only intended to be a moral paper. 'A moral paper!' cry'd he starting, 'and how do you expect to get money by it?' 'I do not propose to get money by it,' said I; upon which he turn'd from me with the air of compassionate Contempt with which good natur'd people look upon those, they suppose *non compos mentis*.

I am now convince'd by these tryals that the Liberty of the press is as much block'd up, by the combination of the Booksellers, printers, pamphlet sellers, Authors etc. or perhaps more, than it would be by an Act of Parliament; and that without bribery or some methods tantamount to it 'tis as impossible for a man to express his thoughts to the public as it would be for one honest Fishmonger to retail Turbots in a plentiful season below the price fix'd on them by the Company.

I have with much ado prevail'd on an obscure printer to publish this plain story, and the poor Fellow is halfe frighted out of his Wits, for fear his Fraterniiy should find out he dares print without their permission.[1]

[The printed essay continues with:]

N.B. Whereas, we have been informed, that Gentlemen have sent to several Booksellers and Pamphlet-shops for this Paper, and have had for Answer, *They had none of them, nor could find any of them*; we are, therefore, obliged to give Gentlemen Notice, That when they receive any such Answer, it is only because the Bookseller, or Pamphlet-seller, will not be at the Pains to send for what they want; for the Publisher of this Paper, where every one may be supply'd, is well known to all the Booksellers and Pamphlet-sellers in Town. In all such Cases it would be easy for Gentlemen to insist upon being supplied with whatever they want by those they usually deal with; for every Bookseller and Pamphlet-seller must know where to find any thing just published, and often advertised.

---

[1] Actually all issues of *The Nonsense of Common-Sense* were printed by James Roberts.

Text H MS. 80. 140–1, 244–5.

THE NONSENSE OF COMMON-SENSE

To be continued as long as the Author thinks fit, and the Publick likes it.

TUESDAY, January 24, 1738[1]

I HAVE allways (as I have allready declar'd) profess'd my selfe a Freind thô I do not aspire to the character of an admirer of the Fair sex; and as such I am warm'd with Indignation at the barbarous treatment they have receiv'd from the Common Sense of January 14. and the false advice that he gives them.[2] He either knows them very little or like an interested Quack prescribes such med'cines as are likely to hurt their Constitutions. 'Tis very plain to me, from the extreme partiality with which he speaks of Operas and the rage with which he attacks both Tragedy and comedy, that the Author is a performer in the Opera; and who ever reads his paper with attention will be of my Opinion. No Thing else alive would assert at the same time, the Innocence of an Entertainment contriv'd wholly to soften the mind and sooth the sense, without any pretence to a moral, and so vehemently declaim against plays, whose end is to shew the fatal Consequences of vice, and warn the Innocent against the snares of a well bred designing Dorimant.[3] You see there to what insults a Woman of Wit, Beauty, and Quality is expos'd that has been seduce'd by the artificial Tenderness of a Vain agreable Gallant; and I beleive that very comedy has given more checks to Ladys in persuit of present pleasures, so closely attended with shame and sorrow, than all the sermons they have ever heard in their Lives.

[1] LM kept a printed copy of this issue (now among the H MSS.), and wrote opposite the date: 'wrote by me M.W.M.'

[2] In the essay cited (written by Lord Chesterfield), women are advised on how to resist various temptations, especially that of succumbing to a love-affair.

[3] Opera is recommended by *Common Sense* for its innocence, but dramatic pieces are condemned because they 'soften the Heart, and inflame the Imagination'. Dorimant is the central character in Etherege's *The Man of Mode*, 1676, and Bellinda the lady he seduces. It had not been played on the London stage since Jan. 1735.

But this Author does not seem to think it possible to stop their propensity to Gallantry by Reason or Refflection; he only desires them to fill up their time with all sort of other triffles: in short he recommends to them, Gosiping, Scandal, Lying, and a whole troop of Follys instead of it, as the only preservatives for their Virtue. I am for treating them with more dignity, and as I profess my selfe a protector of all the oppressed I shall look upon them as my peculiar care. I expect to be told, this is downright Quixotism, and that I am ventureing to engage the strongest part of mankind with a paper Helmet upon my Head. I confess it an undertaking where I cannot foresee any considerable success, and according to an Author I have read somewhere

> The World will still be rule'd by Knaves
> And Fools contending to be slaves.[1]

But however, I keep up to the character I have assume'd, of a Moralist, and shall use my endeavors to releive the distress'd, and defeat vulgar prejudices whatever the event may be. Amongst the most universal Errors I reckon that of treating the weaker sex with a contempt, which has a very bad Influence on their conduct, who, many of them, think it excuse enough to say, they are Women, to indulge any folly that comes into their Heads, and also renders them useless members of the common wealth, and only burdensome to their own Familys, where the Wise Husband thinks he lessens the opinion of his own understanding if he at any time condescends to consult his Wive's. Thus what Reason nature has given them is thrown away, and a blind obedience expected from them by all their ill natur'd Masters, and on the other side, as blind a complaisance shown by those that are indulgent, who say, often, that Women's weakness must be comply'd with, and tis a vain troublesome attempt to make them hear reason.

I attribute a great part of this way of thinking (which is hardly ever controverted) to the Ignorance of Authors who are many of them heavy Collegians that have never been admitted to politer conversations than those of their Bedmakers, or to the design of selling their Works, which is gennerally the only view of writeing, without any regard to Truth or the ill consequences that attend

---

[1] John How (*fl.* 1680), an imitation of Horace Ode II, Lib. 2, in *The History of Adolphus, Prince of Russia . . . With a Collection of Songs and Love-Verses*, By several Hands, 1691. LM repeated this couplet in a letter of 1742 (*Letters*, 2. 294).

the propagation of wrong notions. A paper smartly wrote (thô perhaps only some old conceits dress'd in new words) either in Rhyme or prose: I say Rhyme for I have seen no verses wrote of many years. Such a paper, either to ridicule or declaim against the Ladys, is very welcome to the Coffee houses, where there is hardly one Man in ten but fancys he has one reason or other, to curse some of the Sex most heartily. Perhaps his sisters' fortunes are to run away with the money that would be better bestow'd at the Groom porter's,[1] or an old Mother good for nothing keeps a Jointure from a Hopefull son, that wants to make a settlement on his mistriss; or a Handsome Young Fellow is plague'd with a Wife, that will remain alive to hinder his running away with a great Fortune, haveing 2 or 3 of them in love with him. These are serious misfortunes that are sufficient to exasperate the mildest tempers to a contempt of the sex, not to speak of lesser inconveniencies, which are very provokeing at the time they are felt.

How many pretty Gentlemen have been unmercifully jilted by pert Huzzys, after haveing cursy'd to them at halfe a dozen operas! nay permitted themselves to be led out twice: yet after these encourragements (which amount very near to an engagement) have refus'd to read their *Billet doux*, and perhaps marry'd other men under their noses. How welcome is a couplet or two in scorn of Womankind to such a disapointed Lover! and with what comfort he reads in many profound Authors, that they are never to be pleas'd but by Coxcombs, and consequently he owes his ill success to the brightness of his Understanding, which is beyond Female comprehension! The Country Squire is confirm'd in the Elegant Choice he has made in preferring the conversation of his Hounds to that of his wife, and the Kind Keepers (a numerous sect) find themselves justify'd in throwing away their time and estates on a parcel of Jilts, when they read that neither Birth or Education can make any of the sex rational Creatures; and they can have no value but what is to be seen in their Faces.

Hence springs the Applause with which such Libels are read, but I would ask the applauders if these Notions in their own Nature are likely to produce any good Effect towards the reforming of the vicious, the instructing of the Weak, or the guiding of the Young. I would not every day tell my Footmen (if I kept any) that their whole Fraternity were a pack of Scoundrels, that Lying and Stealing

[1] See p. 71 n. 1 above.

were such inseparable Qualitys to their Cloth that I should think my selfe very happy in them if they confine'd themselves to innocent Lyes, and would only steal candles' ends. On the contrary, I would say in their presence that Birth and Money were accidents of Fortune, and that no man was to be seriously despis'd for wanting either; that an Honest faithfull servant was a character of more value than an Insolent corrupt Lord, that the real Distinction between Man and Man lay in his Integrity, which in one shape or other gennerally met with its reward in the World, but could not fail of giving the highest pleasure, by a consciousness of Virtue which every Man feels that is so happy to possess it.[1]

With this Gentleness would I treat my Inferiors, with much greater Esteem would I speak to that beautifull halfe of Mankind who are distinguish'd by petticoats. If I was a divine I would remember that in their first Creation they were design'd a Help for the other Sex, and nothing was ever made incapable of the end of its Creation. 'Tis true the first Lady had so little experience that she hearken'd to the persuasions of an Impertinent Dangler; and if you mind the story, he succeeded by persuadeing her that she was not so wise as she should be,[2] and I own I suspect something like this device under the raillerys that are so freely apply'd to the Fair Sex.

Men that have not sense enough to shew any superiority in their Arguments hope to be yeilded to by a Faith that as they are men all the Reason that has been allotted to Humankind has falln to their share. I am seriously of another Opinion: as much greatness of Mind may be shewn in submission as in command, and some Women have suffer'd a Life of Hardships with as much Philosophy as Cato travers'd the Desarts of Affrica,[3] and without the support that the veiw of Glory afforded him and which is support enough for the Human mind that is touch'd with it, to go through any toil or Danger. But this is not the Situation of a Woman, whose virtue must only shine to her own recollection, and loses that name when it is ostentatiously expos'd to the World. A Lady who has perform'd her Duty as a Daughter, a Wife, and a Mother, appears to my Eyes with as much veneration as I should look on Socrates or

[1] In later years LM called such democratic beliefs 'silly prejudices' (1753, *Letters* 3. 36).

[2] The printer deleted the rest of the sentence.

[3] LM had once contrasted women's weakness with the fortitude of Cato (see p. 231, line 35, below). Her remarks on female heroism follow those of Mary Astell in *Some Reflections upon Marriage*, 1700.

Xenophon, and much more than I should pay either to Julius Caesar or Cardinal Mazarine, thô the first was the most famous enslaver of his Country, and the other the most successfull plunderer of his Master.[1]

A Woman realy virtuous in the utmost extent of this expression has virtue of a purer kind than any Philosopher has ever shewn, since she knows if she has Sense (and without it there can be no Virtue) that Mankind is too much prejudice'd against her Sex to give her any Degree of that Fame which is so sharp a spur to their Greatest Actions. I have some thoughts of exhibiting a set of Pictures of such meritorious Ladys, where I shall say nothing of the fire of their Eyes or the pureness of their Complexions, but give them such praises as befits a rational sensible Being, Virtues of Choice and not Beautys of Accident. I beg they would not so far mistake me as to think I am undervaluing their Charms: a Beautifull Mind in a Beautifull Body is one of the Finest Objects that is shewn us by Nature. But[2] I would not have them place so much value on a Quality that can be only usefull to one as to neglect that which may be of Benefit to thousands, by precept or by Example. There will be no occasion of amuseing them with triffles when they consider themselves capable of makeing not only the most aimable but the most Estimable Figures in Life. Begin then Ladies by paying those Authors with Scorn and contempt who with the sneer of affected Admiration would throw you below the Dignity of the Human Species.[3]

[1] For LM's essay on Caesar see pp. 150-2 below. Cardinal Mazarin (1602-61) was Prime Minister from Louis XIV's regency in 1643 until his death. Extravagant in his tastes, Mazarin acquired a large fortune through the sale of offices and new taxes.

[2] The printer deleted the word *But*; LM inserted it in her own copy of the printed paper.

[3] Under the title 'An Apology for the LADIES' most of this essay was reprinted in the *London Magazine* of Jan. 1738.

Text H MS. 80. 240–3.

THE NONSENSE OF COMMON-SENSE

To be continued as long as the Author thinks fit, and the
Publick likes it.

TUESDAY, February 14, 1738

I AM very much entertain'd with the variety of Censures that are
pass'd on my harmless paper, which I hear allmost every day with
an Indifferent Face, and to say truth without much violence to my
selfe, not feeling the paternal Affection that most Authors do for
their productions, neither my Fame or Fortune being any way
affected by their Success. My Acquaintance think me no more
qualify'd for a writer than for a General; and even in this Nation of
Partys, I have preserv'd my selfe so unspotted by any of them that
I am not suspected of being engag'd either in Court or Country
Interest. I make use of this expression in compliance with the
Familiar Phrases of the Age, for the Distinction is really absurd:
the Court has no true Interest but the welfare of the Country, and the
safest foundation of the Happyness of the Country is in the support
of the present Government as by law establish'd.

I confess these Refflexions foreign to the principal Design of my
Papers which are only intended as short essays of Morality,[1] without any touch of Politicks. I shall leave to the Authors of Common
Sense the full possession of their puns and ordures both now and
for evermore, and to the Gazetteer the happy talent of such easy
Panegyrick and polite satyr that none of his Readers would be able
to guess what paragraph was design'd for either if he did not with
great Humanity instruct us in his meaning by signifying to us the
names of those he intends to write of.[2] This singular accomplishment can never be sufficiently paid, is really beyond Imitation, and
in my opinion very inoffensive; nor am I so far misled by my
Ambition as to attempt to rival him.

I would willingly renew amongst Readers that taste which was

---

[1] The printer omitted the rest of the sentence.
[2] *The Daily Gazetteer* was the chief paper of the ministry.

once universal when Sir Richard Steele entertain'd, before he appear'd attach'd to any party, but that of Virtue and good sense.[1] That Gentleman had the Glory of pleasing without the assistance either of Lewdness or Malice. I am willing to beleive there yet remains so much politeness in the Kingdom of Great Brittain, a Great number of both Sexes are still capable of being delighted with what is rational rather than what is absurd, and do not want any of those *haut goûts* to relish a paper. It is indeed a proofe of a very deprav'd Appetite when the taste of reading must be excited by coarse raillery or such wretched *double entendres* as can mean but one thing. These Authors seem to have forgot the great Authoritys of the Earl of Roscommon, the Earl of Mulgrave, and Mr. Cowley; the first of these has declar'd,

> The want of Decency is want of Sense[2]

and in the Art of Poetry we find this manner of style mention'd with the greatest scorn:

> Bawdry barefac'd, that poor pretence to Wit.[3]

Mr. Cowley, notwithstanding the roughness of his verse, pleases me with the Justness of his sentiment when he says, speaking of Wit:

> 'Tis not when two words make up one noise,
>   Jests for Dutch men, and English Boys;
> In which who finds out wit, the same may see
> In An'grams and acrostiques poetry.
>   Much less can that have any place
>   At which a Virgin hides her Face.
> Such dross the Fire must purge away, tis Just
> The author blush, there where the Reader must.[4]

'Tis impossible to avoid these refflexions on reading the late productions of the Club of people who think they have monopoliz'd common sense; and if they mean by that pretention the sense of the common people, I agree that they appear possess'd of the

---

[1] In 1713, soon after the *Spectator* was terminated, Steele turned to political pamphleteering (Calhoun Winton, *Captain Steele The Early Career . . .*, 1964, p. 160).

[2] Adapted from the Earl of Roscommon, *An Essay on Translated Verse*, 1684, p. 8.

[3] From Earl of Mulgrave, later Duke of Buckingham, *An Essay upon Poetry*, 1682, p. 6.

[4] From Abraham Cowley, 'Of Wit', *Poems: I. Miscellanies*, 1656, p. 3.

way of thinking that us'd to be peculiar to the lowest of that class. The papers of Jan. [21][1] and Jan. 28 seem to be wrote by the very inspiration of Gin, and calculated for the amusement of all the blind alleys in and about Holbourn, Fleet Ditch, and the 7 Dials. There are scatter'd in them many ancient Water Jokes, which show the author's inclination to Plagiary, thô he wants taste to steal what is valuable, and puts me in mind of the petty larceny dealers, who with great art and contrivance rob country yards of old brooms, broken Glass bottles, and decaid washing tubs. These very fellows would perhaps spare plate or Jewells if they lay in their way, either from ignorance of their value, or not knowing what to do with them, when they had got them; but I do not think the meaness of a mischeif any excuse for committing it. When a Creature does all the harm in its power, (thô that should happen to be very little) it is a very mischeivous Creature; a Flea is as ravenous after Blood as a Lion, and has no better plea for mercy.

Thus I am exasperated by these insults on Modesty, thô I am convince'd the attempts are too dull and too gross to corrupt even the lowest form in a boarding School; and I am more than ever determin'd to write in Defence of Moral Virtue, thô I should be oppos'd by all the Printers, Ministers, and Patriots that flourish in this age, and think with Seneca, *Avida est periculi virtus.*[2]

It is I confess very possible that these my Labours may only be destin'd to line Trunks or preserve rost meat from too feirce a fire, yet in that shape I shall be usefull to my Country. Pies and band boxes will be the better for me; in the meantime, I am pleas'd with my own endeavors to serve the Public, and while I am writeing I chase from my mind many uneasy thoughts that would be very troublesome to my selfe. Thus I do good at Home, if I have not the Happyness of succeeding abroad.[3]

The taste of the Times is wholly turn'd to Jokeing, and the general affectation of it has even introduce'd it into the most serious assemblys and where the most Important matters have been consider'd. The ill consequences of it were not at first foreseen,

---

[1] The date, omitted in the manuscript, was provided by the printer. Horace Walpole wrote that this number of *Common Sense* 'was written by Lord Chesterfield, but I suppose was omitted [from his *Miscellaneous Works*] for its great indecency' (quoted in Roger Coxon, *Chesterfield and his Critics*, 1925, p. 218).

[2] 'Virtue is greedy of danger' (*De Providentia*, Cap. 4).

[3] That these sentiments are truly autobiographical can be seen in LM's letter to Algarotti on 24 Feb. [1738] (*Letters*, 2. 114–15).

but has been very sensibly felt. I am a Freind to Mirth, but I am shock'd with it when it is improperly employ'd, or endeavor'd to be rais'd at the expence of Decency or morality. Tully has said justly[1] *non est hilaritate, nec lascivia, nec risu aut joco comite levitatis, sed saepe etiam tristes firmitate et constantia sunt beati*: that is, Ladys, it is very possible to be extreme happy without being extreme merry; and I have often observ'd the loudest Laughers to be the dullest fellows in the Company. I am not recommending the sort of Gravity which is the Effect of Pride or the Mask of Stupidity. It is a praise not below the highest Genius, to know how to triffle agreably, but when Horace speaks of its delight, he adds, the propriety of place,[2] and I will joyn, a propriety of subject. When Honor, probity, and Freindship are publickly jested with, there requires a very uncommon strength of Mind to dare to avow the practise, or even an Approbation, of sentiments, that are so often the subject of Ridicule.

It is very true that many, many years ago, there was a sort of extravagant Worship paid to them. Some young Gentlemen of more Fire than Refflexion have thrown away their Lives on mistaken punctilios of Honor; and I have read of Nuns that cut off their noses, to hinder temptations ariseing from their Beauty.[3] I confess these mistakes were very fatal to some few, but how inconsiderable was that mischeife in comparison of the Corruption of the Whole? I had rather hear of halfe a dozen Knight Errants clapp'd up in Bedlam, thô they should be of the best Familys, and twenty Hermits gone to end their Days in the mountains of Wales or Scotland, than to hear people of the highest Rank applauding such maxims as one should only expect in the Cells of Newgate, and see papers lying on the Toilets of great Ladys that are only fit to be perus'd by those of Drury Lane.

I will for once address my selfe to the Authors, thô I can hope for small amendment from men who seem to have lost all sense of shame.

---

[1] The printer omitted the Latin quotation (from *De Finibus Bonorum et Malorum*, II. xx. 64–6).

[2] 'dulce est desipere in loco', Horace, *Odes*, IV. xii. 28.

[3] LM had jested at such an expedient during her courtship, chiding W for his jealousy (*Letters*, I. 56). The expedient of cutting off their noses and mangling their faces was used by the nuns of Winchester, during the Danish invasion, to convert the men's lust to pity (*A Present for the Ladies: being an Historical Vindication of the Female Sex*, 1692, pp. 47–8).

My Lords, Gentlemen, and others.

I do verily beleive there is not one amongst you but may in some capacity or other be usefull or ornamental, either to the public or your own Familys. Your very papers (such as they are) shew me you have been at School, and learn'd your books tolerably well. If you will write (from a redundancy of Fancy, or to get money for your *menu plaisirs*[1]), remember that you are then speaking to your Country, that the notions of Virtue (thô you should see through the Fallacy of them your selves) are necessary to be propagated, and without them even you with all your Wit, Beauty, and Learning will be cuckolded and cheated by your Wives and servants. Consider also that if you go on in writeing at this dirty Rate, it will be in the power of a very ordinary Author to outwrite you in your own style, especially if he can afford to keep a Girl that understands her trade; she will furnish several new hints, as you may be inform'd by many old Gentlemen that keep Wenches meerly for their Conversation. But why will you, Wits, Gentlemen, and Polititians, submit to the Imitation of such Jokers? Take my word for it, these stale attempts at Humour, meet with no applause but from the admirers of D'Urfey's Ballads, who sing the Winchester christ'ning, *'cause there is a pretty Jest in't.*[2] Leave then to the miserable writers for Daily Bread the two pences that they collect by such little arts from Green sickness misses and Boys before they have learn'd Latin.[3] I must own I have heard of such a thing as Political Bawdy. I have an ancient manuscript by me of the memoirs of old Hugh Spencer, first minister to Edward the second,[4] where he confesses that he us'd to mix Bawdy in his politick conferences with great Success. He charm'd several country Gentlemen with the familiarity of his expressions, and now and then made some young Fellows forget the Arguments they came prepar'd to oppose by tickling their fancys with the remembrance of their Brothel diversions. But these were his private Arts of Government, and he says in another place that he gave orders to all his Authors in pay never to talk Bawdy without mixing a great deal of Wit with it, and this Injunction was so severe, they never wrote any at all. If you (Common Sense club)

---

[1] LM repeated this gallicism in a letter of Nov. 1738 (*Letters*, 2. 130).

[2] LM quotes from 'The Winchester Christening', the very ballad she is condemning (*A New Collection of Songs and Poems, Part II*, 1687, p. 107).

[3] The rest of the essay was omitted by the printer.

[4] Hugh le Despenser the elder (1262–1326), favourite of Edward II after the banishment and subsequent murder of Gaveston. LM refers to Walpole's known *penchant* for such political bawdy.

would make the same Resolution, I am persuaded that all your Future papers thô they might be very dull, would at least be very decent.[1]

[1] Under the title 'Of indecent Writers' a long extract from this essay was reprinted in the *Gentleman's Magazine* for Feb. 1738; and under the title 'Against immodest Writers' an extract in the *London Magazine* for Feb. 1738.

THE NONSENSE OF COMMON-SENSE

To be continued as long as the Author thinks fit, and the
Publick likes it.

TUESDAY, February 21, 1738

Proverbs Chap. 3. V. 13 and 14 Happy is the man that finds wisdom, and the
man that getteth understanding. For the merchandize of it is better than the
merchandize of silver, and the gain thereof than fine gold.

REAMS of public papers which (out of great Idleness) I have read
for these many years last past have been fill'd with dissertations on
the word LIBERTY, which has been wrested to great variety of
purposes, without one definition of the true signification, and even
the lowest of the people[1] apply it to the service of their own passions,
be they never so irrational and destructive. We can have no greater
Demonstration of this truth than the LIBERTY they now take not
only of evadeing but resisting a late Law that was necessary even for
the preservation of the Human species in these Kingdom[s]: I
mean that, against the common vending Spirituous Liquors; and I
cannot help thinking these public riots in open defiance of the
Legislative power, to be in some measure occasion'd, by ill understood arguments of the pretended patrons of Liberty.[2]

   I am not now going to declaim in Favor of Slavery, but I would
fix a signification to the words *free people* that has not yet enter'd
into the wise heads of any party; and here I shall agree with the
opinion of the Philosopher that asserted that none but a vertuous
man can be a Free man,[3] and it is certain who ever is a slave to his
own vices will quickly be so to those of other people. The real

---

[1] The manuscript continues, in a passage partially crossed out: '(who by a shamefull
prostitution of learning can gennerally write and read)'.

[2] The Opposition had asserted that Walpole's advocacy of excise taxation, which
allowed officers to invade warehouses and even homes to levy the tax, threatened the
liberty of Englishmen. The consequent rioting had caused Walpole to drop the Excise
Bill of 1733; and the Gin Act, in effect on 29 Sept. 1736, again set off riots.

[3] Epictetus, 'Of Freedom', *Discourses*, Book IV, Chapter 1. As a young woman LM
had translated the *Enchiridion* of Epictetus (see pp. 10–11 above).

Tyrants of Mankind are carry'd in their own Bosoms. The same pride that makes an Oyster Wench scold and a Dutchess paint makes them both miserable. I name this Distemper as most Epidemical and the root of the greatest number of others, but there is no vice that carries not some proportion of its punishment along with it, and I beg my Gentle Readers to let me persuade them to be temperate, good natur'd, and above all, Humble, for one fortnight by way of experiment, and I am sure they will find it the most agreable fourteen days they ever spent in their Lives. The highest definition of Worldly Happyness is a sound Mind in a sound Body;[1] that is to say, a good Conscience and a Healthfull Constitution.

> Conscience, thou solemn Bond of Mutual Trust,
> Prop to the Weak and Anchor to the Just,
> Fructiferous Root whence human Virtues spring,
> The subject's Law and safety of the King:
> Appeas'd by thee our inward troubles cease,
> Thou guidst our feet into the paths of peace.
> Fair polar star, whose influenceing Ray
> Directs our toil and manifests our way.
> Should Cloud or storm thy radiant Beams obscure,
> Yet those who hope they follow thee are sure;
> Thô tir'd by Day, they pass the Night in rest
> And going wrong, yet thinking right, are blest.[1]

This last line may look as if I favour'd Enthusiasm, but remember that I first of all recommend Humility. I beleive no Humble man ever carry'd peculiar Notions out of his own Closet; and under that Restriction, I do not know but a small touch of them may be a very innocent Recreation. When ever it breaks out into that Zeal that delights in rending and tearing, I think the people infected with it ought to be taken care of in a proper place, where they can be in no danger of spreading the Contagion.[2] But this is very distant from the temper of mind to which I wish my Freinds[3] reduce'd. I would cure them of that sort of Pride that is tickle'd when they are appeal'd to by designing Men to judge of matters they cannot understand and which makes them so eager to buy all virulent papers against their superiors, be the Writers never so dull.

[1] Juvenal *Sat.* x. 356.
[2] From Prior, 'A Dialogue between the Vicar of Bray, and Sir Thomas More' (*Works*, I. 652–3).
[3] Attacks on Methodism began to appear in 1732, although its full manifestation did not occur until 1738 (see Umphrey Lee, *The Historical Backgrounds of Early Methodist Enthusiasm*, 1931, pp. 120–1).   [4] 'the Plebeians' struck out in MS.

Pride is the source of Envy, and Envy the most terrible sensation that a Human Mind can be afflicted with (not to speak of the many other evils that flow from it). I shall therefore (according to the Original Design of this paper, which is to give comfort) endeavor to take this serpent from their Bosoms by shewing them that these Objects of their Envy have a better right to their pity, and that all superfluitys are misfortunes to the poor Creatures whose birth or Circumstances subjects them to the use of them; and that the real Drudgery of the World is not perform'd by the Artisans and Labourers but the unhappy Men who loll in Coaches and six with more uneasyness than their footmen ride behind them.

How many temptations have these Wretches to Lazyness and Luxury! What distempers of mind and Body are the consequence! The most rational enjoyments of Life are remov'd at a greater distance from them than from the rest of Mankind. They are seldom sensible of the Endearments of Freindship, and Truth is hid from them both by Flattery and Malice. For my part I see no greater Object of Compassion than the Heir to a vast Estate, except it is he who has had so little sense as to acquire one, and genneraly sees the Fruit of his restless nights and toilsome days destind to foolish or ungratefull children, or children that he knows are none of his own, who are to squander what he has dearly purchas'd with the impairing of his Health, and (perhaps) the loss of both his Reputation and Vertue. Such is commonly the result of a Life spent in scenes of Busyness, with the view of Heaping up unnecessary Summs. It must be a cruel Refflection to a man in such miserable Circumstances, that he once was us'd to walk on foot with all the Strength and pleasure of those that have no other way of conveying their persons from one place to another; that he was then courted by nobody, but welcome to every body; that all the Freindly professions made to him were sincere, while it was no one's Interest to be otherwise to him, that he then could perfectly distinguish those that lov'd from those who dislik'd his conversation. His Hours are now past in the Mist rais'd round him by his Money, through which allmost all Objects appear false to him, and none clear. He often embraces where he is cheated and ridicule'd; and if he has any Freind left, is very likely to neglect him because it is the custom of Flatterers to remove any of that sort from the Familiarity of their Patron. If he has any ill or foolish Inclinations riseing up in his Mind (as they intrude sometimes into the wisest Heads) the certainty of applause provokes him to shew them; and there are all-ways people at hand to lead him into any path he pleases to chuse, be it never so destructive to his constitution, peace, or character.

If either accident or excesses throw him into sickness, a whole band of Doctors, Apothecarys, and Surgeons beseige his House, and force their way to his Bed chamber, where if they can prevail on his weakness to take their prescriptions, they are erected[1] into daily visitants; and tis very probable some or other of their med'cines will be found necessary for every future day of his Life, and his mind perplex'd with perpetual apprehensions of distempers that they fill his ears with. I have known a poor man break his Leg, and in a few weeks he was able to return to his Labour. A Rich man of my acquaintance had the same misfortune, and (what is wonderfull in a rich man) had as good a Constitution as the ploughman, yet kept his room as many months; and had it not been for his uncommon sound Constitution, had lost his Life by that unreasonable confine-ment and the variety of tortures that he was put to, for the sake of Fees. I could tell a great number of storys to this purpose, but I beleive all my Readers can recollect some on their own knowledge.

Why then should we envy this wealth, that can only bestow imaginary Happyness, and assuredly brings with it solid incon-veniencies? I beleive no one will dispute (except some crack brain'd stoicks) that pain and shame are the two most dreadfull Calamitys that can touch the Body and the Mind. I have allready shewn you the probabillity of the wealthy suffering a double share of the first. I shall be told (it may be) that it is from their own fault, and that it is possible for a rich man to be as innocent and as abstinent as a poor one. I confess the *possibillity* and perhaps there may be 2 or 3 such instances in the three Kingdoms; but I answer that I had rather drive ten yards from a precipice than within halfe an Inch of it, thô I was the skillfullest Coachman in England; and a frugal meal is the only certain preservative against surfeits.

As to the second point of my Discourse, it is sure that the sense of shame is not only less poignant in the lower stations of Life, but the cure of its consequences only to be found amongst them. If a Great man loses his character, thô by false report, tis hardly possible for him ever to clear it; his name is known every where, and his Infamy is inseparable from it. If a poor man has the ⟨ill⟩ Luck to be defam'd amongst his companions, he has not far to travel to find a

---

[1] *O.E.D.* cites the last use of this meaning as 1709.

new set of Companions, who never heard any mention of him, where he may raise himselfe a new reputation and never be reproach'd for the miscarriages that lost the first.

I have not gone through above halfe the considerations that ought to make us thankfull to the providence that has place'd us in an Industrious or Laborious course of Life; but I have said enough to cure the envy that some of us bear to those who suffer real evils, and abandonn real goods to grasp at Shadows, dificult in the persuit and unpleasing in the Enjoyment.

P.S. I am so impartial to see all the merit of the paper call'd Common Sense of Feb. 11. The Folly expos'd in it is very properly the subject of Ridicule, and ridicule'd with great pleasantry;[1] and as I will allways afford those Authors my praise when they are either entertaining or beneficial to the Public, I shall as freely take notice of whatever absurditys they produce, however dignify'd or distinguish'd.[2]

[1] This paper, by Chesterfield, satirizes excessive attention to cuisine and eating. The satire, however, broadens to attack Walpole, whose gluttony and obesity were often ridiculed by his friends and enemies.

[2] On the verso of the manuscript sheet LM wrote a brief letter to her printer (*Letters*, 2. 114).

Text original printed folio.

THE NONSENSE OF COMMON-SENSE

To be continued as long as the Author thinks fit, and the
Publick likes it.

TUESDAY, March 14, 1738

Nam neque Divitibus contingunt Gaudia solis. Hor.[1]

THERE is one Vice, which I think peculiar to this Age (at least the
Degree of it to which we seem to be arrived) I mean *Impudence.*—
'Tis the Fashion to be asham'd of nothing but *Bashfulness.*—There
certainly have been Nations more dissolute, more cruel, and as venal
as ours; but there was always kept up in Writings and Conversations a Sort of respectful Deference for *Virtue.*—Temperance,
Valour, and Generosity, met with Applause in the utmost Decline
of the *Roman* Empire.—An honest Man is now obliged, under Pain
of being stigmatized with the Reproach of being singular and
whimsical, to *conceal* all Sentiments of Honour or Humanity; and
very polite People compliment one another publickly in a Stile not
much unlike that of the Ladies in the *Beggar's Opera,*[2] and for Actions
altogether as inconsistent with the Maxims of Morality.

Bravery and Chastity, the antient Idols of the two Sexes, are not
only left without Worshippers, but trampled on and despis'd.—I
confess some of their Zealots (the Duellists and Prudes) invented
very extravagant Ceremonies to shew their Homage, which I am
not sorry are abolished; but I could wish that Gentlemen were
ashamed of being abused, and that avowed Strumpets were not
receiv'd into the best Company.—It is now an Excuse for either to
say, he could not resent for fear of losing his Interest; or she could
not refuse having but a small Fortune: Nay, it is a Sort of Merit
in People to get the better of natural Shame, when *Money* is in their
Way; and we have such an Aversion to the very Shadow of *Virtue,*

---

[1] 'For enjoyments fall not to the wealthy alone' (*Epistles*, 1. xvii. 9). The printer
evidently put this motto here instead of at the head of the previous paper.

[2] John Gay's popular ballad-opera, first staged in 1728, attacked Walpole for his
alleged corruption and cynicism. The whores compliment each other on cheating etc. in
II. iv.

that, I believe the very same Actions would still be infamous, if it could be proved, that a young Man put up an Affront, from a Principle of *Christian* Meekness; or a young Woman was debauched, from too much Truth and Tenderness.

All our modern Writers follow this System.—We are always mistaking *Knavery* for *Wisdom*, and *Luxury* for *Politeness.*—I shall be told that I forget the Churches are still open, and that we have Weekly Sermons full of Piety and Morality; but I am afraid they have no farther Influence on our Manners, than the Exercises of the *Militia* have in teaching the *English* Youth the Art of War. 'Tis true, we have our regular training Days, and we may see there the old Methods of mustering, attacking, *&c.* but alas! few are the Spectators, generally of very low Rank, and even those oftner laugh at the Performers, than any way profit by their Show.

The present fashionable Depravity of *Sentiments* (a more proper Expression than Depravity of *Manners*, many *talking* lewdly who *live* soberly) I take to be much heighten'd by the Variety of *stupid Libels*, with which this Age abounds.

> Writing was once a Philosophick Pride:
> Th' inspir'd Poet scorn'd the World beside.
> Now of all Trades, the last and meanest Cheat:
> They praise to drink, and satyrize to eat.[1]

I forbear speaking of the Injuries which such Writings may do occasionally to private Families; but they have one very pernicious Effect on the Publick, I mean lessening the Value People ought to set on *Reputation*, which was once a very great Restraint on Vice, even to those whose ill Dispositions inclined them to the Practice of it.—We see now frequently Heaps of miserable Verses sold by the Help of initial Letters, which are sometimes ingeniously contrived to serve for several Names, that the Reader may apply as best suits his own ill Nature, and the Author perhaps escape beating, by throwing the Application from one to another; and this Propagation of Scandal takes off the Fear of it.[2]

I am not accusing these Writers of any Malice.—I know they only look on Defamation as a Branch of Trade.—The Art of Poetry

---

[1] Apparently written by LM.

[2] Angered by Pope's character of her as Sappho in his first imitation of Horace's satires (1733), LM complained to his friend Lord Peterborough, who in turn wrote to her that Pope 'wonderd how the Town could apply those Lines to any but some noted common woeman' (*Letters*, 2. 97).

is now grown so thoroughly Mechanical, that, if my Conscience would suffer me, I would bind my youngest Son 'Prentice to an eminent Poet; it is sure Bread to a Boy that has a good Memory, and a Knack at *Crambo*.[1]—I have myself observed their Method so nicely, that I have a great Insight into the Mysteries of their Profession.—Sometimes they quarrel amongst themselves, only intending to sell a Paper on both *Sides*.—

> So *Fig* and *Sutton* seem inflamed with spite,
> And charm Spectators with a bloody Fight:
> Yet by the Friendly Battle all they mean,
> To draw a Crowd, and calmly share the Gain.[2]

When the Town will read no more of their *Squabble*, another Club join to Praise one another.—The Doctor's Raillery is so Polite! Mr. What d'y'call'm's Lines are so strong! and Mr. you know who's Stile's so sublime, that we are all Fools, Blockheads, and Scoundrels, that do not see such apparent Beauties.—This judicious Mixture of *Praise* and *Satyr* never fails to get off one Impression.—I cannot help looking upon Poetry (the Mistress of my Youth) with the same Compassion and Abhorrence, the Angel in *Milton* does on *Lucifer*,

> How chang'd! How fall'n![3]

Since *Cowley*, *Wicherley*, *Congreve*, *Addison*, not one Lampoon is extant under their Names; with what Indignation would any of them have received the Proposition of Gain by such Methods? Even out of my humble Cell, (vulgarly called a *Garret*) I can despise these Practitioners of Rhime, and am resolved either to be read innocently, or not read at all.—Like *an honest Courtier* (for I will positively believe the *possible* Existence of such a *Species*) who had rather remain without Advancement, than obtain it by undermining his Patron.—The Race of Libellers will answer me by asserting, That it is their great Zeal against Vice, that provokes them.—Give me leave to tell them, that as there are few in the World *perfectly Good*, there are not many *thoroughly Vicious*; one good Quality is enough to hinder a Character from being compleatly bad, and should save it from publick Infamy; but if they would forbear this stigmatizing a Man's Name, and confine their Censure to single Actions,

---

[1] LM had accused Pope of thinking crambo 'sublime' (see p. 251, line 117 below).

[2] James Figg (d. 1734), the most famous pugilist of his time, was beaten only once—by Ned Sutton (d. 1737), the Pipemaker of Gravesend, whom he fought several times (H. D. Miles, *Pugilistica: The History of British Boxing*, 1906, i. 8–12).

[3] 'O how fall'n! how chang'd' (*Paradise Lost*, i. 84).

even there, it is impossible to judge fairly; except they knew all attending Circumstances which relate to them.—But I do these Creatures too much Honour to speak to them in this Manner, after having given a true Account of the real Motives of their *Satyrs* and *Panegyricks.*—Yet I am afraid Mr. *Dryden*'s Lines are too near Truth.

> On Eagles Wings immortal Scandals fly,
> While virtuous Actions are but born and die.[1]

I will save as many as I can from Oblivion, I will praise, though with the Peril of being insipid; nay, I will praise a *first Minister*, a Minister whom I never saw, nor shall see, who never brib'd either me or any of my Acquaintance; I mean Cardinal *Fleury*,[2] born for a Blessing to his Country, who makes her Greatness and neglects his own: I shall compare him to *Richleu* and *Mazarine*,[3] with as much Impartiality as is to be seen in any of *Plutarch*'s Comparisons, and shew that Power may subsist without degenerating into Tyranny or Luxury.

---

[1] From Juvenal's *Ninth Satire*, translated by Stephen Hervey. This satire is included in *The Satyrs of . . . Juvenal and . . . Persius translated . . . By Mr. Dryden, and several Other Eminent Hands . . .*, 3rd ed., 1702, which LM owned (Sotheby Catalogue, 1 Aug. 1928, p. 90).

[2] Cardinal Fleury (1653–1743), unwilling to follow the examples of Richelieu and Mazarin, refused the title of Prime Minister under Louis XV, yet served from 1726 to 1743. As a peace-loving minister he was able to maintain friendly relations with Walpole. A year later LM praises Fleury's achievements from first-hand observation (*Letters*, 2. 143).

[3] Cardinal Richelieu (1585–1642), Prime Minister under Louis XIII, virtually ruled France from 1624 to 1642. For Mazarin see p. 134, n. 1 above.

Caesar

This dramatic essay grew out of Lady Mary's friendship with Francesco Algarotti (1712–64), the Italian writer; her holograph survives among his manuscripts, endorsed by him 'Cesare'. When she met him in London in 1736 he had already written a prefatory letter to his friend Voltaire's *La Mort de César* (1736). He himself began to write a biography of Caesar in 1739, a year when he again visited London, and he resumed work on it in 1740 and 1741. Since he and Lady Mary were both in Turin in the spring of 1741 she may have written her piece then (if not in 1739). In style Lady Mary's 'Caesar' is very different from Algarotti's heavily documented and densely learned treatise; she would have offered it to him simply as an exercise in wit. Algarotti never completed his biography; a long fragment, that ended before Caesar's assassination, was published posthumously in his works (*Opere*, 1791–4, 17. 149–522).

In this piece Lady Mary invents a dramatic monologue for Brutus to justify himself to the Romans for joining the conspiracy against Caesar. Such a speech does not appear in the histories of Suetonius or Plutarch or in the plays by Voltaire and by the Abbé Conti. But it has close parallels in Shakespeare's *Julius Caesar*, from which Lady Mary adopts and elaborates many of the ideas in Brutus's and Mark Antony's speeches. She thus constructs a rationalistic *apologia* in the oratorical manner of a stage play. She had discussed the Shakespeare play in her essay on *Cato* (see pp. 63, 63–4 above).

Text MS. 1259, Biblioteca Civica, Treviso. *Printed* in Halsband, 'Algarotti as Apollo: His Influence on Lady Mary Wortley Montagu', in *Friendship's Garland: Essays Presented to Mario Praz*, ed. V. Gabrieli, 1966, 1. 234–6.

BEHOLD the Just reward of Murder, Perfidy and Treason—. You seem surpriz'd to hear me call it Just. You still are dazle'd with the Success of this man's arms. You see before you bleeding in the dust, that Conqueror to whose Triumphs you have so oft been Witness. You have seen our daggers hid beneath our Robes drawn all at once against defenceless Caesar. You have seen joyn'd in this Conspiracy his Relations, his Companions and his Freinds. These Circumstances give a Face of Horror to this Action. The Recent memory of his victorys, nay, let me add, his virtues, the Compassion natural to Mankind, the Brand fix'd on Assassins, all plead against us; but let me raise this veil of Prejudice, and learn you to distinguish between false Glory and the True.

I will not strive to lessen any part of that merit which so justly has made him the Object of Admiration. I am my selfe amaz'd when I recollect the number of Advantages with which the Gods endow'd him: His noble Birth, the Graces of his person, his winning Eloquence, that strength of Mind which render'd him patient of Toil and even of adversity, without being vain or Insolent in Prosperity, that Courtesy even to his Enemys, his Clemency in power, his Liberality, that presence of mind which never abandonn'd him in the most difficult occasions, that valour which set him above the Fear of Death, yet that Prudence that never suffer'd him to hazard his Soldiers rashly, that Fire which animated him in Battel, yet so temper'd as to Judge calmly in the heat of it. What Qualitys, Had they been employ'd to serve his Country!

But curse the virtues that have Ruin'd Rome! No Man is valuable from the possession of Talents but from the application of them. Caesar's have not only been fatal to his Country but poison'd halfe Mankind. His example has dignify'd debauchery, while he corrupted our youth, and the Successes of his Wild Ambition gilded over the Horrors of it. Generations yet unborn shall shelter by his Name Projects of Lawless Power; and every narrow mind incapable of seeking true Glory will aim at the False to joyn his Fame to Caesar's. Mistaken Men! who only look on the superficial Glare, nor see the Blackness, nay the misery, attending all unjust persuits. The Gods have so closely connected Happyness with virtue, they are not to be divided by Fortune. You have seen the strongest proofe of it, even in this successfull villain, restless, unsatisfy'd, in the midst of Triumphs, reduce'd by inward discontent to wish for that Death he has now receiv'd, and which has not been given him from any motive of private Malice or Revenge.

Many of us have been oblig'd, none personally injur'd by him. But Rome our common Mother has been enslav'd; we have seen him trample on her sacred Laws, and triumph in the Blood of her best Citizens; we have seen him almost openly avow the Design of establishing a Tyranny. We had no other way of escapeing but that we now have taken with Reluctance. There is no brave Man that is not ready to sacrifice his Life, when ever it is necessary to preserve his Honour; but Honour, precious as it is, must be abandonn'd, when no longer to be kept with Virtue. This is the severest Tryal of a Generous Soul, yet, if I must choose, let me [be] Infamous, but still be honest. We'll bear the Blame of an illjudging Croud (if there be any Blind enough to blame this Action), content with the Plaudit of our own conscious Minds, those secret Judges that are not to be brib'd, the God within us, that still voice which Independant of Applause or Calumny dictates to every Man his Duty. We have done ours by this endeavor to preserve your Liberty. That he endeavor'd the total overthrow of it, you have seen too many proofes. If he refus'd a crown in Public, who offer'd it him? The Loose Antonius, a Man devoted to his service, too well acquainted with his Projects to make such an offer had he not known it was agreable to him. It is true he refus'd it, but How refus'd? A faint Refusal proves a strong Desire. A Patriot son of Rome would have been fir'd at the affront done to his Probity, to suppose him capable of receiveing it, and the prostitute Flatterer would have mourn'd his Insolence in Chains.

If Caesar's victorys have extended the Roman Empire, his sword has thinn'd her Citizens. Is there one Family amongst you that does not bear the loss of a Parent, Son, or Brother falln in his civil wars? If you have seen him bring foreign Treasure to your Capitol, can you forget he still remain'd the master of it? Did you not see him take it by Force, when Metellus your Tribune in vain represented the Infringement of your Laws?[1] Caesar was then a Robber, at Pharsalia a Parracide and Glorious Murderer. Take from his Actions the varnish of success and shine of Power, these are thy Titles, Caesar!

Can you then doubt the Justice of his Death? 'Twas not from want of Numbers, we have undertaken it in this Manner. There still are Men in Rome, thousands of Galant Men, ready to rise on the first Call of Liberty, who would once more have cover'd the Plains with Arms, and disputed with this Tyrant his ill gott Authority. But we would spare your Blood; too much has been shed in our unnatural Wars. Even his mistaken Army (misled by too much fidelity to their General) is dear to us; nor would we destroy so many valiant Men, that may live to boast nobler Conquests than over their fellow Citizens. Neither have we slain him by Night, or in disguise; he has not dy'd by Poison (the Invention of Traitors) but falln a public Sacrifice to Liberty. We own the Fact, and expect your Censure.

---

[1] Caecilius Metellus Creticus, appointed tribune in 49 B.C., yielded the sacred treasury to Caesar only on compulsion.

Carabosse

In this brief *jeu d'esprit* Lady Mary converts the opening section of Charles Perrault's well-known fairy tale 'La Belle au bois dormant' (the sleeping beauty) into a personal essay. In her version as each good fairy bestows a blessing on the infant princess, the evil spirit, Carabosse, nullifies it in turn. As a final curse—evidence of the paradoxical nature of the essay—the princess is endowed with a great fund of tenderness,

Lady Mary addressed her essay to the Abbé Antonio Conti (1677–1749). He was a cosmopolitan savant and littérateur, whom she knew in London in 1715, when he visited the court of George I. During her husband's embassy to Turkey (1716–18) Lady Mary sent the Abbé her most brilliant virtuoso letters. When she retired to Venice in 1739 she resumed her friendship with him, and probably wrote her essay at this time. (See Halsband, 'An Imitation of Perrault in England: Lady Mary Wortley Montagu's "Carabosse"', *Comparative Literature*, 3 (1951), 174–7.) Translation on pp. 383–4.

Text H MS. 80. 290–3; endorsed by LM: 'Carabosse a l'Abbé Conti'. *Printed* 1803.

Il y avoit autre fois un Prince et une Princesse (car c'est ainsi que ma nourice commençoit tous les contes dont elle me berçoit). Le Prince estoit brave et genereux, la Princesse belle et sage; leurs vertû et leur amour reciproque et constant faisoient toute a la fois la Gloire et la honte du siecle. Mais comme il n'y a point de Felicité parfaitte, il leur manquoit des Enfans. Les temples de tous les Dieux estoient chargez de leurs offrandes, et toutes les bonnes fées des environs de leur presents, pour obtenir la seule chose qu'ils avoient a souhaitter. Il y est vrai qu'on ne pût jamais persuader a la Princesse de rechercher les mauvaises, et c'éstoit en vain que le Prince lui representoit que les mechantes pouvoient nuire avec autant de facilité que les bienfaisantes pouvoient servir. Elle disoit toujours que faire la Cour aux Vicieux estoit une espece de Culte rendue au Vice et elle ne pouvoit pas s'ÿ resoudre. On dit même qu'elle s'emancipoit quelque fois a blamer leur conduitte d'une façon un peu temeraire. Enfin ses Vœux furent combléz: elle devint grosse. Elle n'oublia pas de prier a ses couches toutes les Fées de ses amies, et elle leur preparoit de presents digne de leur estre offerte. Donner de Pierreries ou de l'or aux Maitresses des Mines auroit été leur faire un affront; elle sçavoit qu'elles en font si peu de cas qu'elles en comblent souvent les mortels les plus indignes pour en mieux marquer

leur mepris. Elle avoit remassée par des soins infinis des beaux vers
passionez composez par des Amants sincere, le Portrait d'une Belle
religieuse qui n'avoit jamais pensé a l'amour profane, une Phiole
(tres petite a la verite) des larmes versez par une jeune et riche veuve
seule dans son Cabinet, et des Livres de Theologie qui n'avoient
jamais ennuyé personne.[1] Les Fées etoient toute etonnez d'ou elle
auroit pû trouver tant des choses rares et precieu(ses); elles etoient
empressez de temoigner leur reconnoisance en rendant son enfant
la personne du monde la plus accomplie et la plus heureuse. Elle
mit au monde une petite Princesse. A peine avoit elle vû la Lumiere
que la Fée Bellinde s'écria, 'Je la doue d'une Beauté noble et touch-
ante.' Elle n'avoit pas cessée de parler quand on entendoit un bruit
comme de cent cannons dechargez a la fois, un sifflement comme
de mille serpents furieux, et on vit descendre par la Cheminée la
Fée Carabosse[2] montée a Califorçhon sur un enorme Crapaud. Je
ne veux salir mon papier par la Description de sa figure, faitte pour
inspirer le degout et l'horreur. 'Je veux' (crioit-elle d'une voix
rauque) 'que cette Fille cherie perde cette beauté admirable par la
petite verole dans l'age qu'elle commence a sentir ses avantages.'[3]
La Fée Spirituelle se flattant d'adoucir cet malheur, disoit, 'Je la
doûe d'une memoire la plus heureuse qui a jamais été, d'un goût
juste, d'une Vivacité surprenante, temperée par un jugement qui
reglera toutes ses paroles. Elle excellera dans tous les genres
d'écrire; elle seroit sçavante sans vanité, et vive sans étourderie.'
'Cet bel esprit' (repliqua Carabosse, avec un souris dedaigneux) 'ne
servira qu'a lui attirer des ennemis; elle seroit toujours en proye aux
Sots, dechirée par leurs mallices, et importunée par leurs assiduitez.'
'Je veux,' disoit la brillante Argentine en s'avançant, 'que son Pere
soit le Plus riche Seigneur de son Rang, et que son Mari auroit des
millions d'or.' 'Oui,' interompit Carabosse, 'elle vivra au milieu des
Tresors sans en voir jamais a sa disposition.'[4] 'Je lui donne,'
disoit Hygeia, 'une Santé a toute épreuve, que ni les chagrins ni les
Fatigues ne pourront diminuer.' 'Cette Santé,' repondit Carabosse,

---

[1] Lists of such paradoxical elements had been used by witty poets earlier, e.g.
Alexander Pope in *The Rape of the Lock*, v. 113–20.
[2] In Perrault's tale the wicked fairy is nameless; LM chooses a traditional name in
French folklore.
[3] For LM's own attack of smallpox, see p. 35 above.
[4] LM's father, the Duke of Kingston, was a powerful peer, whose wealth went to
his grandson (in 1726); and her husband, who died one of the richest commoners in
England, allowed her only £980 a year when she left England to live abroad in 1739.

'lui inspirera la Hardiesse de tenter des enterprises temeraires, et de risquer des dangers dont elle seroit toujours environnée.' 'Elle aura,' disoit l'aimable Harmonie, 'l'oreille juste et un goût exquis pour la musique—' 'Je lui oste' (crioit Carabosse en lui coupant la parole) 'le pouvoir de chanter pour qu'elle sente toute la rage du Desir et de l'impuisance.' Les bonnes Fées, consternées de voir leur benedictions ainsi empoissonées, se parloit tout bas, et consultoit en quelle maniere on pouvoit vaincre cette malice infernale. Spirituelle crût avoir trouvée un expedient infaillible. 'Il faut lui oster' (disoit elle) 'toutes les vices, et elle se trouvera garentie des malheurs qui en sont la suitte. Je lui oste' (ajouta-elle d'un ton haut et ferme) 'toutes les semences de l'envie et de l'avarice, qui sont les sources des miseres de l'humanité; elle aura l'humeur douce et égalle,—' 'et un grand fond de tendresse,'¹ ⟨s'écria⟩ Cabarosse [*sic*] avec un éclat de rire que faisoit trembler le Palais. Les Fées bienfaisantes s'envolerent ni voiant aucune remede a tant des maux. La Princesse mourût de Chagrin, son Enfant s'embellisoit chaque jour, mais . . .

Ici le Manuscript est deffectueux.

¹ In some verse addressed to Lord Hervey, LM referred to her sensibility, a 'Gift from partial Heaven', as her torment (p. 290 below).

[The Turkey and the Ant]

Lady Mary based this brief prose fable on No. XXXVIII of John Gay's popular verse collection, published in 1728; its theme was apparently original with him. She began a French version in rhyme but evidently abandoned it (H MS. 80. 309). She kept a different, complete poetic version in French not in her autograph (H MS. 81. 275–6). Her piece may also be related to a letter she sent to Francesco Algarotti in 1757 in which she discoursed on a parallel theme, and then told him that she might write an 'epistle' on the subject (*Letters*, 3. 121). Translation on pp. 384–5.

Text H MS. 80. 308–9. *Printed* in Halsband, 'Algarotti as Apollo: His Influence on Lady Mary Wortley Montagu', in *Friendship's Garland: Essays Presented to Mario Praz*, ed. V. Gabrieli, 1966, 1. 237–8.

DANS une belle journée de l'automne un dindon marchoit a la tête de sa troupe avec autant de Fierté qu'un consul Romain a la tête du Senat. 'Mes chers freres' (disoit-il avec une eloquence ciceroniene) 'profitons des delices dont la nature nous pourvoye. Il n'y a point d'espece plus favorisée du Ciel que la nostre. Nous avons la Beauté et l'esprit en partage, et un Goût exquis pour sçavoir joüir de nos avantages, mais Helas! nostre vie est aussi courte que belle. L'homme, ce Tyran cruel de la nature, qui n'est jamais assouvi de sang, ne nous permet que rarement de parvenir a la viellesse; il coupe sans pitie le fil de nos jours. Je le vois deja qui regarde nostre embonpoint d'un oeil de convoitisse, et pour contenter sa volupté brutale, il nous destine peutestre (en peu de jours) les uns a la broche, et les autres a la daube. Nostre foible innocence ne peut pas resister a ses forces. Contentons nous de suivre les maximes de la vraie sagesse: jouissons du present et soumettons nous a l'avenir. Je vois au pied de ce chesne la terre toute noircie d'une foule innombrable de fourmis. Il n'y a point de Gibier plus excellent pour la santé, ni plus delicieux du Goût. Allons, jouissons du bien que les dieux nous envoyent.'

Une Fourmis lui repond—'Et vous Barbare, que vous plaignez de l'homme! Vous croyez qu'il vous est permis de massacrer tout un peuple pour un dejeuner! Sachez que quand nous vous voyons plumé nous regardons cette main meurtriere comme l'instrument de la juste vengeance de la desolation de nostre race.'

Sur la Maxime de Mr de Rochefoûcault.
Qu'il y a des marriages commodes, mais point des *Delicieux*.[1]

In this French essay Lady Mary, whose cynicism often seems akin to La Rochefoucauld's, refutes one of his maxims on marriage. Her 'romantic' view of marriage as a union based on mutual love and esteem is, however, consistent with ideas she had expressed in her letters and verse during and since her courtship. Exactly when she composed this essay is uncertain. It must have been in circulation between 1732 and 1734, for Charles de Montesquieu, in a section of his commonplace book between those dates, copied several brief passages 'D'un manuscrit de milady Wortley Montagu' ('Spicilège' 576, *Œuvres complètes*, ed. R. Caillois, 1951, 2. 1373–4).

By 1740, certainly, the essay was in a completed and polished form; and she showed it to her friends. Her old friend the Abbé Conti, whom she was seeing in Venice, translated it into Italian verse (Conti, *Prose e poesie*, 1739, 1756, 2. 309 ff.). In the summer of 1740 she visited Lady Pomfret in Florence, who sent a copy of the essay to her friend Lady Hertford in England. 'I never read any thing in which more truth, wit, and delicacy, was joined', Lady Hertford replied, thanking her for the 'charming essay' by one who, she said, had more wit than La Rochefoucauld himself (Frances, Countess of Hertford, and Henrietta Louisa, Countess of Pomfret, *Corr.* 1805, 2. 153–4). A few months later, when Lady Mary met Joseph Spence in Rome, she let him read her essay as well (Spence's letter to his mother, 11 Mar. 1741, B.M. Egerton MS. 2234, f. 251). It was evidently a literary work she was particularly pleased with. (A contemporary translation is printed on pp. 385–92.)

Text H MS. 256. MS. transcript by LM in H MS. 80. 295–301; and in Portland MSS., Longleat, 21. 120–8 (probably sent by LM to her friend Lady Oxford). *Printed* 1803; a translation had appeared in the *Annual Register for 1763*, pp. 204–9.

IⅬ paroist bien hardi d'entreprendre de detruire une maxime établie par un bel esprit si celebre que M. de Rochefoucaûlt, et receû avec un foy si aveugle chez une Nation qui se dit le seul parfaitement poli du Monde, et qui a donné depuis si longtemps des Loix de Galanterie a toute l'Europe. Cependant (plein de l'Ardeur qu'inspire la verité) J'ose avancer tout le contraire, et je soutiens hardiment qu'il nÿ a qu'un Amour marié qui peut estre delicieux

[1] François, duc de La Rochefoucauld (1613–80). The maxim actually reads: 'Il y a de bons mariages, mais il n'y en a point de délicieux' (No. 113 in *Réflexions ou sentences et maximes morales*, 2nd ed., 1666).

pour une Ame bien faitte. La Nature nous a presenté des plaisirs propre pour nostre Espèce; on n'a qu'a suivre son Instinct rafiné par le Goût, et relevé par un Imagination vive et douce pour trouver le seul bonheur dont les Mortels sont capable. L'Ambition, L'Avarice, La Vanité ne peuvent donner (dans leur plus grandes Jouisances) que des plaisirs bas, mediocres, et qui ne sont pas capable de toucher un Cœur noble.

On peut regarder les bien faits de la fortune comme des Échaffaûts necessaire pour monter au bonheur, mais on ne peut jamais le trouver, soit en bornant ses souhaits, soit en obtenant ses frivoles faveurs, qui ne sont que les gênes de la vie, quand on le regarde pas comme necessaire pour obtenir ou conserver une felicité plus precieuse. Cette felicité ne se trouve que dans l'Amitie fondé sur un Estime parfaitte, fixé par la reconnoissance, soûtenue par l'Inclination, et éveillé par la tendresse de l'Amour, que les Anciens ont tres bien depeint sous la figure d'un bel enfant. Il se plait dans les jeux enfantins; il est tendre, et delicat, incapable de nuire, charmé de Bagatelles; tous ses desseins se terminent en des plaisirs, mais ces plaisirs sont doux et Innocens. On a representé sous une figure bien different une autre passion trop grossiere pour nommer (mais dont le plus part d'hommes sont seulment capable) je veux dire, celui d'un Satyr, qui est plus bestial qu'humain; et on a exprimé dans cet Animal équivoque le vice et la Brutalité de cet Appetit sensuel, qui est cependant le vrai fondement de tous les beaux procedez de la belle Galanterie. Une passion qui tache de s'assouvir dans la perte de ce qu'elle trouve de plus aimable au monde, qui est fondé sur l'Injustice, soutenue par la tromperie, et suivie des crimes, de remors, de la honte, et du mepris: peut elle estre delicieuse pour un Cœur vertueux? Voila pourtant l'aimable equipage de tous les engagemens illegitimes. On se trouve obligé d'arracher de l'ame tous les sentimens de l'honneur inseparable d'un Education noble, et de vivre miserable dans la poursuitte éternelle de ce qu'on condamne, d'avoir tous ses plaisirs empoisoné de Remors, et d'estre reduit a cet état malheureux de renoncer a la vertu sans pouvoir se plaire dans le vice.[1]

On ne peut gouter les douceurs d'un amour parfait que dans un mariage bien assorti. Rien ne marque tant de petitesse dans l'Esprit que des s'arester aux paroles. Q'importe que la coûtume (pour

---

[1] Most of this sentence was copied by Montesquieu into his commonplace book (pp. 1373-4).

laquelle nous voions d'assez bonnes raissons) a donné un peu de ridicule a ces paroles, de Mari et femme? Un Mari signifie (dans l'interpretation generale) un Jaloux, brutal, grondeur, Tyran, ou bien un bon sot a qui on peut tout imposer; Une femme est un Demon domestique qu'on donne pour tromper ou pour tourmenter ce pauvre homme. La Conduitte de la plus part des Gens justifie assez ces deux Caracteres. Mais encore, qu'importe des paroles? Un Mariage bien reglé ne ressemble pas a ces mariages d'interest ou d'Ambition; ce sont deux Amans qui vivent ensemble. Qu'un Prestre dit de certains paroles, qu'un Notaire signe de certains papiers: je regarde ces preparatifs dans la mesme vûe qu'un Amant, l'echelle de Corde qu'il attache a la fenestre de sa Maitresse.[1] Pourveu qu'on vive ensemble qu'importe a quel prix et par quelles moïens?

Il est impossible qu'un Amour parfait et bien fondé soit heureux que dans la paisible possession de l'Objet aimé, et cet Paix n'oste rien de la douceur ni de la vivacité d'une Passion telle que je scai l'imaginer. Si je voulois m'occuper a faire des Romans, je ne voudrois pas placer les Images du vrai bonheur dans l'Arcadie, ni sur les bords de Lignon.[2] Je ne suis pas assez pre[c]ieuse pour borner la plus delicate tendresse a des Souhaits; je commencerois le Roman par le Mariage de deux personnes unie par l'Esprit, par le Gout, et par l'Inclination. Se peut-il donc rien de plus heureux que d'unir leurs Interests et leurs jours? L'Amant a le plaisir de donner la derniere marque d'Estime et de Confiance a sa Maitresse; et l'Amante lui donne en recompense le soin de son repos et de sa Liberté. Peut on se donner des gages plus chers ou plus tendres? et n'est il pas naturel de souhaitter de donner des preuves incontestable d'une tendresse dont l'Ame est penetrées?

Je scai qu'il y a des faux delicats qui soutiennent que les plaisirs de l'Amour ne sont deu qu'aux difficultez et aux dangers. Ils disent, fort spirituellement, que la rose ne seroit pas rose sans epines, et mille fadaisses de cette nature, qui font si peu d'Impression sur mon Esprit que je suis persuadée que si j'etois Amant, la crainte de nuire a celle que j'aimerois me rendroit Malheureux si sa possession même estoit accompagnée des dangers pour Elle. La vie des Amans

---

[1] This sentence is summarized and quoted in part by Montesquieu (p. 1374).

[2] The shores of the Lignon, a small river in the Loire district, the scene of *L'Astrée*, the seventeenth-century pastoral romance by Honoré d'Urfé. The 1763 translator of LM's essay substituted Hymen (p. 387 below).

mariés est bien differente; ils ont le plaisir de la passer dans une suitte d'Obligations mutuelle et des marques de bien veillance, et on a la joie de voir, qu'on fait le bonheur entier de l'Objet aimé, en quel point je place la Joüisance parfaitte.

Les plus petit soins de l'Œconomie deviennent nobles et delicats, quand ils sont relevez par des sentimens de tendresse. Meubler une chambre n'est pas meubler une chambre, c'est orner un leiu ou j'attens mon Amant; ordonner un Souper, n'est pas simplement donner des Ordres a mon Cuisinier, c'est m'amuser a regaler celui que j'aime. Ces occupations necessaires, regardez dans cette veüe par une amoureuse, sont des plaisirs mille fois plus plus vives et plus touchans que les Spectacles, et le jeu qui font le bonheur de cette foule incapable de la vraie Volupté.

Une passion heureuse et contente adoucit tous les mouvemens de l'ame, et d'ore tous les Objets qu'on voit. Un Amant content (j'entend marié a sa Maitresse) s'il exerce une Charge, les fatigues d'un Camp, l'embarras d'une Cour: tout lui devient agreable en se disant que c'est pour servir celle qu'il aime. Si la Fortune favorable (car cela n'est depend nullement du merite) fait reusir ses desseins, tous les avantages qu'elle lui donne sont des Offrandes qu'il mette aux pieds de sa Charmante Amie, il la remercie de l'Inspiration qu'il doit a ses charmes; et il trouve dans le succes de son Ambition un plaisir plus vif et plus digne d'un honnête homme que celui d'elever sa fortune, et d'etre applaudi du Public. Il ne joüit de la Gloire, du rang, et de la Richesse que par rapport a celle qu'il aime; et c'est son Amant qu'elle entend louer quand il s'attire l'approbation d'un Parliment, l'Applaudisment d'un Armée ou l'Agrement de son Prince. Dans le Malheur, c'est son Consolation de se retirer aupres d'une personne attendrie par ses disgraces, et de se dire, entre ses bras, 'Mon Bonheur ne depend pas du Caprice de la Fortune; ici j'ai un azyle asseuré contre les Chagrins; vostre Estime me rende insensible a l'injustice d'une Cour ou l'Ingratitude d'un Maitre; et j'ai un espece du Plaisir dans la perte de mon bien puisque cette Infortune me donne de nouvelles preuves de vostre vertu et de vostre tendresse. A quoi servent les Grandeurs a des personnes deja heureux?[1] Nous n'avons besoin ni des flatteurs ni des Equipages; je regne dans vostre Coeur, et je possede toutes les delices de la Nature dans vostre personne.'

Enfin il n'y a point de Situation dont la tristresse ne soit capable

---

[1] This sentence is quoted by Montesquieu (p. 1374).

d'estre diminuée par la Compagnie de l'Objet de son Amour. Une Maladie mesme n'est pas sans douceurs quand on a le plaisir d'estre soignée par celle qu'on aime. Je ne finira jamais si j'entreprenois de donner un detail de tous les Agreemens d'un Union ou l'on trouve, a la fois, tout ce qui peut satisfaire un Imagination tendre et delicat, et tout ce qui flatte les sens dans la Volupté la plus pure, et la plus étendue. Mais je ne sçaurois finir sans parler du plaisir de voir croistre tous les jours les aimables marques d'une tendre Amitie et s'occuper (selon leur differens sexes) de les perfectioner. On s'abandonne a cet doux instinct de la Nature, raffiné par l'Amour. On baisse dans une Fille la Beauté de sa Mere, et on respecte dans un Fils, l'Esprit et les apparences d'un probité naturel qu'on estime dans son Pere. C'est un Plaisir auquel Deiu mesme (a ce que dit Moïse)[1] estoit sensible quand voiant ce qu'il avoit fait, il la trouvoit bon.

A propos de Moïse, le premier plan du bonheur a infiniment surpassé tous les autres, et je ne sçaurois former d'Idée d'un Paradis, plus Paradis, que l'Etat ou estoit placé nos premiers Parens; cela n'a pas duré parce qu'ils ne connoissoient pas le Monde, et c'est par la mesme raison qu'on voit si peu des Mariages d'Inclination heureux. Eve estoit une sotte Enfant, et Adam un homme fort peu éclairée. Quand des Gens de cet espece se rencontrent ils ont beau estre amoureux; cela n'est peut pas durer. Ils se forment pendant la fureur de leur Amour, des Idées surnaturelles. Un Homme croit sa Maitresse une Ange parce qu'elle est belle, et une femme est enchanté du Merite de son Amant parce qu'il l'adore. Le premier changement de son teint lui oste son Adoration, et le Mari cessant d'estre Adorateur devienne Haïsable, a celle qui n'a pas eû d'autre fondement de son Amour. Ils se degoutent peu a peu, et a l'Exemple de nos premiers Parens ils ne manquent pas de rejetter l'un sur l'autre le crime de leur mutuelle Foiblesse. Apres le Froideur, le Mepris marche a grand pas et il sont prevenus qu'il faut se haïr puis qu'ils sont mariée. Leurs moindres defauts se grossissent a leur veue, et ils sont aveugle sur les Agremens qui pourroient leur toucher en toute autre personne. Un Commerce établi sur l'usage du sens ne peut pas avoir d'autre suitte.

Un Homme en epousant sa Maitresse doit oublier qu'elle lui paroist adorable, pour considerer que c'est une simple mortelle,

---

[1] Until the middle of the eighteenth century it was commonly believed that Moses was the author of the first five books of the Old Testament.

sujette aux Maladies, aux Caprices, et a la mauvaise humeur. Il doit preparer sa Constance a soûtenir la perte de sa Beauté, et amasser un fonds de Complaisance, qui est necessaire pour la Conversation continuelle de la personne du Monde la plus raisonable, et la moins inegale. La Dame, de son costé, ne doit pas attendre une suitte des Flatteries et d'obeissance; elle doit se disposer elle mesme a Obeïr agreablement, Science tres dificile, et par Consequence, d'un grand merite aupres d'un Homme capable de le sentir. Elle doit tacher de relever les Charmes d'une Maitresse par le bon sens et la solidité d'une Amie. Quand deux personnes, preoccupée par des Sentimens si raisonable, sont uni par des liens Éternels, La Nature entiere leur rit, et les Objets le plus communs leur deviennent charmans.

Il me semble que c'est une vie infiniment plus douce, plus elegante, et plus voluptueuse, que la Galanterie la plus heureuse et la mieux conduitte. Une femme capable de Refflexion ne peut regarder un Amant autrement qu'un Seducteur qui veut profiter de sa foiblesse pour se donner un plaisir d'un moment aux depens de sa gloire, de son repos, et peutestre de sa vie. Un voleur qui met le Pistolet a la Gorge pour enlever une bourse me paroist plus honnête, et moins coupable; et j'ai assez bonne Opinion de moi pour croire que si j'etois homme, je serois aussi capable de former le plan d'un assassinat que celui de corrompre une honnête femme, estimée dans le monde et heureuse dans son menage.[1] Serois-je capable d'empoisonner son Cœur en lui inspirant une passion funeste, a la quelle il faut immoler l'honneur, la Tranquillité et la vertu? Rendrois-je meprisable une personne parce qu'elle me paroist aimable? Doit-je recompenser sa tendresse en lui rendant sa Maison en horreur, ses Enfans indifferens, et son Mari detesté? Je croi que ces Refflexions me paroistront dans la mesme force, si mon Sexe m'avoit rendu excusable dans des pareils procedez, et j'espere que j'aurois été assez sensé pour ne pas croire le vice moins vicieux parce qu'il est a la mode.

J'estime beaucoup les mœurs Turcs (peuple ignorant, mais tres poli, a ma fantaisie). Un Galant convaincu d'avoir debauché une femme mariée est regardé parmi eux avec la mesme horreur qu'une Dame abandonnée chez nous. Il est seure de ne jamais faire Fortune,

---

[1] In her scorn of the immoral gallant LM echoes a passage in Montesquieu's *Lettres persanes*, 1721, Lettre XLVIII (ed. P. Vernière, 1960, pp. 103–4), as well as in a poem of her own (pp. 245–6 below).

et on auroit honte de donner un charge considerable a un homme soupsçonné d'avoir faitte un Injustice si énorme. Que dira-t'on dans cette Nation Morale si on voyoit quelques un de nos Anti-Chevaliers errans qui sont toujours en poursuitte des avantures pour mettre des Filles innocentes en détresse, et pour perdre d'honneur des femmes de Condition;[1] qui ne regardent la Beauté, la Jeunesse, le rang, et la vertu même que comme des Aiguillons pour exciter le desir de les ruiner, et qui mettent toute leur gloire a paroistre des Seducteurs habiles, oubliant qu'avec tout leurs soins ils ne peuvent jamais atteindre qu'au second rang de ce bel Escadron, les Diables ayant été depuis si longtemps en possession du Premier.

J'avoue que nos manieres barbares sont si bien calculées pour l'etablissement du vice et du malheur (qui en est inseparable) qu'il faut avoir des Têtes et des Cœur infiniment au dessus du commun, pour pouvoir joüir de la felicité d'un mariage tel que je viens de le peindre. La Nature est si foible et si portée au changement qu'il est dificile de soutenir la Constance la mieux fondées parmi toutes les disipations que nos Coûtumes ridicules ont rendue inévitable. Un Mari amoureux a peine a voir prendre a sa femme toutes les Libertez du bel usage; il paroist y avoir de la dureté a les refuser, et il se trouve reduit pour se conformer aux mannieres poli de l'Europe, de voir tous les jours ses mains en proye a qui les veut prendre, de l'entendre partager a toute la terre les charmes de son Esprit, la voir montrer sa Gorge en plein midi, se parer pour des bals et pour des Spectacles, s'attirer des Adorateurs, et écouter les fades flatteries de mille et mille sots. Peut-on soûtenir son estime pour une Creature si publique? et ne perd-elle pas (au moins) beaucoup de son prix?

Je reviens toujours a mes mannieres Orientale, ou les plus belles femmes se content de limiter le pouvoir de leurs Charmes a celui à qui il est permis d'en joüir; elles ont trop d'humanité pour souhaitter de faire des miserables, et elles sont trop sinceres pour ne pas avouer qu'elles se croient capable d'exciter des Passions. Je me souviens d'une Conversation que j'ai eû avec une Dame de grande Qualité a Constantinople, la plus aimable Femme que j'ai connu de ma vie, et pour qui j'ai eû ensuitte un tendre Amitié. Elle m'avoua naïvement qu'elle estoit contente de son Mari. 'Que vous etes Liber-

[1] LM expressed this idea more succinctly when she met Joseph Spence in Rome in 1741: 'Sure there cannot be a more detestable set of creatures upon earth than those anti-knight-errants who run about only to ruin as many ladies as they can' (Spence, *Anecdotes*, ed. J. M. Osborn, 1966, 1. 309). She also expressed her detestation of gallantry in letters (e.g. *Letters*, 3. 2) and poems.

tines,' me disoit elle 'vous autres Dames Chrestiennes! Il vous est permis de recevoir les visites d'autant d'hommes que vous voulez, et vos Loix vous permettent, sans bornes, l'usage de l'Amour et du vin.' Je l'assura qu'elle estoit fort mal instruitte, qu'il estoit vrai que nous recevions des visites, mais ces visites estoient plein du respect et de retenu, et que c'estoit un Crime d'entendre parler d'Amour ou d'aimer un Autre que son Mari. 'Vos Maris sont bien bon,' me repliqua-t-elle en riant, 'de se contenter d'une fidelité si borné. Vos yeux, vos mains, vostre Conversation est pour le Publique, et que pretendez vous reserver pour eux? Pardonnez moi ma belle Sultane,' ajouta-t-elle en m'embrassant, 'j'ai toute l'Inclination possible de croire tout ce que vous me dittes, mais vous voulez m'imposer des Impossibillitez. Je sçai les Saletez des Infidelles. Je vois que vous en avez honte, et je ne vous en parlerois plus.'[1]

J'ai trouvé tant de bon sens et de vrai semblance en tout ce qu'elle me disoit que j'avois peine a la contredire; et j'avoua d'abord qu'elle avoit raison de preferer les mœurs Musulman a nos coûtumes ridicule, qui sont une confusion surprenante des Maximes severe du Christianisme avec tout le Libertinage des Lacedemoniens. Et nonobstant nos folles mannieres, je suis du sentiment qu'une femme determinée de faire son bonheur de l'amour de son Mari doit abandonner le desir extravagant de se faire adorer du Public, et qu'un mari qui aime tendrement sa femme doit se priver de la Reputation d'etre galant a la Cour. Vous voyez que je suppose deux personnes bien extrodinaire; il n'est pas donc fort surprenant qu'une telle union soit rare dans les Païs ou il est necessaire de mepriser les Coûtumes le plus établie pour estre heureux.[2]

[1] In her conversation with Spence LM quoted the Turkish lady as saying, 'O my sultana, you can never defend the manners of your country, even with all your wit! But I see you are in pain for them, and shall therefore press it no farther' (Spence, i. 311).

[2] When LM met Joseph Spence in Rome (in 1741) she allowed him to read this 'paper written by her Ladyship on a very odd subject'; she also dazzled him with two paradoxical maxims on marriage (*Letters from the Grand Tour*, ed. S. Klima, 1975, pp. 361–2). In composing his anecdotes Spence apparently misremembered this essay on Rochefoucault as a 'little treatise in prose' based on the two paradoxical maxims (*Anecdotes*, ed. J. M. Osborn, 1966, i. 312). Hence my attribution to LM of an anonymous 'Essay on Marriage' printed by Curll in 1726 (*Life*, pp. 121–2) must be rejected.

[Letter to Anna Maria van Schurman]

Lady Mary composed this spirited feminist essay in the form of a letter while living in Avignon (1742–6). The Latin quotation on this page links it to the Dutch scholar and autobiographer Anna Maria van Schurman (1607–78): her version of her 'thesis' to be proved by logical demonstration is 'Num Foeminae Christianae conveniat studium Litterarum?' (*Dissertatio, De Ingenii muliebris . . .*, 1641, p. 9). Perhaps after she settled in Brescia in 1746, LM amused herself with writing, among other pieces, a cycle of pseudo-historical tales about the court of Louis XIV. She dedicated this English manuscript to a different 'Mademoiselle' with a brief introductory letter (H MS. 257; quoted in Halsband, *LM*, p. 253). Translation on pp. 392–3.

Text H MS. 81. 262–3.

V OUS me faittes bien de l'honneur (Mademoiselle) de penser a moi, dans un situation aussi heureuse que la vostre, et parmi des Illustres qui doivent vous donner beaucoup de mepris pour nous autres miserables vivants. Je voye bien que vous avez profitée infiniment de leur commerce, vostre style étant fort embelli, depuis vostre sejour aux champs élisées. Vos ouvrages terrestes, quoyque tres sçavants, n'approchent pas de la beauté de la Lettre dont vous m'avez honorée. La Pedanterie de vostre Siecle, dont vous etiez peu infectee, a fait place a la Legereté françoise, et a une Badinerie agreable que vous avez pris (peutestre) dans la conversation de Petrone.[1] Je vous felicite de tout mon Cœur de ces nouveaux agrements, que j'estime au dessus de la possession de cent Langues differentes. Je voudrois en troquer six que je possede[2] contre une seule ode d'Horace ou de Rousseau.[3] Je vous croies a pressent assez degagée des Prejuges pour souffrir mesme la Critique de vos œuvres sans impatience, et vous me permettrez de dire librement que vos raisons pour prouver vostre These

'Feminæ christianæ convenit studium Litterarum'[4]

---

[1] Petronius Arbiter (d. A.D. 65), Roman writer, most famous for his *Satyricon*.
[2] Besides English, the languages that LM knew (in varying degrees of competence) were French, Italian, Latin, Spanish, German, and Turkish.
[3] Jean-Baptiste Rousseau (1671–1741), with whom LM had corresponded (*Letters*, 2. 59–60, 67–8).
[4] 'The study of literature is suitable for a Christian woman.'

me semblent quelque fois assez foibles, et toujours debitées d'une façon seche et scholastique. Il est vrai que vous pourriez vous excuser de vous estre servie de les termes de Pedant par la mesme raison que vous avez portée un fraise; c'etoit la mode de vostre Temps d'avoir l'esprit et le Corps guindé, et il faut respecter, mesme se conformer, a la sottise Publique. Ce siecle nous aprende a regarder toutes choses dans une vûe Politique, et c'est par la que je pretendrois prouver que la Science est tres necessaire aux Femmes. Il est sûr que pour peu qu'on sache, on commence á douter, et que la Doute inspire naturellement la Modestie, vertu qui a toujours été recommandée au sexe et dont il ne se pare guere, depuis qu'on l'eleve dans une ignorance si crasse qu'il lui suffit de marmoter des Pâtes nôtres [*sic*], pour se croire inspiré du Ciel, et par consequent digne de tout regler chez elles, de mepriser leur Maris, et de maltraitter leur Domestiques. J'ose avancer hardiment que la Conduitte de la plûspart des Femmes fait plus de mal que du bien. Elles deviennent insensiblement des animaux plus nuisibles qu'utiles. J'attribue cette depravation a la mauvaise education qui éttouffe l'esprit naturel des unes, et augmente la folie des autres. Si les Hommes vouloient seulment nous regarder comme un parti dans l'etat (car je me soumets a l'inferiorité quoyque je pû dire mille qui a écrit comme vous sçavez, pour prouver l'egalite des sexes)[1] ils doivent tacher de mettre a profit tous les Talents. Nôtre delicatesse ne nous permet pas de servir a la Guerre, mais cette mesme delicatesse nous fournit un grand loisir pour l'étude. Celles qui reüssiront pourront ajouter a la Republique des Lettres, et celles qui ne reussiront pas éviteront au moins l'oisiveté avec toute sa suitte. On ne sera pas obligé de faire un provision de Fadaisses avant d'oser parler dans les Conversations du Bel air, ou on brille a l'heure qu'il est, uniquement par la Science de la Toilette ou du tapis verd. Vous ⟨?⟩ assez justement d'avoir donné dans ces ⟨?⟩ qui font la honte de l'humanité.[2]

Plaignez moi, Mademoiselle, il n'y a point ici d'academie de cavaliers ou de dames. Je n'ai pas de relais des yeux; quand ils sont fatiguez je suis forcée d'écouter et de parler des pertes et des Gains, qui sont les seuls sujets interessants pour l'Avignon moderne. Si j'avois l'honneur d'avoir une compagnie comme la vostre je renon-

---

[1] *De l'égalité des deux sexes*, 1673, is a work by François Poullain de La Barre, which LM had in her library in 1739 (Wh MS 135, f. 12).

[2] When writing to her daughter (in 1753) LM repeated several of her ideas from this essay (*Letters*, 3. 40).

cerois avec plaisir a tous mes barbares, et m'apliquerois a cultiver la bonté que vous m'avez temoigné avec toute la reconnoisance et respect que vous meritez de la part

de

Mlle

etc.

Je suis si charmée de vostre cotterie[1] que si vous me donnez parole de m'y admettre immediatement j'irai me jetter dans le Rhône pour vous trouver, moitie par desire de vous voir, et moitie d'ennuy de tous ceux que je vois.

[1] Schurman belonged to a religious community, and wrote to an English female friend of her desire to live together for the sake of study and affection.

POEMS

INTRODUCTION

THROUGHOUT her life Lady Mary liked to refer to herself as a poet, often with a touch of irony or self-deprecation. At fifteen or so she confessed to the folly of having 'trespass'd wickedly in Rhime', her confession taking the form of an eight-line poem. At sixty-nine she described herself as 'haunted . . . by the Dæmon of Poesie'.[1]

Her contemporaries took her verse seriously. John Sheffield, Duke of Buckingham, referred to her fame in a 'sessions of the poets' piece.[2] Many of the voices raised to honour her are suspect—seekers for her patronage or protesters against Pope's satire. Admirers who carry more weight included the young Pope himself, who longed to read her 'Sonnets'; Lord Hervey, who got her verses by heart; Horace Walpole, who found them at first 'too womanish' but later 'excessively good'; the distinguished foreigners Antonio Conti, who translated them into Italian, and Voltaire and Algarotti, who quoted them; and perhaps most surprising of all, Lord Auchinleck, father of James Boswell.[3] Late in this chorus of praise, resisting the new definitions of poetry to which he had himself contributed, came Byron, demanding of the fourth stanza of 'The Lover', 'Is not her *"Champaigne and Chicken"* worth a forest or two? Is it not poetry?'[4] The nineteenth century in general (Wordsworth, Leigh Hunt, Walter Bagehot) thought it was not. George Saintsbury ruled out poetry, the true diamond, when he wrote that her 'verse flashes with the very best paste in Dodsley'.[5]

Yet today Lady Mary's poems need no apology. She herself would not have claimed diamond quality for them, though she did claim to have inscribed eleven lines on a window pane with a diamond. This rather unlikely verve and facility, this small scale, was what she aimed at in poetry. She had the habit of dashing off verse extempore. Her poems demonstrate the continuing vitality of the Augustan

[1] H MS. 250. 5; *Letters*, 3. 183.
[2] Buckingham, *Works*, 1723, I. 199.
[3] Pope, *Corr*. I. 494; Hervey MS., Bury St. Edmunds, 47/2, p. 14; Walpole, *Corr*. 13. 234; 19. 450; H MS. 81. 256–61; Voltaire, *Corr*., ed. T. Besterman, 1953–64, 5. 67; Algarotti, *Opere*, Leghorn, 1764–5, 8. 134; *Boswell in Holland 1763–1764*, ed. F. A. Pottle, 1952, p. 214.
[4] *Letters and Journals*, ed. R. E. Prothero, 1898–1901, 5. 566.
[5] *The Peace of the Augustans*, 1916, p. 215.

tradition within which she wrote, its power to shape the voice and even the thinking of a minor talent. The tradition supplied her not only with forms but with satirical or moral stances based on inheritance from or reaction against the past. She had the gift of successfully embodying her idiosyncratic opinions and attitudes in a verse style heavily influenced by her contemporaries and immediate predecessors, especially Dryden and the Pope of the 1717 *Works*.

Packed with allusion, echoes, parody, her verse is none the less distinctively her own. Its range is remarkable: Ovidian and Horatian epistles, mock-eclogue, mock-epic, songs and ballads, description, meditation, and translation. Despite her reference to the daemon of poesie, most of her poems owe their existence to the provocation of some outside stimulus, some love-affair, political issue, or debating point to be made.

As a woman and an aristocrat, Lady Mary frequently expressed horror at the idea of writing for print. Yet she may well have connived at or even arranged for the publication of her verse attacks on Pope and Swift. Perhaps for reasons of prudence, she copied neither of these printed poems into the album, now Harrowby MS. 256, which bore her claim, 'all the verses and Prose in this Book were wrote by me, without the assistance of one Line from any other. Mary Wortley Montagu.' This volume contains most of her more successful poems, but with some notable omissions. Others she kept in rough draft, in separate copies, or not at all. Individual poems strayed into print in her lifetime, beginning with the three eclogues stolen and printed anonymously by Curll in 1716.[1] The first collection was published by Horace Walpole in 1747, with her initials on the title-page. He and Joseph Spence had both read her poems, probably in what is now H MS. 256, in Italy; Spence had many of them copied into a volume which he corrected himself.[2] The number of pieces in print as hers was enlarged by the *London Magazine* and by Dodsley's *Collection*, 1748. Dodsley's second edition, published later that year, transferred Lady Mary's poems from volume three to volume one; later editions added a few more poems. Isaac Reed gathered most of what was available from these sources in a volume of *Poetical Works*, 1768; James Dallaway enlarged the canon in the last volume of his edition of Lady Mary's *Works*, 1803.

[1] *Court Poems*: 'Monday', 'Thursday', and 'Friday'. See p. 182 below.
[2] Rare Book Department, Cornell University Library, Ithaca, N.Y.: MS. E 6004.

Despite her family's permission to use her papers he reproduced existing inaccurate printed texts, and when printing from MS. adapted freely. Later editors of her works added only a few poems and corrected none. Nor did they explain the grounds on which they accepted or rejected attributions to her.

The present collection is as far as possible and within certain definable limits complete. She wrote other poems of which no copies survive, as comments by her contemporaries indicate. She also adapted other people's work. I have printed such poems as 'A Satyr', modelled on Boileau but substantially an original piece, while omitting some in which Lady Mary made only the most minimal alterations to her source. These include poems previously printed among her works, like 'The Bride in the Country' (which she adapted from another satirical ballad to apply to the marriage of her niece), 'A Character' (adapted from verse by Robert Wolseley and William Wharton), and 'To the Same' ('Thô old in ill, the Traitor sure shall find', which she condensed from Creech's translation of Juvenal). An imitation of Dorset's famous ballad, beginning 'To all you ladies now at Bath' and entitled 'Farewell to Bath', appeared in the *Gentleman's Magazine* in 1731 as by 'Lady M. Montagu', and has been anthologized as Lady Mary's. I have omitted it since even if the ascription is accurate, Lady Mary's name was extremely unlikely to be formulated this way except on the Continent. The designation fits at least two other ladies, daughters of Charles Montagu, Earl of Halifax, and the 2nd Duke of Montagu.

I have omitted the poems from Lady Mary's two juvenile albums, composed at the age of fourteen or a little older. These are interesting as late re-workings of various seventeenth-century conventions, but have too little relation to her other work and too great length to justify inclusion.[1] I have omitted fragments and insignificant separate couplets, except those already printed. Passages of verse available among her *Complete Letters* (mainly epistles to Hervey and fragments to Algarotti) are likewise not included here. I have, however, reprinted her poetic rendering 'Turkish Verses', and her epitaph on the lovers struck by lightning, which readers may expect to find among her poems.

The problem of attribution is a tricky one. I have printed, with brief comment, poems in which other writers besides Lady Mary shared, like the 'Friday' eclogue, *Dunciad* imitations, and the *Verses*

[1] I have described them in an article in *The Yearbook of English Studies*, 7, 1977.

to the Imitator of Horace. There can be little doubt about the poems from H MS. 256, and these are all included here. A few poems in another album (H MS. 255) are marked with her monogram MWM; yet two of these come under the category of adaptations made by the substitution of only a word here and there. Of these one seemed worth inclusion, the other not. The same volume yields a few unmarked poems which seem to be by Lady Mary.[1]

She transcribed many poems without giving any author's name, and she also saved copies made by other people. Some of these poems may be by her, but without further evidence I have supposed that they are not. Sometimes heavy correction in her hand supplies evidence of authorship. I have accepted some but not all of the attributions of those with fairly close knowledge of her: Horace Walpole, Sir James Caldwell, and Lady Oxford and her daughter the Duchess of Portland. This volume therefore contains only poems which are almost certainly by Lady Mary, without the many which *may* be by her, or which have been wrongly attributed to her.

For copy-text (identified in the headnote to each poem) I have used H MS. 256 wherever possible, as representing the form which Lady Mary wished to preserve. For poems not in this album I have chosen MSS. in her hand where they exist, and wherever I have used a MS. in another hand I have said so. I have reproduced MS. spelling and (except at the beginnings of lines and occasionally in titles) capitalization, but I have to some extent modified Lady Mary's use of punctuation and apostrophes. Ampersands and contractions are expanded. I have silently corrected obvious slips of the pen (such as an omitted word present in another copy, *be* for *by*, etc.), and have in similar circumstances made emendations to printed texts. [ ] indicates editorial emendations or insertions, ⟨ ⟩ indicates doubtful readings.

Variants from printed texts (none of which has any authority) are ignored; so are minor or irrelevant MS. variants. On the whole the textual notes are concerned with interesting revisions or substantial deletions.

As far as possible I have arranged the poems in order of composition, since so many are linked to particular events. Where no exact date is known, the piece appears under the latest date at which it is likely to have been written. The headnote gives a brief statement of this evidence, together with the date the copy-text was made, if

[1] Page-numbers for this volume are editorial.

this is significantly different. Some poems written in Lady Mary's youth were not transcribed until many years later, as is shown by their position in the albums. I have also given the date of first printing, where it exists; but I have not listed re-printings or other MS. copies, which are in some cases numerous.

I should like to express my gratitude first of all to my co-editor, who introduced me to Lady Mary. Other scholars also have been generous with consultation and advice; they are too many to name, but I have relied particularly on the encyclopedic knowledge of David Foxon of Wadham College, Oxford. I have met with much kindness from owners of manuscripts, pre-eminently the Earl of Harrowby, and with patient help from the staff at the Bodleian and many other libraries. I am grateful, more than I can say, to them, to my relations, friends, and colleagues, and to my sister Janet Orr, who did the typing.

I. M. G.

London,
June 1975

Julia to Ovid

Wrote at 12 Years of Age in Imitation of Ovid's Epistles

Text H MS. 256. 57–8, copied after 1755, probably much revised; *written* 1701–2; *printed* 1803. This and the following poem are fairly representative of Lady Mary's adolescent verse, of which two albums in her hand survive as H MSS. 250 and 251. Other poets had already treated the love of the poet and the emperor's daughter.

Are Love and Power incapable to meet,
And must they all be wretched who are great?
Enslav'd by Titles, and by Forms confin'd,
For wretched Victims to the State design'd.
   What Rural Maid that my sad Fortune knows   5
Would quit her cottage to embrace my Woes?
Would be this cursed Sacrifice to Power,
This wretched Daughter of Rome's Emperour?
   When sick with Sighs to absent Ovid given,
I tire with Vows the unrelenting Heaven,   10
Drown'd in my Tears, and with my Sorrows pale,
What then do all my kindred Gods avail?
   Let proud Augustus place his joys in Power,
I have no Happiness but being Yours:
With nobler Pride I can on Thrones look down,   15
Can court your Love, and can despise a Crown.
   Oh Love, thou Pleasure never dearly bought,
Whose Joys exceed the very Lover's thought!
Of that soft Passion when you teach the Art
In gentle Sounds it steals into the Heart,   20
With such sweet Magick does the Soul surprize
'Tis only taught us better by your Eyes.
   Oh Ovid, first of the inspired Train!
Speak but to Heaven in that inchanting Strain,
So sweet a Voice can never plead in Vain;   25
Apollo will protect his favourite Son

12 Augustus claimed descent from Venus; his great-uncle Caesar, himself, and other relations were deified.
19–20 Referring to Ovid's *Ars Amatoria.*

And all the little Loves unto thy Succour run.
The Loves and Muses in thy Praier shall joyn
And all their wishes, and their Vows be thine,
Some God will soften my Hard Father's Breast   30
And work a Miracle to make thee blest.

. . . . .

Hard as this is, I even this could bear,
But greater ills than what I feel, I fear.
My Fame, my Ovid, both for ever fled;
What greater Evil is there left to dread?   35
Yes; there is one—
(Avert it Gods, who do my Sorrows see;
Avert it thou, who art a God to me!)
When back to Rome your wishing Eyes are cast
And on the lessening Towers gaze your last,   40
When Fancy shall recall into your view
The Pleasures now for ever lost to you,
The Shineing Court, and all the Thousand Waies
To melt the Nights, and pass the happy Days,
Will you not sigh and hate the wretched Maid,   45
Whose fatal Love your safety has betraid?
Say that from me your Banishment does come
And Curse the Eyes that have expell'd you Rome?
Those Eyes which now are weeping for your Woes
The Sleep of Death shall then for ever close.   50

After 31 *LM wrote* some lines lost

27 Referring to Ovid's *Amores.*

Written at 14 Years of Age
Irregular Verses
To Truth

Text H MS. 256. 55 (variants from a tattered copy in Lady Mary's early hand, H MS. 81. 62–3), copied after 1736; *written* 1703–4; *printed* 1803.

Where Lovely Goddess dost thou dwell,
   In what remote and silent Shade?
Within what Cave or lonely Cell,
   With what old Hermit, or unpractis'd Maid?
In vain I've sought thee all around;   5
   But thy unfashionable Sound
   In Crouds was never heard,
Nor ever has thy form in Court or Town appear'd.

The Sanctuary is not safe for thee,
   Chas'd thence by endless Mystery;   10
Thy own Proffessors chase thee thence
And wage eternal War, with thee, and sence,
Then in perplexing comments lost
Even when they would be thought to shew thee most.

   Most Beautiful when most distress'd,   15
   Descend my Goddess to my Breast,
     There thou maist reign, unrivall'd and alone,
My thoughts thy Subjects, and my Heart thy Throne.

After 14 another stanza follows in H MS. 81:

> Even in this tempestuous Age
>   Now Discord and the Furys reign
> And with unintermitting rage
>   Eternal Strife and war maintain,
> In this alone we all agree,
> In hateing and commending Thee;
> No Faction yet was ever known
> Thy long neglected sway to own.

After 16 another couplet follows in H MS. 81:

> On safety there you may depend,
> My Guide, my Goddesse, and my Freind,

Song

Text H MS. 256. 57, copied after 1755; *written* probably before 1713; *printed* 1803.

> How happy is the Harden'd Heart
>   Where Interest is the only view,
> Can sigh and meet, or smile and part,
>   Nor pleas'd nor greiv'd, nor false; nor True.
> Yet have they truly peace of mind?   5
>   Or do they ever truly know
> The bliss sincerer tempers find
>   Which Truth and Virtue can bestow?

Written ex tempore in Company in a Glass Window the first year I was marry'd

Text H MS. 256. 55, copied after 1736; *written* 1712–13; *printed* (inaccurately) as 'The Lady's Resolve' in Aaron Hill's *Plain Dealer*, 27 Apr. 1724, and often reprinted. One reply was published with it by Hill; another, variously ascribed to Pope and to Sir William Yonge, accompanies it in some copies.

> While Thirst of Power, and desire of Fame,
> In every Age is every Woman's Aim;
> Of Beauty Vain, of silly Toasters proud,
> Fond of a Train, and happy in a Croud,
> On every Fop bestowing a kind Glance,   5
> Each Conquest owing to some loose Advance,
> Affect to Fly, in hopes to be persu'd,
> And think they're Virtuous, if not grossly Lewd:
> Let this sure Maxim be my Virtue's Guide,   ⎫
> In part to blame she is, who has been try'd; ⎬   10
> Too near he has approach'd, who is deny'd.   ⎭

7 Cf. Dryden's *Don Sebastian*, 1689, IV. i: 'And look'd behind in hopes to be pursu'd' (*Works*, 6. 90).

Epilogue
To the Tragedy of Cato

Text 1803, 5. 145–6; *written* spring–summer 1713; never used, though Addison acted on some of the hints which Lady Mary gave in her critique of his play (see pp. 62–68 above). The epilogue spoken was by Samuel Garth.

You see in ancient Rome what folly reign'd;
A folly British men would have disdain'd.
Here's none so weak to pity Cato's case,
Who might have liv'd, and had a handsome place;
But rashly vain, and insolently great,   5
He perish'd by his fault and not his fate.
Thank Heav'n! our patriots better ends pursue,
With something more than glory in their view.
Poets write morals—priests for martyrs preach—
Neither such fools to practise what they teach.   10
   Tho' your dear country much you wish to serve,
For bonny Britons 'tis too hard to starve;
Or what's all one, to any generous mind,
From girls, Champagne, and gaming, be confin'd;
Portius might well obey his sire's command,   15
Returning to his small paternal land;
A low estate was ample to support
His private life, far distant from the court;
Far from the crowd of emulating beaux,
Where Martia never wanted birth-day clothes.   20
   For you, who live in these more polish'd days,
To spend your money, lo! ten thousand ways;
Dice may run ill, or duns demand their due,
And ways to get (God knows) are very few;
In times so differing, who shall harshly blame   25
Our modern heroes, not to act the same.

4 News that Cato is wanted to lead the Spanish army comes in the last scene, just before his suicide is discovered.

5 Cf. Pope's prologue, which calls Caesar 'Ignobly vain and impotently great' (*Poems*, 6. 98).

Text   MS. draft inside back cover of first volume of J. B. Rousseau's *Œuvres*,
Rotterdam, 1712, now at Sandon Hall. *Written* probably in 1715, freely adapted
from Catullus's fifth epigram.

Let us live my Lesbia and Love,
When Dear desires our bosoms move
And their Quick Zest to pleasures give
Tis then we may be said to live.

2

Kiss me soft my Lovely Love,   5
Soft and melting as the Dove,
Fondly eager, kind, and sweet,
Thus our mixing Souls may meet,
Let thy gentle
The short transporting Joy prolong.   10

3

Do not yet thy lips remove,
Kiss me on, my charming Love.
I dye with every pointed kiss,
Oh let me dye in such a bliss,
Renew again the Amorous play   15
And kiss my ravish'd Soul away.

9 *line unfinished.*

ECLOGUES

Lady Mary's six town eclogues, which she herself called simply 'Eclogues', are the product of her friendship with Pope and Gay, which began when both these poets had been experimenting with 'mock' forms for several years. Three of Lady Mary's eclogues were printed illicitly by Curll in 1716, all six by Horace Walpole in 1747. 'Thursday' was widely attributed to Pope, but his beautiful transcript shows clearly that he believed this poem to be hers (New York Public Library, Arents Collection: ed. R. Halsband, 1976). Pope was among those who thought 'Friday' to be 'almost wholly Gay's' (Spence, *Anecdotes*, ed. J. M. Osborn, 1966, 1. 104); but Gay's version of it, printed among his *Poems on Several Occasions*, 1720, really amounts to a different poem. Walpole judged that 'all six are by the same hand' (note in his copy of 1748: B.M. C. 117.aa.16). The eclogues are given here in their final order, which is not that of composition.

Except where otherwise specified, identifications of people in the eclogues come from Walpole's notes, generally supported by those made by Joseph Spence in his scribal transcript from Lady Mary's album (Cornell University MS. E 6004; see p. 172 above) and by a contemporary annotator of the 1747 edition (Huntington Library).

Monday

Roxana

Or the Drawing-room

Text H MS. 256. 23–5, copied after 1730; *written* Feb.–Dec. 1715; *printed* in part in 1716, in full in 1747.

Lord Oxford's copy of 'Monday' gives the date '1714/15' (B.M. Lansdowne MS. 852. 184–5); Spence's dates it 'On the coming over of the Hanover family: soon after which the others were wrote'. Lady Mary finished it before falling ill with smallpox (Halsband, *PMLA*, 68, 1953, p. 244, where the story is told in more detail).

Roxana was Mary Ker (1677–1718), Duchess of Roxburghe, a Tory as well as a prude.

> Roxana from the Court returning late
> Sigh'd her soft sorrows at St James's Gate;
> Such heavy thoughts lay brooding in her Breast
> Not her own Chairmen with more weight oppress'd;

1 Here Pope's note quoted the opening of Virgil's eclogue ii (NYPL MS.).
3–4 This couplet echoes Pope's *Iliad*, x. 3–4, and *The Rape of the Lock*, ii. 53–4 and iv. 1–2, thus calling up a whole complex of classical echoes.

They groan the cruel load they're doom'd to bear, 5
She, in these gentler Sounds, express'd her Care.
   Was it for this, that I these Roses wear,
For this, new set my Jewells for my Hair?
Ah Princesse, with what Zeal have I persu'd!
Almost forgot the Dutys of a Prude, 10
Thinking I never could attend too soon,
I've miss'd my Prayers to get dress'd by noon.
For thee, Ah what for Thee did I resign!
My Pleasures, Passions, all that e're was mine.
I sacrificed both modesty and ease, 15
Left Operas, and run to filthy Plays;
Double Entendres shock'd my tender Ear,
Yet even this for thee I chose to bear.
In glowing Youth when Nature bids, be Gay,
And ev'ry Joy of Life before me lay, 20
By Honor prompted, and by Pride restrain'd,
The Pleasures of the Young my Soul disdain'd,
Sermons I sought, and with a mein severe
Censured my Neighbours, and said daily Pray'r.
Alas how chang'd! With the same sermon meen 25
That once I pray'd, the What d'ee callt I've seen.
Ah cruel Princesse! for thy sake I've lost
That Reputation which so dear had cost.
I, who avoided every Public place
When Bloom, and Beauty bid me shew my Face, 30
Now near thee constant ev'ry Night abide
With never failing Duty by thy side:
My selfe and Daughters standing on a row
To all the foreigners a goodly Show!

7–8 Cf. *The Rape of the Lock*, iv. 97–100, and Gay's town eclogue 'Araminta', 1714 (line 33: *Poetry and Prose*, ed. V. A. Dearing and C. E. Beckwith, 1974, 1. 84).

9 Caroline, Princess of Wales: see p. 27 above.

16 In Feb. 1715 Lady Cowper recorded the Duchess's moral disapproval of a play which the Princess enjoyed (*Diary 1714–20*, ed. S. Cowper, 2nd ed., 1865, p. 46).

24 'She does not care what she says of Anybody to wreak her Malice or Revenge' (Lady Cowper, *Diary*, p. 78).

25 Cf. *Aeneid*, ii. 247, and *Paradise Lost*, i. 84.

26 '*The Name of a Farce, which some Prudes Scrupled to go to, on the score of the Title*' (Pope's note)—which was supposed to allude to Gay's classification of his play as a 'Tragi-Comi-Pastoral Farce'. The Prince and Princess of Wales saw it in Feb. 1715.

33 The Duchess had three daughters by her first husband.

Oft had your drawing room been sadly thin   35
And Merchants' Wives close by the Chair had been,
Had not I amply fill'd the empty Space
And sav'd your Highness from the dire Disgrace.
Yet Coquettilla's Artifice prevails
When all my Merit and my Duty fails,   40
That Coquettilla, whose deluding airs
Corrupts our Virgins, and our Youth ensnares:
So sunk her Character, so lost her Fame,
Scarce visited before your Highness came,
Yet for the Bed chamber, 'tis her you chuse,   45
When Zeal, and fame, and virtue you refuse.
Ah worthy Choice! not one of all your Train
Whom Censure blasts not, or Dishonors stain.
Let the Nice Hind now suckle dirty Pigs
And the Proud Peahen hatch the Cuckow's Eggs,   50
Let Iris leave her Paint, and own her Age,
And Grave Suffolkia wed a giddy Page,
A great[er] Miracle is daily veiw'd,
A vertuous Princesse with a Court so lewd.
I know thee, Court! with all thy treacherous wiles,   55
Thy false Carreses and undoing smiles!
Ah Princesse! learn'd in all the courtly Arts,
To cheat our Hopes, and yet to gain our Hearts!
    Large lovely Bribes are the great Statesman's Aim
And the neglected Patriot follows Fame,   60

49–54 *omitted 1716 and early MS. copies.*
59–66 *omitted 1716 and early MS. copies.*

---

39 *Coquettilla.* Adelaide Paleotti, Duchess of Shrewsbury, was Lady of the Bed-chamber to the Princess of Wales from Oct. 1714 till her death in 1726. 'She had a wonderful Art at entertaining and diverting People, though she would sometimes exceed the Bounds of Decency.... she was the most cunning, designing Woman alive, obliging to People in Prosperity, and a great Party-woman' (Lady Cowper, *Diary*, pp. 8–9).
47 Here Pope quoted Virgil's eclogue viii. 32.
49 Here Pope quoted Virgil's eclogue viii. 27 and 52, which Gay had copied in his 'Wednesday', line 59.
52 There were two elderly Lady Suffolks, widows of the 3rd and 5th Earls.
55 Here Pope quoted Virgil's eclogue viii. 43, which he had echoed in 'Autumn', line 89, and Gay in his 'Wednesday', line 89. A fragment which LM wrote inside a volume of Rousseau's *Œuvres* (cf. previous poem) begins with almost the same couplet.
59 Here Pope quoted Virgil's eclogue ii. 63, 65.

The Prince is *ogle'd*, some the King persue,
But your Roxana only follows you.
    Despis'd Roxana, cease, and try to find
Some other, since the Princesse proves unkind,
Perhaps it is not hard to find at Court,   65
Thô not a greater, a more firm support.

61 This helped to make the poem politically suspect, for the breach between George I
and his son was not yet open.
61-2 Cf. Pope's 'Summer', line 70.
63 Here Pope quoted Virgil's eclogue ii. 69, 73.

Tuesday

St James's Coffee-house
Silliander and Patch

Text H MS. 256. 25-6, copied after 1730; *written* Jan.–July 1716; *printed*
1747.
    Silliander was John Campbell (*c.* 1693–1770), Duke of Argyll 1761. Patch was
Algernon Seymour (1684–1750), styled Earl of Hertford until he became Duke
of Somerset, 1748.

Thou who so many Favours hast receiv'd,
Wondrous to tell and hard to be beleiv'd,
Oh H——d, to my Lays Attention lend,
Hear how two Lovers boastingly contend,
Like thee successfull, such their bloomy Youth,   5
Renown'd alike for Gallantry and Truth.
    St James's bell had toll'd some wretches in,
As tatter'd Riding hoods alone could sin,
The happier Sinners now their Charms recruit
And to their Manteaus their Complexions suit.   10
    The Opera Queens had finish'd halfe their Faces
And City Dames allready taken Places,

After 8 *an extra couplet in Pope's transcript:*
            Nice Ladies loath with such a Crowd to mix,
            For none but ragged Matrons pray at Six.

3 Probably Charles Howard (d. 1765), younger son of the 3rd Earl of Carlisle, with
whose family LM was intimate.
11 ff. The curtain usually rose at 6 p.m.

Fops of all kinds to see the Lion run,
The Beauties wait till the first Act's begun
And Beaux step home to put fresh Linnen on.   15
No well dress'd Youth in Coffee house remain'd,
But pensive Patch, who on the Window lean'd,
And Silliander, that Alert and gay,
First pick'd his Teeth and then began to say.

Silliander

Why all these sighs, ah why so pensive grown?   20
Some cause there is that thus you sit alone.
Does hopeless Passion all this Sorrow move?
Or dost thou Envy, where the Ladies love?

Patch

If whom they love, my envy must persue,
'Tis sure at least I never envy you.   25

Silliander

No, I'm unhappy, you are in the right,
'Tis you they favour, and tis me they slight.
Yet I could tell—but that I hate to boast—
A Club of Ladies, where 'tis me they toast.

Patch

Toasting does seldom any favour prove,   30
Like us they never toast the Thing they love.
A certain Duke one night my health begun,
With cheerfull Pledges round the Room it run,
Till the young Silvia, press'd to drink it too,
Started, and vow'd she knew not what to do: 35
What, drink a fellow's health! she dy'd with Shame,
Yet blush'd when ever she pronounced my Name.

---

13 'A famous Scene in the Opera of Hydaspes, where Nicolini kills a Lyon' (Pope's
note). LM had seen this opera (by Mancini) in 1710; it had several performances at the
King's Theatre in 1715 (*Letters*, 1. 22; *London Stage*, 2, 1960, ed. E. L. Avery).

18 *alert*. Except in its military sense, this word was a recent borrowing from French;
Addison in *Spectator* No. 403 had written it *alerte* (ed. D. F. Bond, 1965, 3. 507).

Silliander

Ill fate persue me, may I never find
The dice propitious or the Ladys kind
If fair Miss Flippy's fan I did not tear,   40
And one from me she condescends to wear.

Patch

Women are allways ready to receive,
'Tis then a favour when the Sex will give.
A Lady (but she is too great to name,
Beauteous in Person, spotless in her Fame)   45
With gentle Strugglings let me force this Ring,
Another Day may give Another Thing.

Silliander

I could say something—see this Billet doux—
And as for presents—look upon my shooe—
These Buckles were not forc'd, and halfe a Theft,   50
But a young Countess fondly made the Gift.

Patch

My Countess is more nice, more artfull too,
Affects to fly, that I may fierce persue.
This Snuff box, while I begg'd, she still deny'd,
And when I strove to snatch it, seem'd to hide,   55
She laugh'd, and fled, and as I sought to seize
With Affectation cramm'd it down her Stays:
Yet hoped she did not place it there unseen;
I press'd her Breasts, and pull'd it from between.

After 39 *an extra couplet in Pope's transcript:*
        Or what's yet worse to each well-judging Spark,
        My Wigg be ruffled when I walk the Park!

47 Here Pope quoted Virgil's eclogue iii. 71.
48–51 Cf. *The Rape of the Lock*, ii. 39–41.
53 ff. Here Pope quoted Virgil's eclogue iii. 64–6, which he had echoed in 'Spring',
line 58.

Silliander

Last Night as I stood ogling of her Grace,   60
Drinking Delicious Poison from her Face,
The soft Enchantress did that face decline
Nor ever rais'd her Eyes to meet with mine,
With sudden art some secret did pretend,
Lean'd cross two chairs to whisper to a Freind,   65
While the stiff whalebone with the motion rose
And thousand Beauties to my sight expose.

Patch

Early this morn (but I was ask'd to come)
I drunk Bohea in Cœlia's dressing room,
Warm from her Bed, to me alone within,   70
Her Nightgown fasten'd with a single Pin,
Her Nightcloaths tumbled with resistless Grace
And her bright Hair play'd careless round her Face.
Reaching the Kettle, made her Gown unpin,
She wore no Wastcoat, and her Shift was thin.   75

Silliander

See Titiana driving to the Park,
Hast, let us follow, 'tis not yet too Dark,
In her all Beauties of the Spring are seen,
Her Cheeks are rosy, and her mantua Green.

61 Cf. *Eloisa to Abelard*, line 122: 'Still drink delicious poison from thy eye'. LM apparently believed that Pope took his cue from her, since she annotated his line in her copy of his *Works*, 1717, with the word 'mine' (Halsband, *LM*, p. 76).

66–7 Cf. Gay's 'Monday', lines 105–6 (added after the first edition: *Poetry and Prose*, I. 100).

71–3 These lines reappear as lines 78–80 of 'Epistle from Arthur Gray' (p. 223 below).

76, 80 The names, from Titian and Tintoretto, allude to the use of cosmetics.

78–9 Cf. 'Verses on Mrs. Susanna Townley' to Fossile's wife in *Three Hours after Marriage* (pub. 21 Jan. 1717, after LM had left for Turkey):

> In you the beauties of the spring are seen,
> Your cheeks are roses, and your dress is green.

Fossile comments 'A poor dog of a poet! I fear him not' (ed. J. H. Smith, 1961, p. 164).

79, 83 *mantua*: a corruption of *manteau* from association with the Italian town, where silk was made (*O.E.D.*).

Patch

See, Tintoretta to the Opera goes,   80
Hast, or the Croud will not permit our Bows,
In her the Glory of the Heavens we view,
Her Eyes are star-like, and her mantua blue.

Silliander

What Colour does in Cœlia's stockings shine?
Reveal that secret and the Prize is thine.   85

Patch

What are her Garters? tell me if you can,
I'll freely own thee for the happy man.
    Thus Patch continu'd his Heroic Strain
While Silliander but contends in vain.
After a Conquest so important gain'd   90
Unrivall'd Patch in ev'ry Ruelle reign'd.

84 Here Pope quoted Virgil's eclogue iii. 104, which he had echoed in 'Spring',
line 85 ff.
84–7 *Spectator* No. 492 had described such a test with stockings and garters.
88–9 Here Pope quoted Virgil's eclogue vii. 69–70.

Wednesday
The Tête à Tête

Text H MS. 256. 28–31, copied after 1730; *written* Jan.–July 1716; *printed*
1747. The lovers in this poem remain unidentified with real people.

No; fair Dancinda no; You strive in vain,
To calm my Care, and mitigate my Pain,
If all my sighs, my tears can fail to move,
Ah, sooth me not with fruitless vows of Love.—
    Thus Strephon spoke, Dancinda thus reply'd: 5
What must I do to gratify your Pride?
Too well you know (ungratefull as thou art)
How much you triumph in this tender Heart.
What proofe of Love remains for me to grant?
Yet still you teize me with some new Complaint!   10

Oh, would to Heaven (but the fond wish is vain)
Too many favours had not made it plain!
But such a passion breaks through all disguise,
Love reddens on my Cheek, and wishes in my Eyes.
    Is't not enough, Inhuman and unkind! 15
I own the secret conflict of my Mind?
You cannot know what torturing Pain I prove,
When I with burning Blushes own, I love.
You see my artless Joy at your Approach,
I sigh, I faint, I tremble at your touch, 20
And in your Absence, all the World I shun,
I hate Mankind, and curse the cheering Sun;
Still as I fly, ten thousand Swains persue;
Ten thousand Swains I sacrifice to you:
I shew you all my Heart, without Disguise: 25
But these are tender proofes that you despise—
I see too well what Wishes you persue;
You would not only Conquer, but undo.
You, Cruel Victor, weary of your Flame,
Would seek a Cure in my Eternal Shame; 30
And not content my Honor to subdue,
Now strive to triumph o're my Virtue too.
    Oh Love! A God indeed to Womankind!
(Whose Arrows burn me, and whose fetters bind)
Avenge thy Altars, vindicate thy fame, 35
And blast these Traitors who prophane thy Name,
Who by pretending to thy sacred Fire,
Raise Cursed Trophys to impure Desire!
    Have you forgot, with what ensnaring Art
You first seduced this fond, uncautious Heart? 40
Then as I fled, did you not, kneeling, cry,
Turn, Cruel Beauty! whither would you fly?
Why all these doubts, why this distrustfull Fear?
No impious Wishes shall offend your Ear,
Nor ever shall my boldest Hopes pretend 45
Above the Title of a tender Freind.
Blest if my Lovely Goddess will permit
My humble vow, thus sighing at her feet!
The Tyrant Love that in my Bosom reigns,
The God himselfe submits to wear your chains, 50

You shall direct his Course, his Ardour tame,
And check the Fury of his wildest Flame.
  Unpractis'd Youth is easily deceiv'd,
Sooth'd by such sounds, I listen'd, and beleiv'd:
Now quite forgot that soft submissive Fear,   55
You dare to ask, what I must blush to hear.
  Could I forget the Honor of my Race,
And meet your wishes, fearless of Disgrace;
Could Passion o're my tender Youth prevail,
And all my Mother's pious Maxims fail: 60
Yet to preserve your Heart (which still must be,
False as it is, for ever dear to me)
This fatal proofe of Love, I would not give,
Which you contemn the moment you receive.
The wretched she who yeilds to guilty Joys,   65
A Man may pity, but he must despise.
  Your Ardour ceas'd, I then should see you shun
The wretched victim by your Arts undone,
Yet if I could that cold Indifference bear,
What more would strike me with the last Despair,   70
With this Refflection would my Soul be torn,
To know I merited your cruel Scorn.
  Has Love no pleasures free from Guilt or Fear?
Pleasures less feirce, more lasting, more sincere?
Thus let us gently kiss, and fondly Gaze,   75
Love is a Child, and like a Child he plays.
  Oh Strephon! if you would continu Just,
If Love be something more than Brutal Lust;
Forbear to ask, what I must still deny,
This bitter Pleasure, this Destructive Joy;   80
So closely follow'd by the Dismal Train
Of cutting Shame, and Guilt's heart peirceing Pain.

65–6 *omitted by Pope in his transcript and inserted by LM.*

75–6 Spence admiringly quoted this couplet (*Polymetis*, 1747, p. 70); so did Frances
Brooke (*The History of Emily Montague*, 1769, letter 156). The thought comes from the
Remedia Amoris (Tate's translation, *Ovid's Art of Love*, 1709, p. 269), and was used
elsewhere by LM without irony (p. 158 above).
  81–2 This couplet was quoted in an anonymous imitation of Horace's ode iii. 28,
perhaps by LM or copied from her (*Fog's Weekly Journal*, 7 Nov. 1730).

She paus'd; and fix'd her Eyes upon her Fan,
He took a pinch of snuff, and thus began,
Madam, if Love—but he could say no more   85
For Made'moiselle came rapping to the Door.
The dangerous Moments no Adieus afford,
Begone, she crys, I'm sure I hear my Lord.
The Lover starts from his unfinish'd Loves,
To snatch his Hat, and seek his scatter'd Gloves,   90
The sighing Dame to meet her Dear prepares;
While Strephon cursing slips down the back Stairs.

89 Loves] *altered by LM from* joys *Pope's transcript.*
90–2 *substituted by LM for three lines which she struck out, Pope's transcript:*
> The Lady ⟨?⟩ with a ⟨?Look⟩, and cries,
> Ah thoughtless Youth! what ⟨?moments⟩ have you mist?
> You have but ⟨listen'd⟩ when you should have kist!

89 Cf. George Villiers, Duke of Buckingham's *The Rehearsal*, 1671, Act I:
> Boar beckons sow to trot in chestnut groves,
> And there consummate their unfinished loves.
For an alternative ending see next poem.

[Alternative ending to 'Wednesday']

Text H MS. 255. 11. This passage, headed in MS. 'Eclogue', was perhaps rejected by one of Lady Mary's associates (cf. the ending transcribed by Pope but rejected by her).

Madam, if Love could touch that Gentle Breast
With halfe that ardour with which mine's oppress'd,
You would not blast my more than vestal Fire
And call it Brutal, or impure Desire.
The Lusty Bull professes not, nor vows,   5
But Bellows equal for a Herd of Cows,
The Stately Horse persues no chosen Fair,
But neighs, and prances for each common Mare.
This is impure desire, this Brutal Lust,
Man sighs for One, and to that One is just.   10
Why, Lovely Delia, do these sighs arise?
Why heaves your Breast? why sparkle thus your Eyes?
Examine your own Heart, and you will find
Some Wish still left unsatisfy'd behind.
Oh take me, press me to your panting Breast!   15
Let me be now, and I'm for ever blest.

He spoke, and on her Bosom laid his Cheek,
Fair Delia sigh'd, but had no power to speak,
Fair Delia blush'd, while he put out the Light,
And all that follow'd was Eternal Night. 20

Thursday
The Bassette Table
Smilinda, Cardelia

Text H MS. 256. 31–4, copied after 1730; *written* before 26 Jan. 1716, probably before 20 Dec. 1715 (Halsband, *PMLA*, 1953, pp. 243–4). *Printed* 1716.
Smilinda was identified by Walpole and Spence as Lady Mary herself. Cardelia was Elizabeth Hervey (1676–1741), Countess of Bristol, whose passion for play is a frequent topic in her husband John Hervey's *Letter-Books*, 1894, *passim*.

Cardelia

The Bassette Table spread, the Tallier come,
Why stays Smilinda in the dressing room?
Rise, pensive Nymph! The Tallier stays for you—

Smilinda

Ah Madam! since my Sharper is untrue,
I joyless make my once ador'd Alpieu. 5
I saw him stand behind Ombrelia's Chair,
And whisper with that soft deluding Air
And those feign'd sighs that cheat the list'ning Fair.

1 'The *Talliere* is he that keeps the Bank.' He frequently made a large profit ([Charles Cotton], *The Compleat Gamester . . . to which is added, the Game at Basset*, 1709, pp. 178, 184).
4 *Sharper*: identified by Walpole and Spence as John Dalrymple (1673–1747), 2nd Earl of Stair. Walpole suggested twice (with some discrepancy in the stories) that LM was his mistress (*Corr.* 14. 243; James Prior, *Life of Malone*, 1860, p. 149).
5 *Alpieu*: decision to raise the stake after an initial win, signalled 'by turning up, or crooking the corner of the winning Card' (*Compleat Gamester*, p. 180).
6 *Ombrelia*: 'Mrs Hanbury' (Walpole's note), probably Bridget (d. 1741), wife of 'Major' John Hanbury and mother of Sir Charles Hanbury Williams.

Cardelia

Is this the cause of your Romantic Strains?
A mightier greife my heavy Heart sustains;   10
As you by Love, so I by Fortune crost,
In one bad deal three sept le va's I lost.

Smilinda

Is that a Greife that you compare with mine?
With ease the Smiles of Fortune I resign,
Would all my Gold in one bad Deal were gone   15
Were lovely Sharper mine, and mine alone.

Cardelia

A Lover lost is but a common Care
And prudent Nymphs against the Change prepare.
The Queen of Clubs thrice lost! Oh, who could guess
This fatal stroke, this unforeseen distress?   20

Smilinda

See Betty Loveit, very a propos!
She all the pains of Love and Play does know,
Deeply experienced many years ago.
Dear Betty shall th'Important point decide,
Betty, who oft the pains of each has try'd;   25
Impartial she shall say who suffers most,
By Cards' ill usage, or by Lovers lost.

Loveit

Tell, tell your Greife, attentive will I stay,
Tho' Time is precious, and I want some Tea.

12 *deal*: single hand of cards (*O.E.D.*). '*Sept-et-le-va*' is a successful 'second Chance' which pays seven times the stake (*Compleat Gamester*, p. 180).

21 *Betty Loveit*: Elizabeth, daughter of Sir Robert Southwell, a gambling friend of Lady Bristol (Hervey, *Letter-Books*, 2. 152).

24–5 Cf. Ovid, translated by Addison:

> *Tiresias* therefore must the cause decide,
> Having the Pleasure of both Sexes try'd

(1704, *Misc. Works*, ed. A. C. Guthkelch, 1914, 1. 115); also *Aeneid*, vi. 448, translated by Prior (*Works*, 1. 614).

Cardelia

Behold this Equipage by Mathers wrought,   30
With fifty Guineas (a great pen'north) bought.
See, on the Tooth pick Mars and Cupid strive,
And both the struggling Figures seem alive.
Upon the bottom, see the Queen's bright Face,
A Myrtle Foliage round the Thimble Case.   35
Jove, Jove himselfe does on the Scissars shine;
The Metal, and the Workmanship Divine!

Smilinda

This Snuff box once the Pledge of Sharper's love
When Rival Beauties for the present strove,
(At Corticelli's he the Raffle won,   40
There first his Passion was in Public shown,
Hazardia blush'd, and turn'd her Head aside,
A Rival's envy, all in vain, to hide)
This Snuff box—on the hinge see Brillants shine!
This Snuff box will I stake, the Prize is mine.   45

Cardelia

Alas! far lesser Losses than I bear,
Have made a Soldier sigh, a Lover swear.
But oh what makes the Disapointment hard,
'Twas my own Lord, who drew the Fatal Card!
In complaisance I took the Queen he gave,   50
Thô my own secret Wish was for the Knave:
The Knave won Sonica that I had chose
And the next pull, my sept le va I lose.

30 *Equipage. O.E.D.* quotes: 'a little case which held a thimble, scissors, a pencil, and other such little matters, and . . . hung to the girdle.' Charles Mather had a toyshop at Temple Bar. Pope quoted here Virgil's eclogue iii. 36–7; cf. 'Spring', lines 33–40.

31 *pen'north*: a buyer's bargain, a favourite word of LM's.

37 Cf. 'The Workman, and the Workmanship Divine!' (translation of Theocritus' first idyll: *Sylvae*, 1685, p. 358).

40 *Corticelli's*: 'a fashi⟨onab⟩le Indian Warehouse at the upper End of Suffolk Street, ⟨and⟩ a rendezvous of galantry' (Walpole's note), once suggested to LM as a possible meeting-place during her courtship (*Letters*, 1. 75–6).

49 Lord Bristol made resolutions against gaming for himself and his wife in 1703 and 1721 (*Diary*, 1894, p. 39; Hervey, *Letter-Books*, 2. 157).

52 *Sonica*: card having an immediate effect on the game (*O.E.D.*).

53 *pull. O.E.D.* quotes LM as its only example of this word meaning the act of drawing a card. Spence thought she meant 'pool', i.e. a round or game.

Smilinda

But ah, what agravates the killing smart,
The cruel thought that stabs me to the Heart: 55
This curst Ombrelia, this undoing Fair,
By whose vile arts this heavy Greife I bear,
She, at whose Name, I shed these spitefull Tears,
She owes to me the very Charms she wears.
An aukard Thing when first she came to Town,   60
Her Shape unfashion'd, and her Face unknown,
She was my Freind; I taught her first to spread
Upon her sallow cheeks enlivening Red.
I introduced her to the Parks and Plays,
And by my Interest Cosins made her Stays.   65
Ungratefull Wretch! with Mimic airs grown pert,
She dares to steal my Fav'rite Lover's Heart.

Cardelia

Wretch that I was! how often have I swore
When Winnall tally'd, I would punt no more?
I know the Bite, yet to my ruin run,   70
And see the Folly which I cannot shun.

Smilinda

How many Maids have Sharper's vows deceiv'd?
How many curs'd the moment they beleiv'd?
Yet his known Falsehood could no warning prove,
Ah what are Warnings to a Maid in Love!   75

Cardelia

But of what Marble must that Breast be form'd,
Can gaze on Bassette and remain unwarm'd?
When Kings, Queens, Knaves, are set in decent Rank,
Expos'd in Glorious heaps, the tempting Bank!
Guineas, halfe guineas, all the shineing Train,   80
The Winners Pleasure, and the Losers pain;
In bright Confusion open Rouleaus lie,

82 *Rouleaus*: defined by Mary Evelyn as 'forty nine guineas, made up in a paper roll,
which Monsieur F——, Sir J——, and Father B——, lend to losing gamesters that are
good men, and have fifty in return' (*Mundus Muliebris*, 1690: John Evelyn, *Misc.
Writings*, ed. W. Upcott, 1825, p. 712).

They strike the Soul, and glitter in the Eye:
Fir'd by the sight, all Reason I disdain,
My passions rise, and will not bear the Rein.   85
Look upon Bassette, you who reason boast,
And see if Reason may not there be lost!

Smilinda

What more than Marble must the Breast compose
That listens coldly to my Sharper's vows?
Then, when he trembles, when his Blushes rise,   90
When Awfull Love seems melting in his Eyes!
With eager Beats, his Mechlin Cravat moves:
He loves! I whisper to my selfe, He loves!
Such unfeign'd Passion in his Looks appears,
I lose all mem'ry of my former Fears;   95
My panting Heart confesses all his Charms,
I yeild at once, and sink into his Arms.
Think of that Moment, you who Prudence boast;
For such a Moment, Prudence well were lost!

Cardelia

At the Groom Porter's, batter'd Bullys play;   100
Some Dukes at Marrow bone bowl Time away.
But who the Bowl or rattling Dice compares
To Bassette's heavenly Joys, and pleasing Cares?

Smilinda

Soft Semplicetta doats upon a Beau,
Prudina likes a Man, and laughs at Shew.   105
Their several graces in my Sharper meet,
Strong as the Footman, as the Master sweet.

Loveit

Cease your Contention, which has been too long,
I grow Impatient, and the Tea too strong,

100 Here Pope quoted Virgil's eclogues iii. 82, 83; vii. 61, 65. For the groom-porter,
see p. 71 above.
101 John Sheffield, Duke of Buckingham, went regularly to the bowling green at
Marylebone (Sheffield, *Works*, 1723, 2. 278), which was also spelt 'Marrowbone'.

Attend and Yeild to what I now Decide,   110
The Equipage shall grace Smilinda's side,
The Snuff Box to Cardelia I decree:
So, leave Complaining, and begin your Tea.

    110 ff. Cf. the closing passage of Pope's 'Spring'.

Friday
The Toilette
Lydia

Text H MS. 256. 35–7, copied after 1730; *written* before 1716. *Printed*: 76-line text, fairly close to LM's MS., 1716; 106-line text, of which only 43 agree word for word with Lady Mary's copy, in Gay's *Poems on Several Occasions*, 1720; a version close to this, 1747. For variants from Gay's text, not given here, see his *Poetry and Prose*, 1. 181–5. See also Ann Messenger, *His and Hers: Essays in Restoration and Eighteenth-Century Literature*, 1986, pp. 84–107.

    Lydia was Mary (d. 1724), wife of Thomas Coke, Vice-Chamberlain to Queen Anne and to George I. Lady Mary apparently alluded to her death in a doggerel imitation of Prior (*Letters*, 2. 41).

Now twenty Springs had cloath'd the Park with Green
Since Lydia knew the blossom of Fiveteen.
No Lovers now her morning Hours molest
And catch her at her Toilette halfe undrest,
The thundering Knocker wakes the street no more,   5
Nor Chairs, nor Coaches, croud the silent door;
Now at the Window all her mornings pass,
Or at the dumb Devotion of her Glass.
Reclin'd upon her Arm she pensive sate,
And curst th'Inconstancy of Man, too late.   10
    Oh Youth! Oh spring of Life, for ever lost,
No more my Name shall reign the fav'rite Toast,
On Glass no more the Di'mond grave my Name,
And Lines mispelt record my Lovers Flame,
Nor shall side boxes watch my wand'ring Eyes,   15
And as they catch the Glance in rows arise

    15 ff. 'Ladies at that time sat in the front boxes, men in the side' (Walpole's note). Cf. *The Rape of the Lock*, 1717 revision, v. 13–14:
        Why round our Coaches crowd the white-glov'd Beaus,
        Why bows the Side-box from its inmost Rows?

With humble Bows, nor white Glov'd Beaux incroach
In crouds behind to guard me to my Coach.
  What shall I do to spend the hatefull Day?
At Chappel shall I wear the Morn away?   20
Who there appears at these unmodish hours,
But ancient Matrons with their frizled Tours,
And grey religious Maids? My presence there
Amidst that sober Train, would own Dispair;
Nor am I yet so old, nor is my Glance   25
As yet fix'd wholly on Devotion's Trance.
  Strait then I'll dress and take my wonted Range,
Through India shops, to Motteux's, or the Change,
Where the Tall Jar erects his stately Pride
With Antick Shapes in China's Azure dy'd,   30
There careless lyes a rich Brocard unroll'd,
Here shines a Cabinet with burnish'd Gold;
But then, Alas! I must be forc'd to pay,
Or bring no Pen'norths, not a Fan away.
  How am I curs'd! unhappy and forlorn,   35
My Lover's Triumph, and my Sexes Scorn!
False is the pompous Greife of youthfull Heirs,
False are the loose Coquettes inveigling airs,
False is the crafty Courtier's plighted word,
False are the Dice when Gamesters stamp the Board,   40
False is the sprightly Widow's public Tear,
Yet these to Damon's Oaths are all sincere.
  For what young Flirt, Base Man! am I abus'd?
To please your Wife am I unkindly us'd?
'Tis true her Face may boast the Peaches bloom,   45
But does her nearer whisper breathe Perfume?

22 *O.E.D.* s.v. 'tour' cites this line for the meaning 'A crescent front of false hair',
but also gives a possible alternative—the tall head-dress of pasteboard, muslin, lace
and ribbons fashionable in the reigns of William III and Anne. Both were old-fashioned
(*Spectator* No. 98).
  28 Peter Anthony Motteux (1663–1718), French refugee, author, and shopkeeper,
published a letter in *Spectator* No. 288, puffing his shop in Leadenhall Street. The New
Exchange was a fashionable bazaar.
  42 *Damon*: James, 3rd Earl of Berkeley (d. 1736). Lady Cowper had written in 1714
that Mrs. Coke's last child was actually his (*Diary*, 1865, pp. 15–16). Walpole noted, 'the
beautifull ballad of blackeyd Susan was made on Mrs Coke and James Earl of Berkeley'.
  44 Berkeley had married (1711) Lady Louisa Lenox (1694–1717), to whom LM had
written a juvenile verse compliment.

I own her taper Shape is form'd to please,
But don't you see her unconfin'd by Stays?
She doubly to fiveteen may claim pretence,
Alike we read it, in her Face, and sense.   50
Insipid servile Thing! whom I disdain,
Her Phlegm can best support the Marriage Chain.
Damon is practis'd in the modish Life,
Can Hate and yet be Civil to his Wife.
He Games, he drinks, he swears, he fights, he roves,   55
Yet Cloe can beleive he fondly Loves;
Mistriss and Wife by turns supply his need,
A Miss for pleasure and a Wife for breed.
Powder'd with Di'monds, free from Spleen or Care
She can a sullen Husband's humour bear,   60
Her Credulous Freindship, and her Stupid Ease,
Have often been my Jest in happier Days.
Now Cloe boasts and triumphs in my Pains,
To her he's Faithfull, 'tis to me he feigns.
Am I that stupid Thing to bear Neglect   65
And force a smile, not daring to Suspect?
No perjur'd Man! a Wife may be content,
But you shall find a Mistriss can resent—
    Thus Lovesick Lydia rav'd; her Maid appears,
And in her faithfull Hand, the Band box bears,   70
(The Cestos that reform'd Inconstant Jove,
Not better fill'd with what allures to Love).
How well this Riband's Gloss becomes your Face,
She crys in Rapture! Then so sweet a Lace!
How charmingly you look! so bright! so fair!   75
'Tis to your Eyes the Head dress owes its Air!
    Strait Lydia smil'd; the Comb adjusts her Locks
And at the Play House, Harry keeps her Box.

49 i.e. she makes two separate claims to the desirable age of fifteen.
71-2 This story from *Iliad* xiv had been re-told in *Tatler* No. 147.

Satturday

The Small Pox
Flavia

Text H MS. 256. 37–40, copied after 1730; *written* Jan.–July 1716; *printed* 1747. Lady Mary later said she had expressed her own feelings in this poem (see p. 35 above). In it she made some use of her juvenile imitation of Virgil's tenth eclogue (H MS. 251. 28–9).

The wretched Flavia, on her Couch reclin'd,
Thus breath'd the Anguish of a wounded mind.
A Glass revers'd in her right hand she bore;
For now she shunn'd the Face she sought before.
    How am I chang'd! Alas, how am I grown   5
A frightfull Spectre to my selfe unknown!
Where's my Complexion, where the radiant bloom
That promis'd Happyness for Years to come?
Then, with what Pleasure I this Face survey'd!
To look once more, my Visits oft delay'd!   10
Charm'd with the veiw, a fresher red would rise,
And a new Life shot sparkling from my Eyes.
Ah Faithless Glass, my wonted bloom restore!
Alas, I rave! that bloom is now no more!
    The Greatest Good the Gods on Men bestow,   15
Even Youth it selfe to me is useless now.
There was a Time, (Oh that I could forget!)
When Opera Tickets pour'd before my Feet,
And at the Ring where brightest Beauties shine,
The earliest Cherrys of the Park were mine.   20
Wittness oh Lilly! and thou Motteux tell!
How much Japan these Eyes have made you sell,
With what contempt you saw me oft despise
The humble Offer of the raffled Prize:

4 Cf. Pope's 'Summer', line 30.
14 Like Pope in 'Winter', LM uses the refrain ending 'no more' seven times; but she does not modify it on its last appearance.
19 The Ring, in Hyde Park, was used for social parade in coaches.
21 Charles Lillie, perfumer, kept a shop in Beaufort Buildings, Strand. For Motteux see p. 199 above.

For at each raffle still the Prize I bore,   ) 25
With Scorn rejected, or with Triumph wore:)
Now Beautie's Fled, and Presents are no more.   )
   For me, the Patriot has the House forsook,
And left debates to catch a passing look,
For me, the Soldier has soft verses writ,   30
For me, the Beau has aim'd to be a Wit,
For me, the Wit to Nonsense was betraid,   )
The Gamester has for me his Dun delaid,   )
And overseen the Card, I would have paid.   )
The bold and Haughty, by Success made vain,   35
Aw'd by my Eyes has trembled to complain,
The bashfull 'Squire touch'd with a wish unknown
Has dar'd to speak with Spirit not his own,
Fir'd by one Wish, all did alike Adore,
Now Beauty's fled, and Lovers are no more.   40
   As round the Room I turn my weeping Eyes,
New unaffected Scenes of Sorrow rise;
Far from my Sight that killing Picture bear,
The Face disfigure, or the Canvas tear!
That Picture, which with Pride I us'd to show,   45
The lost ressemblance but upbraids me now.
And thou my Toilette! where I oft have sate,
While Hours unheeded pass'd in deep Debate,
How Curls should fall, or where a Patch to place,
If Blue or Scarlet best became my Face;   50
Now on some happier Nymph thy Aid bestow,
On Fairer Heads, ye useless Jewells, glow!
No borrow'd Lustre can my Charms restore,
Beauty is fled, and Dress is now no more.
   Ye meaner Beauties, I permit you, shine,   55
Go triumph in the Hearts, that once were mine,
But midst your Triumphs, with Confusion know,
'Tis to my Ruin all your Charms ye owe.
Would pitying Heaven restore my wonted mein,
You still might move, unthought of, and unseen—   60

33–4 'at Basset' (Walpole's note). 'The *Pay* is when the *Punter* has won the *Couch* or
first Stake . . . and being fearful . . . leaves off' (Cotton, *Compleat Gamester*, 1709 ed.,
p. 179). Flavia's admirer was underwriting her next bet.
50 Cf. 'If Pink or Purple best become his face' (Dryden's epilogue to *All for Love*).

Satturday
The Small Pox
Flavia

The wretched Flavia on her Couch reclin'd,
Thus breath'd ye Anguish of a wounded mind.
A Glass revers'd in her right hand she bore;
For now she shunn'd ye Face she sought before.

How am I chang'd! Alas, how am I grown
A frightfull Spectre to my selfe unknown!
Where's my Complexion, where the radiant Bloom
That promis'd Happyness for years to come?
Then, wth what Pleasure I this Face survey'd!
To look once more, my Visits oft delay'd!
Charm'd wth ye view a fresher red would rise,
And a new Life still sparkling from my Eyes.
Ah! faithless Glass my wonted Bloom restore!
Alas I rave! that Bloom is now no more.

3. Opening lines of 'Satturday', 1716 (copied after 1730), in Lady Mary's autograph
See page 201

VERSES

Address'd to the

IMITATOR

OF THE

FIRST SATIRE

OF THE

Second Book of HORACE.

By a LADY.

LONDON:

Printed for A. DODD, and fold at all the Pamphlet-Shops in Town.

(Price Six-pence.)

4. Title-page of *Verses Address'd to the Imitator of . . . Horace*, published through Anne Dodd, 1733. Lord Oxford's copy

But oh, how vain, how wretched is the boast,
Of Beauty faded, and of Empire lost!
What now is left, but weeping to Deplore
My Beauty fled, and Empire now no more!
Ye cruel Chymists, what with held your Aid? 65
Could no Pomatums save a trembling Maid?
How false and triffling is that Art you boast;
No Art can give me back my Beauty lost!
In tears surrounded by my Freinds I lay,
Mask'd o're, and trembling at the light of Day, 70
Mirmillo came my Fortune to deplore
(A golden headed Cane, well carv'd he bore),
Cordials, he cry'd, my Spirits must restore,—
Beauty is fled, and Spirit is no more!
Galen the Grave, Officious Squirt was there, 75
With fruitless Greife and unavailing Care;
Machaon too, the Great Machaon, known
By his red Cloak, and his Superior frown,
And why (he cry'd) this Greife, and this Dispair?
You shall again be well, again be fair, 80
Beleive my Oath (with that an Oath he swore),
False was his Oath! my Beauty is no more.
    Cease hapless Maid, no more thy Tale persue,
Forsake Mankind, and bid the World Adieu.
Monarchs, and Beauties rule with equal sway, 85
All strive to serve, and Glory to obey,
Alike unpity'd when depos'd they grow,

87-8 *omitted by Pope in his transcript and inserted by LM.*

---

71 Walpole and Spence identified Mirmillo as Sir Hans Sloane, who was a contender with Dr. William Gibbons for the doubtful honour of this name in Garth's *Dispensary*, 1699; LM, however, probably intended Mirmillo for Richard Mead, who published a letter on smallpox in 1716. He generally carried a golden-headed cane given him by Radcliffe in 1714, bearing the coats of arms of both men ([William MacMichael], *The Golden-Headed Cane*, 1827, pp. 54–5 and *passim*).

71 ff. Here Pope quoted Virgil's eclogue x. 19–27 *passim*.

75 *Galen*: famous physician of the second century A.D. LM may intend John Woodward (1665–1728), who was professionally interested in smallpox; Gay also called him Galen in 1725 (*Poetry and Prose*, 1. 293, 2. 615).

Officious Squirt: a character with this name and epithet figures in *Dispensary*, cantos ii and iii.

77 *Machaon*: the name of the *Dispensary*'s doctor-hero, frequently applied to its author, Samuel Garth (1661–1719), friend and physician to LM's family.

85–8 LM re-used these lines in 'An Epilogue to Mary Queen of Scots' (p. 241 below).

Men mock the Idol of their Former vow.
Adieu ye Parks, in some obscure recess,
Where Gentle streams will weep at my Distress,   90
Where no false Freind will in my Greife take part,
And mourn my Ruin with a Joyfull Heart,
There let me live, in some deserted Place,
There hide in shades this lost Inglorious Face.
Ye Operas, Circles, I no more must view!   95
My Toilette, Patches, all the Wo⟨rl⟩d Adieu!

95 *Circles*. *O.E.D.* quotes this line for the sense of a tier in a theatre, but a more likely meaning is that of an assembly.

Turkish Verses
Address'd to the Sultana
Eldest Daughter of S[ultan] Achmet 3d.

Text H MS. 253. 253–5, copied before 1718; *written* about 1 Apr. 1717; *printed* 1763, *Letters of the Right Honourable Lady M——y W——y M——e.* Lady Mary's interpreters supplied her with a literal translation (*Letters*, 1. 333–7) of verses written by the Sultan's favourite Ibrahim Pasha (*c.* 1666–1730) to his bride Princess Fatma (1704–33). The marriage had taken place in Feb., but consummation was postponed for reasons of state. Lady Mary, sending her version in 'the stile of English Poetry' to Pope, suggests that she produced it extempore.

Stanza I

Now Philomel renews her tender strain,
Indulging all the night her pleasing Pain.
I sought the Groves to hear the Wanton sing,
There saw a face more beauteous than the Spring,
Your large stag's-eyes where 1000 glorys play,   5
As bright, as Lively, but as wild as they.

2

In vain I'm promis'd such a heavenly prize,
Ah Cruel Sultan who delays my Joys!
While pierceing charms transfix my Amorous Heart
I dare not snatch one kiss to ease the smart.   10
Those Eyes like etc.

3

Your wretched Lover in these lines complains,
From those dear Beautys rise his killing pains.
When will the Hour of wish'd-for Bliss arrive?   15
Must I wait longer? Can I wait and live?
Ah bright Sultana! Maid divinely fair!
Can you unpitying see the pain I bear?

Stanza 4th

The Heavens relenting hear my peircing Crys,
I loath the Light, and Sleep forsakes my Eyes. ⎱ 20
Turn thee Sultana e're thy Lover dyes. ⎰
Sinking to Earth, I sigh the last Adeiu—
Call me my Goddesse and my Life renew.
My Queen! my Angel! my fond Heart's desire, ⎱
I rave—my bosom burns with Heavenly fire. ⎰ 25
Pity that Passion which thy Charms inspire. ⎰

Constantinople
To [William Feilding]

Text H MS. 256. 2–4: lines 1–37 in the hand of a scribe Lady Mary employed
in her Embassy Letter albums; copied soon after composition. *Written* 26 Dec.
1717 (MS. in contemporary hand, once owned by Sir Charles Hanbury Williams:
Lewis Walpole Library, Farmington, Conn.), just over three weeks before the
birth of Lady Mary's daughter. Copying this poem at the end of Pope's transcript
of her eclogues (MS. in New York Public Library, Arents Collection), Lady
Mary gave its date in New Style, and also specified the place of composition:
the kiosk or summer-house of the British Palace at Pera, overlooking Constantinople. *Printed* in *A New Miscellany* [ed. A. Hammond], 1720, through the indiscretion of her uncle William Feilding (see p. 10 above; *Letters*, 3. 169),
whose name was probably that obliterated in the title.

Give me, Great God (said I) a Little Farm
In Summer shady and in Winter warm,
Where a clear Spring gives birth to a cool brook
By nature sliding down a Mossy rock,
Not artfully in Leaden Pipes convey'd ⎱ 5
Nor greatly falling in a forc'd Cascade, ⎰
Pure and unsulli'd winding through the Shade. ⎰
All-Bounteous Heaven has added to my Prayer
A softer Climat and a Purer air.
  Our frozen Isle now chiling winter binds, 10
Deform'd with rains and rough with blasting winds,

1 Cf. the opening of Horace's satire ii. vi. One of LM's juvenile poems, 'My Wish',
began 'Give mee, my God, some close obscure retreat' (H MS. 251. 13).
5 For the thought cf. Pope's *Epistle to Bathurst*, lines 255–8.

The wither'd woods grown white with hoary froast
By driving Storms their verdent Beauty's lost,
The trembling Birds their leafless coverts shun
And seek in Distant Climes a warmer Sun,   15
The water Nimphs their Silenc'd urns deplore,
Even Thames benum'd, a river now no more;
The barren meadows give no more delight,
By Glistening Snow made painfull to the Sight.
   Here Summer reigns with one Eternal Smile,   20
And Double Harvests bless the happy Soil.
Fair, fertile, fields! to whom indulgent Heaven
Has every charm of every Season given,
No killing Cold deforms the beauteous year,
The Springing flowers no comeing winter fear,   25
But as the Parent rose decayes and dyes
The infant buds with brighter collours rise
And with fresh Sweets the Mother's-Scent Supplies.
Near them the Vi'let glows with odours blest
And blooms in more than Tyrian Purple drest,   30
The rich Jonquills their golden gleem display
And shine in glory emulating day.
These chearfull groves their Living Leaves retain,
The streams still murmur undefil'd by rain,
And rising green adorns the fruitfull plain.   35
The warbling Kind uninterrupted Sing,
Warm'd with enjoyment of perpetual Spring.
   Here from my Window I at once survey
The crouded City, and Resounding Sea,

12–13 Cf. Pope's 'Winter', lines 9–10.

16 Cf. Addison's translation from Ovid, 'The Story of Phaeton': 'The water-nymphs lament their empty urns' (1704, *Misc. Works*, ed. A. C. Guthkelch, 1914, I. 73).

17 LM's most recent London winter had been of 'greater Severity than had been known in the Memory of Man. The River *Thames* was quite frozen up, and abundance of Booths were built upon it' (*Historical Register for the Year 1716*, 1717, p. 115).

26–8 Cf. Prior's 'Celia to Damon':

    And when the Parent Rose decays, and dies;
    With a resembling Face the Daughter-Buds arise

(1705, *Works*, I. 212), and E. Vernon's verse compliment to LM before her marriage as 'the Nymph . . . of Acton':

    Then beaming will a young Maria rise,
    Whose spring of Beauty shall with fresh supplys
    Maintain the Empire of her Mother's Eyes

(H MS. 255. 15; printed in Halsband, *LM*, p. 19).

In Distant views see Asian Mountains rise   40
And lose their Snowy Summits in the Skies.
Above those Mountains high Olympus tow'rs
(The Parliamental seat of heavenly Pow'rs).
New to the sight, my ravish'd Eyes admire
Each gilded Crescent and each antique Spire,   45
The Marble Mosques beneath whose ample Domes
Fierce Warlike Sultans sleep in peacefull Tombs.
Those lofty Structures, once the Christian boast,
Their Names, their Glorys, and their Beautys lost,
Those Altars bright with Gold, with Sculpture grac'd,   50
By Barbarous Zeal of Savage Foes defac'd:
Sophia alone her Ancient Sound retains
Thô unbeleiving Vows her shrine prophanes.
Where Holy Saints have dy'd, in Sacred Cells
Where Monarchs pray'd, the Frantic Derviche dwells.   55
How art thou falln, Imperial City, low!
Where are thy Hopes of Roman Glory now?
Where are thy Palaces by Prelates rais'd;
Where preistly Pomp in Purple Lustre blaz'd?
Where Grecian Artists all their Skill display'd   60
Before the Happy Sciences decay'd,
So vast, that youthfull Kings might there reside,
So splendid, to content a Patriarch's pride,
Convents where Emperours profess'd of Old,
The Labour'd Pillars that their Triumphs told   65
(Vain Monuments of Men that once were great!)
Sunk undistinguish'd in one common Fate!
　　One Little Spot the small Fenar contains,
Of Greek Nobillity, the poor remains,

45 *followed by two extra lines in NYPL:*

　　　The Fair Serail where sunk in Idle ease
　　　The Lazy Monarch melts his thoughtless Days.

---

41 Cf. Gay's translation from Ovid, 'The Story of Arachne', line 131: 'And lose their less'ning summits in the skies' (1712, *Poetry and Prose*, 1. 34).

51 LM later wrote that stories about the defacement of churches were untrue (*Letters*, 1. 398–9).

61 *Happy Sciences*: the arts of civilized life.

65 The 'Historical Pillar . . . dropp'd down about 2 year befor I came' (*Letters*, 1. 402).

68 The Greek quarter of Constantinople was called Fanar or Phanar from a lighthouse on the Golden Horn.

Where other Helens show like powerfull Charms   70
As once engag'd the Warring World in Arms,
Those Names which Royal Auncestry can boast
In mean Mechanic arts obscurely lost,
Those Eyes a second Homer might inspire,
Fix'd at the loom, destroy their useless Fire.   75
  Greiv'd at a view which strikes upon my Mind
The short-liv'd Vanity of Humankind,
In Gaudy Objects I indulge my Sight
And turn where Eastern Pomp gives Gay Delight.
See; the vast Train in Various Habits drest,   }   80
By the bright Scimetar and sable vest,
The Vizier proud, distinguish'd o're the rest.
Six slaves in gay Attire his Bridle hold,
His Bridle rich with Gems, his stirrups Gold,
His snowy Steed adorn'd with Lavish Pride,   }   85
Whole troops of Soldiers mounted by his Side,
These toss the Plumy Crest, Arabian Coursers guide.
With awfull Duty, all decline their Eyes,
No Bellowing Shouts of noisie crouds arise,
Silence, in solemn state the March attends   90
Till at the Dread Divan the slow Procession ends.
  Yet not these prospects, all profusely Gay,
The gilded Navy that adorns the Sea,
The rising City in Confusion fair,
Magnificently form'd irregular,   95
Where Woods and Palaces at once surprise,   }
Gardens, on Gardens, Domes on Domes arise,
And endless Beauties tire the wandring Eyes,
So sooths my wishes or so charms my Mind
As this retreat, secure from Human kind,   100
No Knave's successfull craft does Spleen excite,
No Coxcomb's Tawdry Splendour shocks my Sight,
No Mob Alarm awakes my Female Fears,
No unrewarded Merit asks my Tears,
Nor Praise my Mind, nor Envy hurts my Ear,   105
Even Fame it selfe can hardly reach me here,

82–4 Voltaire quoted these lines, apparently from H MS. 256, in a letter of Feb. 1736
(*Corr.*, ed. T. Besterman, 1953–64, 5. 67).
97–8 Cf. Pope's *Essay on Criticism*, lines 231–2.

Impertinence with all her tattling train,
Fair sounding Flattery's delicious bane,
Censorious Folly, noisy Party rage,
The thousand Tongues with which she must engage   } 110
Who dare have Virtue in a vicious Age.

A Satyr

Text H MS. 81. 205–9; *written* June 1717–June 1718. On the leaf preceding
this adaptation from Boileau's tenth satire (otherwise blank and of the same
paper as the following leaves) Lady Mary later noted, 'Wrote at Constantinople'.
As an attack on women, it stands out oddly among her works.

Sated with Pleasure you no more will rove
But fix your Fortune, and confine your Love;
Tis thus you say—Determind at the last,
The Choice is made, the word of Honnour past,
The portion, that material point, agreed,   5
Advice comes late, I cannot now recede.
To say the truth, tir'd with my rambling Life
I wish the solid Comfort of a Wife,
To pass in peace My now declineing years
And disapoint the hopes of Greedy heirs,   10
And then I think, what pleasure it will be
A Little riseing Family to see,
To view my Image in an Infant face
And see renew'd the honnours of my Race.
In search of happyness we blindly stray,   15
Tis heaven alone directs the proper way,
And Man can only boast of true Delight
When Law confines the wand'ring Appetite.
    Have you then thought, oh unrefflecting Freind,
On every Chance that does that Choice attend?   20
In Silence will you Sullenly repent
Or have you gaind the Skill to be content?
Methinks I hear you toast your beauteous bride
And wish each Freind the happy State had tryd,
Yet when the parting hour, tho' late, is come   25
You sit the last and tremble to go home.

Go cheerfull on, perhaps you need not fear,
'Tis ten to one, you do not meet her there.
'Tis true yon red appears the Break of Day
But yet my Lady mayn't be ris from Play,   30
Still crouds of Hacks attend at Damon's Door
And waiting Chairmen on the Benches snore
While well-bred Footmen with repeated Knocks
Repay the Echo of the upper Box.
When she returns, blest Husband as you are,   35
You must your tender Consort's sorrows share
And kindly listen while the sighing Dame
Tells by what strange Surprize she lost the Game,
By what unthought of Chance, unheard before,
When 7 the main some Devil brought up 4.   40
Such cursed Fortune cannot allways last,
One Lucky Night may recompence the past.
Wise Arguments like these must needs prevail, ⎫
Mortgage your land or set your House to Sale, ⎬
Debts must be paid or Madam's Credit Fail.   ⎭   45
   Yet rather may you meet this moderate Fate,
Mourning at worst the loss of your Estate,
Then wed a frugal manager like some
Who dare not ask a Freind to dine at home,
But Starve at home with a dear carefull spouse   50
Whose good Oeconnomy no Fire allows,
Or if you stir, must trust it in the wet
Till Coach is call'd, on t'other side the Street,
Give strict accounts even of your pocket Gold
⟨And⟩ see the short allowance often told.   55
Nor vainly think this wife your wealth assures,
Money indeed is heap'd, but tis not yours,
Dearly you pay for all your easy hours
Till her insatiate hand the whole Devours.
Then should your fortune frown and freinds desert   60
Hope not to see return'd the smallest part,
Unpitying She beholds you drag'd to Jail
And at your vain Expence does loudly rail,

33–4 The upper row of boxes was below the footmen's gallery.
40 *main.* 'In the game of hazard, a number . . . called by the "caster" before the dice are thrown' (*O.E.D.*).

Your vanish'd Fortune plac'd you know not where
Rewards the Lady for her prudent Care.—   65
  Quick you reply, The Maid I make my Choice,
Incapable of such detested vice,
In Sweet retirement wastes her virgin Days, ⎫
Unknown at Court, and rarely seen at plays, ⎬
Avoids the Dang'rous pride of Public praise. ⎭   · 70
A Pious Mother's care directs her Youth
In Paths of Virtue, Modesty and Truth.
Pleas'd she submits to her experienced Guide,
Fond of her Guard and ever by her side.
  Suppose this true, yet have you never known   75
An artless Innocence brought up to Town,
Led by her Spouse, for thither she must come,
To Plays, assemblys, Church and Drawing room,
Soon grow Polite, all sense of Shame laid by
(Or but asham'd of Rustic Modesty)   80
She hears, not only hears, but gay, Coquette,
With pert advances all Mankind are met.
Freely she raillys on her ruind fame
And proudly Triumphs in a madcap's Name
Till to the last extremes of Lewdness run   85
She Courts your Footman, or corrupts your Son.
  Happy for you, if vicious without Art
Her Conduct furnishes pretexts to part,
But more I fear, for that we often see
Her tast confind to modish Gallantry.   90
Then round her Toilet waiting Lovers stand,
One gains a Glance, and one the pritty hand,
While her glad Eyes the sighing Croud surveys,
Charm'd with the Incense of Insipid praise.
Here every fulsome Fop is welcome seen,   95
When you approach, my Lady has the Spleen.
To morning Hours no Husband has a right,
Tis Just you should expect the happy Night,
Then you may see the careless fair undressd,
Her Day Complexion on the Toilet plac'd,   100
Some rare Pomatum shrouds her shineing Charms,

101 LM had recently tried the famous Balm of Mecca, with unfortunate results
(*Letters*, I. 368–9).

And so prepar'd receive her to your Arms.
Thus is the Beauty by her Spouse enjoy'd,
For others all inviteing Arts employ'd,
For them, selects her silks with nicest care,   105
For them in vary'd Curles she sets her hair,
With Hoops and heads of every form and size
Follows the Protean Fashion as it flys,
And should you murmur at the vain Expence
What a loud torrent of Impertinence!   110
Was ever tender Wife so coarsly us'd?
Was ever virtuous Love so much abus'd?
And after all of what do you complain?
Is't not your Credit that she should be clean?
In spite of Birthday suits and lace grown dear   115
She shifts with bare 500 [pounds] a year.
I see you mov'd with such pathetic crys
And some new Jewel future Quiet buys.

But there are Ladys not so soon appeasd,
Who are most happy seeming most displeas'd,   120
Fond of Occasions to exert their Power,
The wretched Husband knows no Silent hour,
The House a Scene of strong perpetual Noise,
The Servants' Curses or the Children's Cries.

Yet these are Gentle to those Furious Dames   125
Whose Hearts the rage of Jealousie enflames.
Then is the time to know the Sexes Fire,
What vengeance Vain Suspicion can inspire,
In every Street you meet her watchfull Spies   ⎫
And oft her selfe mobd in some odd Disguise   ⎬   130
With Thunder on her Tongue and Light'ning in her Eyes. ⎭

You sigh and think this very hard to bear
But would you rather Chuse a sickly fair?
In Dishabillé allways on the bed,
Now groans, the Cholic, now laments her Head,   135

115–16 £500 in 'pin-money', not living expenses. LM's annual allowance as an unmarried girl had been £200; in old age she claimed that she and her husband had lived several years on under £800 p.a. (*Letters*, 1. 134 n. 1; 3. 257). Lace was an extravagance, with 'heads' at £30 and £40; in 1712 one lady spent £1,418. 14s. on lace (Mrs. Bury Palliser, *History of Lace*, 1865, p. 324).

130–1 Cf. 'Now with fresh vigour Morn her Light displays', lines 87–92 (p. 254 below).

In spite of hartshorn 20 times a day
Oppress'd with Vapours, allmost faints away.
What can such Languishments and sighings mean?
Some Dire distress must cause the mournfull Scene,
A Fever, sure, attacks the fondled Heir   140
And can you Justly blame a Mother's fear?
No, tis some servant she would have displac'd,
For too much sense abhor'd, with too much favour gracd,
Or to prevent some Journey you design'd,
Better to Dye, than be from Town confind.   145
   But leaving to her tears this tender Dame,
Persue my Muse a more exalted Theme,
The Learned She, who makes her wise remarks
On Whiston's Lectures or on Dr Clark's,
And quite dispiseing mean Domestic Cares   150
Only regards the motions of the Stars.
A Gilded Telescope oft fills her hand,
An Orrery does on her Toilet stand,
New Systems seeks, will all Dark points explore,
Charm'd with Opinions never heard before,   155
Boldly derideing Superstitious fear,
Raillys the mysterys she should revere,
Mistakeing what she cannot comprehend
In downright Atheism her Studys end.
   With Joy this odious Charecter I quit   160
To shew more comical pretence to Wit,
The Politician whose fantastic Zeal
Impairs her Health to mind the Public weal,
Makes grave Refflections on the weekly Lies,
Reads all the Pamphlets Grubstreet can devise,   165
Even at her Tea instead of female Chat
With matchiavilian Art reforms the State,
Proffess'd a Champion of her Party's Cause
Raillys our Rulers, and arraigns the Laws.

149 Samuel Clarke (1675–1729) and his friend and biographer William Whiston (1667–1752) were religious controversialists suspected of deism.
   153 The orrery was invented *c*. 1700. *O.E.D.*'s first examples of the word, 1713 and 1720, show awareness that it is novel.

To —— Esqr

Text H MS. 255. 8o, copied after 1743; *written* 18–30 Sept. 1718, during Lady Mary's brief and hectic stay in Paris on her way home from Turkey (*Letters*, 1. 438, 441). As the recipient of this compliment phrased it,

> Nor in your way would you Lutetia spare,
> Amongst the rest your faithfull Slave was there.

Lady Mary also transcribed his answer to these lines, which expatiates on her oriental conquests, and his 'Postcript by the Same Hand', which compares himself to a merchant hoping to profit on the exchange. He may have been connected with the Mississippi Scheme, which was expected to benefit French, Negroes, and Indians (*The Flying-Post, or, The Post-Master*, 18 Sept. 1718).

> Oh worthy endless Fame! (if True Desert
> Can seek Applause but from the conscious Heart)
> Who makest the Savage Social Tyes approve,
> And bid'st divided Faiths consent to Love!
> While different Worlds consent to one great End, 5
> Nor take a Master, but embrace a Freind.
>   The only Spot, where Nature's Sons yet claim
>   Their Rights, and Christian is no dreadfull Name!

Epitaph

Text H MS. 254. 39–40; *written* Sept. 1718; *printed* 1763, *Letters of the Right Honourable Lady M——y W——y M——e*. On 1 Sept. 1718 Pope sent Lady Mary his two sentimental epitaphs on the lovers killed by lightning at Stanton Harcourt (*Corr*. 1. 493–6). She was roused by his suggestions that the pair would otherwise have lived in pastoral bliss, that their death was a reward for virtue, and that it in turn would be rewarded by 'a Tear from the finest eyes in the world'. Her poem addresses itself less to the lovers' death than to Pope's celebration.

> Here lyes John Hughs and Sarah Drew.
> Perhaps you'l say, what's that to you?
> Believe me Freind much may be said
> On this poor Couple that are dead.
> On Sunday next they should have marry'd; 5
> But see how oddly things are carry'd.
> On Thursday last it rain'd and Lighten'd,
> These tender Lovers sadly frighten'd

Shelter'd beneath the cocking Hay
In Hopes to pass the Storm away.   10
But the bold Thunder found them out
(Commission'd for that end no Doubt)
And seizing on their trembling Breath
Consign'd them to the Shades of Death.
Who knows if 'twas not kindly done?   15
For had they seen the next Year's Sun
A Beaten Wife and Cuckold Swain
Had jointly curs'd the marriage chain.
Now they are happy in their Doom
For P. has wrote upon their Tomb.   20

Virtue in Danger
A Lamentable Story how a vertuous Lady had like to have been Ravished by her Sister's Footman.
To the Tune of The Children in the Wood.

Text B.M. Harley MS. 7316. 137–8, copied by a scribe of Lord Oxford's;
written 21 Oct.–5 Dec. 1721; *printed* as a broadside ballad, *Virtue in Danger: Or
Arthur Gray's last Farewell to the World. Written by a Gentleman at St. James's;*
(*Tune, of Chivy Chase.*) n.d. Unique copy in Huntington Library.
    See Lady Louisa Stuart's account of this episode involving Mrs. Griselda
Murray and Arthur Gray the footman (pp. 41–2 above). Lady Lansdowne
wrote from Paris on 5 Dec.: 'We have here an excellent new ballad, sent from
England by the lady herself [Mrs. Murray] to her dear friend L[ady] M[ar]'
(Henrietta Howard, Lady Suffolk, *Letters* [ed. J. W. Croker], 1824, 1. 84–5).
By March 1725 Mrs. Murray was convinced that the ballad was by Lady Mary,
who defied her to prove it but noticeably refrained from actual denial (*Letters,*
2. 49–50).

I

Now ponder well ye Ladys fair,
These words that I shall write,

1–2 Cf. the opening of 'The Children in the Wood':

> Now ponder well you Parents dear,
> These Words which I shall write

(*A Collection of Old Ballads,* 1723, p. 221).

I'le tell a Tale shall make you stare
Of a poor Lady's fright.

2

She lay'd her down all in her Bed;   5
And soon began to snore;
It never came into her head
To lock her Chamber door.

3

A Footman of her Sister dear,
A Sturdy Scot was he   10
Without a Sense of Godly fear,
Bethought him wickedly.

4

Thought he, this Lady Lyes alone,
I like her comely face,
It would most gallantly be done,   15
Her body to embrace.

5

In order to this bold Attempt
He ran up Stairs apace;
While the poor Lady nothing dreamt,
Or dream't it was his *Grace*.   20

6

The Candle flaring in her Eyes
Made her full soon awake,
He scorn'd to do it by Surprize,
Or her a Sleeping take.

7–8 At Gray's trial some time was devoted to the catch and lock on Mrs. Murray's door (*Select Trials at the . . . Old-Bailey*, 1742, 1. 98–101).

20 *his* Grace: identified by Walpole as the Duke of Athol (G. Sherburn, 'Walpole's Marginalia in *Additions to Pope* (1776)', *Huntington Library Quarterly*, 1 (1938), 482).

7

A Sword he had and it hard by   25
   A thing appear'd with all
Which we for very Modesty
   A Pistol chuse to call.

8

This Pistol in one hand he took
   And thus began to woo her,   30
Oh how this tender Creature shooke
   When he presented to her!

9

Lady quoth he, I must obtain
   For I have lov'd you long;
Would you know how my heart you gaind   35
   You had it for a Song.

10

Resolve to quench my present flame
   Or you shall murderd be:
It were those pretty Eyes, fair Dame,
   That first have murder'd me.   40

11

The Lady Lookt with fear around,
   As in her Bed she lay,
And thô half dying in a Swound,
   Thus to her Self did say.

12

Who rashly judge (it is a Rule)   45
   Do often judge amiss,
I thought this fellow was a Fool,
   But there's some Sense in this.

25-8 omitted in the broadside.

13

She then recover'd heart of grace,
   And did to him reply,   50
Sure Arthur you've forgot your place,
   Or know not that 'tis I.

14

Do you consider who it is
   That you thus rudely treat:
'Tis not for scoundrell Scrubs to wish   55
   To tast their Master's Meat.

15

Tut, tut quoth he, I do not care;
   And so pull'd down the Clothes:
Uncover'd lay the Lady fair
   From bubby to her toes.   60

16

O Arthur, cover me, She said,
   Or sure I shall get cold:
Which presently the Rogue obey'd;
   He could not hear her Scold.

17

He lay'd his Sword close by her side;   65
   Her heart went pit a pat:
You've but one weapon left, She cry'd,
   Sure I can deal with that.

18

She saw the Looby frighted stand,
   Out of the Bed jumpt She,   70
Catch'd hold of his so furious hand:
   A Sight it was to See!

19

His Pistol hand she held fast clos'd
As She remembers well;
But how the other was dispos'd   75
There's none alive can tell.

20

The Sword full to his heart she lay'd
But yet did not him Slay;
For when he saw the Shining blade
G–d wot he run away.   80

21

When She was sure the Knave was gone
Out of her Father's Hall,
This vertuous Lady straight begun
Most grievously to bawl.

22

In came Papa and Mama dear,   85
Who wonder'd to behold:
Out Grisle! What a noise is here!
Why stand you in the Cold?

23

Mama, She said (and then She wept),
I have a Battle won;   90
But if that I had soundly Slept,
My honour had been gone.

24

A Footman of my Sister, he—
A footman? cry'd Mama,
Dear Daughter, this must never be,   95
Z——ds we must go to Law.

96 For the legal proceedings see Halsband in *History Today*, Oct. 1967.

25

This Lady's fame shall ever last
And live in British Song:
For She was like Lucretia chast,
And eke was much more strong.   100

99–100 A comment on 'And with fam'd *Lucrece* let her vye in Glory' (verse in praise
of Mrs. Murray printed in *The Weekly Journal: or, British Gazetteer*, 21 Oct. 1721).

Epistle From Arthur G[ra]y to Mrs M[urra]y

Text H MS. 256. 10–13, copied after 1730; *written* Oct.–Dec. 1721; *printed*
1747. Here Lady Mary transforms the unsuccessful rapist into a romantic
Ovidian suitor. She kept a copy of someone else's poem on the same subject
(H MS. 81. 16–17).

Read, Lovely Nymph, and tremble not to read,
I have no more to wish, nor you to dread.
I ask not Life, for Life to me were vain
And Death a refuge from severer Pain,
My only Hope in these last lines I try,   5
I would be pity'd, and I then would die.
    Long had I liv'd, as sordid as my Fate,
Nor curst the Destiny that made me wait,
A servile Slave: content with homely food,
The Grose instinct of Appetite persu'd;   10
Youth gave me Sleep at Night, and warmth of Blood.
Ambition yet had never touch'd my Breast,
My lordly Master knew no sounder rest;
With Labour healthy, in Obedience blest.
But when I saw! (oh had I never seen   15
That wounding softness, that engaging Mien!)
The mist of wretched Education flys,
Shame, Fear, Desire, Despair, and Love arise,
The new Creation of those Beauteous Eyes.

3 Cf. Lansdowne's *The British Enchanters*, III. ii: 'I ask not Life, for Life were
Cruelty' (*Poems upon Several Occasions*, 1712, p. 233).
    3–4 The question of a reprieve troubled Mrs. Murray's family: mercy urged them
to obtain one, but they also feared this would suggest that they doubted the justice of
the conviction.
    13 *lordly Master*: Lord Binning, Mrs. Murray's brother-in-law.

But yet that Love persu'd no Guilty Aim,   20
Deep in my Heart I hid the secret flame;
I never hop'd my fond Desire to tell,
And all my Wishes were to serve you well.
Heaven! how I flew when wing'd by your command,
And kiss'd the Letters given me by your Hand.   25
How pleas'd, how proud, how fond was I to wait,
Present the sparkling Wine, or change your Plate!
How when you sung my Soul devour'd the Sound,
And every Sense was in the Rapture drown'd!
Tho bid to go, I quite forgot to move,   30
You knew not that Stupidity was Love.
But oh the torment not to be express'd,
The Greife, the Rage, the Hell that fir'd my Breast,
When my Great Rivals in Embrodiery Gay,
Sat by your Side, or led you from the Play;   35
I still contriv'd, near as I could to stand
(The Flambeau trembled in my shaking hand),
I saw (or thought I saw) those fingers press'd; ⎫
For thus their Passion by my own I guess'd,   ⎬
And Jealous Fury all my Soul possess'd.   ⎭   40
Like Torrents, Love and Indignation meet,
And Madness would have thrown me at your Feet.
   Turn, Lovely Nymph (for so I would have said),
Turn from those Trifflers that make Love a Trade,
This is true Passion in my Eyes you see,   45
They cannot, no, they cannot, love like me.
Frequent Debauch has pall'd their sickly taste,
Faint their Desire, and in a Moment past.
They sigh not from the Heart, but from the Brain,
Vapours of Vanity and strong Champaign.   50
Too dull to feel what Forms like yours inspire, ⎫
After long talking of their painted Fire,   ⎬
To some lewd Brothel they at Night retire.   ⎭
There pleas'd with fancyd Quality and Charms,
Enjoy your Beautys in a Strumpet's Arms.   55

28-9 Gay called her 'Sweet Tongu'd *Murray*' ('Mr. Pope's Welcome from Greece',
Poetry and Prose, I. 256).

47 Cf. Rowe's 'Frequent Enjoyment pall'd your sprightly Taste' ('Prologue to the
Gamster [*sic*]', *Poetical Works*, 1720, p. 66).

Such are the Joys these Toasters have in View ⎫
And such the Wit and Pleasure they persue, ⎬
But is this Love that ought to merit you? ⎭
Each Opera Night a new Address begun,
They swear to Thousands what they swear to one.   60
Not thus I sigh—But all my sighs are vain, ⎫
Dye wretched Arthur, and conceal thy Pain; ⎬
Tis Impudence to wish, and Madness to complain. ⎭
   Fix'd on this View, my only hope of Ease,
I waited not the Aid of slow Disease,   65
The keenest Instruments of Death I sought,
And Death alone employ'd my Lab'ring Thought,
This all the Night—when I remember well
The charming Tinkle of your morning Bell,
Fir'd by the Sound, I hasten'd with your Tea,   70
For one last look to smooth the darksome way,
But oh how dear that fatal Look has cost,
In that fond Moment my Resolves were lost!
Hence all my Guilt, and all your sorrows rise,
I saw the languid softness of your Eyes,   75
I saw the dear Disorder of your Bed,
Your Cheek all glowing with a tempting red,
Your Nightcloaths tumbled with resistless Grace,
Your flowing Hair plaid careless round your Face,
Your Nightgown fastned with a single pin,   80
Fancy improv'd the wondrous charms within,
I fix'd my Eyes upon that heaving Breast
And hardly, hardly, I forbore the rest.

66–7 LM invented Gray's plan of suicide to provide a reason for his procuring the
pistol and sword with which he entered Mrs. Murray's room.
  72 Cf. Pope's 'How dear, O Kings! this fatal Day has cost!' (*Iliad*, vii. 392).
  78–80 LM adapted these lines from her own 'Tuesday', lines 71–3.
  80–1 LM's admirer Algarotti later used this couplet in his 'A Lesbia':

> D'un gentil zamberlucco il seno involta,
> Che un sol ago tenea dinanzi chiuso

(*Opere*, Leghorn, 1764–5, 8. 134. A footnote quotes the lines from 'Epistle from Arthur
G.Y. to Ms. M.Y.' without naming its author).
  82–3 Cf. Stephen Hervey's 'Jupiter and Europa':

> Impetuous Fires now struggled in his Breast,
> And hardly, hardly he forbore the rest

(from Ovid's *Metamorphoses: The Annual Miscellany*, 1694, p. 257).

Eager to Gaze, unsatisfy'd with sight,
My Head grew giddy with the near Delight—   85
Too well you know the fatal following Night.

　Th'extremest proofe of my Desire I give,
And since you will not love, I will not live.
Condemn'd by you I wait the righteous Doom,
Careless and fearless of the woes to come.   90

　Yet when you see me waver in the Wind,
My Guilty Flame extinct, my Soul resign'd,
Sure you may pity, what you can't approve,
The cruel Consequence of Furious Love.

　Think the bold Wretch, that could so greatly dare,   95
Was Tender, Faithfull, Ardent, and sincere.
Think, when I held the Pistol to your Breast,
Had I been of the World's large rule possess'd
That World had then been yours, and I been blest.

Think that my Life was quite below my Care,   100
Nor fear'd I any Hell beyond Despair.

　If these Refflections (tho they seize you late)
Give some Compassion for your Arthur's fate,
Enough you give, nor ought I to complain,
You pay my Pangs, nor have I dy'd in vain.   105

86 LM here passes over the actual attempt at rape.
91 Cf. Pope's 'Wife of Bath her Prologue', lines 395–6:
　　　　　On which three Wives successively had twin'd
　　　　　A sliding Noose, and waver'd in the Wind

(*Poems*, 2. 76). The sentence of death was reported on 9 Dec.; news of a reprieve (at the intercession of some of the family) was published on 23 Dec. (*The Post Man* and other papers).

John Duke of Marlborough

Text 1803, 5. 156; *written* June–Aug. 1722; last four lines *printed* 19 Jan. 1731 in the *London Evening-Post* and *Whitehall Evening-Post*, as an epitaph on Anne Oldfield. The Duke of Marlborough died on 16 June 1722 and was buried with great pomp on 9 Aug. Lady Mary was a friend of his wife and of two of his daughters.

　　When the proud Frenchman's strong rapacious hand
　　Spread over Europe ruin and command,

Our sinking temples and expiring law
With trembling dread the rolling tempest saw,
Destined a province to insulting Gaul;   5
This Genius rose, and stopp'd the ponderous fall.
His temperate valour form'd no giddy scheme,
No victory rais'd him to a rage of fame;
The happy temper of his even mind
No danger e'er could shock, or conquest blind.   10
Fashion'd alike, by Nature and by Art,
To please, engage, and interest, every heart.
In public life by all who saw approv'd,
In private hours by all who knew him lov'd.

Text Pierpont Morgan MS. M.A. 347: verso of item 23, an incomplete copy of 'L. [Peter]borough's Verses on Mrs. Howard. 1723—' in an unknown hand. *Written* Oct.–Nov. 1723. *Printed* in *Philological Quarterly*, 48 (1969), p. 194 (as by Pope). For Lady Mary's connection with Peterborough's 'I said to my heart between sleeping and waking', upon which this is a comment, see Grundy in *Review of English Studies*, new ser. 20 (1969), 461–8.

Here's a fine Declaration of Whimsical Love
That nor Beauty, nor Spirit, nor Virtue can move,
He would mortify none, lampoon'd he ten more,
For who but a Bawd will design on Threescore?

2 LM is identified on her copy of Peterborough's poem as the representative of wit, who like 'Mrs Harvy' (beauty) and 'Miss Meadows' (virtue), fails to arouse his love.
4 Charles Mordaunt (d. 1735), 3rd Earl of Peterborough, was born in 1658.

On a Lady mistaking a Dy[e]ing Trader for a Dying Lover.

On Mrs. Lowther, Lord Lonsdale's Sister.

Text B.M. Harley MS. 7316. 167–8, copied by Lord Oxford's scribe; *written* before spring 1723; *printed* 1729: James Ralph, *Miscellaneous Poems, By Several Hands*, pp. 277–9. MS. copies of the poem include shorter versions. Lady Mary denied writing '2 vile ballads' on this episode, about which its heroine quarrelled with her (*Letters*, 2. 23); but this piece, attributed to her by Oxford's scribe and by Spence (Cornell MS. E 6004), is no ballad. Jane Lowther died unmarried in 1752.

As Chloris on her downy Pillow lay,
'Twixt sleep and wake the morning slid away,
Soft at her Chamber door a tap she heard,
She listen'd, and again; no one appear'd.
Who's there? the sprightly Nymph with courage cries.   5
Ma'am, 'tis one who for your La'ship *dies*.
Sure 'Tis delusion! what, a dying Lover?
Yet speak once more, what is't you say however.
A second time, these Accents pierc'd the air;
Sweet was the sound, transported was the Fair.   10
At length mankind are just, her La'ship said,
Threw on her Gown, and steping out of Bed
Look'd in her Glass, confess'd him in the right.
Who thinks me not a Beauty, 'tis meer spight.
'Assemble you Coquets! with envy burn   15
'To see the wonders that my eyes have done.
'In vain your pert and forward airs you try, ⎞
'Mankind the more you Court the farther fly, ⎬
'And 'tis for me and only me they dye. ⎠
But how shall I receive him? cry'd the dame,   20
Prudence allows not pitty, I must blame.
Perhaps poor Soul! has sigh'd in Secret long
E'er the presumptuous thought fell from his tongue.
I am the cause, yet Innocent by Heav'n,
Why were these Eyes for such destruction giv'n?   25
'Tis not my fault, I did not make one feature.'
Then turn'd the look to view the dying Creature.
But ah! who should the enamour'd Swain now prove?
A wretch who dyes by Trade and not by Love.
No mortal pen can figure her surprize,   30
Willing to trust her Ears but not her Eyes,
The approaching Storm her swelling bosom show'd,
A while now pale, then Red with anger glow'd.
She wept, she rav'd, invok'd the powers above
Who give no Ear when old Maids talk of Love,   35
Fruitless her prayers and impotent her rage
Yet fierce as when two Females do engage.

At length the fire was spent, all was serene,
A calm succeeded this tempestuous Scene,
And thus She spoke.   40
'Ye blooming Maids! let my example prove
'How oft your Sex mistaken are in Love.
'When young we're cruel and with beauty play
'Which while we vainly Parly fades away,
'When old, to'increase the rigour of our fate,   45
'We wish and talk of Lovers when too late.
'As idle travellers who've lost the day
'And hope in Night thrô shades to find the way,
'Forlorn they tread the thorny paths in vain,
'Not of themselves but their hard fate complain,   50
'So peevish Maids when past their youthful bloom
'On sad remains and fancy'd charms presume,
'Lonely they wander, no companion find,
'Then rail and quarrel with all humankind.
'But let us to our selves for once be just   55
'And see our own decays and wrinkles first,
'When e'er to melting sighs we lend an ear
'Think youth and beauty make the Man sincere,
'No other powers their stubborn hearts can move,
'Did ever Vertue light the torch of Love?   60
'From sad experience I this truth declare,
'I'm now abandon'd, thô I once was Fair.'

Miss Cooper to ——

Text H MS. 81. 41-2; *written* Oct.–Nov. 1723. Judith Cowper (1702–81) m. (Dec. 1723) Capt. Martin Madan (1700–56). In the first years of her marriage she addressed poems to her husband under the name of Lysander; he is probably the fickle lover Lady Mary writes of.

If Wealth could bribe me, or if Beauty move,
I need not sigh (Lysander) for your Love!

1-2 Cf. a verse passage in Arabella Plantin's 'The Ingrateful: Or, The Just Revenge':
     If Honour, or if Gratitude, should move,
     How strong my Claim, to my *Lysander*'s Love!

(*Whartoniana*, 1727, 2. 138.)

The Croud still follows where I please to pass
Nor need I dread the Censure of my Glass,
The Heaven-born Muses in my Bosom dwell,   5
Not Sapho's selfe express'd their sense so well,
And what should most engage you to be true,
A Heart that languishes, and dyes for You.
But You (False Man) no Gratitude can warm
And Fatal Kindness sullys every charm.   10
These Eyes, the Source of all your Joy and Pain,
(For so you swore) now melt in Tears in vain.
The strong Disorders on my Vitals prey,
I weep all night, yet Hate the dawning Day,
The Day restores me to the Cursed Care   15
To hide a Torment which I cannot bear,
Cheiffly from you, I should the pain conceal,
Who cannot pity, what you cannot feel.
     From Fair, to Fair, with Idle vows you rove
And Repetitions of unmeaning Love,   20
A new pink Cornet makes you wish to day,
A Brillant Buckle takes that wish away,
Harvey, How, Howard, please you in their Turn,
You sigh for Ribands, and for Tippets burn.
Where these are Merits, oh how vain I plead   25
A tender Heart, and a refflecting Head!
Yet such a Heart, so fond, so nicely true,
Would force Esteem from any Man but You.
     By sly Design, or by Affected chance
Can you accuse me of one Guilty Glance?   30
Too much my Tenderness my Faith secures,

5–6 Judith Cowper had already written 'Abelard to Eloisa', 1720 (in reply to Pope),
and 'The Progress of Poetry', 1721.
   10 Judith Cowper's courtship letters sometimes mention her lover's neglect and her
jealousy (Falconer Madan, *The Madan Family*, 1933, pp. 87, 97).
   13–14 Cf. variant and note, p. 296 below.
   18 Cf. 'Abelard to Eloisa': 'Nor can you pity what you never felt' (*Letters of Abelard
and Heloise*, 1782, p. 139). Judith Cowper suffered from nervous disorders (*Madan
Family*, p. 78).
   21 *Cornet*: defined by Mary Evelyn as 'The upper pinner, dangling about the cheeks
like hounds ears' (*Mundus Muliebris*, 1690: John Evelyn, *Misc. Writings*, 1825, p. 710).
   23 All ornaments of the court: Lady Hervey (see p. 40 above); Mary, daughter of
1st Viscount Howe, who m. (1725) Lord Pembroke; Henrietta Howard, later Countess of
Suffolk. Judith Cowper thought that Mrs. Howe was in love with Madan (*Madan Family*,
p. 87).

My Cares, my Wishes, and my Soul are yours,
For You I dress, for you to Shades retire
And curse the feeble Charms that Crouds admire.
   Take back, ye Gods, this useless pow'r to please,   35
It gains no Glory, and it gives no Ease!
While at my Feet neglected Lovers lie
'Tis I that languish, and 'tis I that dye.
With silent sorrow they reproach my Scorn,
With more than equal pangs this Heart is torn,   40
And when I see you ('tis not to be told)
I see you Careless, Insolent, or Cold,
What ere you say, you say with too much ease,
No fear to lose me, nor no Care to please.
Dull common Courtship comes not from the Heart,   45
No Rapture when we meet, no pain to part.
   With what dead weight is then my Soul oppress'd!
Love, Shame, and Indignation rend my Breast,
Fain would I tell—but cannot force my Voice
To say, How I repent my worthless Choice.   50
Rack'd, and Tormented, ruin'd, and undone,
I see my Doatage—and I yet doat on.
   Go Faithless Man, this wretched Victim leave,
I cannot more be lost, or you deceive.
Persue the dirty Paths that lead to Gold   55
And like a Common Prostitute be sold.
Are these the Steps by which to Power you move?
Is this the Picture of the Man I love?
   By Heaven, I will this mean Desire controul,
I'll tear this hated Passion from my Soul,   60
I will not thus be toss'd—Desire—Despise,
Contemn your Folly, yet adore your Eyes.
   For what strange Curse has Nature form'd my Mind
So different from the rest of Womankind?
Shew, Dress and Danceing are their sole delights,   65

After 56 *six lines heavily obliterated, apparently identical with lines 71–6 of 'Epistle from Mrs. Y[onge]' (p. 232 below). Unconnected words and names of some of LM's acquaintance have been written over the lines.*

55–8 It does not appear that Madan was unusually ambitious. He was promoted captain in 1721, held court posts, and sat in Parliament 1747–54 (*Madan Family*, pp. 73–6; Spencer Cowper, *Letters 1746–74*, ed. E. Hughes, 1956, p. 140, n. 4).

In visits lose the Day, in play they waste the Nigh⟨ts⟩,
But I had rather from the Croud retir'd,
Be lov'd by One, than be by all admir'd.
Through ⟨?⟩ the World is there no hope to find
One faithfull Partner to a tender mind,   70
Gentle and Just, and without feigning, Kind?
None, ⟨there⟩ is none, the fond persuit is vain,
A Fan⟨cy'd⟩ Bliss I never can obtain.

Epistle from Mrs. Y[onge] to her Husband
1724

Text H MS. 256. 8–10; *written* July–Dec. 1724; *printed* and discussed by
Grundy in *Review of English Studies*, new ser. 23 (1972), 417–28. Mary (b. 1696),
daughter and heiress of Samuel Heathcote, m. (1716) the libertine and universally
detested William Yonge (*c.* 1693–1755, Bart. 1731). Although she was already
separated from Yonge at the time of her adultery, he recovered damages from
her lover on 30 June 1724 (£1,500 with costs), after a hearing well attended by
the public. Her love-letters were read to the House of Lords in November. The
king gave his consent on 16 Dec. to a divorce which left Yonge with most of her
fortune (*The Evening Post*, 17 Dec.).

Think not this Paper comes with vain pretence
To move your Pity, or to mourn th'offence.
Too well I know that hard Obdurate Heart;
No soft'ning mercy there will take my part,
Nor can a Woman's Arguments prevail,   5
When even your Patron's wise Example fails,
But this last privelege I still retain,
Th'Oppress'd and Injur'd allways may complain.
   Too, too severely Laws of Honour bind
The Weak Submissive Sex of Woman-kind.   10
If sighs have gain'd or force compell'd our Hand,
Deceiv'd by Art, or urg'd by stern Command,
What ever Motive binds the fatal Tye,

6 Yonge followed the example of his patron, Sir Robert Walpole, in extra-marital
affairs, but not in tolerance for those of his wife.
11–12 Cf. *The Rape of the Lock*, ii. 33–4:

> For when Success a Lover's Toil attends,
> Few ask, if Fraud or Force attain'd his Ends.

The Judging World expects our Constancy.
   Just Heaven! (for sure in Heaven does Justice reign   15
Thô Tricks below that sacred Name prophane)
To you appealing I submit my Cause
Nor fear a Judgment from Impartial Laws.
All Bargains but conditional are made,
The Purchase void, the Creditor unpaid,   20
Defrauded Servants are from Service free,
A wounded Slave regains his Liberty.
For Wives ill us'd no remedy remains,
To daily Racks condemn'd, and to eternal Chains.
   From whence is this unjust Distinction grown?   25
Are we not form'd with Passions like your own?
Nature with equal Fire our Souls endu'd,
Our Minds as Haughty, and as warm our blood,
O're the wide World your pleasures you persue, ⎫
The Change is justify'd by something new;   ⎬   30
But we must sigh in Silence—and be true.   ⎭
Our Sexes Weakness you expose and blame
(Of every Prattling Fop the common Theme),
Yet from this Weakness you suppose is due
Sublimer Virtu than your Cato knew.   35
Had Heaven design'd us Tryals so severe,
It would have form'd our Tempers then to bear.
   And I have born (o what have I not born!)
The pang of Jealousie, th'Insults of Scorn.
Weary'd at length, I from your sight remove,   40
And place my Future Hopes, in Secret Love.
In the gay Bloom of glowing Youth retir'd,
I quit the Woman's Joy to be admir'd,
With that small Pension your hard Heart allows,
Renounce your Fortune, and release your Vows.   45
To Custom (thô unjust) so much is due,
I hide my Frailty, from the Public view.
My Conscience clear, yet sensible of Shame,
My Life I hazard, to preserve my Fame.

25–31, 32–5 LM quoted these lines many years later (*Letters*, 3. 219).
   38 Cf. Dryden's *Troilus*, III. ii (*Works*, 5. 73): 'For I have lost (oh what have I not
lost!)'—a line LM had already imitated in a juvenile poem (H MS. 251, f. 31).

And I prefer this low inglorious State, ⎫ 50
To vile dependance on the Thing I hate— ⎬
—But you persue me to this last retreat. ⎭
Dragg'd into Light, my tender Crime is shown
And every Circumstance of Fondness known.
Beneath the Shelter of the Law you stand, 55
And urge my Ruin with a cruel Hand.
While to my Fault thus rigidly severe,
Tamely Submissive to the Man you fear.
    This wretched Out-cast, this abandonn'd Wife,
Has yet this Joy to sweeten shamefull Life, 60
By your mean Conduct, infamously loose,
You are at once m'Accuser, and Excuse.
Let me be damn'd by the Censorious Prude
(Stupidly Dull, or Spiritually Lewd),
My hapless Case will surely Pity find 65
From every Just and reasonable Mind,
When to the final Sentence I submit,
The Lips condemn me, but their Souls acquit.
    No more my Husband, to your Pleasures go,
The Sweets of your recover'd Freedom know, 70
Go; Court the brittle Freindship of the Great,
Smile at his Board, or at his Levée wait
And when dismiss'd to Madam's Toilet fly,
More than her Chambermaids, or Glasses, Lye,
Tell her how Young she looks, how heavenly fair, 75
Admire the Lillys, and the Roses, there,
Your high Ambition may be gratify'd,
Some Cousin of her own be made your Bride,
And you the Father of a Glorious Race
Endow'd with Ch——l's strength and Low—r's face. 80

71–6 LM rejected these lines from 'Miss Cooper to —— ' (p. 229 above).

75 The capital points the pun.

78 In 1729 Yonge married his second wife, a daughter of the 7th Baron Howard of Effingham. In Dec. 1724 his ex-wife, as 'Mrs. Mary Heathcote', married Patrick Macmahon, Esq., of Co. Tipperary (G. E. C[okayne], *Complete Baronetage*, 1900–9). The line comes from Rochester's account of a rich booby: lest he choose a wife who might improve the stock 'his friends provide / A cousin of his own to be his bride' ('A Letter from Artemisia in the Town to Cloe in the Country': *Complete Poems*, ed. D. M. Vieth, 1968, p. 111).

80 Probably Churchill and Lowther. For Churchill and Lady Walpole see p. 57, n. 3, above. Antony Lowther (d. 1741) was the gallant later blamed for the death of Sophia Howe.

Written ex tempore on the Death of Mrs Bowes

Text H MS. 256. 7; *written* 14 Dec. 1724 (date given at first publication); *printed* 26 Dec., in *The Weekly Journal or Saturday's-Post*, as 'extempore upon a Card, in a great deal of Company'; often reprinted with various scurrilous replies. All texts except those copied by Lady Mary or by her daughter (Portland MSS., Longleat) give four extra lines after line 4. The 'Company' perhaps included Mary Astell, whose twelve-line poem on Mrs Bowes sounds like debate with this (Ruth Perry, *The Celebrated Mary Astell*, 1986, p. 504).

George Bowes (1701–60) m. (1 Oct. 1724) Elizabeth or Eleanor Verney, not yet fifteen years old, who died less than eleven weeks later, on 14 Dec. Lady Mary's verse was vehemently attacked, probably because of gossip noted by Horace Walpole: the bride 'was said to die of the violence of the Bridegroom's embraces' (G. Sherburn, *Huntington Library Quarterly*, i (1938), 482).

Hail happy Bride, for thou art truly blest!
Three Months of Rapture crown'd with endless Rest!
You had not yet the fatal Change deplor'd,
The tender Lover, for th'imperious Lord,
Nor felt the Pangs that jealous Fondness brings,   5
Nor wept the Coldness from Possession springs;
Above your Sex, distinguish'd in your Fate,
You trusted, yet experienced no Deceit.
Soft were your Hours, and wing'd with Pleasure flew;
No vain Repentance gave a sigh to you.   10
And if Superior Bliss Heaven can bestow
With fellow Angels you enjoy it now.

3–4 Cf. Pope's 'To a Young Lady, with the Works of Voiture':
> Whole Years neglected for some Months ador'd,
> The fawning Servant turns a haughty Lord

(*Poems*, 6. 63.)

9 Cf. William Bowles's 'Pharmaceutria': 'Now swift the hours, and wing'd with pleasure flew' (*Miscellany Poems*, 1684, p. 251); and Rochester's 'Letter from Artemisia to Cloe': 'Gay were the hours, and winged with joys they flew' (*Poems*, p. 110).

A Man in Love
L'homme qui ne se trouve point, et ne se trouvera jamais

Text H MS. 256. 18, copied after 1730; *written* 1721–5; *printed* Jan. 1750, *London Magazine*. The man is probably Robert Walpole, since Molly (last line) must be Lady Mary's friend Maria Skerrett (see p. 26 above), his mistress by 1724 and later his wife. The motto comes from the title of an essay by Saint-Évremond on an ideal woman (*Œuvres en prose*, 1962-9, 2. 46).

The Man who feels the dear Disease
Forgets himselfe, neglects to please,
The croud avoids, and seeks the Groves,
And much he thinks, when much he loves,
Press'd with alternate Hope and Fear   5
Sighs in her Absence, sighs when she is near;
    The Gay, the fond, the Fair and young, ⎫
Those Trifflers pass unseen along,   ⎬
To him, a pert insipid throng.   ⎭
But most he shuns the vain Coquette,   10
Contemns her false affected Wit,
The Minstrels Sound, the flowing Bowl,
Oppress and hurt the Amorous Soul;
'Tis Solitude alone can please,
And give some Intervals of ease.   15
He feeds the soft distemper there
And fondly courts the distant Fair,
To Balls the silent shade prefers
And hates all other charms but Hers.
When thus your absent Swain can do   20
Molly; you may beleive him true.

4 Cf. Prior's *Henry and Emma*: 'And much He meditates; for much He loves' (1708: *Works*, 1. 283).

The Lover
a Ballad

Text H MS. 256. 18-19; copied after 1730; *written* probably 1721-5; *printed* 1747. This poem describes an ideal lover, not yet found. Lady Mary's MS. addresses the description to her friend Molly Skerrett, and it seems likely that she wrote it while she and Molly were on confidential terms. One copy in the Osborn Collection calls it 'a song as wrote from Miss Skerrett to Sir Robert Walpole and made by Lady Mary Wortley', another 'address'd to Miss S——t'. Walpole and Spence, however, believed that it was addressed to Richard Chandler (1703?-69), who m. Elizabeth Cavendish in 1732 and took her name on her father's death. Lady Mary addressed other verses to him (p. 260 below). Walpole wrote, 'One of her many amours was with Mr Chandler, eldest son to the

Bishop of Durham, to whom she wrote that admirable Description of a Lover
... though in the copies which she gives now she writes (Molly)' (*Corr.* 14. 245;
Spence's copy, Cornell MS. E 6004). Where 1747 printed 'C——', 1803 printed
'Congreve', thus originating an unfounded rumour.

I

At length by so much Importunity press'd,
Take (Molly) at once the Inside of my Breast,
This stupid Indifference so often you blame
Is not owing to Nature, to fear, or to Shame,
I am not as cold as a Virgin in Lead   5
Nor is Sunday's Sermon so strong in my Head,
I know but too well how Time flys along,
That we live but few Years and yet fewer are young.

2

But I hate to be cheated, and never will buy
Long years of Repentance for moments of Joy,   10
Oh was there a Man (but where shall I find
Good sense, and good Nature so equally joyn'd?)
Would value his pleasure, contribute to mine,
Not meanly would boast, nor lewdly design,
Not over severe, yet not stupidly vain,   15
For I would have the power thô not give the pain.

3

No Pedant yet learned, not rakehelly Gay
Or laughing because he has nothing to say,
To all my whole sex, obliging and Free,
Yet never be fond of any but me.   20
In public preserve the Decorums are just
And shew in his Eyes he is true to his Trust,
Then rarely approach, and respectfully Bow,
Yet not fulsomely pert, nor yet foppishly low.

4

But when the long hours of Public are past   25
And we meet with Champaign and a Chicken at last,

26 The line Byron admired (see p. 171 above).

May every fond Pleasure that hour endear,
Be banish'd afar both Discretion and Fear,
Forgetting or scorning the Airs of the Croud
He may cease to be formal, and I to be proud,   30
Till lost in the Joy we confess that we live
And he may be rude, and yet I may forgive.

5

And that my Delight may be solidly fix'd
Let the Freind, and the Lover be handsomly mix'd,
In whose tender Bosom my Soul might confide,   35
Whose kindness can sooth me, whose Councel could guide,
From such a dear Lover as here I describe
No danger should fright me, no Millions should bribe,
But till this astonishing Creature I know
As I long have liv'd Chaste I will keep my selfe so.   40

6

I never will share with the wanton Coquette
Or be caught by a vain affectation of Wit.
The Toasters, and Songsters may try all their Art
But never shall enter the pass of my Heart;
I loath the Lewd Rake, the dress'd Fopling despise,   45
Before such persuers the nice Virgin flys,
And as Ovid has sweetly in Parables told
We harden like Trees, and like Rivers are cold.

47–8 e.g. the stories of Daphne and Arethusa.

The Mistriss

Text H MS. 255. 31–2, copied after 1730; *written* probably 1721–5. According to Horace Walpole, Lady Mary 'suppressed' this companion piece 'as from Chandler' to the previous poem (*Corr.* 14. 245).

I

If e're passion in hopes of refining Delight
Shall engage me beyond the Amour of a Night

To seek dearer Arms, and a faithfuller kiss,
May it [be] for such Charms, such a Mistriss as this.
May her Face and her Mind to alure me conspire   5
And what one begun may the other raise higher,
Relenting her Nature and moving her Air
With Eyes of Desire to keep Hearts from Despair.

2

May She neither be easy, nor yet too severe,
But with Handsome Resistance her Yeilding endear,   10
By Winning Delays, pleasing Hope lead along,
And her Honnour grow weak, as my passion grows Strong,
Till soft to the Flame all the rigour remove,
Till she melt in a fusion of pleasure and Love,
To make me rejoyce that I once did complain,   15
To requite for the Stay and to pay for the pain.

3

When thus she is mine, may she be mine alone,
And want in Return to have me all her own,
Not vain of her Power, or Quick to Distrust,
May her prudence and Faith teach her Swain to be just, 20
May all her Endearments discover her Heart
From the smile when we meet, to the sigh when we part,
While ravish'd I see in each Look of her Eye
She for me would live, and she with me could die.

4

May she know to suit Love, in his every way,   25
To Languish, to Toy, to be eager and Gay.
In the Hours of Delight may she nothing forbear
That can Pleasure impart, or can Pleasure Declare,
Yet sometimes sweet blushes should follow to tell
The Wanton asham'd of her Loving so well   30
Till warm'd by a Kiss she in Whisper confess
She may Love too well, but she would not Love less.

5

In Public may no loose Demeanor betray
The Freedom she loves, and the Game she does play,
Yet nothing constrain'd least I learn to beleive   35
She has cunning to Feign and a Will to deceive,
But all her behaviour let Decency guide
Enrich'd by such worth, and good Humour beside,
That the World may not see, or not censure her Flame
But so much find to praise that they nothing dare blame.   40

6

To ennoble the rest may she Freindship adjoyn
And the Play of her Love have no under design,
Whilst easy and safe in the down of her Breast
May my Secrets all sink, and my Cares may all rest,
Thus may she be all a fond Heart can require,   45
Have much to Esteem, and yet more to Desire,
Then blest in her Arms, perhaps I may find
That a Woman can give more than halfe Womankind.

Wrote in Answer to a Letter in Verse sent me by Mr. H. after having met Miss S. and me accidentally on the road and carry'd us to his Country House.

He compar'd us to Venus and Pallas.

Text H MS. 256. 53, copied after 1736; *written* probably 1721–5. The place and people connected with this verse remain a mystery.

To Froyle the Muses sweetest seat
    My Thanks I will express,
That with such tender care releiv'd
    Poor damsels in distress.

In Ancient Time when Errant Knight   5
    Some wand'ring Nymph did find,
He lightly leap'd from off his Steed
    And set her up behind.

And while with Tears she told a Tale
  Of strange Disastrous Fate 10
She quench'd her thirst from Limpid Streams
  And Sallads were the Treat.

But You more hospitably kind
  Receive the Stranger Guest,
Scarce knowing what or whence they were, 15
  Unfreinded and undress'd.

While at a neat well furnish'd Board
  You elegantly dine
You garnish out the rich repaste
  With Music, Mirth, and Wine. 20

'Tis well for you no Goddesses
  Conceal'd their heavenly Shapes
As once, 'tis said, they often did
  In form of Mortal Trapes.

Celestial Dames, as Ovid sings 25
  (Who was, you know, inspir'd),
Cannot bear Rivals upon Earth
  And are with Envy fir'd.

Had Pallas seen the Loom at Froyle
  And heard the sounding Lyre 30
She surely had the Canvas tore
  And broke the Silver wire.

Venus no less enrag'd had view'd
  Fair Amarillis' Youth,
She has not halfe so bright a Bloom 35
  Nor such a melting Mouth.

But leaving these Heroic Strains
  We beg you condescend
To bear the Filthy Town once more
  And see your faithful Freind. 40

25 ff. The moral of the story of Arachne (*Metamorphoses*, vi).

Text 'the first leaf' of a copy of *Paradise Lost*, 9th ed., 1711, given to Lady
Mary by the Duke of Wharton, which she later gave to Molly Skerrett, and
which is now in the Lewis Walpole Library, Farmington, Conn. *Written* 1722–5,
during Lady Mary's friendships with Wharton and Molly Skerrett; *printed*
1837, 3. 426–7, with many variants, and seven unexplained extra lines.

> This pair a certain Happyness might prove,
> Confin'd to constancy and mutual Love.
> Heaven to one object limited his vows,
> The only safety faithless Nature knows,
> ⟨ ? ⟩ saw his wand'ring appetite would range   5
> And wisely kept him from the power to change,
> ⟨ ? ⟩ the world peopled falsehood soon began,
> Through ev'ry age the swift Contagion ran,
> This makes the censure of the world more just
> That brands with shame the weakness of a trust.   10

An Epilogue to a new Play of M[ary] Queen of Scots design'd to be spoke by Mrs Oldfield

Text H MS. 256. 6–7; *written* 1722–5; *printed* 1748. The 'new Play' was begun
but never finished by Lady Mary's friend Philip, Duke of Wharton; in 1726
Curll managed to elicit only four lines of it from a correspondent (Walpole,
Catalogue of Royal and Noble Authors: Works, 1798, 1. 445; *Whartoniana*, 1727,
2, Appendix, p. 21). Anne Oldfield (1683–1730), well known to have been mistress to Arthur Maynwaring and later to Charles Churchill, showed a special
flair for the mocking epilogues which frequently followed serious roles.

> What could Luxurious Woman wish for more
> To fix her Joys, or to extend her Power?
> Their every Wish was in this Mary seen,
> Gay, Witty, Youthful, Beauteous and a Queen!
> Vain useless Blessings with ill Conduct joyn'd!   5
> Light as the Air, and Fleeting as the Wind.
> What ever Poets write, or Lovers vow;
> Beauty, what poor Omnipotence hast thou!

8 Cf. Dryden's *Spanish Friar*, II. i (*Works*, 5. 145):

> > Love! What a poor omnipotence hast thou
> > When Gold and Titles buy thee?

(quoted by LM in 1712, *Letters*, 1. 119).

Queen Bess had Wisdom, Councel, Power, and Laws;
How few espous'd a Wretched Beauty's Cause!   10
Learn hence, ye Fair, more solid charms to prize,
Contemn the Idle Flatterers of your Eyes.
The brightest Object shines but while 'tis new,
That Influence lessens by Familiar View.
Monarchs and Beauties rule with equal sway,   15
All strive to serve, and glory to Obey;
Alike unpity'd when depos'd they grow,
Men mock the Idol of their former Vow.
   Two great Examples have been shewn to Day:
To what sure Ruin, Passion does betray,   20
What long Repentance to short Joys is due;
When Reason rules what Glory does ensue.
   If you will Love, love like Eliza then,
Love for Amusement like those Traitors, Men.
Think that the Pastime of a Leisure Hour   25
She favour'd oft—but never shar'd her Power.
   The Traveller by Desart Wolves persu'd,
If by his Art the savage Foe's subdu'd,
The World will still the noble Act applaud,
Tho' Victory was gain'd by needfull Fraud.   30
   Such is (my tender Sex) our helpless Case
And such the barbarous Heart, hid by the begging Face.
By Passion fir'd, and not with held by Shame,
They cruel Hunters are, we trembling Game.
Trust me, Dear Ladys (for I know 'em well),   35
They burn to Triumph, and they sigh—to tell.
Cruel to them that Yeild, Cullys to them that sell.
Beleive me tis by far the wiser Course,
Superior Art should meet superior force.
Hear; but be faithfull to your Interest still,   40
Secure your Hearts, then Fool with who you will.

15-18 Repeated from 'Satturday', lines 85-8.
  32 Cf. 'An Answer to a Love Letter in verse', line 30 (p. 245 below), and a note in
LM's commonplace-book, 'Lovers, common Beggars' (Fisher Library, University of
Sydney, f. 5).

Epistle [to Lord Bathurst]

Text H MS. 256. 14–16, copied after 1730; *written* probably in 1725 as a result of Bathurst's flirtation with Mrs. Howard (*Letters*, 2. 55–7); *printed* 1748. Lady Mary addressed this epistle to Allen, 1st Baron Bathurst (1684–1775), with whom in 1724 she had been 'well and ill ten times within this two months' (*Letters*, 2. 53). For their relationship and Bathurst's schemes and volatility, see Pope, *Corr.* 2. 82, 258, 292, 315; 3. 130, 134, 136.

How happy you who vary'd Joys persue,
And every Hour presents you something new!
Plans, Schemes, and Models, all Palladio's Art
For six long Months has gain'd upon your Heart,
Of Colonades, and Corridores you talk,   5
The winding Stair case, and the cover'd Walk,
Proportion'd Colums strikes before your Eye,
Corinthian Beauty, Ionian Majesty,
You blend the Orders with Vitruvian Toil
And raise with wondrous Joy the fancy'd Pile.   10
    But the dull Workman's slow-performing Hand
But coldly executes his Lord's command,
With Dirt and Mortar soon you grow displeas'd,
Planting Succeeds, and Avenues are rais'd,
Canals are cut, and Mountains Level made,   15
Bowers of retreat, and Gallerys of shade.
The shaven Turf presents a living Green,
The bordering Flowers in Mystic knots are seen.
With study'd Art on Nature you refine—
The Spring beheld you warm in this Design,   20
But scarce the cold attacks your favourite Trees,
Your Inclinations fail, and wishes freeze,
You quit the Grove, so lately so admir'd,
With other views your eager Hopes are fir'd,

3 Andrea Palladio (1518–80), architectural ideal of Lord Burlington's school.

9 Marcus Vitruvius Pollio, Roman architect of the Augustan age, author of *De Architectura*, the major source of knowledge of classical building.

15 Pope joked about Bathurst's supposed scheme for joining the Thames and Severn ([May] 1722, *Corr.* 2. 116).

22–3 Hervey apparently identified Bathurst with Villario in Pope's *Epistle to Burlington*, who creates a fine estate only to find 'at last he better likes a Field' (*Poems*, 3. 2. 145–6, 181).

Post to the City you direct your way,   25
Not blooming Paradice would bribe your stay,
Ambition shows you Power's brightest Side,
'Tis meanly poor in Solitude to hide,
Tho certain Pain attends the Cares of State,
A Good Man owes his Country to be great,   30
Should act abroad the high distinguish'd Part,
Or shew at least the purpose of his Heart;
With Thoughts like these, the shining Court you seek
Full of new projects for—allmost a Week.
You then Despise the Tinsel glittering Snare;   35
Think vile Mankind below a serious Care:
Life is too short for any distant Aim,
And cold the dull reward of Future Fame.
Be happy then; while yet you have to live:
And Love is all the Blessing Heaven can give;   40
Fir'd by new passion you address the fair,
Survey the Opera as a gay Parterre,
Young Cloe's bloom had made you certain Prize
But for a sidelong Glance of Cœlia's Eyes,
Your beating Heart acknowledges her power,   45
Your eager Eyes her lovely form devour,
You feel the Poison swelling in your Breast
And all your Soul by fond Desire possess'd.
In dying sighs a long three hours is past,
To some Assembly with Impatient haste,   50
With trembling Hope and doubtfull Fear you move,
Resolv'd to tempt your Fate, and own your Love:
But there Bellinda meets you on the Stairs.
Easy, her Shape, attracting all her Airs,
A smile she gives, and with a smile can wound,   55
Her melting voice has Music in the Sound,
Her every Motion wears resistless Grace,
Wit in her Mien, and Pleasure in her Face;
Here while you vow Eternity of Love,
Cloe and Cœlia unregarded move.   60
   Thus on the Sands of Affric's burning plains
However deeply made no long Impress remains,
The lightest Leaf can leave its figure there,
The strongest Form is scatter'd by the Air,

So yeilding the Warm temper of your Mind,⎫ 65
So touch'd by every Eye; so toss'd by every Wind,⎬
O how unlike has Heaven my Soul design'd!⎭

   Unseen, unheard, the Throng around me move,
Not wishing Praise, insensible of Love,
No Whispers soften, nor no Beautys Fire, 70
Careless I see the Dance, and coldly hear the Lyre.

   So numerous Herds are driven o're the Rock,
No print is left of all the passing Flock,
So sings the Wind around the solid stone,
So vainly beats the Waves with fruitless moan, 75
Tedious the Toil, and great the Workman's care
Who dare attempt to fix Impressions there.
But should some Swain more skillfull than the rest
Engrave his Name on this cold Marble Breast
Not rolling ages could deface that Name— 80
Through all the storms of Life tis still the same,
Tho length of Years with moss may shade the Ground
Deep thô unseen remains the secret wound.

68–71 Quoted by Walpole, who denied that it was an accurate portrait of her ('Anecdotes of Lady Mary Wortley Montagu': *Corr.* 14. 242).

An Answer to a Love Letter in Verse

Text H MS. 256. 5–6; *written* probably in the 1720s; *printed* Apr. 1750, *London Magazine.* Lady Mary was replying to a letter from a 'Mr. T.' or 'Mr. T——n' (Cornell MS. E 6004; Osborn Collection f c 51). One 'sad-lamenting' suitor sent her a verse epistle dated 31 May 1725 (H MS. 81. 121); there were no doubt others.

Is it to me, this sad-lamenting Strain?
Are Heaven's choicest gifts bestow'd in vain?
A Plenteous Fortune, and a Beauteous Bride,
Your Love rewarded, and content your Pride!
Yet leaving her—'tis me that you persu, 5
Without one single charm, but being New.
   How vile is Man! How I detest the Ways
Of Artfull Falsehood, and designing Praise!

Tastless, an easy Happyness you slight,
Ruin your Joy, and Mischeif your Delight.   10
Why should poor Pug (the Mimic of your kind)
Wear a rough Chain, and be to Box confin'd?
Some Cup perhaps he breaks, or tears a Fan,
While moves unpunish'd the Destroyer, Man.
Not bound by vows, and unrestrain'd by Shame,   15
In sport you break the Heart, and rend the Fame.
Not that your Art can be successfull here,
Th'allready Plunder'd need no Robber fear,
Nor Sighs, nor Charms, nor Flattery can move,
Too well secur'd against a second Love.   20
Once, and but Once, that Devil charm'd my Mind,
To Reason deaf, to Observation blind,
I Idly hop'd (what cannot Love persuade?)
My Fondness equall'd, and my Truth repaid,
Slow to Distrust, and willing to beleive,   25
Long hush'd my Doubts, and would my selfe deceive;
But Oh too soon—this Tale would ever last,
Sleep, sleep my wrongs and let me think 'em past.
   For you who mourn with counterfeited Greife
And ask so boldly like a begging Theife;   30
May soon some other Nymph inflict the Pain
You know so well, with cruel Art to feign,
Tho' long you've sported with Don Cupid's Dart,
You may see Eyes, and you may feel a Heart.
   So the Brisk Wits who stop the Evening Coach   35
Laugh at the Fear that follows their approach,

---

11 *Pug*: a monkey.
17 Cf. Prior's *Solomon*, 2. 268: 'Not that those Arts can here successful prove' (*Works*, 1. 340).
19–20 Cf. 'Part of Virgils 4th Georgick' (*Sylvæ*, 1685, p. 153):
> No face cou'd win him, and no charms cou'd move,
> He fled the heinous thoughts of second Love.
21 Cf. Pope's early version of the *Epistle to Arbuthnot* (*Poems*, 4, p. xvi):
> Once, and but once, his heedless youth was bit
> And lik'd that dang'rous thing, a female wit.
23 Cf. 'Part of Virgils 4th Georgick': 'He stopt, look'd back, (what cannot love perswade?)' (*Sylvæ*, p. 150).
25–6 Cf. Prior's *Solomon*, iii. 222–3 (*Works*, 1. 367):
> Hoping at least She may Her self deceive,
> Against Experience willing to believe.

With Idle Mirth, and Haughty Scorn despise
The Passengers pale Cheek, and staring Eyes;
But seiz'd by Justice, find a Fright no Jest
And all the Terror doubled in their Breast.   40

To the Memory of Mr Congreve

Text H MS. 81. 128; *written* Jan.–Feb. 1729. Lines 5–6, 11–12, occur in a
fragmentary draft by Lady Mary on the back of an earlier note to her from Pope
(*Corr.* 2. 22–33; now at Sandon Hall), and were probably composed in 1720.
Printed K. M. Lynch, *A Congreve Gallery*, 1951, pp. 6–7. Congreve died on
19 Jan. 1729.

Farewell the best and loveliest of Mankind
Where Nature with a happy hand had joyn'd
The softest temper with the strongest mind,
In pain could counsel and could charm when blind.

In this Lewd Age when Honor is a Jest   5
He found a refuge in his Congreve's breast,
Superior there, unsully'd, and entire;
And only could with the last breath expire.

His wit was never by his Malice stain'd,
No rival writer of his Verse complain'd,   10
For neither party drew a venal pen
To praise bad measures or to blast good men.

A Queen indeed he mourn'd, but such a Queen
Where Virtue mix'd with royal Blood was seen,

After 8 a stanza struck out:

> How keen his Wit, how pierceing, and how bright,
> The smallest error could not 'scape his sight
> Yet such a gentlenesse his Judgment rein'd
> His verses never were by Malice stain'd.

1 Cf. Dryden's *Tyrannick Love*, Act v: 'Farewel, the best and bravest of Mankind'
(*Works*, 2. 390).

4 *blind*: perhaps an exaggeration, but Congreve had had trouble with his eyes since
1710 (John C. Hodges, *William Congreve the Man*, 1941, pp. 104–5).

13–16 Congreve's 'The Mourning Muse of Alexis', 1695, lamented Queen Mary's
death from smallpox the previous year; her piety and submission to her husband were
famous.

With equal merit grac'd each Scene of Life   15
An Humble Regent and Obedient Wife.

If in a Distant State blest Spirits know
The Scenes of Sorrow of a World below,
This little Tribute to thy Fame approve,
A Triffling Instance of a boundless Love.   20

Text H MS. 81. 36–40, draft; *written* probably summer 1729. This mock-heroic episode and the other following it were conceived as a riposte to the *Dunciad*. Lady Mary composed them in conjunction with a similar attempt by her cousin Henry Fielding (H MS. 81. 172–85; printed in *PMLA*, 87 (1972), 219–45). Fielding was in England between Aug. and Oct. 1728, and again from the summer of 1729, when he composed the greater part of his verse. Lady Mary's poems are backdated, events from 1714 onwards being prophesied for the future. *Printed* 1803.

Her Palace placed beneath a muddy road   ⎫
And such the Influence of the dull Abode,   ⎬
The Carrier's Horse above can scarsely drag his Load. ⎭
   Here chose the Goddess her belov'd Retreat
Which Phoebus trys in vain to penetrate,   5
Adorn'd within by Shells of small expence
(Emblems of tinsel Rhime, and triffleing Sense),
Perpetual fogs enclose the sacred Cave,
The neighbouring Sinks their fragrant Odours gave.
In Contemplation here she pass'd her Hours   10
Closely attended by Subservient pow'rs:
Bold Prophanation with a Brazen brow,
Much to this great Ally does Dullness owe;
But still more near the Goddess you attend,
Naked Obscenity her darling Freind!   15
To thee for shelter all the dull still fly,
Pert double meanings even at School we try.
What Numerous writers owe their praise to thee!
No Sex, no Age, is from thy Influence free!

1–9 Pope's grotto beneath the London–Hampton Court road, 'finished with Shells interspersed with Pieces of Looking-glass in angular forms' (Pope, *Corr.* 2. 297).
7 From the *Dunciad*: 'Emblem of Music caus'd by Emptiness' (1729: i. 30).

By thee how bright appears the senseless song,   20
By thee, the Book is sold, the Lines are strong,
The Heaviest poet by thy powerfull Aid
Warms the Brisk Youth, and charms the sprightly Maid.
Where breaths the Mortal has not prov'd thy force
In well bred Pun, and waiting room discourse?   25
  Such were the cheifs adorn'd the gloomy Court,
Her Pride, her Ornament, and her Support,
Behind attended such a numerous Croud   ⎫
Of Quibbles strain'd, odd Rhimes, and Laughter loud, ⎬
Such Throngs as might have made a Goddess proud. ⎭   30
Yet pensive thoughts lay brooding in her Breast
And Fear (the Mate of Pow'r) her mind oppress'd.
Oft she revolv'd, for oh too well she knew
What Merlin sung, and part long since prov'd true.
'When Harry's Brows the Diadem adorn   35
From Reformation, Learning shall be born,
Slowly in Strength the infant shall improve
The parents glory and its Country's love,
Free from the thraldom of Monastic Rhimes,
In bright progression bless succeeding Times,   40
Milton free Poetry from the Monkish Chain,
And Adisson that Milton shall explain,
Point out the Beauties of each living Page,
Reform the taste of a degenerate Age,
Shew that True Wit disdains all little Art   45
And can at once engage, and mend the Heart,
Knows even Popular Applause to gain
Yet not malicious, Bawdy or Prophane.'

34 The astrologer Partridge had been publishing his almanac *Merlinus Liberatus* since the previous century. Cf. Swift's 'A Famous Prediction of Merlin', 1709 (*Poems*, ed. H. Williams, 1937, 1. 101–5).

35–6 Henry VIII: cf. Fielding's related verse (*PMLA*, 1972, p. 220):

> But soon as Reformation first prevail'd
> My [Dullness's] cause and Popery's together fail'd.

39 Cf. 'The Monkish days! those glorious Days of Rhime!' (ibid., p. 219).

41 *Chain*: i.e. of rhyme. Fielding's verse makes Pope offspring of Dullness and the god of Rhime, contrasting him with Milton (ibid., pp. 224–5).

42 Addison did this in his series of Saturday *Spectators* begun on 5 Jan. 1712. Fielding's verse shows traces of an abandoned plan to make Addison the chief opponent of Pope (*PMLA*, 1972, p. 224).

45 In *Spectator* No. 62.

This Prophecy perplex'd her Anxious Head,
And yawning thrice thus to her Sons she said: 50
When such an Author does abroad appear
'Tis sure the Hour of our Destruction's near,
And public Rumour now aloud proclaims
At Universal Monarchy he aims.
What to this Hero? what shall we oppose?   55
A strong Confedracy of Stupid Foes!
Such Brave Allys as are by Nature fit
To stop the progress of o'reflowing Wit,
Where Envy, and where Impudence are joyn'd
To contradict the Voice of Humankind,   60
At Dacier's Ignorance shall gravely smile
And blame the coarseness of Spectator's style,
Shall swear that Tickell understands not Greek,
That Adison can't write, nor Walpole speak.
  Fir'd by this Project, Prophanation rose:—   65
One Leader, Goddess, let me here propose,
In a near Realm that owns thy Gentle Sway
My darling Son now chaunts his pleasing Lay,
Trampling on Order, Decency, and Laws,
And boasts himselfe the Champion of my Cause.   70
Him will I bring, to teach the Callow Youth
To scorn dry Morals, laugh at sacred Truth,
All Fears of Future reckn'ings he shall quench,
And Bid them bravely drink, and boldly Wench,
By his Example much, by precept more,   75
He learns, 'tis wit to swear, and safe to Whore.
Mocks Newton's Schemes, and Tillotson's Discourse

61 Pope sometimes contradicts the French critic Mme Dacier in his preface and notes to Homer (e.g. *Iliad*, i. 41 and 268).
  62 Swift refers to the 'Flatness' of Steele's *Spectator* essays (*The Publick Spirit of the Whigs*, 1714: *Works*, ed. H. Davis, 1939–68, 8. 36).
  63–4 Tickell's translation of *Iliad*, book i, is cited in *The Art of Sinking in Poetry*, xii (ed. E. L. Steeves, 1952, pp. 60–1), and mentioned in Pope's lines on Addison as Atticus (printed 1722: Pope, *Poems*, 6. 143); Addison is quoted in *The Art of Sinking*, xi, xii (pp. 58, 61).
  67 *near Realm*: Ireland.
  68 *darling Son*: Swift.
  77 Swift had disagreed with Newton over Wood's coinage in 1722; in Glubb-dubdrib, the ghost of Aristotle predicts that Newton's doctrines will be exploded (*Gulliver's Travels*, III. viii). Swift had given ironical praise to Archbishop Tillotson in *Mr. Collins's Discourse of Free-Thinking*, 1713 (*Prose Works*, ed. H. Davis, 1939–64, 4. 34–5).

And Imitates the Virtue of a Horse.
With this Design, to add to his renown,
He wears the reverend dress of Band and Gown.   80
    The Goddess pleas'd bestow'd a gracious Grin
When thus, does fair Obscœnity begin.
My Humbler Subjects are not plac'd so high,
They Joke in Kitchins, and in Cellars ply,
Yet one I have (bred in those worthy Schools)   85
Admir'd by Shoals of Male and female Fools,
In ballads what I dictate he shall sing
And troops of Converts to my Banners bring.
    Despise not, Glorious Goddess, my releife,
I have a Leader worthy to be cheife,   90
My Images are all he knows of Wit!
How Vomits look, what Quantitys are spet,
By his profession skill'd in Terms like these
His usefull writeings cannot fail to please,
Such foul Description all his poem fills,   95
To Stomachs nice, he saves th'expence of Squills,
Born in that Realm where Nastyness gives Joy
And scratching all the solitary hours employ.
    Here —— ceas'd, the Goddess smil'd, and round ⎞
Applauses issue from the deep profound,   ⎬   100
Hoarse murmurs of Applause the Caves resound.   ⎠
But who (she cry'd) where equal Merits plead,
Who can point out the Captain fit to Lead?
This Task be mine; thô hard, it seems, to find
A Soul where all these several gifts are joyn'd,   105
Bold in Obscœnity, prophanely dull,
With smooth unmeaning Rhime the Town shall lull,
Shall sing of Worms in great Arbuthnott's strain,

---

78 Cf. Shakespeare's *Henry V*, III. i. 6.

85 Gay's family were unquestionably gentlefolk, but he had been apprentice to a silk-mercer and domestic steward to the Duchess of Monmouth.

87 Fielding's verse also accuses *The Beggar's Opera*, 1728, of 'Ribaldry' (*PMLA*, 1972, pp. 227–8).

89 A deleted version of this line—'The cheife, said Cloacina, I commend'—indicates that a different character is under discussion: probably Dr. Arbuthnot, a Scot and alleged author of 'The Life and Adventures of Don Bilioso de l'Estomac', 1719.

96 *Squills*: a vomit.

99 Cloacina, not Obscenity, fits the Alexandrine line.

108–10 *To the Ingenious Mr. Moore, Author of the Celebrated Worm-Powder*, 1716,

In Lewd Burlesque the Sacred Psalms prophane,
To maids of Honor bawdy Songs address   110
Nor need we doubt his wonderfull Success.
Long have I watch'd this Genius yet unknown,
Inspir'd his Rhime, and mark'd him for my own;
His early Youth in Superstition bred
And monkish Legends all the Books he read.   115
Tinctur'd by these, proceeds his Love to Rhime,
Milton he scorns, but Crambo thinks sublime,
And oh 'tis sure, (our Foes confess this truth)
The old Crambonians yeild to this Stupendous Youth,
But present want obscures the Poet's Name,   120
Be it my charge to talk him into fame.
My Lansdown (whose Love-songs so smoothly run,
My Darling Author, and my Favourite Son),
He shall protect the Man that I inspire,
And Windsor Forest openly admire,   125
And Bolingbrook with flattry Gay shall bribe
Till the charm'd Lord most nobly shall subscribe
And Hostile Adison too late shall find
'Tis easier to corrupt than Mend Mankind,
The town (which now revolts) once more Obey   130
And the whole Island own my pristine Sway.
  She said, and slowly leaves the realms of Night,
While the Curst Phantoms bless and praise her flight.

A Roman Catholick Version of the First Psalm, 1716, *The Court Ballad*, 1717, and its
accompanying epigrams on the Maids of Honour were all firmly attributed to Pope
but never acknowledged (*Poems*, 6. 161–5, 180–6).
  117 *Crambo: bouts rimés*, or verse composed to fit given rhymes.
  122–3 This is LM's only disparagement of George Granville (1666–1735), Lord
Lansdowne, whose poems she owned and quoted (*Letters*, 3. 170 and n. 1).
  125 Pope dedicated *Windsor Forest*, 1713, to Lansdowne, to whom he said he had
'particular obligations' (*Corr.* 1. 375).
  126 Gay dedicated his *Shepherd's Week*, 1714, to Bolingbroke, who subscribed for
ten sets of Pope's *Iliad*, but not for Gay's *Poems*, 1720.
  130 Under the influence of the *Spectator*, 1711–12.

Text H MS. 81. 45–7, draft; *written* probably summer 1729; *printed* 1803. See
headnote to previous poem.

  Now with fresh vigour Morn her Light displays
  And the glad Birds salute her rising rays,

The opening Buds confess the Sun's return
And rouz'd from Night, all Nature seems new born,
When Pondrous Dullness slowly wing'd her way   5
And with thick Fogs oppos'd the rising day.
Phœbus retir'd (as from Thyestes' Feast)
Droop'd all the Flow'rs, the airial music ceas'd.
Pleas'd with her Influence, she exults with Pride,
Shall Mortals then escape my pow'r? (she cry'd)   10
Nay, in this Town where smoak, and mists conspire
To cloud the head, and damp the Poet's Fire,
Shall Adison my Empire here dispute,
So justly founded, lov'd, and Absolute?
Explode my Children, Ribaldry and Rhime,   15
Rever'd from Chaucer down to Dryden's Time,
Distinguish twixt false humour and the true
And Wit make Lovely to the vulgar Veiw?
No; Better things my Destiny Ordains,
For Oxford has the Wand, and Anna reigns.   20
    She ended, and assum'd Duke Disney's grin,   ⎫
With broad plump Face, pert Eyes, and ruddy skin,   ⎬
Which shew'd the stupid Jokes that lurk'd within.   ⎭
    In this lov'd form she knock'd at St John's gate
Where Crouds allready for his Levée wait,   25
And wait they may, those wretches who appear
To talk of service past, and long arrear,
But the proud partner of his pleasures goes,
Through crouds of envious Eyes, and servile bows,
And now approaching where the Statesman lay   30

15 Addison had judged blank verse better than rhyme for tragedy (*Spectator* No. 39),
and used it for *Cato*, 1713.

17 *Spectator* No. 35.

20 *Wand*: symbol of office of the Lord High Treasurer, held by Lord Oxford, 1711–
14. Cf. Garth's *Dispensary*, iii: 'For *S——rs* has the Seal, and *Nassau* reigns' (4th ed.
1700, p. 37).

21–3 Cf. the dummy poet (originally intended to be Gay), offered as a prize to the
booksellers in *Dunciad*, ii. 31 ff. The facetious Henry Disney or Desaulnais (d. 1731)
was known to his intimates as 'the Duke'.

24 ff. Henry St. John, Lord Bolingbroke, Secretary of State 1710–14. This scene
owes something to that in Boileau's *Le Lutrin*, canto i, where Discord in disguise rouses
the sleepy prelate.

26–7 Swift wrote, 'in my Time . . . there was always a huge list of Names in Arrears
at the Treasury, which would take up, at least take up, your Seven years expedient to
discharge even one half' (*Corr.*, ed. H. Williams, 1963–5, 2. 443).

To his unwilling Eyes reveal'd the Day,
Starting he waked, and wakeing swore, By God
This early visit Freind is wondrous odd.
Scarse have I rested full 2 hours in Bed
And Fumes of Wine oppress my aking Head,   35
By thee I'm sure my Soul is understood
Too well, to plague me for the Public good,
Let stupid Patriots toil to serve the Brutes,
And waste the fleeting hours in vain Disputes,
The use of Power supreme I better know,   40
Nor will I lose the Joys the Gods bestow;
The sparkling Glass, soft flute, and willing Fair,
Alternate guard me from th'Attacks of Care,
'Tis the Prerogative of Wit like Mine
To Emulate in Ease the Pow'rs divine   45
And while I revel, leave the busy Fools,
To plot like Chymists, or to drudge like Tools.
    Beleive me Lord, replys his seeming Freind,
Some Difficulties every State attend,
Cares must surround the Men that Wealth possess   50
And Sorrows mingle even with Love's Success,
Great as you are, no Greatness long is sure,
Advancement is but pain, if not secure,
All your long Schemes may vanish in an hour,
Oh, tremble at the sad reverse of Pow'r!   55
How will those slaves that waiting watch your Eye
Insulting smile, or pass regardless by!
Nor is this thought the Creature of my Fears,
Signs of approaching Ruin strong appears.
Men must be dull who passively Obey   60
And Ignorance fixes Arbitrary Sway,
Think of this Maxim, and no more permit
A dangerous writer to retale his Wit.
The Consequence of Sense is Liberty
And if Men think aright they will be free,   65

34–5 In 1731 Bolingbroke wrote, 'It is now, six in the morning. I recal the time, and
am glad it is over, when about this hour I used to be going to bed, Surfeited with pleasure,
or jaded with business' (Swift, *Corr.* 3. 448).
    63 Addison.
    64–5 Fielding's related verse also connected political liberty with wit and learning
(*PMLA*, 1972, pp. 230–1).

Encourrage you the Poet I shall bring, ⎫
Your Granville he allready trys to sing, ⎬
The mountains Echo, and the vallys ring. ⎭
Nor think my Lord I only recommend
An Able Author but a usefull Freind,   70
In verse his Phlegm, in Puns he shews his fire
And skill'd in pimping to your heart's desire.

I thank thee Duke, replys the drousy peer,
But cannot listen to thy childish Fear,
This Adison, 'tis true (debauch'd in Schools)   75
Will sometimes oddly talk of Musty Rules,
Yet here, and there, I see a Master line,
I feel, and I Confess the power divine,
In spite of Intrest charm'd into Applause
I wish for such a Champion to our Cause,   80
Nor shall your Reasons force me to submit
To patronise a Bard of meaner Wit,
Men can but say Wit did my Judgment blind
And Wit's the noblest frailty of the mind.

The disapointed Goddess swell'd with Spite,   85
Dropping the Borrow'd form appears in open light,
So the Sly Nymph in masquerade disguise
The Faith of her suspected Lover trys
But when the perjury too plain appears
Her eyes are fill'd with mingled rage and tears,   90
No more remembers the affected Tone,
Sinks the feign'd voice, and thunders in her own.

How hast thou dar'd, my party then to Quit?
Or dost thou Wretch, presume thou art a Wit?
Read thy own Verse, consider well each line,   95
In each Dull page, how papaply [*sic*] I shine,

67–8 Pope praised Lansdowne's poetry in 'Spring', line 46, and *Windsor Forest*,
lines 292 ff. Cf. 'The Woods shall answer, and their Echo ring' ('Summer', line 16).

79–80 *Applause*: Bolingbroke gave Booth fifty guineas for his part in *Cato*, but he
hoped thereby to stress the play's possible Tory interpretation. He and Addison dined
together on 3 Apr. 1713 and 'talkt in a friendly manner of Party' (Swift, *Journal to
Stella*, ed. H. Williams, 1948, 2. 652).

83–4 Borrowed from Dryden, *The Indian Emperour*, II. ii (*Works*, I. 293):

Men can but say Love did his reason blind,
And Love's the noblest frailty of the mind.

95 Bolingbroke's early poetical attempts included complimentary verses printed with
Dryden's translation of the *Aeneid*.

'Tis me that to thy Eloquence affords
Such Empty thoughts wrap'd in superfluous Words,
To me alone your Pamphlet-praise you owe,
Tis I, your Tropes, and Florid Style, bestow.   100
After such wreaths bestow'd, such service done,
Dare you refuse protection to my Son?
The time shall come (thô now at Court ador'd)
When still a Writer, thô no more a Lord,
On Common Stalls thy darling Works be spread   105
And thou shall't answer 'em to make 'em read.
    She said and turning shew'd her wrinkled neck
In scales and colour like a Roaches back.

104 He forfeited his titles when he fled to France in 1715.
107-8 This couplet appears also in Fielding's related verse, in a passage parodying
Aeneas's meeting with Venus, which was published separately in Fielding's *Miscellanies*, 1743 (ed. H. K. Miller, 1972, p. 81).

Text H MS. 81. 152; *written* in summer, probably addressed to Lord Hervey
(see pp. 39-40 above), who was travelling for his health in the summer of 1729
(Halsband, *Hervey*, pp. 82-4). *Printed* 1803. Other verse from Lady Mary to
Hervey is published in her *Letters*, 2. 98-9, 112-13, 238-9.

From this vile Town immers'd in Dust and Care,
To you who brighten in a purer Air;
Your Faithfull Freind conveys her tenderest thought
(Thô now perhaps neglected and forgot)
May blooming Health your wonted Mirth restore   5
And every Pleasure crown your every hour
Carress'd, esteem'd, and lov'd, your Merit known
And Foreign Lands adore you like your own,
While I in silence various Tortures bear
Distracted with the rage of Bosom-War.   10
My restless Fever tears my changing Brain
With mix'd Ideas of Delight and Pain,
Sometimes soft views my morning Dreams employ
In the faint Dawn of Visionary Joy
Which Rigid Reason quickly drives away,   15
I seek the Shade and curse the rising Day,

9 ff. Pope had struck at LM in the *Dunciad* (ii. 127-8); hostile pamphlets on both
sides followed the publication of the Variorum version in Apr. 1729. LM was also en-
gaged in family strife over her mentally deranged sister (Halsband, *LM*, pp. 133-5).

In pleasing Madness meet some Moments Ease,
And fondly cherish my belov'd Disease.
    If Female weakness melts my Woman's mind
At least no weakness in the Choice I find.   20
Not sooth'd to softness by a warbling Flute
Or the bought Merit of a Birth-Day suit,
Nor lost my Heart, by the surprizing skill
In Opera Tunes, in danceing, or Quadrille,
The only charm my Inclination moves,   25
Is such a Virtue Heaven it selfe approves,
A Soul superior to each vulgar view;
Great, steady, Gentle, Generous and True.
    How I regret my triffling hours past,
And look with horror on the Dreary Waste!   30
In False persuits and Vanity bestow'd
The perfect image of a dirty Road.
Through puddles oft, o're craggy Rocks I stray
A tiresome, dull, uncomfortable way;
And after toiling long throû thick and thin   35
To reach some meanly mercenary Inn,
The Bills are high, and very coarse the Fare,
I curse the wretched Entertainment there;
And jogging on, resolve to stop no more
When Gaudy Signs invite me to the Door.   40

32 ff. The same image opens 'Address'd To ——' (p. 290 below).
34 Cf. 'A long, forlorn, uncomfortable Way!' (Pope's *Iliad*, vi. 248.)

Text H MS. 81. 66–7, drafted at the bottom of a scribal copy of Hervey's 'To Mr Fox Written at Florence 1729', which extols country retirement (Dodsley's *Collection*, 1748, 1st ed., 3. 240–2). *Written* in Oct. 1729 and sent to Hervey in France, where, however, it missed him (Hervey MS., Bury St. Edmunds, 47/2. 37–40, 44). *Printed* 1803.

So sung the Poet in an Humble Strain
With Empty pockets and a Head in pain
Where the soft Clime enclin'd the Soul to rest
And Pastoral Images inspir'd the Breast!
Apollo listen'd from his heavenly Bow⟨er⟩   5
And in his Health restor'd express'd his power.
Pygmalion thus before the Paphian shrine

With trembling vows address'd the power divine,
Durst hardly make his hopeless wishes known,
And scarce a greater Miracle was shewn,   10
Returning Vigour glow'd in every Vein
And gay Ideas flutter in the Brain,
Back he returns to breathe his Native Air
And all his firm resolves are melted there.

12 Cf. 'Then gay Ideas crowd the vacant Brain' (*The Rape of the Lock*, i. 83).
13–14 LM judged her friend's character correctly; in 1730 he was appointed Vice-Chamberlain to the King, and became increasingly Walpole's right-hand man at court.

Text Commonplace-book MS., Fisher Library, University of Sydney, f. 7, copied during the 1750s; probably *written* in the 1720s if, as Dallaway says (1803, 1. 74), it was shown to Pope. *Printed* 1803. Lady Mary, like Fielding in 1729 (*PMLA*, 1972, p. 230), turns against Pope his own lines on Settle ('To the Author of a Poem, intitled, Successio', 1712: *Poems*, 6. 15–16).

Sure P[ope] like Orph[eus] was alike inspir'd,
The Blocks and Beasts flock'd round them and admir'd.

Song

Text H MS. 256, 13–14; *written* 6 Apr. ?1730; *printed* 1748. The alternative title, 'A Receit to Cure the Vapours', may originate with Lady Mary, since it occurs in Spence's copy (Cornell MS. E 6004). Lady Anne Howard (before 1696–1764), daughter of the 3rd Earl of Carlisle, m. (1717) Lord Irwin, who died four years later. On 8 April [?1730] she told her father that Lady Mary 'was here two nights ago; the conversation turned upon constancy; Lady Mary immediately attacked me for a practice so inconsistent with reason and nature; called for a pen and ink; said she found herself inspired for my service, and writ, as she pretended, the enclosed off hand' (H.M.C., *Carlisle MSS.*, 1897, p. 71). In several MS. copies Lady Irwin's reply accompanies the song, which by 1781 had been 'Sung at Ranelagh' (*The Vocal Magazine*, 1781, poem no. 1216).

Why will Delia thus retire
And languish Life away?
While the sighing Crowds admire
'Tis too soon for Hartshorn Tea.

All these dismal looks and fretting   5
  Cannot Damon's life restore,
Long ago the Worms have eat him,
  You can never see him more.

Once again consult your Toilet,
  In the Glass your Face review,   10
So much weeping soon will spoil it
  And no Spring your Charms renew.

I like you was born a Woman—
  Well I know what Vapours mean,
The Disease alas! is common,   15
  Single we have all the Spleen.

All the Morals that they tell us
  Never cur'd Sorrow yet,
Chuse among the pretty Fellows
  One of humour, Youth, and Wit.   20

Prithee hear him ev'ry Morning
  At least an hour or two,
Once again at Nights returning,
  I beleive the Dose will do.

6 Rich Ingram (1688–1721), 5th Viscount Irwin or Irvine; LM had described him
in 1714 as 'much a prittyer sort of Gentleman . . .' (*Letters*, 1. 220).
   14 In old age LM boasted that she had never suffered from hysterical complaints
(*Letters*, 3. 171).
   20 In 1737 Lady Irwin married, against the wishes of her family, Col. William Douglas
(d. 1747: Charles Dalton, *George the First's Army*, 1910–12, 1. 179 n. 5).

An Answer to a Lady
Advising me to Retirement

Text H MS. 256. 6; many copies survive. *Written* shortly before 16 Sept.
1730, when Hervey quoted from it (Hervey MS., Bury St. Edmunds, 47/4. 137).
Printed May 1750, *London Magazine*.

You little know the Heart that you advise,
I view this various Scene with equal Eyes,

In crouded Court I find my selfe alone,
And pay my Worship to a nobler Throne.

Long since the value of this World I know,   5
Pity the Madness, and despise the Show,
Well as I can, my tedious part I bear
And wait Dismission without painfull Fear.

Seldom I mark Mankind's detested ways
Not hearing Censure, nor Affecting Praise,   10
And unconcern'd my Future Fate I trust;
To that sole Being, Mercifull and Just.

Song

Text H MS. 256. 10; *written* probably before the death (May 1731) of Lady
Mary's friend Mary Astell (see p. 33 above), who wrote or transcribed a
related 'Anti-Song' (separate, smaller leaf bound into H MS. 255), which concludes:

> To some fond Girl display your Art,
>   My Heart is vow'd away and gone,
> Nor shall from Honor's Laws depart;
>   Nor be the purchase of a Song.

Printed 1803. Another song ascribed to Lady Mary, 'Blame not that Love too
cruel Fair', is almost certainly a reply by the 'too lovely Swain' (1861, 2. 498).

Fond Wishes you persue in vain,
My Heart is vow'd away and gone,
Forbear thy sighs too lovely Swain,
Those dying Airs that you put on;
Go, try on other Maids thy Art,   5
Ah! leave this lost unworthy Heart
But you must leave it soon.

Such sighs as these you should bestow
On some unpractis'd blooming Fair
Where Rosy Youth does warmly glow,   10
Whose Eyes forbid you to Despair.
Not all thy wondrous Charms can move
A Heart that must refuse thy Love
Or not deserve thy Care.

Lady Mary Wortley to Mr Cavendish on his first Addresses

Text Portland MS. (Longleat) 19. 94, unknown hand, with title from another copy (18. 58) made after 1752, when Lady Mary's friend Richard Chandler (see p. 234 above) took the name of Cavendish. *Written* before (perhaps long before) his marriage in 1732. No copy of this poem survives in Lady Mary's hand, but it can safely be regarded as hers since her friends' collection ascribes it to her and it echoes other verse by her.

Go Lovely Youth, some happier fair Address,
If she has merit you must meet Success,
On such a form none ever Coldly Gazed,
She must be Stupid or she must be pleased.
Lost to delight thus far Even I am Moved,   5
I see one Object worthy to be Loved,
No Longer left at Liberty to Chuse
Wish when I gaze and sigh when I refuse,
Yet Arm'd with reason firmly I withstand
Your pleading Eyes, your softly pressing hand.   10
But Let not this Confession of my Mind
Sooth a Vain hope I shall be one day kind,
Not like the Gay Coquet who seems to fly,
Fly's to be follow'd, Courted wou'd Comply,
A Double Meaning dwells in Every Glance   15
And Each denial is a Strong Advance.
   Passion like mine's a Stranger to all art,
Without disguise my toungue declares my Heart,
So Lovely Youth does my Affections bear,
Soft are my Meanings and my Soul Sincere,   20
But least thy presence my resolves shou'd shake
And I for thee My Honour shou'd forsake
Without reserve by Every power I swore
On No Occation I wou'd see you More.

13–15 Cf. 'Written ex tempore in a Glass Window', lines 5–8, p. 179 above.
20 Cf. Congreve's translation of Ovid's *Art of Love*, iii: 'Mild are his [a poet's] Manners, and his Heart sincere' (*Complete Works*, ed. M. Summers, 1923, 4. 106), quoted by LM in 1758 (*Letters*, 3. 170).
23–4 One of LM's juvenile poems ends very similarly (H MS. 251. 26).

Text H MS. 81. 48–9; *written* after Lord Hervey's threat (summer 1732) to discredit his ex-mistress Anne Vane (d. 1736) with her new lover, Frederick, Prince of Wales. *Printed* 1803. Lady Mary kept copies of other verse squibs on the Prince's amour with Miss Vane. Hervey's scheme for separating them misfired; he remained in disgrace with all the royal family until early the next year, and his friendship with the Prince never recovered (Halsband, *Hervey*, pp. 135–6).

Ungodly papers every week
  Poor simple Souls persuade
That Courtiers good for nothing are
  Or but for mischeif made.

But I who know their worthy hearts　　　　　　5
  Pronounce tis we are blind
Who disapoint their honest schemes
  Who would be just and kind.

For in this vile degenerate Age
  Tis dang'rous to do good,　　　　　　　　10
Which will when I have told my Tale
  Be better understood.

A puppy Gamesome blithe and young
  Who plaid about the Court
Was destin'd by unlucky boys　　　　　　　15
  To be their noon-day's sport.

With Flattering words they him enticed,
  Words such as much prevail,
And then with cruel art they ty'd
  A Bottle to his Tail.　　　　　　　　　20

Lord Harvy at a window stood
  Detesting of the Fact
And cry'd aloud with all his might,
  I know that bottle's crack'd.

13 *puppy*: the Prince.
20 *Bottle*: Miss Vane.

Do not to such a dirty hole   25
 Let them your Tail apply,
Alas, you cannot know these things
 One halfe so well as I.

Harmless and young you dont suspect
 The Venom of this deed   30
But I see through the whole design
 Which is to make you bleed.

This good advice was cast away,
 The puppy saw it shine
And tamely lick'd their treacherous hands   35
 And thought himselfe grown fine.

But long he had not worn the Gemm
 But as Lord Harvy said,
He run and bled, the more he run
 Alas the more he bled.   40

Greiv'd to the Soul this Gallant Lord
 Tripp'd hastily down stairs,
With courage and compassion fir'd
 To set him free prepares.

But such was his Ingratitude   45
 To that most noble Lord
He bit his lilly hand quite through
 As he unty'd the Cord.

Next day the maids of H[onou]r came
 As I heard people tell,   50
They wash'd the wound with brinish tears
 And yet it is not well.

40 The Prince had just furnished a house for Miss Vane and settled £1,600 p.a.
on her (Halsband, *Hervey*, p. 135).
49–52 Parody of a stanza of 'Chevy Chase':

  Next Day did many Widows come
   Their Husbands to bewail,
  They wash'd their Wounds in brinish Tears,
   But all would not prevail

(quoted in *Spectator* No. 74).

Oh Generous Youth my Councel take
    And warlike Acts forbear,
Put on White Gloves and lead folks out   55
    For that is your affair.

Never attempt to take away
    Bottles from others' Tails
For that is what no Soul will bear
    From Italy to Wales.   60

55 *White Gloves*: insignia of Hervey's position as Vice-Chamberlain.
60 Wales indicates the Prince; Hervey had recently returned from Italy.

Answer'd
by Me. M. W. M.

Text   H MS. 255. 65; *written* extempore early in 1733, as a reply, on behalf of
Lord William Hamilton (d. 1734), to a verse appeal, 'Dear Colin, prevent my
warm blushes', said to be addressed to him by Frances (1699–1754), daughter
of Henry Thynne, herself a poet, who had m. (1715) the Earl of Hertford, the
'Patch' of Lady Mary's 'Tuesday'. *Printed* Dodsley's *Collection*, 6th ed., 1758,
6. 230–1 (with an extra stanza having no authority), as a reply by Sir William
Yonge to Lady Hertford's verse, which Dodsley attributed to Lady Mary. To
her intense indignation Lady Mary therefore found herself appearing in print
in the role she had herself designed for Lady Hertford, that of a middle-aged
lady humiliated by the young man she had approached. See *Letters*, 3. 187.

Good Madam when Ladys are willing
    A Man must needs look like a Fool,
For me I would not give a shilling,
    For one that will love out of Rule.

You should leave us to guess by your blushing   5
    And not speak the matter so plain,
'Tis ours to write, and be pushing,
    'Tis yours to affect a disdain.

That you are in a terrible takeing
    By all these sweet Oglings I see,   10
But the Fruit that can fall without shakeing
    Indeed is too mellow for me.

Text H MS. 81. 33, on scribal copy of Lord Lyttelton's 'Advise to a Lady'; *written* 1731–3, perhaps before Lyttelton's poem was published, 12 Mar. 1733. *Printed* 1803.

Be plain in Dress and sober in your Diet;
In short my Dearee, kiss me, and be quiet.

VERSES
Address'd to the
IMITATOR
OF THE
FIRST SATIRE
OF THE
Second Book of Horace

Text Bod. Godwin Pamph. 1661, second edition (20 Mar. 1733) of the version published through Anne Dodd. *Written* (probably jointly by Lady Mary and Lord Hervey, and possibly in part by William Windham as well), between 15 Feb., when Pope published his *First Satire of the Second Book of Horace*, and early Mar. 1733. The provocation was a couplet in Pope's poem:

> From furious Sappho scarce a milder Fate [than poison or hanging],
> P-x'd her Love, or libell'd by her Hate

(lines 83–4: this follows directly on an insult to Windham's future wife Lady Delorain; a milder insult to Hervey occupies lines 5–6). Many people had been lovingly [small-]poxed by Lady Mary through inoculation. *Printed* in two slightly different texts through Dodd and James Roberts, who were both primarily pamphlet sellers, regularly used by authors who wished not be traced. Both editions were advertised as 'This Day' published on 8 Mar. 1733. There are four small verbal variants in their texts and one in the title. Dodd's second edition is followed here since it introduces an extra couplet and three verbal changes which must have been made by someone closely connected with the composition. The publication of Pope's *Epistle to Arbuthnot* in 1735 provoked a Dodd 'Fifth Edition' with only one verbal variant.

Hervey's part in the collaboration is proved, since he made MS. corrections on a copy of the Roberts edition, now at Ickworth, and on a scribal copy (B.M. MS. Add. 35335, a volume of material collected by Horace Walpôle, ff. 53–4), and wrote a MS. preface '*To the Reader*' (bound in the Ickworth copy). Lady Mary firmly denied that she had any part in the poem (*Letters*, 2. 100). Dodd's title-page, however, ascribes it to 'a Lady'; two contemporary copies, one owned by her friends, ascribe it to her alone (Bod. MS. Eng. misc. c. 399. 76–7; Portland MS., Longleat, 19. 149–50); most contemporaries, including Pope, ascribed it to her and Hervey equally; and modern scholarly opinion is inclined to attribute the dominant role to her (Halsband, *LM*, pp. 141–4; *Hervey*, pp. 143–4). See further Grundy, '*Verses Address'd to the Imitator of Horace*: A Skirmish between Pope and some Persons of Rank and Fortune', *Studies in Bibliography*, 30 (1977).

In two large Columns, on thy motly Page,
Where *Roman* Wit is stripe'd with *English* Rage;

1–6 Pope's imitations of Horace were printed with the Latin text on the left-hand page and the imitation on the right.

Where Ribaldry to Satire makes pretence;
And modern Scandal rolls with ancient Sense:
Whilst on one side we see how *Horace* thought;　　5
And on the other, how he never wrote:
Who can believe, who view the bad and good,
That the dull Copi'st better understood
That *Spirit*, he pretends to imitate,
Than heretofore that *Greek* he did translate?　　10
　　Thine is just such an Image of *his* Pen,
As thou thy self art of the Sons of Men:
Where our own Species in Burlesque we trace, ⎫
A Sign-Post Likeness of the noble Race; ⎬
That is at once Resemblance and Disgrace. ⎭　　15
　　Horace can laugh, is delicate, is clear;
You, only coarsely rail, or darkly sneer:
His Style is elegant, his Diction pure, ⎫
Whilst none thy crabbed Numbers can endure; ⎬
Hard as thy Heart, and as thy Birth obscure. ⎭　　20

9–10 *Hervey substituted 6 lines for this couplet in his MS. (B.M.); first 4 only in his printed copy (Ickworth):*

> Horace than Homer? or was less to seek,
> In Latin Spirit than in verbal Greek?
> For this like that thou shoudst have ask'd Broome's Aid,
> Who writes that Verse for which great Pope is pay'd,
> Broome would have told thee and have told thee true
> That whilst the Paths of Horace you pursue

---

4 Cf. Hervey's *Epistle From a Nobleman to a Doctor of Divinity*, Nov. 1733, of Pope: 'But a few modern words for ancient Sense' (p. 7).

13–15 Cf. Fielding's 'For thou art Surely not of human Race' ('Epistle to Mr Lyttleton'—written on the same occasion as the *Verses*—line 41: *PMLA*, 1972, p. 241). Hervey commented that Pope's body

> seems the Counterpart by Heav'n design'd
> A Symbol and a Warning to Mankind:
> As at some Door we find hung out a Sign,
> Type of the Monster to be found within

(*The Difference Between Verbal and Practical Virtue*, 1742, pp. 5–6).

16 Cf. Pope's 'But *Horace*, Sir, was delicate, was nice' ('Epilogue to the Satires: Dialogue I', 1738, line 11).

19 Perhaps recalled by Pope in 'And *Congreve* lov'd, and *Swift* endur'd my Lays' (*Epistle to Arbuthnot*, line 138), which in turn aroused LM's indignation (*Letters*, 2. 100).

20 Pope's *Epistle to Arbuthnot*, line 381, replied to this charge and carried a footnote referring to the *Verses*; he replied further in lines 388 ff. and in his *Letter to a Noble Lord* (*Works*, ed. Elwin and Courthope, 1871–89, 5. 433).

If *He* has Thorns, they all on Roses grow;
Thine like rude Thistles, and mean Brambles show
With this Exception, that tho' rank the Soil,
Weeds, as they are, they seem produc'd by Toil.
Satire shou'd, like a polish'd Razor keen,   25
Wound with a Touch, that's scarcely felt or seen,
Thine is an Oyster-Knife, that hacks and hews; ⎫
The Rage, but not the Talent to Abuse;   ⎬
And is in *Hate*, what *Love* is in the Stews.   ⎭
'Tis the gross *Lust* of Hate, that still annoys,   30
Without Distinction, as gross Love enjoys:
Neither to Folly, nor to Vice confin'd;
The Object of thy Spleen is Human Kind:
It preys on all, who yield or who resist;
To Thee 'tis Provocation to exist.   35
    But if thou see'st a great and gen'rous Heart,
Thy Bow is doubly bent to force a Dart.
Nor Dignity nor Innocence is spar'd,
Nor Age, nor Sex, nor Thrones, nor Graves rever'd.
Nor only Justice vainly we demand,   40
But even Benefits can't rein thy Hand:
To this or that alike in vain we trust,
Nor find Thee less Ungrateful than Unjust.
    Not even Youth and Beauty can controul
The universal Rancour of thy Soul;   45
Charms that might soften Superstition's Rage,
Might humble Pride, or thaw the Ice of Age.

38–9 *Omitted by Roberts and Dodd 1st ed., supplied by Hervey in Ickworth.*
40–3 *Struck out by Hervey in B.M. and Ickworth.*

---

36 ff. Both editions and Hervey's MS. have notes here citing Pope's *Epistle to Bur-lington*—i.e. the passage on Timon's villa, lines 99 ff. The identification of Timon with James Brydges, 1st Duke of Chandos, was widely made (e.g. by Hervey: Halsband, *Hervey*, pp. 141–2), though by 1733 Pope had several times publicly denied it (to the Duke's own satisfaction) and modern scholarly opinion bears him out (*Poems*, 3. 2, pp. xxvi–xxix, 170–4).
38–9 Cf. Hervey's poem, 'The Adventures of Telemachus in the Island Ogygia taken from the French of Fenelon' (n.d.: Hervey MS., Bury St. Edmunds, 47/17. 6):

> Horrid Confusion! Age nor Sex is spared;
> Nor Royal Heads, nor ev'n their Gods rever'd.

44 ff. These lines, taken by Courthope as written by Hervey of LM ('Life of Pope', *Works*, 5. 261), could be the work of Windham, referring to Lady Delorain.

But how should'st thou by Beauty's Force be mov'd,
No more for loving made, than to be lov'd?
It was the Equity of righteous Heav'n,   50
That such a Soul to such a Form was giv'n;
And shews the Uniformity of Fate,
That one so odious, shou'd be born to hate.
   When God created Thee, one would believe,
He said the same as to *the Snake of Eve*;   55
To human Race Antipathy declare,
'Twixt them and Thee be everlasting War.
But oh! the Sequel of the Sentence dread,
And whilst you *bruise their Heel*, beware your Head.
   Nor think thy Weakness shall be thy Defence;   60
The Female Scold's Protection in Offence.
Sure 'tis as fair to beat who cannot fight,
As 'tis to libel those who cannot write.
And if thou drawst thy Pen to aid the Law,
Others a Cudgel, or a Rod, may draw.   65
   If none with Vengeance yet thy Crimes pursue,
Or give thy manifold Affronts their due;
If Limbs unbroken, Skin without a Stain, ⎫
Unwhipt, unblanketed, unkick'd, unslain; ⎬
That wretched little Carcass you retain: ⎭   70
The Reason is, not that the World wants Eyes;
But thou'rt so mean, they see, and they despise.
When fretful *Porcupine*, with rancorous Will,
From mounted Back shoots forth a harmless Quill,
Cool the Spectators stand; and all the while,   75
Upon the angry little Monster smile.

49–51 Fielding and Hervey both accused Pope of sexual impotence; the latter also
agreed that his bodily shape was a just judgement ('Epistle to Lyttleton', line 39,
PMLA, p. 241; *The Difference Between Verbal and Practical Virtue*, pp. 5–6).
   55 Dodd's '5th ed.', 1735, refers here to the *Epistle to Arbuthnot*—i.e. line 319, 'Or
at the ear of *Eve*, familiar Toad', where Pope's note carefully owns that he took this
hint for Sporus from the *Verses*.
   59 From Genesis 3: 15.
   64–5 In Dec. 1731 Hervey reported Pope's having been told 'a Year or two ago':
          In black & White whilst Satyr you pursue,
          Take Heed the Answer is not Black & Blue.
The couplet may be LM's: Walpole recorded a similar phrase as hers (Halsband,
Hervey, p. 142; Walpole, *Corr.* 14. 243 n. 7; James Prior, *Life of Malone*, 1860, p. 437).
   73 From 'quills upon the fretful porpentine' (*Hamlet*, I. v. 20).

Thus 'tis with thee:—whilst impotently safe,
You strike unwounding, we unhurt can laugh.
Who but must laugh, this Bully when he sees,
A puny Insect shiv'ring at a Breeze?   80
One over-match'd by ev'ry Blast of Wind,
Insulting and provoking all Mankind.
   Is this the *Thing* to keep Mankind in awe,
To make those tremble who escape the Law?
Is this *the Ridicule* to live so long,   85
The deathless Satire, and *immortal Song?*
No: like thy self-blown Praise, thy Scandal flies;
And, as we're told of Wasps, it stings and dies.
   If none do yet return th'intended Blow;
You all your Safety, to your Dullness owe: 90
But whilst that Armour thy poor Corps defends,
'Twill make thy Readers few, as are thy Friends;
Those, who thy Nature loath'd, yet lov'd thy Art,
Who lik'd thy Head, and yet abhor'd thy Heart;
Chose thee, to read, but never to converse,   95
And scorn'd in Prose, him whom they priz'd in Verse.
Even they shall now their partial Error see,
Shall shun thy Writings like thy Company;
And to thy Books shall ope their Eyes no more,
Than to thy Person they wou'd do their Door.   100
   Nor thou the Justice of the World disown,
That leaves Thee thus an Out-cast, and alone;

79–82 Struck out by Hervey, B.M.; 81–2 only struck out, Ickworth.
99–100 Hervey substituted a different couplet in Ickworth:
> Or thy late Works for Dormitives shall keep,
> And to thy *Taste* and *Riches* nightly sleep.

79–80 From Pope's *Epistle to Burlington*, lines 107–8, on Timon.
84 From Pope's *First Satire of the Second Book*, line 118. Cf. Fielding's
> Shew me the Man above the Laws accus'd,
> The lawless Pow'r which Laws defend abus'd

('Epistle to Lyttleton', lines 148–9; *PMLA*, p. 244).
85–6 From Pope's *First Satire*, lines 69, 79–80.
88 Again Pope took the hint (*Epistle to Arbuthnot*, lines 309–10):
> Yet let me flap this Bug with gilded wings,
> This painted Child of Dirt that stinks and stings.

  93–4 Cf. Hervey's *The Difference Between Verbal and Practical Virtue* (p. 7):
  90 Cf. last line of Catharine Trotter, *Agnes de Castro*, 1696: 'Thus to our Frailty, we our Safety owe.'
> Whilst not one Man who likes his rhyming Art,
> Allows him Genius, or defends his Heart.

For tho' in Law, to murder be to kill,
In Equity the Murder's in the Will:
Then whilst with Coward Hand you stab a Name,   105
And try at least t'assassinate our Fame;
Like the first bold Assassin's be thy Lot,
Ne'er be thy Guilt forgiven, or forgot;
But as thou hate'st, be hated by Mankind,
And with the Emblem of thy crooked Mind,   110
Mark'd on thy Back, like *Cain*, by God's own Hand;
Wander like him, accursed through the Land.

106 Cf. Fielding's 'Epistle to Lyttleton': 'As he who durst assassinate thy [LM's] Fame' (line 33: *PMLA*, p. 241).
111 Genesis 4:15. John Ozell had called Pope 'that second CAIN, *whose Hand is against every Body*' (quoted in *Poems*, 5. 450).

The ANSWER to the foregoing ELEGY

Text   An Elegy To A Young Lady, In the Manner of Ovid. With an Answer: By a Lady, Author of the Verses to the Imitator of Horace, 1733; *written* probably shortly before it was *printed* with the *Elegy* on 29 Mar. 1733. The *Answer* is almost certainly by Lady Mary, though its heading says only 'By the Author of the Verses to the Imitator of Horace', and this led to their ascription to Hervey in Dodsley's *Collection* (4, 1755, p. 79) and later reprints. Dodsley first named the author of the *Elegy* (p. 77) as James Hammond (1710–42). Lady Mary kept two copies of an unpublished ballad ascribed to Hammond (H MS. 81. 157; 255. 67–8). The *Elegy* was not collected with Hammond's other elegies, which were 'written in the Year 1732', all except the last addressed to Catherine Dashwood, who died unmarried in 1779. Horace Walpole said that she, 'finding he did not mean marriage, broke off all connection, though much in love with him' (notes pub. in *Miscellanies of the Philobiblon Society*, 11, 1867–8, p. 17); Lady Corke, a friend of Miss Dashwood, told in old age a different story: that she 'had at first accepted, but afterwards rejected him, on [as her contemporaries thought] *prudential* reasons' (Hervey, *Memoirs*, ed. J. W. Croker, 1848, 1. xxx, n. 16).

Too well these Lines that fatal Truth declare,
Which long I've known, yet now I blush to hear—
    But say, What hopes thy fond, ill-fated Love?
What can it hope, tho' mutual it should prove?
This little Form is fair in vain for you;   5
In vain for me, thy honest Heart is true,

5 Catherine Dashwood was known to her circle as 'dear little Dash' (Mrs. Delany, *Autobiography and Corr.*, ed. Lady Llanover, 1861, 1. 563).

For would'st thou fix Dishonour on my Name,
And give me up to Penitence and Shame!
Or gild my Ruin with the Name of Wife,
And make me a poor *Virtuous* Wretch for Life?   10
    Could'st thou submit to wear the Marriage-Chain,
(Too sure a Cure for all thy present Pain)
No Safron Robe for us the Godhead wears,
His Torch inverted, and his Face in Tears;
Tho' ev'ry softer Wish were amply crown'd,   15
Love soon would cease to smile, when *Fortune* frown'd.
    Then would thy Soul my fond Consent deplore,
And blame what it sollicited before:
Thy own exhausted, would reproach my Truth,
And say, I had undone thy blinded Youth;   20
That I had damp'd *Ambition*'s nobler Flame,
Eclips'd thy Talents, and obscur'd thy Name:
To *Madrigales* and *Odes* that Wit confin'd,
That might in *Senates* or in *Courts* have shin'd;
Gloriously active in thy Country's Cause,   25
Asserting Freedom, and enacting Laws.
    Or say at best, that negatively kind,
You inly mourn'd, and silently repin'd:
The jealous Demons in my own fond Breast,   ⎫
Would all these Thoughts incessantly suggest,   ⎬ 30
And tell what Sense must feel, tho' Pity had supprest. ⎭
    Yet added—Grief my Apprehension fills,
(If there can be Addition to those Ills:)
When *they* shall cry, whose harsh Reproof I dread,
'*Twas thy own Deed; thy Folly on thy Head.*   35
    Age knows not to allow for thoughtless Youth,
Nor pities Tenderness, nor honours Truth:
Holds it romantick to confess a Heart;
And says, those Virgins act the wiser Part,
Who *Hospitals* and *Bedlams* would explore,   40
To find the Rich, and only dread the Poor;
Who *legal Prostitutes* for Interest's sake,
Clodios and *Timons* to their Bosom take;

21 ff. Hammond, a protégé of Chesterfield's, became an equerry to the Prince of
Wales in 1733, and was elected M.P. the year before his death.
43 Clodio typifies unscrupulousness; Pope applied the name to LM's friend the

And (if avenging Heav'n permit Increase)
People the World with Folly and Disease.   45
    Those, *Titles, Deeds,* and *Rent-Rolls* only wed,
Whilst the best Bidder mounts their venal Bed;
And the grave *Aunt* and formal *Sire* approve
This Nuptial Sale, this *Auction* of their Love.
    But if Regard to Worth or Sense is shewn,   50
That poor *degenerate* Child her Friends disown,
Who dares to deviate, by a virtuous Choice,
From her great Name's hereditary Vice.
    These Scenes my Prudence ushers to my Mind,
Of all the Storms and Quicksands I must find,   55
If I imbark upon this Summer-Sea,
Where Flatt'ry smooths, and Pleasure gilds the Way.
    Had our ill Fate ne'er blown thy dang'rous Flame
Beyond the Limits of a Friend's cold Name,
I might, upon that score, thy Heart receive,   60
And with that guiltless Name *my own* deceive.
That Commerce now in vain you recommend,
I dread the latent Lover in the Friend:
Of Ignorance I want the poor Excuse,
And know I both must take, or both refuse.   65
    Hear then the safe, the firm Resolve I make,
Ne'er to encourage one I must forsake.
Whilst other Maids a shameless Path pursue,
Neither to Honour, nor to Int'rest true;
And proud to swell the Triumphs of their Eyes,   70
Exult in Love from Lovers they despise;
Their Maxims all revers'd, I mean to prove,
And tho' I like the Lover quit the Love.

Duke of Wharton (*Epistle to Cobham*, 1734, lines 179 ff.). For Timon cf. previous
poem, line 36 note.
  48 These traditional figures existed in LM's own family (*Letters*, 1. 160, 216).
  59–60 Referring to Hammond's *Elegy*, lines 31–2:

> And now (for more I never must pretend)
> Hear me not as thy Lover, but thy Friend.

The Reasons that Induced Dr S[wift] to write a Poem call'd the Lady's Dressing room

Text H MS. 81. 13–15; textual notes record passages rejected from a draft, H MS. 81. 25–6. *Written* after June 1732, when Swift published his poem, and before 8 Feb. 1734, when hers was *printed* as *The Dean's Provocation For Writing the Lady's Dressing-Room.* See Halsband, ' "The Lady's Dressing-Room" Explicated by a Contemporary' in *The Augustan Milieu, Essays presented to Louis A. Landa,* ed. H. K. Miller, E. Rothstein, G. S. Rousseau, 1970, pp. 225–31. Lady Mary always disliked Swift: here she skilfully assumes his own poetic manner to lampoon him.

> The Doctor in a clean starch'd band,
> His Golden Snuff box in his hand,
> With care his Di'mond Ring displays
> And Artfull shews its various Rays,
> While Grave he stalks down —— —— Street   5
> His dearest Betty —— to meet.
>   Long had he waited for this Hour,
> Nor gain'd Admittance to the Bower,
> Had jok'd and punn'd, and swore and writ,
> Try'd all his Galantry and Wit,   10
> Had told her oft what part he bore
> In Oxford's Schemes in days of yore,
> But Bawdy, Politicks nor Satyr
> Could move this dull hard hearted Creatu⟨re.⟩
> Jenny her Maid could taste a Rhyme   15
> And greiv'd to see him lose his Time,
> Had kindly whisper'd in his Ear,
> For twice two pound you enter here,
> My Lady vows without that Summ
> It is in vain you write or come.   20
>   The Destin'd Offering now he brought

2–3 Swift's will mentions a tortoiseshell and gold snuff-box and gold rings (*Prose Works,* ed. H. Davis, 1939–68, 13. 153). A diamond ring said to have been his was left by Enid Starkie to Somerville College, Oxford (Joanna Richardson, *Enid Starkie,* 1973, p. 214).

6 LM took the maid's name (*Lady's Dressing-Room,* line 6) for the mistress, whom Swift called Celia. The printed text of her poem has a blank.

9–10 From *Cadenus and Vanessa,* 1726, lines 542–3: Cadenus

> Had sigh'd and languish'd, vow'd, and writ,
> For Pastime, or to shew his Wit.

And in a paradise of thought
With a low Bow approach'd the Dame
Who smileing heard him preach his Flame.
His Gold she takes (such proofes as these   25
Convince most unbeleiving shees)
And in her trunk rose up to lock it
(Too wise to trust it in her pocket)
And then return'd with Blushing Grace
Expects the Doctor's warm Embrace.   30
   But now this is the proper place
Where morals Stare me in the Face
And for the sake of fine Expression
I'm forc'd to make a small digression.
Alas for wretched Humankind,   35
With Learning Mad, with wisdom blind!
The Ox thinks he's for Saddle fit
(As long ago Freind Horace writ)
And Men their Talents still mistakeing,
The stutterer fancys his is speaking.   40
With Admiration oft we see
Hard Features heighten'd by Toupée,
The Beau affects the Politician,
Wit is the citizen's Ambition,
Poor Pope Philosophy displays on   45
With so much Rhime and little reason,
And thô he argues ne'er so long
That, all is right, his Head is wrong.
   None strive to know their proper merit
But strain for Wisdom, Beauty, Spirit,   50

After 30 *four lines struck out in H MS. draft:*

But oh how vain are human Joys!
Those views that wisest heads employs
The Luckless hand of Chance o're turns
And all our prudent Caution scorns.

31 ff. H MS. 81 draft shows how this digression gradually expanded from 4 to 62 lines, copying a device used by Swift in prose and verse (e.g. *A Tale of a Tub*, 1704; *On Poetry, A Rapsody*, 31 Dec. 1733, line 61: 'And here a *Simile* comes Pat in').

37–8 'Optat ephippia bos' (*Epist*. I. xiv. 43).

39 A favourite phrase of Swift's, repeated in the title, 'Advertisement', and line 206 of his 'The Beasts Confession to the Priest, on Observing how most Men mistake their own Talents. Written in the Year 1732', not published till 1738 (*Poems*, 3. 599).

48 From *An Essay on Man*, 1733. Cf. 'Pope to Bolingbroke', line 66, p. 283 below.

And lose the Praise that is their due
While they've th'impossible in view.
So have I seen the Injudicious Heir
To add one Window the whole House impair.
    Instinct the Hound does better teach   55
Who never undertook to preach,
The frighted Hare from Dogs does run
But not attempts to bear a Gun.
Here many Noble thoughts occur
But I prolixity abhor,   60
And will persue th'instructive Tale
To shew the Wise in some things fail.
    The Reverend Lover with surprize ⎱
Peeps in her Bubbys, and her Eyes, ⎱
And kisses both, and trys—and trys. ⎰   65
The Evening in this Hellish Play,
Beside his Guineas thrown away,
Provok'd the Preist to that degree
He swore, the Fault is not [in] me.
Your damn'd Close stool so near my Nose,   70
Your Dirty Smock, and Stinking Toes
Would make a Hercules as tame
As any Beau that you can name.
    The nymph grown Furious roar'd by God
The blame lyes all in Sixty odd   75
And scornfull pointing to the door
Cry'd, Fumbler see my Face no more.
With all my Heart I'll go away
But nothing done, I'll nothing pay.
Give back the Money—How, cry'd she,   80

After 54 *four extra lines in* H MS. *draft and printed text:*
    Nature to every thing alive
    Points out the path to shine or thrive
    But Man, Vain Man, who grasps the whole
    Shews in all Heads a touch of Fool.

55–8 Swift frequently appealed ironically to the order of the animal kingdom, notably
in *On Poetry, A Rapsody*, lines 13–20.
  70–1 From *The Lady's Dressing-Room*, lines 11–14, 51–2, 69 ff.
  75 Swift was sixty-five on 30 Nov. 1732.

> Would you palm such a cheat on me!
> For poor 4 pound to roar and bellow,
> Why sure you want some new Prunella?
> I'll be reveng'd you saucy Quean
> (Replys the disapointed Dean)   85
> I'll so describe your dressing room
> The very Irish shall not come.
> She answer'd short, I'm glad you'l write,
> You'l furnish paper when I shite.

After 81 an extra couplet in H MS. draft and printed text:

> I lock'd it in the Trunk stands there
> And break it open if you dare.

82 Last line in H MS. fair copy; the rest torn away.
82–3 Omitted in H MS. draft. Line 83 comes from printed text, where 6 lines follow which the MSS. omit:

> What if your Verses have not sold,
> Must therefore I return your Gold?
> Perhaps you have no better Luck in
> The Knack of Rhyming than of ——
> I won't give back one single Crown,
> To wash your Band, or turn your Gown.

84–9 From H MS. draft.
The margin of the draft bears a couplet never worked into the text:

> The port of universal Trade,
> That Anvil where Mankind [?is] Ma⟨de⟩.

---

83 Prunella has double significance: as a fabric used in gowns for the clergy, and as the eponymous heroine of Richard Estcourt's *Prunella: An Interlude*, 1708, a grocer's daughter 'something given to Love'.
89 Cf. *The Lady's Dressing-Room*, line 118: 'Oh! Celia, Celia, Celia shits!'
Marginal couplet: adapted from Rochester's *Sodom*, III. i:

> This is the ware house of the world's chief Trade,
> On this soft anvil all mankind was made.

Cf. also Pope's 'Phryne', ll. 2–3 (*Poems*, 6. 49).

Occasion'd by the Sight of a Picture

Text H MS. 81. 154; *written* probably after Robert Walpole's peak of unpopularity over the Excise crisis (spring 1733). It may be an answer to a verse attack on him in *Fog's Weekly Journal*, 20 July 1734, which its closing lines echo. *Printed* 1803. This must be one of Lady Mary's impromptu exercises; the state of the MS. suggests that it may have been written in a moving vehicle. It is useless to speculate as to which picture inspired her verse; many of the seventy-odd known portraits of Walpole fit her description. For Lady Mary's early acquaintance with him and his family, see pp. 22-7 above.

> Such were the lively eyes and rosy hue
> Of Robin's face when first I Robin knew,
> The gay Companion and the favourite Guest,
> Lov'd without awe and without veiws carress'd.
> This chearfull Smile and open honest Look   5
> Added new Graces to the sense he spoke,
> Then every man found something to Commend,
> The pleasant Neighbour and the worthy freind,
> The Generous Master of a private house,
> The tender Father and th'Indulgent Spouse.   10
> The hardest censurers, at the worst beleiv'd
> A [*sic*] temper was too easily deceiv'd
> (A consequential ill good nature draws,
> A bad Effect but from a noble Cause).
> Whence then these clamours of the Judging croud,   15
> Suspicious, gripeing, Insolently proud,
> Rapacious, cruel, violent, unjust,
> False to his freind and Traitor to his trust?

9 This contrasts the old manor of Houghton with the mansion which Walpole began planning to replace it in 1720 (J. H. Plumb, *Sir Robert Walpole*, 1956, 1960, 1. 92, 359).

10 For Walpole's marital and paternal indulgence see pp. 25-6 above.

12 Hervey, though, thought him 'under a seeming openness and negligence, devilish artful' (Lord Ilchester, *Lord Hervey and His Friends*, 1950, p. 131).

13-14 From Prior's *A Letter to Monsieur Boileau Despreaux* (*Works*, 1. 226).

18 Townshend, Walpole's brother-in-law and ally, quarrelled openly with him in 1728 and resigned in May 1730 (Plumb, 2. 196, 199).

An Elegy on Mrs. T[hompso]n

Text Portland MSS. (Longleat), 20. 31, unknown hand. Since the Duchess of Portland had a copy in Nov. 1734 (Mrs. Delany, *Autobiography and Corr.*, ed. Lady Llanover, 1861, 1. 522), this probably pre-dates publication. *Written* 21 Oct.–Nov. 1734; *printed* (some variants) June 1735, *Gentleman's Magazine*, with a censorious verse reply. The title comes from the first printing.

Arabella, daughter of Edmund Dunch, m. (1725) Edward Thompson (*Letters*, 2. 45-6). Her husband 'rusticated' her 'for Gallantrys' in June [1727], but apparently later condoned her adultery with his brother-in-law Sir George

Oxenden (R. E. Tickell, *Thomas Tickell*, 1931, p. 131; H.M.C., *Egmont Diary*, 2. 225). She died (Hervey said in adulterous childbed, the papers 'after a tedious Indisposition') in Oct. 1734 (Hervey, *Memoirs*, 2. 741-2; *Daily Post-Boy*, 21 Oct.).

> Unhappy fair, by fatal love betrayed,
> Must then thy beauties thus untimely fade,
> And all thy bloomy, soft, inspiring charms
> Become a prey to Death's destructive Arms?
> Tho' short thy day and transient like the Wind,   5
> How far more blessed than those yet left behind!
> Safe in the grave with thee thy griefes remain,
> And life's tempestuous billows break in Vain.
>
> Ye tender Nymphs in lawless passions gay,
> Who heedless down the paths of pleasure stray,   10
> Tho' now secure with blissfull joy elate,
> Yet pause, and think of Annabella's [*sic*] fate;
> For such may be thy unexpected doom,
> And thy next slumber lull thee in the tomb.
>
> But let it be the Muses gentle care   15
> To sheild from envious rage the mouldring fair,
> To draw a vail o'er faults she can't commend,
> And what prudes half devoured, leave time to end.
> Be it her part to pay a pitying tear,
> And heave a sigh of sorrow o'er thy beare.   20
> Nor shall thy woes long glad th'illnatured crowd,
> Silent in praise and in detraction loud.
> For Scandal that thro' life each worth destroys
> And malice, that Imbitters all our joys,
> Shall in some ill-starr'd wretch find later staines,   25
> And let thine rest forgot, as thy remaines.

Text Pierpont Morgan Library MS. M.A. 347, item 24; *written* probably in 1734, when relations between George II and his heir were deteriorating and the patriot opposition becoming augmented with disaffected Whigs.

> While fruitfull Nile ador'd his horned Queen
> And mitred Preists were at her Altars seen,

1 *horned Queen*: Isis.
2 Several bishops enjoyed Queen Caroline's special patronage.

Compell'd to Worship, and yet hardly fed;
Afflicted Israel from the Idol fled.
But when grown hungry in the desart waste   5
They sigh'd for shows, and thought of Flesh pots past
(Isis processions were like Birth days fine
And they at Festivals were ask'd to dine),
Her Gracious help they now wish'd to implore
And would have made a Goddess to adore,   10
But such her size, their gold but form'd her half,
Their Deity was lessen'd to a Calfe.
So haughty Patriots missing of their Aim
Left their Devotion to their Royal Dame,
Yet still desirous in some court to shine,   15
Paid their addresses to the Prince's shrine.

5–6 Exodus 16: 3.
9–12 Exodus 32: 1–6, which does not say they had too little gold; this is a taunt at the Queen's bulk.

Epigram
1734

Text Pierpont Morgan Library MS. M.A. 347, item 24, probably the earliest copy; title from H MS. 255, where Lady Mary transcribed it after 1738. *Printed* 1861.
    Lady Mary adapted this quatrain to the 1734 elections (at which Walpole and the Whigs were returned to power after some suspense and with a reduced majority), modelling it very closely on an epigram printed in *Poems on Affairs of State* as 'On the French Subjects' (1707, p. 459). Apparently she told Algarotti that she adapted it extempore (Bod. MS. Don. c. 56. 36).

Born to be slaves, our Fathers freedom sought,
And with their blood the valu'd treasure bought,
We their mean offspring our own bondage plot,
And born to Freedom, for our chains we vote.

P[ope] to Bolingbroke

Text H MS. 256. 60–1, scribal transcript, copied after 1755; *written* July 1734–June 1735, after Pope published not only *An Essay on Man*, addressed to

Bolingbroke, but also his *Second Satire of the Second Book of Horace*, and probably before Bolingbroke's departure from England. *Printed* 1803. Lady Mary was evidently familiar with the anonymous verse *Epistle From the late Lord Bo——ke to the Duke of W[harto]n*, 1730. An early draft of her poem, H MS. 81. 43–4, includes some interesting lines later omitted.

> Confess dear Lælius, Pious, Just, and Wise,
> Some self-content does in that bosom rise,
> When you reflect (as sure you sometimes must)
> What Tallents Heaven does to thy Virtue trust;
> While with Contempt you view poor human-kind   5
> Weak, willful, Sensual, Passionate and blind;
> Amidst these Errours thou art faultless found,
> (The Moon takes Lustre from the Darkness round)
> Permit me too, a small attendant Star, ⎫
> To twinkle, tho' in a more distant Sphere, ⎬   10
> Small Things with great we Poets oft compare. ⎭
> With Admiration all your steps I view,
> And almost Envy what I can't pursue.
> The World must grant (and 'tis no common Fame)
> My Courage and my probity the same.   15
> But you, great Lord, to nobler scenes was born,
> Your early Youth did Anna's court adorn.
> Let *Oxford* own, let *Catalonia* tell,
> What various victims to your wisdom fell.

After 6 *an extra couplet in draft:*
> Sure all these Follys by the Hand divine
> Were placed express, to shew how bright you shine.

12–23 *omitted in draft.*

---

1 *An Essay on Man*, i, began in the 1733 eds.: 'Awake, my Lælius!' Pope later changed the name of his 'guide, philosopher, and friend' to 'St. John'.

9 Apparently recalling Pope's 'little bark attendant' on Bolingbroke (*Essay on Man*, iv. 385–6).

11 A cliché which goes back to Virgil's first eclogue.

18–19 Cf. Garth's *Dispensary*, iv (4th ed. 1700, p. 47):
> *Oxford* and all her passing Bells can tell,
> By this Right Arm, what mighty Numbers fell.

Hervey held that Bolingbroke was taken up by Oxford 'whom he undermined, supplanted in the Queen's favour, and turned out'. An anonymous writer claimed that Bolingbroke alone among the Cabinet had sought—unsuccessfully—some guarantee in the Treaty of Utrecht for the Catalonians' safety (*Memoirs*, 1. 9; 'A Short Character of John Sheffield late Duke of Buckinghamshire' in his *Works*, 4th ed., 1753, 2. 246).

Let Vows, or benefits, the Vulgar bind,   20
Such Ties can never chain th'intrepid mind.
  Recorded be that memorable hour,
When, to elude exasperated Pow'r,
With blushless front you durst your Friends betray,
Advise the whole confed'racy to stay,   25
And brave the danger of th'enquiring day,
While, with sly Courage, you ran brisk away.
  By a deserted court with joy reciev'd,
Your projects all admir'd, your Oaths believ'd,
Some Trust obtain'd, of which good use you made   30
To gain a Pardon where you first betray'd.
But what is Pardon to th'aspiring breast?
You should have been first Minister at least.
Failing of that, forsaken and deprest,
Sure any Soul but Yours had sought for rest!   35
And mourn'd in shades, far from the publick Eye,
Successless Fraud, and useless Infamy.
  And here (My Lord) let all mankind admire
The bold Efforts of unexhausted fire.
You stand the Champion of the People's cause,   40
And bid the Mob reform defective Laws.
  Oh, was your Pow'r like your Intention good,

34–41 *draft has a triplet:*

> Failing in that, your Country grows your Care, ⎫
> You curse all Measures where you do not share ⎬
> And kick'd from Court, turn grave Philosopher. ⎭

Before 42 *draft inserts:*

> Greatly Mischeivous you bold Treasons write,
> To Arms the madding Multitude excite.

22 Two paragraphs open similarly in *An Epistle From the late Lord Bo——ke to the Duke of W——n*, 1730: 'Forgot for ever, be that luckless Hour' and 'Be blotted from the Day, that spiteful Hour' (pp. 20, 22).
28–31 The *Epistle* also gives an account of double treachery (p. 11):

> Whene'er at Courts, by Art, or seeming Grace,
> For both are mine, I wriggled into Place,
> Neither by Gratitude, nor Conscience sway'd,
> Each Sov'reign that I own'd, I still betray'd.

33 Horace Walpole tells of Bolingbroke's attempt to supplant Sir Robert, and how many believed—mistakenly—that he would have succeeded had George I not died ('Reminiscences': *Works*, 1798, 4. 277–9).

Your native Land would stream with civil blood.
I own, these glorious schemes I view with pain,
My little Mischiefs to myself seem mean,   45
My ills are humble tho' my heart is great,
All I can do is flatter, lie, and cheat.
Yet I may say, 'tis plain that you preside   ⎱
O'er all my morals, and 'tis much my Pride   ⎬
To tread, with steps unequal, where you guide.   ⎭   50
My first Subscribers I have first defam'd,
And when detected never was asham'd:
Rais'd all the Storms I could in private Life,
Whisper'd the Husband to correct the Wife;
Outwitted Lintot in his very trade,   55
And Charity with infamy repaid:
Yet, while you preach in prose, I scold in Rhimes,
Against th'Injustice of flagitious Times.

After 43 draft inserts:

> While you Endeavour to embroil a state
> In private Familys I sow debate.

After 54 draft inserts:

> And if the Blockhead will not take the hint
> Give him an Item of the Joke in print.

55–96 omitted from draft, which concludes:

> The weakness should protect that Sex from wrongs
> But more exposes to our blasting tongues,
> Tis known to all what Conquests you have gaind
> And I insinuate joys I ne'er obtain'd,
> When dear Miss Cooper my retreat has blest
> How sweet her Lips! how downy was her breast!
> Tell in what raptures our soft hours are spent,
> Thô me deform'd, and You thought impotent.
> And in the Midst of these Heroic strains
> We seek for Mistrisses in dirty Lanes,
> Even there superior, there it often happ'd
> My Lord was pox'd, when I was only clapp'd.

51 This charge goes back to Curll's *The Catholick Poet*, 1716.

55 The complexities of Pope's financial dealings with Bernard Lintot (d. 1736) have been unravelled by David Foxon in the Lyell Lectures, 1976.

Variant after 56 Pope's period of boasting his amatory conquests was long past. He may never have met his correspondent Judith Cowper (*Corr.* 2. 210 n. 1; p. 227 above). For the concluding couplet cf. *An Epistle From the late Lord Bo——ke*, 'The P-x cou'd then my Piety commend' (p. 19). LM may have known of Pope's alternative ending to his epistle to Martha Blount after the Coronation, written *c.* 1715 though not printed till 1775 (*Poems*, 6. 232).

You, learned Doctor of the publick Stage,
Give gilded poison to corrupt the Age;　　　　　60
Your poor Toad-eater I, around me scatter
My scurril jests, and gaping Crouds bespatter.
This may seem Envy, to the formal Fools
Who talk of Virtue's bounds, and honour's rules:
We, who with piercing Eyes look Nature through,　65
We know that all is right in all we do.
　　Reason's erroneous, honest Instinct right.
Monkeys were made to grin, and Fleas to bite.
Using the Spight by the Creator given,
We only tread the Path that's mark'd by heaven.　70
And sure with Justice 'tis that we exclaim,
Such wrongs must e'en your Modesty inflame.
While Blockheads Court rewards and honours share,⎫
You, Poet, Patriot, and Philosopher,　　　　　　⎬
No Bills in Pocket, nor no Garter wear.　　　　　⎭ 75
　　When I see smoaking on a Booby's board
Fat Ortalans, and Pies of Perigord,
My self am mov'd to high poetick rage
(The Homer, and the Horace of the Age).
Puppies! who have the insolence to dine　　　　　80
With smiling beauties, and with sparkling wine,
While I retire, plagu'd with an Empty Purse,
Eat Brocoli, and kiss my antient Nurse.

65 Pope wrote of Aristotle doing this (*Temple of Fame*, lines 236–7).

66 From *An Essay on Man*, i. 294 and iv. 394.

67 What Pope says (with qualifications) is that instinct 'must go right' while reason 'may go wrong' (*Essay on Man*, iii. 79–98).

68 From Pope's version of Horace, *Sat.* II. i, lines 85–8 (a passage LM was especially apt to remember, since it follows the insult to herself):

> Its proper Pow'r to hurt, each Creature feels,
> Bulls aim their horns, and Asses lift their heels,
> 'Tis a Bear's Talent not to kick, but hug,
> And no man wonders he's not stung by Pug.

73–5 Cf. *An Epistle From the late Lord Bo——ke*: 'No Place I yet possess, no Staff survey' (p. 4). Walpole had received the Garter in 1726.

76 ff. Pope made gluttony the main theme of *Sat.* II. ii.

83 Cf. ibid. 137–8:

> Content with little, I can piddle here
> On Broccoli and mutton, round the year.

Pope's old nurse, Mary Beach, had died in 1725.

But had we flourish'd when stern Henry reign'⟨d⟩
Our good Designs had been but ill explain'd;   85
The Ax had cut your solid Reasoning short,
I, in the Porter's Lodge, been scourg'd at Court,
To better Times kind heaven reserv'd our Bir⟨th,⟩
Happy for us that Coxcombs are on Earth.

Mean Spirits seek their Villany to hide,   ⎫   90
We shew our venom'd Souls with noble Pride,   ⎬
And, in bold strokes, have all Mankind defy'd;   ⎭
Past o'er the bounds that keep Mankind in aw⟨e,⟩
And laugh'd at Justice, Gratitude and Law:
While our Admirers stare with dumb surprize   95
Treason, and Scandal, we monopolize.
Yet this remains our more peculiar boast,
You scape the Block, and I the Whipping-Post.

84 Henry VIII (cf. p. 248 above).
86 Swift had believed Bolingbroke's head in danger in 1715 (*Corr.*, ed. H. Williams, 1963–5, 2. 176).
88–9 Referring to Horace, *Sat.* II. ii. 97–8:

> Why had not I in those good times my birth,
> E're Coxcomb-pyes or Coxcombs were on earth?

1736
The 9th Ode of the 3d Book of Horace Imitated

Text H MS. 256. 52; *written* 1736; *printed* 1803. This ode had been applied to Walpole and William Pulteney by other poets in unrelated verses (e.g. B.M. Harley MS. 7318, f. 69, *c.* 1727–30; *Gentleman's Magazine*, May 1733, p. 263). Pulteney had supported Walpole before 1726; according to Hervey he never forgave the Prime Minister for not making him Secretary of State; in 1736 he was thought to be 'weary of the opposing part he had so long unsuccessfully acted' (Hervey, *Memoirs*, 1. 9; 2. 529).

Sir R. W.

While in all my Schemes you most heartily joyn'd
And help'd the worst Jobs that I ever design'd,
In Pamphlets, in Ballads, in Senate, at Table
Thy Satyr was witty, thy Council was Able.

3–4 Pulteney 'had as much lively ready wit as ever man was master of, and was, before politics soured his temper and engrossed his thoughts, the most agreeable and coveted companion of his time' (Hervey, *Memoirs*, 1. 7). He sat in the Commons 1705–42.

W. P.

While with me you divided both profit and Care   5
And the Plunder and Glory did equally share
Assur'd of his Place, if my Fat Freind should die,
The Prince of Wales was not so happy as I.

Sir R. W.

Harry Pelham is now my Support and Delight,
Whom we bubble all Day, we joke on at Night,   10
His Head is well furnish'd, his Lungs have their Merit,
I would venture the Rope to advance such a Spirit.

W. P.

I too have a Harry more usefull than yours;
Writes verses like mad, and will talk you whole hours,
I would bleed by the Hatchet or swing in the Cord   15
To see him once more in his robes, like a Lord.

Sir R. W.

But what if this Quarrel was kindly made up?
Would you my dear Willy accept of a Sop?
If the Queen should confess, you had long been her Choice
And you knew it was I, that spoke in her Voice.   20

W. P.

Thô my Harry so gay, so polite, and so Civil,
You rude as a Bear, and more proud than a Devil,
I gladly would drop him, and laugh in your Ear
At the Fools we have made for this last dozen year.

7 *Fat Freind*: Walpole himself.
8 At the time referred to, the Prince of Wales was the future George II.
9 For the support given by Pelham (1695?–1754) to Walpole against Pulteney, see
J. W. Wilkes, *A Whig in Power, The Political Career of Henry Pelham*, 1964, pp. 9–11.
13–16 Henry St. John, Lord Bolingbroke. His Viscountcy was restored 'in blood
only' (G. E. C[okayne] *et al.*, *Complete Peerage*, 1910–59), but he was forbidden to sit
in the Lords.

Impromptu to a young Lady singing

Text H MS. 255. 70, copied after 1738; *written* perhaps either Sept. 1721 or May–July 1736; *printed* 1803. If Lady Mary composed this poem in autumn 1721, when she wrote both of her unease and of the consolation of music, the singer may have been Maria Skerrett (p. 26 above) and the 'raging Passions' caused by Rémond's threats of blackmail (*Letters*, 2. 1–14). More likely, however, the singer was her daughter (cf. *Letters*, 3. 124), and she was writing during her unhappy love for Algarotti (see p. 150 above).

> Sing Gentle Maid, reform my Breast
>   And soften all my Care,
> Thus I can be some moments blest
>   And easy in Despair,
> The Power of Orpheus lives in you,   5
> The raging Passions of my Soul subdue
> And tame the Lions, and the Tygers there.

Text H MS. 81. 216–17, where Lady Mary's hand and Hervey's alternate; marginal notation taken from Hervey's transcript (Hervey MS., Bury St. Edmunds, 47/2. 70–1). For another copy of lines 44–73 (Bod. MS Eng. misc. b. 169, f. 61), see Isobel Grundy, '"New" Verse by Lady Mary Wortley Montagu', *Bodleian Library Record*, 10, 1981, pp. 237–49. *Written* 21 or 25 Sept. 1736.

During the summer of 1736 Lady Mary fell in love with Francesco Algarotti, who was visiting England and left on 6 Sept. In a note dated 'Saturday' [18 Sept.] Hervey offered to call on her that evening or 'next Saturday' (Hervey MS. 47/2. 15). Two days later she wrote to Algarotti of her intention of seeing Hervey (*Letters*, 2. 107). After the painful meeting she sent another anxious note to Hervey, who mentioned in reply his promise to 'behave and write to —— as if Tuesday and Saturday had never been and that the last week had had but five Days in it. . . . as for the first Part of the Dialogue I have it not here but will write it out as well as I can from my Memory' (Monday [27 Sept.], Hervey MS. 47/2. 69–71). Apparently Lady Mary visited Hervey on 21 Sept., leaving after six hours at 1 a.m.; on 25 Sept. he visited her. Each reported to Algarotti on Lady Mary's embarrassed attempts to ask for news of him, she writing with reproachful dignity and Hervey with unkind hilarity (*Letters*, 2. 108; Halsband, *Hervey*, p. 201); but neither mentioned this extraordinary conversation in verse. The suppressed couplet at the end seems proof of genuine extemporaneity.

> L. H.   What is this Secret you'd so fain impart?
>   Open your own, rely upon my Heart.
>
> L. M.   I wish to tell, but I would have you guess,
>   And think at least that it would pain me less.

L. H.   This Preface to your Question is refined,   ⎫ 5
         And should I *guess* when I should *read* your Mind;   ⎬
         You'd fear some other might your Secret find.   ⎭

L. M.   My secret can be guess'd, by only you,
         You see my trust—but see my Folly too.

L. H.   You might be wise, and yet that Folly chuse;   ⎫ 10
         Ask then, nor fear your Suit I shall refuse,   ⎬
         Or that your Trust I ever can abuse.   ⎭
         I own you're rather form'd by Heav'n to grant,
         But Heav'n can only know what 'tis we want;
         Mortals tho e'er so willing all to give,   15
         Must for a welcome Gift, some Hint recieve.
         You may perhaps this wary Silence blame,
         But won't you chide me more if I should name?

L. M.   My Question short, but long will be the pain,   ⎫
         I ask to one that can too well explain,   ⎬ 20
         My Heart demands, you answer from the brain.   ⎭

L. H.   Tis true I answer only from the Brain
         Fearing my Answer should be thought too plain
         For since you wish to know yet fear to read
         Cautious the winding Precipice I tread,   25
         I combate Nature, have recourse to Art
         And rack my Head that I may spare your Heart.
         Like Rivers turn'd my Numbers useless grow,
         Say shall they in their nat'ral Channel flow?

L. M.   He laughs at scars who never felt a wound   30
         (This truth long since the Gentle Romeo found)
         The time may come to feel th'exstatic smart,
         You may see Eyes and you may feel a Heart.

9 Hervey kept LM's trust: in describing their meeting to Algarotti, he added, 'elle m'a dit des choses, que comme elle m'a fait promettre avant que de les dire que je ne les redirois point, je ne veux pas vous les communiquer' (MS. owned by Mr. John Murray, London).
    30 *Romeo and Juliet*, II. ii. 1.
    33 Borrowed from her own 'Answer to a Love Letter', line 34 (p. 245 above).

L. H.   A little longer yet your Pain endure,
        Nature who made the Wound, will give the Cure;   35
        For as the Characters in Sand we trace,
        If unrenew'd (tho e'er so deep) will pass;
        So all Impressions which our Passions make,
        By Absence smooth'd, an even Surface take;
        Thus Heav'n at once both covetuous and kind,   40
        Has constituted ev'ry human Mind,
        For as we lose the Merit to be true,
        In recompense we lose the Mis'ry too.

L. M.   A little Love deserves not passion's name,
        A Taper's light is hardly call'd a Flame,   45
        A Transient Wind extinguishes the Fire
        And a short Absence cools a small desire,
        But when the Heat on the whole Vitals preys
        Even Tempests but encrease the powerfull Blaze.

L. H.   *As Poysons other Poysons will remove,*   50
        So love may be expel'd by other Love.
        This Doctrine Cleopatra held was true;
        Won't Cleopatra's Medcines do for You?

L. M.   Go bid the thirsty, overlabour'd swains
        Seek Grecian Vines on Caledonian plains,   55
        With equal Hope you sooth my restless mind   }
        (To this cold Climate cursedly confin'd)
        To meet a second lovely of the Kind.   }

L. H.   These Thoughts are not from Nature but a Book,
        Into our Conduct, not our Writings look;   60
        There Men and Women equally you'll see,   }
        Form'd by Receipts you've heard explain'd by me, }
        I tell you what they are, You what they ought to be. }

44–9 In the Bodleian MS, LM wrote these six lines as if to stand alone, heading them:
'Epigram written extempore in a dispute whether Absence ended Love.' Despite a line
drawn below the epigram, she and Hervey pursued the dialogue on the verso of the sheet.

    50–1 Paraphrase of a remark insincerely made by Dryden's Cleopatra (*All for Love*,
Act IV: *Works*, 4. 234). When LM's infatuation ended (1741), she received the same
advice again from Hervey (*Letters*, 2. 240–1).

L. M.   Sway'd by no moral, or affected Rules
      (By Knaves invented and observ'd by Fools)   65
      Judge of my Future Actions by my past
      And call my Conduct, nicety of Taste.

L. H.   In vain you talk of what you love and hate
      For when you're hungry and have Food you'll eat.

L. M.   Hunger's the Motive of the unbred Clown   70
      To whose coarse Palate, all rank meat goes down
      But Hunger never rais'd the Pain I feel
      Which only one can give, and only One could heal.

After 73 an extra couplet in Hervey's hand, heavily scribbled over by LM:
I'm tired of all this fine poetic Stuff;
Now call for Supper, we have writ enough.

October 1736

Text (first 12 lines) H MS. 256. 51; (remainder) H MS. 81. 214, in which
Hervey's hand follows Lady Mary's. *Printed* (first 12 lines) 1803. The first
section of this poem was intended to stand alone; Hervey converted one copy
of it into a dialogue. Lady Mary had been at Twickenham for the first part of
Oct. 1736, but saw Hervey at court on 20 or 21 Oct. (*Letters*, 2. 108, 110).
Copies in Cornell and the Osborn Collection claim the poem was written on her
daughter's marriage, of which she disapproved.

If Age and Sickness, poverty, and Pain,
    Should each assault me with Alternate Plagu⟨es⟩
I know Mankind is destin'd to complain
    And I submit to Torment, and Fatigues,
But here I murmur against Heaven's decree   5
That Miracles must rise to ruin me.

The Pious Farmer that ne'er misses pray'rs
    With Patience suffers unexpected Rain,
He blesses Heaven for what its Bounty spares
    And sees, resign'd, a crop of blighted Grain   10

But ('spite of Sermons) Farmers would blaspheme
If a Star fell to set their Thatch on Flame.

[Hervey] In Sicily alone an Ætna burns,
        But what Sicilian Ætna's Fury mourns?
        He knows the Warmth which from the Mountain glows,
        His plenteous Olives and his Vines bestows: 16
        Ægypt alone is never blest with Rains
        And the same Nile that spares the Plowman's Pains,
        By Miracles to Ægypt only known,
        Gives these rich Harvests to her Sons alone.   20
        Thus neither Country weeps the Fire or Flood
        But bare the Bad, contented with the Good.

[LM]   Suppose it true (which I can scarce suppose)
        That with uncommon Fire this Bosom glows
        Yet what avails this Gift from partial Heaven   25
        Not for my Pleasure but my Torment given,
        This sensibillity which oft you praise
        Serves but to plague me in unusual ways.

1736
Address'd To ——

Text H MS. 256. 51–2; *written* late 1736; *printed*, with a disapproving editor's note, June 1749, *London Magazine*. Lady Mary must have addressed this poem to either Algarotti or Hervey during the period of despair which followed the former's departure. She showed it to a few select friends. In 1740 Lady Pomfret sent a transcript under seal of secrecy to Lady Hertford; she thought it written 'so feelingly that all who read must know it comes from the heart!' Both ladies were shocked by the recommendation of suicide (*Corr.*, 1805, 2. 116, 170–1, 175). J. Lane, meeting Lady Mary almost on her death-bed, wrote a fulsome reply (H MS. 81. 120).

        With toilsome steps I pass through Life's dull Road,
        No Pack Horse halfe so weary of his Load;
        And when this dirty Journey will conclude,
        To what new Realms is then my Way persu'd?

Say; then does the unbody'd Spirit fly,   5
To happier climes and to a better Sky;
Or sinking, mixes with its kindred clay,
And sleeps a whole Eternity away?
Or shall this Form be once again renew'd,
With all its Frailties, and its Hopes endu'd;   10
Acting once more on this detested Stage,
Passions of Youth, Infirmities of Age?
 I see in Tully what the Ancients thought
And read unprejudiced what moderns taught
But no Conviction from my reading springs,   15
Most dubious, on the most important things.
 Yet one short moment would at once explain, ⎫
What all Philosophy has sought in vain,   ⎬
Would clear all doubt, and terminate all pain. ⎭
 Why then not hasten that decisive Hour,   20
Still in my view, and ever in my power?
Why should I drag along this Life I hate
Without one thought to mitigate the weight?
Whence this misterious bearing to exist,
When every Joy is lost, and every Hope dismist?   25
In chains and darkness wherefore should I stay
And mourn in Prison while I keep the Key?

5 ff. This passage is a complex of echoes from Dryden: 'And here and there th'un-
bodied Spirit flies' ('Of the Pythagorean Philosophy', *Poems*, ed. J. Kinsley, 1958, 4.
1724); 'To some new Clime, or to thy native Sky' (*Aureng-Zebe*, 1: *Works*, 4. 97) and
   Is there no smooth descent? no painless way
   Of kindly mixing with our native clay?
(*The State of Innocence*, v: *Works*, 3. 460). LM was also recalling Pope's *Elegy to the
Memory of an Unfortunate Lady*, lines 24–6:
   Fate snatch'd her early to the pitying sky.
   As into air the purer spirits flow,
   And sep'rate from their kindred dregs below.

 12 LM noted in her commonplace-book, 'passions insepr[able] to youth and in-
firmitys to age' (Fisher Library, University of Sydney, f. 6).

For four 'new' poems see Appendix I, below, p. 381.

Text H MS. 378, typescript supplied by Sir Shane Leslie, Bt., from Lady Mary's holograph, which Lord Wharncliffe gave to Lady Constance Leslie in 1889. *Written* after the birth of Sir Robert Walpole's grandson in Apr. 1730, and before Hervey quoted from this dialogue in Aug. 1737. The first speaker is a member of the Opposition; the second is Walpole.

> When rolling time brings on the golden hour
> Shall shew my Monarch in the shine of Pow'r,
> He shall consign to this capacious Hand
> At least the Key, perhaps the Treasurer['s] wand.
> ⟨?⟩ my old woman of her — has dy'd,   5
> Betty shall then come forth, avow'd my Bride,
> Venus may bless the Nuptials she has made
> If with a lovely Boy my prayers be paid.
>
>   When Europe sees the Blessing of my Schemes
> And all my Blunders are forgot like dreams,   10
> Then full of years and Honor I retreat
> And leave to duller Heads the toils of state,
> Then my old Kate shall yield my Molly place,
> How I shall smile, when she is styl'd, Her Grace!
> From distant shires the nobles shall repair   15
> To Houghton Hall to worship Venus there,
> But far, oh far, be Oxenden removed,
> Bold to attack and skillfull to be loved,
>
> To other shores let him his steps convey
>
> Triumph enough for that enchanting Face!   20
> That my damnation must enrich his Race,
> May he permit that quiet, without fears
> I clasp this Joy of my declining years,
> Nor she shall think her selfe too much confined
> When I except but him of all mankind.   25

2 *my Monarch*: Frederick, Prince of Wales.

4 *Key*: badge of office of the Vice-Chamberlain, since 1730 Lord Hervey.

13 Walpole m. LM's friend Maria Skerrett shortly before 3 Mar. 1738, six months after Catherine Walpole's death.

14 Walpole was created an earl in 1742, but never a duke.

17–18 Sir George Oxenden (pp. 277–8 above) had had an affair with Walpole's daughter-in-law, and her only son was rumoured to be his (Hervey, *Memoirs*, 3. 742).

20–1 i.e. Walpole will be damned for the avarice which will eventually enrich his spurious grandson. Hervey quoted this couplet in 1737 (ibid.).

The Politicians

Text 1803, 5. 234–5; *written* probably during one of Walpole's periods of acute political struggle: 1733–4 or 1737–8. Addison had recounted this fable in prose in *Tatler* No. 229, Sept. 1710.

In ancient days when ev'ry brute
To human privilege had right;
Could reason, wrangle, or dispute,
As well as scratch, and tear, and bite.

When Phœbus shone his brightest ray, 5
The rip'ning corn his pow'r confess'd;
His cheering beams made Nature gay,
The eagle in his warmth was blest.

But mal-contents e'en then arose
The birds who love the dolesome night; 10
The darkest grove with care they chose,
And there caball'd against the light.

The screech-owl, with ill-boding cry,
Portends strange things, old women say:
Stops ev'ry fool that passes by, 15
And frights the school-boy from his play.

The raven and the double bat,
With families of owls combine;
In close consult they rail and chat,
And curse aloud the glorious shine. 20

While the great planet, all serene,
Heedless pursues his destin'd way;
He asks not what these murmurs mean,
But runs his course, and gives us day.

17 The bat may be Bolingbroke, whom LM regarded as doubly a turncoat; cf. 'a Trimmer like a Bat will be eaten by Beasts and Birds' (commonplace-book MS., f. 8).

Verses wrote under General Churchill's Pictour

Text Bagshawe MS., John Rylands Library, Manchester, 3/7/5, copied by Sir James Caldwell, 1746 (Halsband, *LM*, p. 233); *written* after 1737, when Jean-Baptiste Vanloo, French painter of the picture in question, arrived in London; *printed* July 1738, *London Magazine*. Caldwell, Horace Walpole, and others ascribed these lines to Lady Mary, though Walpole later believed she had 'seized' them from David Mallet (*Corr.* 14. 246 and n. 22). Mallet first claimed them in 1759, twenty-one years after their composition and first printing, and in his *Poems*, 1779, he added six introductory lines which change the whole point of the epigram. Lady Mary had earlier hinted (p. 232 above) at the amorous exploits of Charles Churchill (*c.* 1679–1745), who must have been over fifty-four when Vanloo painted him.

> Still hovering round the fair at fifty four,
> Unfit to Love, unable to give o'er,
> A flesh fly that still flutters on the Wing
> Awake to Buz, but not alive to Sting,
> Brisk where he cannot, backward where he can,   5
> The teazing Ghost of the departed Man.

6 Hanbury Williams wrote that the ageing Churchill 'yet / Grasps at the shade of his departed wit' (*Works*, 1822, 1. 77).

Text preliminary pages of Algarotti's *Il Newtonianismo per le dame*, Naples, 1739; *written* perhaps in July 1738 (*Letters*, 2. 117).

> Such various learning in this Work appears,
> As seems the slow result of length of years;
> Yet these dark Truths explain'd in such a way,
> As only youth cou'd write a stile so gay.
>
> While life so short, and Art so long we mourn,   5
> Science in you appears not taught, but born.
> While *Newton's* deep Philosophy you tell,
> You show the pleasing gift to trifle well.
>
> So *Eden* rose, as we in *Moses* find,
> (The only Emblem of thy happy mind)   10
> Where ev'ry charm of ev'ry season meets,
> The Fruit of Autumn mix'd with vernal sweets.

9 ff. Simultaneous fruit and flowers occur not in the biblical account of Eden but in that of Milton (*Paradise Lost*, iv. 148).

Text MS. 1259, Biblioteca Civica, Treviso; *written* probably either summer 1736 or Apr.–May 1739, based very closely on part of Lord Lansdowne's 'To Myra' (*Poems Upon Several Occasions*, 1712, p. 73). *Printed* 1956: Halsband, *LM*, pp. 176–7. Other verse Lady Mary sent to Algarotti is printed in her *Letters*, 2. 106 and 148.

Prepar'd to rail, and quite resolv'd to part,
What magick is it awes my trembling Heart?
At that fair vision all resentments fly,
And on my tongue halfe-form'd reproaches dye,
My melting Soul one tender Glance disarms,   5
I faint—and find all Heaven within his arms.

Text H MS. 81. 51. If it refers to Algarotti it must have been *written* in summer 1736 or Apr.–10 May 1739.

Ye soft Ideas leave this tortur'd Breast
And thou fond Heart, go beat thy selfe to rest.
Reason (if once I offer'd at thy Shrine)
Now bring thy Aid, exert thy right Divine,
Subdue these Passions that resist thy sway   5
And teach my Rebel Wishes to obey.
   Come calm Oblivion chase away my Cares,
Quiet this throbbing Pulse, repel my tears,
Blot out this Imagery of Joy and pain,
These mix'd emotions that confuse my Brain,   10
Which poetry it selfe cannot reveal,
Which only he could raise, and I can feel.
   He comes!—'twas nothing but the rustling Wind,
He has forgot, is faithless, is unkind—
While expectation rends my labouring mind.   15
   Can all the pleasures that he brings me pay
For the long sighing of this tedious day?
Thou watchfull Taper by whose silent Light
I lonely pass the melancholy night,
Thou faithfull Wittness of my secret pain   20
To whom alone I venture to complain

18–21 From Congreve's 'To a Candle. Elegy' (*Complete Works*, ed. M. Summers, 1923, 4. 147).

Text H MS. 81. 156; Algarotti made himself a copy (Bod. MS. Don. c. 56. 36); *written* before 10 May 1739, remodelled from an early version (H MS. 81. 69) whose second stanza closely followed Addison's rendering of Horace's Ode I. xiii, on jealousy (*Misc. Works*, ed. A. C. Guthkelch, 1914, 2. 143).

Between your sheets you soundly sleep
Nor dream of Vigils that we Lovers keep
While all the night, I waking sigh your name,
The tender sound does every nerve inflame,
Imagination shews me all your charms,   5
The plenteous silken hair, and waxen Arms,
The well turn'd neck, and snowy rising breast
And all the Beauties that supinely rest
    between your sheets.

Ah Lindamira, could you see my Heart,
How fond, how true, how free from fraudfull Art, 10
The warmest glances poorly doe explain
The eager wish, the melting throbbing pain
Which through my very blood and soul I feel,
Which you cannot beleive nor I reveal,
Which every Metaphor must render less   15
And yet (methinks) which I could well express
    between your sheets.

3–6 *early version:*
While wakeing I indulge the pain
Of Fruitless Pasion oft declar'd in vain,
Too lively Fancy paints your Flowing Hair,
Your killing Eyes that give dispair,

9–14 *represented by four lines in early version:*
Ah would some God my songs inspire
With warmth to show the strong desire
Does on my heart and vitals prey
And wastes my very Soul away,

Text H MS. 81, f. 56; *written* probably before Lady Mary left England in July 1739; *printed* 1803.

Finish, these Languors make me sick,
Of dying airs I know the Trick,

Long since I've learnt to well explain
Th'unmeaning Cant of Fire and pain
And see thrô all the senseless Lyes   5
Of burning darts from killing Eyes,
I'm tir'd with this continual Rout
Of bowing low and leading out,
                    Finish.

Finish this tedious dangling Trade
By which so many Fools are made,   10
For Fools they are, who you can please
With such affected ⟨arts⟩ as these.
At Operas ⟨ ? ⟩ to stand
And slyly press the given hand,
Thus you may wait whole years in vain   15
But sure you would, were you in pain,
                    Finish.

Text H MS. 81. 170; *written* probably before July 1739; *printed* 1803.

Why should you think I live unpleas'd
    Because I am not pleas'd with you?
My mind is not so far diseas'd
    To yeild when pouder'd Fops persue.

My Vanity can find no charm   5
    In common prostituted vows,
Nor can you raise a wish that's warm
    In one that your true value knows.

While cold and careless thus I shun
    The Buz and Flutter that you make   10
Perhaps some giddy Girl may run
    To catch the Prize that I forsake.

So brightly shines the glittering Glare
    In unexperienced children's Eyes
When they with little Arts ensnare   15
    The ⟨Tawdry⟩ painted ⟨butt⟩erflys.

While they with Pride a Conquest boast
And think the Chase deserving Fame,
Those scorn the useless Toil it cost
Who're us'd to more substantial Game.   20

Apollo and Daphne

Text H MS. 255. 28; *written* before July 1739, probably on the occasion of
one of the scandals concerning Oxenden (cf. pp. 277–8, 292 above).

  This *Metamorphoses* incident was burlesqued by other writers (*The Hive*,
1724, pp. 226–7; Prior, *Works*, 1. 413–17; Tickell, *Poems*, 1779, p. 146). Lady
Mary transcribed the first two with her own version, and probably knew the
last.

I am, cry'd Apollo, and run as he spoke
But the skittish young Damsel ne'er turn'd back to look,
I am the great God Tenedos Adores
And Delos does also acknowledge my power.

Round my Head the Sun beams you may glittering see   5
And no man alive can make Ballads like me,
All Physic I know—she mended her pace
And his Godhead halfe tir'd was quitting the Chase.

Had Apollo known Women, as well as I know 'em,
He would not have talk'd of a potion or poem,   10
But he had appear'd in O[xenden']s Shape,
By my Soul little Daphne had suffer'd the Rape.

  9 For this reference to her sex, cf. p. 109 above.

A Billet to invite to Suppers

Text H MS. 255. 76, signed with Lady Mary's initials MWM; *written* before
July 1739. She probably addressed this invitation to Hervey, although she had
other ambitious friends.

Come ——, and pertake my Frugal meal,
Some easy moments from Ambition steal,

Here you may freely laugh where you despise
And shew the Honest Soul without Disguise;
And if you please, be an establish'd Rule   5
At every Supper sacrifice a Fool,
Yet free our mirth from any real offence,
Still true to Freindship, modesty and sense.

Epithalamium

Text   1803, 5. 227; *written* probably before 1739, about an unidentified couple.

Since you, Mr. H**d, will marry black Kate,
Accept of good wishes for that blessed state:
May you fight all the day like a dog and a cat,
And yet ev'ry year produce a new brat.
                        Fal la!

May she never be honest—you never be sound;   5
May her tongue like a clapper be heard a mile round;
Till abandon'd by joy, and deserted by grace,
You hang yourselves both in the very same place.
                        Fal la!

Epigram to L. H.

Text H MS. 255. 77, copied after 1738, signed 'MWM'; *written* probably
before July 1739. Lady Mary's personal expenses (about £160 p.a. in the 1720s,
of which £100 went on clothes: Halsband, *LM*, p. 124) were very low for one
of her rank.

When Lycé enters so exactly dress'd
My last year's Habit is her constant Jest,
Lycé with reason you my cloaths upbraid,
They are old fashion'd, but my Bills are paid.

Hymn to the Moon
Written in July in an Arbor

Text H MS. 256. 22, copied after 1730; *written* before Aug. 1740, by which date the Abbé Conti made Italian translations of this and others of Lady Mary's poems (H MS. 81. 256–61; Conti, *Prose e poesie*, 2, 1756, pp. xiii–xxii). *Printed* May 1750, *London Magazine*. Algarotti in 1758 requested a copy of this poem, which he published among his 'Pensieri Diversi' with a graceful compliment to its author (*Letters*, 3. 150; *Opere*, Leghorn, 1764–5, 7. 70–1).

Thou silver Deity of secret Night,
   Direct my footsteps through the Woodland Shade,
Thou conscious Witness of unknown delight,
   The Lovers Guardian, and the Muses Aid.

By thy pale beams I solitary rove,   5
   To thee my tender Greife confide,
Serenely sweet you gild the silent Grove,
   My Freind, my Goddess and my Guide.

Even thee fair Queen from thy amazing height
   The Charms of young Endimion drew,   10
Veil'd with the Mantle of concealing Night,
   With all thy Greatness, and thy Coldness too.

Verses Written in a Garden

Text H MS. 256. 16–17; *written* before Aug. 1740 (cf. headnote to previous poem); *printed* July 1750, *London Magazine*. Lady Mary kept copies of a group of French verse fables in an unidentified hand (H MS. 81. 241–85 *passim*), including three slightly differing but very closely related renderings of this poem. One was printed in 1803 as 'Translated by herself', which is unlikely.

See how that pair of billing Doves
With open Murmurs own their Loves;
And heedless of censorious Eyes,
Persue their unpolluted Joys.
No fears of Future Want molest   5
The downy Quiet of their Nest,

No Interest joyn'd the happy Pair,
Securely blest in Nature's Care,
While her dear dictates they persue,
For Constancy is Nature too. 10
Can all the Doctrine of our Schools
Our Moral Maxims, our Religious Rules,
Can Learning to our Lives ensure
Virtu so bright, or Bliss so pure?
The great Creator's happy Hand 15
Virtue and Pleasure ever blends,
In vain the Church and Court have try'd
Th'united Essence to divide;
Alike they find their wild mistake,
The Pedant Preist, and Giddy Rake. 20

Fragment to ✱✱✱

Text 1803, 5. 153; *written* from Venice, Sept. 1739–Aug. 1740, probably to Hervey.

Let mules and asses in that circle tread,
And proud of trappings toss a feather'd head;
Leave you the stupid business of the state,
Strive to be happy, and despise the great:
Come where the Graces guide the gentle day, 5
Where Venus rules amidst her native sea,
Where at her altar gallantries appear,
And even Wisdom dares not shew severe.
* * * * * * * *
* * * * * * * *

6 ff. LM praised the permissive Venetian society in prose (*Letters*, 2. 159).

The 5th Ode of Horace Imitated

Text H MS. 256. 20, copied after 1730; *written* before (perhaps long before)
Lady Mary left Rome (8 Feb. 1741), where the Cornell copy (MS. E 6004) was
made for Spence; *printed* Sept. 1750, *London Magazine*.

For whom are now your Airs put on?
And what new Beauty doom'd to be undone?
　That careless Elegance of Dress,
　　This Essence that perfumes the Wind,
　Your every motion does confess　　　　　　5
　　Some secret Conquest is design'd.

Alas the poor unhappy Maid,
To what a train of ills betraid!
　What fears! what pangs shall rend her Breast!
　　How will her eyes disolve in Tears!　　　10
　That now with glowing Joy is blest,
　　Charm'd with the faithless vows she hears.

So the young Sailor on the Summer Sea
Gaily persues his destin'd way,
　Fearless and careless on the deck he stands　　15
　　Till sudden storms arise, and Thunders rowl,
　In vain he casts his Eye to distant Lands,
　　Distracting Terror tears his timerous Soul.

For me, secure I view the raging Main,
Past are my Dangers, and forgot my Pain,　　　20
　My Votive Tablet in the temple shews
　　The Monument of Folly past,
　I paid the bounteous God my gratefull vows
　　Who snatch'd from Ruin sav'd me at the last.

Ballad
to the Irish Howl

Text H MS. 256, ff. 21–2, copied after 1730; *written* before 8 Feb. 1741; *printed* June 1749, *London Magazine*. 'The Irish Howl' was a popular tune.

To that dear Nymph, whose powerfull Name
Does ev'ry throbbing Nerve inflame
(As the soft sound I low repeat
My pulse unequal measures beat),
Whose Eyes I never more shall see   5
That once so sweetly shin'd on me,
Go Gentle Wind, and kindly bear
My tender wishes to the fair,
         Oh ho, ho, etc.

Amidst her pleasures let her know
The secret Anguish of my Woe,   10
The midnight pang, the Jealous Hell
Does in this tortur'd bosom dwell
While laughing she, and full of play
Is with her young Companions gay
Or hearing in some fragrant bower   15
Her Lovers sighs, and Beauty's power,
         Oh ho, ho etc.

Lost and forgotten may I be,
Oh may no pitying thought of me
Disturb the Joy that she may find
When Love is crown'd, and fortune kind.   20
May that blest Swain (whom yet I hate)
Be proud of his distinguish'd Fate;
Each happy Night be like the first
And she be blest, as I am curst,
         Oh ho, ho etc.

1–2 Cf. 'Between your sheets you soundly sleep', lines 3–4, p. 296 above.
7–8 Cf. Pope's 'Autumn', line 17 etc.: 'Go gentle Gales, and bear my Sighs away!'

While in these pathless Woods I stray   25
And lose my Solitary way,
Talk to the Stars, to Trees complain
And tell the senseless rocks my pain,
But madness spares that sacred Name
Nor dares the hidden wound proclaim   30
Which secret rankling, sure, and slow
Shall close in endless peace my Woe.
   Oh ho, ho etc.

When this fond Heart shall ake no more
And all the ills of Life are o'er
(If Gods by Lovers' prayers are mov'd,   35
As ev'ry God in Heaven has lov'd)
Instead of bright Elyzian Joys
That unknown something in the skies
In recompence of all my pain
The only Heaven I would obtain,   40
May I the Guardian of her charms
Preserve that Paradise from harms.

30 ff. Cf. 'Epistle [to Lord Bathurst]', lines 82–3, p. 244 above.

A ma Raison

Text   MS. 1259, Biblioteca Civica, Treviso, among Algarotti's papers; *written* probably before the early 1740s; *printed* 1966: Halsband, 'Algarotti as Apollo: His Influence on Lady Mary Wortley Montagu' (*Friendship's Garland: Essays Presented to Mario Praz*, ed. V. Gabrieli, Rome, 1966, 1. 240). Translation on pp. 393–4.

C'en est fait, je me cede, soumettons nous au sort—
Et vous Raison! quittez vos inutiles efforts—
En soupirs, en regrets, en d'erreurs, en desirs,
Je promene mon esprit, et je fonde en plaisirs.
C'est ridicule vous dittes—j'en conviens, mais helas!   5
La sagesse des humains aussi ne l'est elle pas?
C'est une Folie sans doute, mais ma Folie m'est chere—
Preceptes, et Refflections, je vous prie de vous taire.

Ces Princes, ces Ministres dont on vantent le Genie,
Qui consument en vain projets, des jours plein d'ennuy,   10
Eh sont-ils donc Sage, et moi je suis Folle
Quand je forme dans ma tête un Aimable Idole?
Mais j'enrage (je l'avoue) quand mon Cœur me dit bas,
Songez y bien Manon, il vous aimerois pas,
Jugez en par son Air, jugez en par vous mesme,   15
On se connoit que trop en Amour quand on aime.
—De cette triste verité ma gloire est offensé—
Je l'oublie, et Philante n'est plus dans ma pensée.

Text H MS. 81. 68; *written* probably before the early 1740s, if, as seems likely, the 'Youth' is Algarotti and the friend addressed is Hervey.

So often seen, it should be nothing new,
That miracles can be perform'd by you;
And yet surpriz'd I read these pleaseing lines;
Where lively Wit, in native sweetness shines,
My long-lost spirit you know how to raise,   5
And thô I would not like, you force my praise.
Beyond my Praise, you force my Freindship too,
I feel the Gratitude, you make your due,
And warmly wish that Heaven would shew the way
At any price that Gratitude to pay.—   10
But if there is a pleasure that proceeds
From recollection of good natur'd deeds,
May that be thine,—may every joy attend
The generous Heart that knows to be a Freind,
Can view my weakness with indulgent Eyes   15
And sooth a Folly which you must despise.
My artless thanks ('tis all I can) receive;
And Blessings, such as wretched Bankrupts give.
The Gods (if Gods can destiny controul,
And view the strugglings of a gratefull Soul)   20
May point some path, as yet unguess'd by me,
To do a service worthy thanks from thee.
But you, of every Grace, and Good, possess'd,
Can feel no want, nor be (like me) distress'd.
O let me learn the happy courtly Art   25

To please my Eyes, and not engage my Heart—
Too late, alas! is made this fond request,
The Fatal Form too deeply is impress'd.
This Youth (Delightfull Vision of a day!)
Has snatch'd my reason, and my Soul away.   30
Lethean Draughts my Quiet must restore,
O were I wafted to that silent Shore
Where I should sigh, and he should charm no more.

31–3 A parallel to Hervey's 'Monimia to Philocles':

No—grief shall swell my sails, and speed me o'er
(Despair my pilot) to that quiet shore
Where I can trust, and thou betray no more

(Dodsley's *Collection*, 4, 1755, p. 88; LM's transcript H MS. 255. 48).

Answer to an impromptu Song
Address'd to me at Avignon by the Count——
to the same Tune.

Text H MS. 256. 59; *written* May 1742–Aug. 1746. Translation on p. 394.

Chantez, chantez vostre tendresse,
    Arachez moi mon Cœur par Force ou par Adresse,
Tachez de le gagner, pour moi je le permets,
    Je n'ai point encore fait d'Efforts pour le defendre,
Mais vous n'avez pas scu le prendre   5
    Et ferez aussi bien de m'en parler jamais.

Wrote in the Year 1755 at Louvere

Text H MS. 256. 57; *printed* 1803.

Wisdom! slow product of experienced Years,
The only Fruit that Life's cold Winter bears!
Thy sacred seeds in vain in Youth we lay
By the Fierce storms of Passion torn away;

Wrote in the Year 1755 at Louvere

Wisdom! slow product of experienc'd Years,
The only Fruit that Life's cold Winter bears!
Thy sacred seeds in vain in Youth we lay
By the Fierce storms of Passion torn away;
Should some remain in a rich Generous soil
They long lie hid, & must be rais'd with Toil;
Faintly they struggle with inclement skies,
No sooner born, than the poor Planter dyes

Song

How happy is the harden'd Heart
where Interest is the only view
Can sigh and meet, or smile & part
nor pleas'd, nor griev'd, nor false; nor True.

Yet have they truly peace of mind?
Or do they ever truly know,
The Bliss sincerer tempers find
Which Truth & virtue can bestow?

5. Lady Mary's late hand. *See pages 306, 178–9*

has not been able to resist your Eyes

B. but I shall be able to resist this discourse – Adieu for —

S. stay, it is not Sir William that begs it of you

B. who then?

S. At Lucy you shall judge in what distractions I have been

B. you distract me.

S. my honor obliges me at present to discover ye real state
of things, it is not m^r Gaymore. who is now courting
y^r Lady

B. not Gaymore!

S. his footman

B. who then am I talking to? quick

S. him selfe

B. aside) my spirit is saved.

S. I thought in this disguise. to find out ye true character
of the woman propos'd to me. for a wife, my father was
so good to consent to this stratagem at my earnest
request, & ye Event has turn'd my head, I despise the Lady
I came to marry, & I adore. the chambermaid, that should
have been my servant, I am sorry for the sake of S^r
John Leary's family to add; that his daughter has so little
taste to grow fond of my footman, & if I don't put
a stop to it, is very likely to marry him. what shall
I do? you shall advise me Lucy.

B. aside) I will have ye pleasure of teazing him (aloud)
Your affairs are in a very odd situation, but S^r in
the first place I beg your pardon if I have not behav'd
my selfe to you with ye respect that I ought

S. Dear Lucy you might have omitted a compliment wch only serves
to put me in mind that we are. not so equal as I
could wish

B. is y^r Inclination for me serious enough to make that
uneasy to you?

Should some remain in a rich Generous Soil 5
They long lie hid, and must be rais'd with Toil;
Faintly they struggle with inclement skies,
No sooner born, than the poor Planter dyes.

6-8 LM has combined two quotations: John Sheffield, Duke of Buckingham's
Men toil for Fame, which no Man lives to find;
Long ripening under-ground this *China* lies;
Fame bears no Fruit, till the vain Planter dies,
and Congreve's 'No sooner born, but the Vile Parent dies' ('On Mr. Hobbs and His
Writings', *Works*, 1723, 1. 181; last line of *The Double Dealer*, 1694).

Text H MS. 81. 61; *written* May–Oct. 1757; *printed* 1803 with corrections by
Dallaway, the result of his failure to recognize the irony of the praise. Fulke
Greville (*c.* 1717–*c.* 1806), who visited Lady Mary in Venice, presented her
with a copy of 'his curious Book', *Maxims, Characters, and Reflections, Critical,
Satyrical, and Moral* (1756). To her daughter she compared it with Edward
Howard's 'incomparable, incomprehensible poem' satirically praised by Lord
Dorset (*Letters*, 3. 127, 137). Here she vies with Dorset in ostensible pane-
gyric.

For ever blest be the prolific Brain
Could not this store of Images contain,
Such various Talents were by Heaven design'd ⎫
(Too vast a Treasure for a single mind!) ⎬
To please, astonish, and instruct Mankind. ⎭ 5
Thus the charg'd Trees with blooming odors crown'd ⎫
Shed their fair Blossoms with profusion round, ⎬
The rich manure improves the barren Ground. ⎭
So swells the Brook with heaven descended Rain
And flows meandering on the thirsty Plain. 10
   With a delight, not to be told, I veiw
Themes long exhausted, in your Hands grow new.
Past all describing, your descriptions are,
So full, so just, so wild and regular.
The Style so vary'd that it wants a Name, 15
Which ever differing, ever is the same.

1-8 Greville himself suggested to LM her manure image. He compares the mind to
fertile soil in many of his maxims, including the first and last. LM alludes particularly
to his confession in his Preface, that he had 'thrown' his papers into the world to 'relieve'
and 'discharge' his mind (pp. iii–iv).
   12 Greville admits that he shares many ideas with other maxim writers, but claims
that he thought of them independently (pp. iv–v).

You raise, or calm our Passions, as you please,
The Human Heart your powerfull Pen obeys,
When eager Trasimond persues the Course,
We hear the Whip, and see the Foaming Horse,   20
With soft Sophronia, we have wept and smiled,
So soon offended, sooner reconcil'd.
    Go on, great Author, that the World may see ⎫
How bright, when from Pedantic fetters free   ⎬
True Genius shines, and shines alone in thee. ⎭   25
Give new Editions, with a noble Scorn
Of Insect Critics would Obscure thy Morn,
Neglect their Censures, nor thy Work delay,
The Owls still sicken at the sight of Day.

19-20 LM has conflated two characters: Torismond, the passionate amateur jockey, and Trasimond, the uncouth squire (pp. 115-18, 235-7).

21-2 Greville tells a lengthy sentimental anecdote of Sophronia, which in his second edition he omitted 'partly in compliance with the tastes and opinions of some particular persons' (p. xxii).

23-5 Alluding to Greville's comparison: 'SENSE, like a winged insect, flutters through the mists that surround this dark spot at a small distance from its surface; GENIUS, like a planet, takes a wide circuit through the pure expanse of nature, and visits not regions only, but whole worlds which SENSE does not know to exist' (pp. 266-7).

26-7 In his Preface Greville promised to heed criticism by changes in any later edition. The second, 1757, had 'Alterations Additions and explanatory Notes' and a 'Preface To the Second Edition By the Editor' which compares critics to insects (p. xxii).

Advice

Text H MS. 255. 71, copied after 1738; *printed* 1803.

Cease Fond Shepherd, cease desiring
    What you never must enjoy,
She derides your vain aspiring,
    She to all your Sex is coy.

Cunning Damon once persu'd her   5
    Yet she never would encline,
Strephon too as vainly woo'd her
    Thô his Flocks were more than thine.

At Diana's shrine she's vow'd
By the Zone about her waste,   10
Thrice she bow'd, and thrice she vow'd
Like the Goddess to be chaste.

Answer

Text etc. as previous poem.

Thô I never get possession
'Tis a pleasure to adore,
Hope the Wretches only blessing
May in time procure me more.

Constant Courtship may obtain her   5
Where both Wealth and Merit fail
And the lucky minute gain her,
Fate and Fancy must prevail.

At Diana's shrine she's vow'd
By the Bow and by the Quiver   10
Thrice she bow'd and thrice she vow'd
Once to love and that for ever.

Text inside cover of Saint-Évremond's *Œuvres meslées*, London, 1705, vol. i
(now at Sandon Hall). The juvenile *nom de plume* in line 6 suggests an early
date (H MS. 251), the parallel with the exiled poet a late one. *Printed* (first 4
lines) *T.L.S.*, 1928, p. 596. Saint-Évremond (1610–1703) spent the last thirty
years of his life in exile in England.

Exil'd, grown old, in Poverty and Pain;
    Philosophy could calm the Poet's Breast:
But oh! what cure for those who wish in Vain?
    What Lesson is it must restore my Rest?

Let others court the mighty Idol Fame;   5
Let all the World forget Clarinda's Name,
    I could lose all that Avarice requires

Or all that Beauty that the World admires,
This only greife I cannot bear or cure,
    The firmness of my Soul gives way,   10
Some pitying Power behold what I endure

The Fourth Ode of the First Book of Horace, Imitated
'Solvitur acris hyems grata vice veris,' &c.

Text 1803, 5. 201–2.

Sharp winter now dissolved, the linnets sing,
The grateful breath of pleasing Zephyrs bring
The welcome joys of long desired spring.

The gallies now for open sea prepare,
The herds forsake their stalls for balmy air,   5
The fields adorn'd with green th'approaching sun
                             declare.

In shining nights the charming Venus leads
Her troop of Graces, and her lovely maids
Who gaily trip the ground in myrtle shades.

The blazing forge her husband Vulcan heats,   10
And thunderlike the labouring hammer beats,
While toiling Cyclops every stroke repeats.

Of myrtle new the chearful wreath compose,
Or various flowers which opening spring bestows,
Till coming June presents the blushing rose.   15

Pay your vow'd offering to God Faunus' bower!
Then, happy Sestius, seize the present hour,
'Tis all that nature leaves to mortal power.

The equal hand of strong impartial fate,
Levels the peasant and th'imperious great,   20
Nor will that doom on human projects wait.

To the dark mansions of the senseless dead,
With daily steps our destined path we tread,
Realms still unknown, of which so much is said.

Ended your schemes of pleasure and of pride,   25
In joyous feasts no one will there preside,
Torn from your Lycidas' beloved side;

Whose tender youth does now our eyes engage,
And soon will give in his maturer age,
Sighs to our virgins—to our matrons rage.   30

27, 30 *Here text follows punctuation of 1805 reissue.*

A Motto to a Graveing
representing the Death of William Rufus

Text H MS. 256. 56, copied after 1741. The unpopular William II was killed by an arrow in 1100, cf. Pope, *Windsor Forest*, lines 83–4.

Behold with Joy, the Heaven-directed Reed;
A Tyrant dying, and a Nation Freed!

A COMEDY

SIMPLICITY

Simplicity, a Comedy

AMONG Lady Mary's manuscripts is a fair copy, in her own hand, of a three-act play entitled *A Comedy / Simplicity*. It is undated, bears no indication of source, and was apparently never published or staged. (In 1967 it was produced on the stage at Columbia University. In 1988 Co-Producers presented it professionally in six English towns and lastly in London.) It is actually a translation–adaptation of *Le Jeu de l'amour et du hasard*, subtitled *Arlequin maître et valet*, by Pierre de Marivaux (1688–1763), first staged in Paris in 1730, printed the same year and reprinted 1732. When a French company of actors visited London in the autumn of 1734, playing at the Little Theatre in the Haymarket, they performed it several times. It is likely that Lady Mary saw the play, read it, and then made her translation. Whether or not she hoped to see her version produced on the stage—not, of course, under her own name—we do not know. The manuscript remained among her papers, unnoticed by previous editors, biographers, and even the cataloguer for Sotheby's in 1928.

In relation to Marivaux's play, *Simplicity* is something between a literal translation and a free adaptation. Lady Mary transposes Marivaux's setting: instead of Paris she chose not its equivalent London but the English countryside—which easily makes the plot about four disguised characters more credible. She also naturalizes the cast, converting all the French names, several of them borrowed from the *commedia dell'arte*, into realistic English ones. She made one important change in the plot. In Marivaux it is the heroine who suggests to her father that she disguise herself as her maid in order to test her suitor, and he agrees; in Lady Mary's more convincing version the father suggests the disguise to his daughter because he already knows that her suitor will arrive disguised as his own valet. And where Marivaux ends his play with a witty remark by the valet, after which the company breaks into dance, Lady Mary ends hers more soberly with a sententious comment by the heroine's father, in prose and then heroic couplets.

Lady Mary's most pervasive alteration, of course, can be seen in her treatment of the dialogue. She approaches the French text with respectful freedom, translating verbatim when the idiom and rhythm have English equivalents. Occasionally she conflates separated passages, or transposes a speech from one character to another, or adds and deletes bits of dialogue. In tone her changes transform Marivaux's subtle and delicately sentimental style (*marivaudage*) into robust, practical English. The most striking example of this transformation is the crucial scene of the play: when the suitor reveals his true identity the heroine says in an aside, 'Ah! je vois clair dans mon cœur' (Ah! I see clearly into my heart). How does Lady Mary translate it? 'My life is saved.' In rough proportions, about a quarter of her play is a literal translation of Marivaux, about half is a free translation, and about a quarter is original. Yet not a single phrase or sentence in *Simplicity* has the sound of translation; nowhere does the English betray a foreign origin.

Although Marivaux's comedy was recklessly imitated by William Popple in *The Double Deceit* (1737) and freely looted by Isaac Bickerstaffe in his comic opera *Love in a Village* (1762), Lady Mary's version is the only direct translation of the French comedy made in the eighteenth century. In its own right *Simplicity* wins admiration—not merely as an example of Lady Mary's versatility and as a specimen of comparative comedy but as a worthy addition to English dramatic literature.

Text H MS. 80. 160–87. (Dramatis Personæ and Scene have been provided by the editor. LM's stage directions throughout have been italicized and enclosed in parentheses.)

DRAMATIS PERSONÆ

MEN

SIR JOHN HEARTY
NED, his son
GAYMORE, son of Sir John's old friend
WILLIAM, Gaymore's footman
FOOTMAN, in Sir John's household

WOMEN

BELLINDA, Sir John's daughter
LUCY, her maid

SCENE, *Sir John's house in the country*

[Act I.]

Bellinda, Lucy

Bellinda

What busyness had you to say all those Impertinencys to my
Father? I over heard you—

Lucy

Realy, Madam, I spoke for the best, and I did not at all doubt but
you would thank me for it. I am sure any other Lady of your Age
would. Says my Master, says he, 'Lucy, your mistriss loves you.
You know her thoughts. Young Women tell one another. Is not my
Girl heartily glad that she is going to be marry'd?' 'Yes, Sir,' says I.
What could a body say else? I'm sure 'No' would have sounded
very unnatural.

Bellinda

Very unnatural! Horrid Creature! You think a Husband a fine
thing then?

Lucy

Why yes, again, I don't know what to say else.

Bellinda

Hold your tongue. A fine way of judging, to guess my thoughts by
your own!

Lucy

I am sure I think like a woman almost out of her teens and all the women of that age I ever talk'd with, and I think one must be of a very odd temper and very—

Bellinda

If I did not stop you, you would add 'whimsical,' I suppose.

Lucy

Why realy, Madam, if I durst, and if I was upon a foot to be a little sincere—

Bellinda

You grow downright Impertinent.

Lucy

But pray, Madam, a little patience if you please, and without all this anger. Let me know what harm I have done you in letting your Father beleive you are glad to be marry'd.

Bellinda

In the first place it is false. I am not weary of a single Life.

Lucy

Why, this is again a very odd temper.

Bellinda

In the next place, my Father thinking to oblige me may hurry on things and make preparations, perhaps for nothing after all.

Lucy

How, Madam, will you disoblige good Sir John, and refuse the Husband he has provided for you?

Bellinda

How do I know whether I shall like him? We are not perhaps made for one another.

Lucy

Every body says that the young Esquire that is coming to fall in love with you is genteel, handsome, well bred, witty, Generous, good natur'd. Tis impossible to give a Man a finer character. I should think such a husband a very delicious present—

Bellinda

Delicious! Was there ever such an Expression! What an Idea it gives one!

Lucy

Bless me, Madame, you would make one mad with your nicetys and your scrupules. I beg your pardon, but I must tell you once more that you are very lucky to have such a man propos'd to you, and those sort of Men don't use to marry in these days, and I could not blame you, if you were getting out of the Garret Window to him. Well shap'd, Genteel and Handsome: there's for your taste; witty and good natur'd: there's for your Conversation. In my Conscience, such a kind of man would be welcome to me by day or by Night; he is both usefull and agreable.

Bellinda

Why, what you have said of him is agreable, that's true, and I have heard other people say the same thing, but I seldom found my opinion on what people say. He may be all the fashion, and yet I not like him. For example, they say he is handsome; that is gennerally so much the worse.

Lucy

So much the worse! so much the worse! Was there ever such Heterodox notions?

Bellinda

I tell you tis a very reasonable notion. All the handsome men I have seen are Fops.

Lucy

To be sure, a man is mightily in the wrong to be a Fop, but he is mightily in the right to be handsome.

Bellinda

Then, say they, he is genteel, but so far I can forgive.

Lucy

Yes; I think that may be pardonn'd.

Bellinda

As to his Shape and Face, if they are handsome tis a very superfluous piece of merit, in my mind.

Lucy

Now by my troth, when I fall in Love I shall find those superfluitys very necessary.

Bellinda

—because thou'rt a fool. It is more necessary to have a reasonable Husband than a Handsome one. In short, I will not marry but to a Character I can esteem, and that is not so easy to be found. I would go upon sure grounds when I fix my Opinion. People speak well of him: are not people often in the wrong? He has wit, they say: do not men of wit conceal ill Qualitys from the world, that make their Houses the Image of Hell, and their poor wives suffer all the torments of Purgatory? Is not a woman very happy to see her Husband all Complaisance, and good breeding abroad when at home nothing can please him, and she must endure perpetual reprimands in a brutal style? These different behaviours seem very extrodinary, and yet is not this the picture of Sir William our next Neighbour?

Lucy

Oh, but he is a whimsical halfe witted animal.

Bellinda

Pray, is my schoolfellow now Mrs Watchit happier in her Husband? —who does not honor her with 6 words in a month, who when he dines with her hardly seems to know she is in the room, who consults her in nothing, and has allways an air of distrust and melancholy that freezes people that look upon him.

Lucy

I freeze to hear of him, but I think my Lady Gentle who has such a fine Equipage—

Bellinda

Yes, she has a fine Equipage, and a pretty Gentleman as people say. I went tother day to visit this happy Lady, and her pretty Gentleman met me in the Court, with so open a Countenance, so engageing a smile I durst have sworn that man had never said a shocking thing in his Life, such a settle'd content on his pretty Features! Ah, the cheat! I find his poor Lady with her face pale as ashes, her Eyes halfe swell'd out of her Head, and not able to conceal a trembling concern when he came into the room, the very figure that perhaps thou wilt see me. Ah, Lucy, what is a Husband!

Lucy

Why realy, madam, the word Husband gives me an Idea that has made me forget all the rest of your discourse.

(*Enter Sir John and his Son Ned.*)

Sir John

Good morrow, my Bell, I hope I bring good news with me. Your Lover will be here to day, Child. I have just receiv'd a Letter from his father to acquaint me with it—Heyday, are you dumb? and Lucy too? What's the meaning of this? Speak, one of you.

Lucy

Realy, Sir, I am recollecting a man that makes one tremble, another that freezes, a poor woman dying with fear, her eyes swell'd out of her head. These are the pictures we have been collecting.

Sir John

What Nonsense is all this? Have you got the vapours, both of you?

Bellinda

Sir, I was talking with Lucy of the misfortune of living with a disagreable Husband, and I was making some refflections on the unhappyness that I see through all the Glitter in my Lady Gentle's way of living.

Ned

My dear Sister, you have never been in London and you know no Examples but those of our Country Neighbours. Go to Town, get introduce'd to my Lady Tatly's assembly, make an Intimacy with Lady Betty Fidget, pretty Mrs Wriggle and about some 50 more I could name to you, and I'll engage they'll soon convince you that it ought to be very indifferent to you what sort of Man your Husband is since he will probably be the man you will seldomest converse with.

Sir John

Indeed, Ned, I am not so well satisfy'd with your Town breeding to desire your Sister should have a share of it. I am very well pleas'd to see her in this unfashionable way of thinking, and it gives me so much esteem for her that I am resolv'd never to constrain her Inclinations because I am persuaded they will allways be reasonable.

You know, my dear Girl, when I went to London last term this match was propos'd to me by Gaymore's Father, who is my old Freind, but it was conditionally you lik'd one another when you met. I can have no partiallity to the young man, for I have never seen him. He was then on the road home from his travells, and his Father is too fond of him to propose a marriage on any other condition. He has the same concern for his happyness that I have for yours.

Bellinda

My dear Papa, I know not how to thank you enough for an Indulgence that I am sensible few parents have for their Children but—

Sir John

But what—are you not satisfy'd?

Bellinda

Men are such dissemblers. I shall see him either before you, whom it is his interest to oblige, or playing over the tricks of one that designs to please me. The Liberty of choice that his father leaves him does not satisfy me. He may be impatient to have a settlement, as commonly men of his age are.

Sir John

You are very hard to please, methinks, but I am in mighty good humour, and you shall be pleas'd one way or other. Let me see— what if you chang'd places with Lucy. Let her represent you. He won't think it worth his while to disguise his temper to a chamber maid, and you may draw out of his footman all that he knows of his Master, for servants keep no secrets from one another.

Ned

Ha, ha, ha! now you are pleas'd, I am sure. This is so like a stratagem in your dear Romances and beloved play books that I see allready you are charm'd with it. I can't help laughing at the Imagination! Ha, ha, ha!

Bellinda

I am sure it is an Imagination so full of goodness to me that I am ready to throw my selfe at my Father's feet to make my Acknowledgments.

Ned

I told you so, ha, ha, ha, and do you realy think my Father so extravagant to expose a man of Gaymore's rank to the conversation of Mrs Lucy? A pretty figure he'll make after he has sigh'd his passion to her with all the respect in the world, and he'll certainly like you the better when he comes to know that his footman has been his proxy with you.

Sir John

You go too fast, Ned. If I had seen any thing so monstrously ridiculous in this proposal I should not have made it, and I desire your respect for me would moderate your censures.

Ned

My respect for you may impose Silence upon me, but I beleive you would your selfe be surpriz'd at my aprobation, and I can hardly beleive yet you are in earnest—

Sir John

(*turning to Bellinda*) Go, go, child. Put on a clean Apron, and dress Lucy in your silver Lutestring. What say you, Lucy, can you mimick a fine Lady?

Lucy

Lard, Sir! thô I say it—why, I liv'd 3 year with my Lady Millamant! You shall see, I can either represent her, or any of her acquaintance, which were halfe the fine Ladys in Town. Do you like the nice, the sickly, the noisy or the Sullen sort? (*walks about in various figure*) This is my Lady Languishe's walk, this is Mrs Dainty's waddle. This is Lady ⟨Rompabout's⟩ run, and I can stand still exactly like the Dutchess of Stiffrump.

Sir John

(*laughing*) Nay, nay, you are admirably qualifyd, I see. Go, get dress'd, both of you.

(*They run out jumping.*)

Sir John

You are out of humour, Ned, and I see begin to suspect me capable of dotage allready, but I beleive I shall bring you over to my opinion. Tis very true what I told your sister; Gaymore will be here to day but he comes disguis'd.

Ned

Disguis'd! what, does he make his first visit in Masquerade?

Sir John

Patience, let me read you part of his father's letter that I have just receiv'd—(*reads*) 'I am afraid you will contemn my Indulgence, but I have not been able to resist my Son's earnest solicitations, that he might wait on you disguis'd like his footman, who will be with him like the Master. He imagines by this contrivance to be perfectly acquainted with your daughter's Character. I am so well persuaded of her merit that I do not doubt his finding it to his satisfaction, and I hope you will think this odd whim proceeds from a design of founding his Happyness in his wive's conversation, but thô I have had this Complaisance for a Young Man's fancy, I thought my selfe oblig'd to give you a private notice of it, that you may act upon it, as you shall judge proper.' Now, Son, what say you?

Ned

Why, I say Gaymore has read as many Romances as my Sister.

Sir John

Well, what do you advise me?

Ned

I beg your pardon for my rashness, and own what you have thought, the most reasonable method to prevent my sister's being expos'd to his footman's impertinencies, and I hope in the Lord, Gaymore will fall in Love with her, in her Chambermaid's cloaths, and that will be a punishment for his folly. Here she comes, highly delighted with her metamorphosis.

(*Bellinda runs in.*)

You have made haste, Sister.

Bellinda

Well, Papa, am not I like a Chambermaid? What think you, Brother?

Ned

I think the poor Footman a dead man, and I don't know but Gaymore himselfe may like you better than your mistriss.

Bellinda

I own I should not be sorry for it. At least I should beleive my person was to his taste, and beside I should have better opportunitys of observing upon his temper. As to the Footman, You shall see me carry it with such an Air the scoundrel shall'nt dare to speak to me.

Ned

Good words, Bellinda; that scoundrel will be your Equal.

Sir John

And ten to one makes Love to thee.

Bellinda

Well, if he does, I shall more easily get out of him all he knows of the Life and character of his Master.

(A Footman comes in.)

Footman

Sir, here is a servant in a Lac'd Livery and a Vine what dee call Wig, an't please your worship, follow'd by a groom with a portmanteau.

Sir John

Let him come in—this is certainly Gaymore's servant; I suppose his Master follows immediately. Where's Lucy?

Bellinda

Oh, at her Looking Glass with great devotion, and smileing to her selfe at my Imprudence in suffering my Lover to come near so many charms.

Sir John

Hush! here is the servant.

(Enter Gaymore in a Livery.)

Gaymore

Is it Sir John Hearty that I have the Honour to see?

Sir John

That is my Name, Freind.

Gaymore

Mr Gaymore, Sir, whom I serve, sent me before him to assure you of his Respects, and will be here presently himselfe to wait on you.

Sir John

You deliver your message with a very good air. What say you, Lucy?

Bellinda

He is very wellcome, Sir, and speaks as he ought.

Gaymore

You are very good to me, Madam. I endeavor at least to do my Duty.

Ned

A Handsome Fellow, Lucy, take care of thy little Heart.

Bellinda

Oh, my Heart! That is a new Question!

Gaymore

Don't be angry, Madam, the Gentleman's raillery won't encourrage me to any Impertinence.

Bellinda

I am pleas'd with your Modesty; pray don't lose it.

Ned

Very well on both sides, but I think these grave Airs don't become people of your rank, and this Madam that he calls you, has too much distance between fellow Servants as you are like to be. You have a name, Lucy, and what's yours, Freind?

Gaymore

William, Sir, at your service.

Bellinda

Well, William be it then.

Gaymore

I am not less your humble servant, Mrs Lucy.

(*Sir John and Ned Laugh.*)

Bellinda

(*aside to her Brother*) You are very merry with my disguise. I see you would teize me, but I'll divert my selfe with it. (*aloud*) Well, Freind William, let us be more Familiar since these Gentlemen will have it so.

Gaymore

I am much oblig'd to you, Mrs Lucy, and very sensible of the Honour you do me.

Sir John

Now, good people, when you begin to love one Another, you are oblig'd to us for haveing broke the Ice between you.

Ned

Oh pray, Sir, not so fast. Lucy has been my mist⟨ress⟩ this halfe year, and thô I can't brag of much success I won't suffer William to run away with her Heart in halfe an hour.

Bellinda

If there is no other objection, I declare I will have William for my Lover from this minute.

Gaymore

There is no occasion of giving me your orders upon that Subject.

Ned

Ho, brave Galantry, faith! Where didst thou steal that?

Gaymore

I have taken all my Galantry, Sir, from her Eyes.

Ned

This is worse and worse. Do you hear, Freind, I charge you to have no wit when you talk with Lucy.

Bellinda

You will not have the less for it, and if my Eyes inspire William with any agreable thoughts I shall be very glad to hear them.

Sir John

As far as I perceive, Son, you'l have a dangerous Rival—but let us go tell my daughter of Gaymore's Arrival, and you, Lucy, shew William his Master's chamber.

(They go out.)

Bellinda

(*aside*) This Fellow is no fool, and if I was a real Chamber maid, I should think I had good Luck to meet with him. He looks in the mind to make Love to ⟨me⟩ but I'll bear with that and try to make him talk of his Master.

Gaymore

(*aside*) This Girl has something strangely agreable in her air. I have seen few women of Quality look so like one. (*aloud*) My dear Lucy, since Ceremony is to be laid aside between us, permit me to ask you one Question. Is thy Mistriss as pretty as thou art? She must have a very good Opinion of her own Beauty to trust yours near her.

Bellinda

This Question convinces me that you came hither with a design of saying fine things to me. Is it not true, William?

Gaymore

No, I'll swear to you; and thô I wear a Livery I have hitherto had very little acquaintance with Chambermaids. I do not use to taste their Conversation, but I know not what's the matter; you appear to me with quite another air, I dare hardly be familiar with you. I keep my distance in spite of my selfe, and you impose a respect upon me I know not how to account for. There is something nobler in your mein than ever I saw in the front Boxes.

Bellinda

Look you, Freind, all the footmen that ever saw me have had the same respect for me.

Gaymore

And all their Masters too, I beleive.

Bellinda

To shorten the Conversation, I must tell thee I never hear of Love from your Habit.

Gaymore

This dress of mine does not please thee then.

Bellinda

Not at all, William, therefore think no more of Love, but let us remain freinds as fellow servants.

Gaymore

This Treaty between us has a strong Impossibillity in the first article.

Bellinda

(*aside*) This is a wonderfull footman. (*to him*) You must perform it thô. I had my fortune told me once that I should marry a Gentleman, and I have sworn since never to hearken to any other.

Gaymore

This is pleasant, by my Faith, for you must know that I have sworn never to marry any but a Woman well born, and perhaps I am not much out of my way at present. You may be a very good Gentlewoman and know nothing of the matter.

Bellinda

I should be much oblig'd to you for your Complement if it was not at my Mother's expence.

Gaymore

You may revenge your selfe upon mine if you think me well made enough to deserve it.

Bellinda

(*aside*) I seriously beleive it. (*to him*) Raillery apart, it is a Gentleman the stars have destin'd for me, and I will think of nothing below one.

Gaymore

If I was one I should be terribly afraid of this prediction, but it would not be the Influence of the stars I should fear, but that of your Eyes.

Bellinda

The prediction is nothing to you since you are excluded by it.

Gaymore

No prediction can hinder me from loving thee.

Bellinda

No, but it is destin'd you will not be the happier, and I assure you of it.

Gaymore

These airs of disdain to a Livery are very charming, Lucy, and I can't help thinking they become you, thô I am undone by them. I thought you too lovely to be address'd to by one in my Shape the first moment I cast my eyes on you, and I am contented with my ruine since it is necessary to compleat your Merit.

Bellinda

(*aside*) This fellow surprizes me. (*to him*) But tell me who you are that talk in this style.

Gaymore

The Son of Honest parents that were not rich—

Bellinda

I wish you better fortune, and to say truth, I think you deserve it.

Gaymore

I had rather hear a more tender Sentiment, and it would please me more to have hopes of touching your Heart than to make the most shineing Fortune.

Bellinda

(*aside*) This grows too warm. (*to him*) I cannot be reasonably angry with you, William, for what you say, but I desire to change the Subject. Let me hear a little about your Master. I suppose you can talk of other things beside Love.

Gaymore

Yes, if I could think of any thing else in thy Company.

Bellinda

You will make me angry at last. Once more, have done with your Love, I say.

Gaymore

I say, leave off your Beauty.

Bellinda

(*aside*) He makes me laugh whither I will or no. (*to him*) I must leave you, I see. (*aside*) I should have done it an hour ago.

Gaymore

Stay, Lucy, I had some Questions to ask thee, but I cannot remember 'em.

Bellinda

You ⟨have⟩ provok'd me so, I have forgot what I intended to say to you.

Gaymore

My Question was whither your Mistrisse deserves such a servant as you are.

Bellinda

And I wanted to know if your master has many good Qualitys. At least he has a good taste in chusing you for his servant, and if he was quite a Sot I think you would not serve him.

Gaymore

How shall I thank you for the obliging Complement You make me?

Bellinda

Oh, pray forget it. I did not mind what I said.

Gaymore

This little disdain charms me. I can resist you no longer, and who would resist the most aimable creature he ever saw?

Bellinda

I can't imagine why I stay here to hearken to all thy Follys. There is something very extrodinary in my patience.

Gaymore

And more reason for it than you know, perhaps.

Bellinda

(*aside*) This is very ridiculous in me. I am asham'd of my selfe. (*to him*) Adieu, William.

Gaymore

Stay at least and tell me what you would know of me.

Bellinda

I would know nothing. I will observe your Master for my Lady's
sake without your assistance. His room is that way—

Gaymore

And here he comes—

(*Enter William.*)

William

Oh Will, you are arriv'd I see. How have you been receiv'd?

Gaymore

Tis impossible to be otherwise than well receiv'd here.

William

A Servant shew'd me in here, and is gone to see for my Father in
law, who they say is in my Wive's chamber.

Bellinda

I suppose, Sir, you mean Sir John Hearty and his daughter?

William

Yes, yes, why I come to be marry'd, don't I? There remains
nothing but a little Ceremony to finish the affair, and what signifys
Ceremony amongst Freinds? I am resolv'd to call her Wife to day
since she is to be so to morrow.

Bellinda

That ceremony is important enough to deserve very serious thoughts.

William

Oh, the people that think of it seriously don't care for thinking of
it at all.

Bellinda

(*aside to Gaymore*) Why have not you taught politeness to your
master?

William

What are you saying to my Footman, pretty one?

Bellinda
Nothing, Sir, I say I'll only call Sir John Hearty.

William
My Father in law you mean.

Bellinda
I don't mean so, Sir, because he is not so yet.

Gaymore
Sir, you forget you are not yet marry'd.

William
Here's a rout indeed. Where's the great difference between to day and to morrow?

Bellinda
Right, Sir, it is very indifferent whether you are marry'd or no. Let me go then and tell your Father in law you are here.

William
And my Wife too prithee, but in the mean time tell mee, pretty creature, are not you her maid?

Bellinda
Yes, Sir.

William
I am glad to hear it. Do you think your Lady will like me? For example, how do you like me?

Bellinda
Me! you make me smile, Sir.

William
That's a good sign, and you may hear farther because you continue to smile.

Bellinda
I don't doubt you'l give me cause, Sir—but certainly they have not inform'd your Father in law of your arival and I must go do it.

William
Tell him I am fond of him allready.

Bellinda

(*aside*) How capricious is Fortune? Why cannot these men change places?

(*goes out*)

William

Well, Sir, you see me well receiv'd by one part of the Family.

Gaymore

You great Blockhead!

William

Have not I behav'd my selfe very genteely?

Gaymore

Very gentile, truly! with thy senseless Familiaritys, after I have taken so much pains to instruct you! I see my own Folly in trusting thee.

William

Realy, Sir, I don't know what your Honour would have. Shall I be silent?

Gaymore

My head is turn'd, and I know not what I would have.

William

Is not this a pretty, pert Wench?

Gaymore

Hold your tongue. Here comes Sir John.

(*Enter Sir John.*)

Sir John

(*embraceing him*) Dear Sir, you are heartily wellcome. I hope you have not waited for me. I beg a thousand pardons.

William

That is too many for one fault.

Sir John

I hope you will not accuse me of another. I'll assure you, I wish'd to see you with great Impatience.

William

I should have come at the same time with Will but I staid to powder at the next Inn that your daughter might be sure to like me.

Sir John

Oh, that can't fail. She is setting her selfe out too. In the mean time will you taste a Glass of Wine?

William

Dear Father in law, you shall see how heartily I'll drink your Health.

Sir John

(*going out*) William, take care of your selfe.

William

The fellow knows good Wine. He'll find out the best you have.

Sir John

I hope he won't spare it.

Act 2.

(*Enter Sir John Hearty, follow'd by Lucy.*)

Sir John

Well, Lucy, what's thy great busyness with me?

Lucy

I beg halfe an hour's audience.

Sir John

What's the matter?

Lucy

I think my selfe oblig'd, Sir, to mention a few things to you because the Consequences may not be laid at my door.

Sir John

You begin very seriously.

Lucy

Sir, I am very serious. You know you propos'd misse's disguise your selfe, and realy at that time I thought it a very innocent frolick.

Sir John

And don't you think so still?

Lucy

Why realy, Sir, I am asham'd to tell you, and you may think it very vain in me, but I am oblig'd in Conscience to tell you, if there is no stop put to your son in law's Inclinations he will have none left to bestow upon your daughter. They are all at my service, and if she does not declare her selfe quickly, he may be engag'd so far that—

Sir John

Why, what will he find to dislike in my Daughter?

Lucy

Lard, Sir, that is not it—but he may find so much to like in your humble servant (*curtsying*) perhaps he mayn't be able to withdraw his Affections.

Sir John

Ha, ha, ha, I wish you joy with all my heart, pretty Lucy.

Lucy

'Tis very well, Sir, I see you are pleas'd to laugh at me, and give me leave to tell you, neither you nor miss will laugh at the long run. I have discharg'd my Conscience, and you can't blame me for what follows.

Sir John

I won't blame thee, upon my Honour, Lucy, let what will be the Consequence.

Lucy

You don't beleive me, you are not at all alarm'd, but the plain truth shall out. I please Mr Gaymore at first sight, he will love me passionately before night, and to morrow I may do what I will with him. I don't pretend to deserve so much honour. You will wonder at his ill fancy, but t'will be, t'will be, Sir, and to morrow (mind what I say) to morrow I do what I please with him.

Sir John

Well, e'en marry him if his Love is so desperate.

Lucy

What! will you permit it?

Sir John

I shall not be at all concern'd if it is his choice.

Lucy

I am sure I have done my Duty. Hitherto I have not aim'd at the Conquest, but since you are pleas'd to shew your selfe so Indifferent about it I shall give my selfe my best airs, and see what will become of his Heart. Poor Man! I shall burn it as black as a shoe. You won't be able to set him to rights; his wits are just going as it is.

Sir John

Display all your Artillery. Burn, ravage, and destroy; in short, marry him if thou canst. I won't hinder it.

Lucy

My Fortune is made. I'll answer for it—

Sir John

But prithee, Lucy, what says my daughter of him?

Lucy

I have hardly had time to speak [to] her, for the young Gentleman is allways at my Heels. Good Lord, How he follows me! But I can see she looks melancholy and unquiet. I suppose she intends to order me to refuse him in her Name.

Sir John

Don't be too hasty in that matter. I would have the disguise last some time that nothing may be resolv'd on rashly. How does his footman behave himselfe? Does he not make love to Bellinda?

Lucy

That is a pleasant Fellow. I can see he gives himselfe gentlemanlike airs because he is handsome. He looks at her with so much softness, I warrant you, and sighs so sweetly.

Sir John

She laughs at him heartily, I suppose.

Lucy

I don't know—she blushes—

Sir John

You don't know what you say, Lucy. My daughter so much concern'd at the looks of a footman!

Lucy

She blushes, Sir—

Sir John

'Tis with anger, then.

Lucy

May be so.

Sir John

However, when you have an Opertunity tell her you suspect the footman of prejudiceing her against his Master. I don't doubt she'll be angry, but follow my Orders, and I'll take care of the rest— Oh, here comes your Lover to seek after you.

(*Enter William.*)

William

My charming Fair, I have sought you all over the House. Your humble servant, dear Father in law.

Sir John

I'll leave you together, children. You ought to love one another before you marry.

William

Sir, I'll do both at a time if you please.

Sir John

Oh, you must not be so impatient—

(*Exit.*)

William

The good man talks at his ease. These old Fellows are no judges of Impatiencies.

Lucy

Indeed, sir, I have much ado to beleive your Love so violent. You have not been 3 hours in the house. At most it can only be a flame just kindle'd.

William

Ah, little wonder of Nature, the fires that you kindle blaze at a great rate. The first glance of your Eye threw Sparks into my breast, and your Breathe has blow'd it into the Flame of a bon-fire. Since it is your own kindling you should voushafe to throw upon it the fuel of a few favors.

Lucy

Do you think I go about to extinguish it?

William

Let me touch then that pretty hand; it will be of the full Effect of a Load of Faggot—

Lucy

(*giving her hand*) I own I would keep it alive.

William

(*kissing it*) Ah, sweet, honey, sugar, stronger than port, and more delicious than rasberry brandy.

Lucy

(*withdrawing her hand*) You are too greedy.

William

I can never hold out without these cordials.

Lucy

Your reason should moderate the violence of your passion.

William

Madam, your Theivish Eyes have stoln my reason, and I cannot tell where to find it.

Lucy

But is it possible in so short a time—?

William

I never trouble my head about what's possible. I am in Love up to the Ears, and your Glass will tell you that I am in the right.

Lucy

My Glass does not flatter me so much.

William

This humility is very becoming in the midst of so many charms—

Lucy

What would this footman of yours have?

(*Enter Gaymore.*)

Gaymore

Sir, I beg leave to speak to you.

William

Don't you see I am very busy?

Lucy

Pray hear what he has to say.

Gaymore

'Tis but one word, Sir.

William

Madam, if he troubles me with two he shan't outlive a third.

Gaymore

(*to him aside*) Blockhead, come when I call you.

William

Presently. Go out and I'll wait on you.

(*Exit Gaymore.*)

William

(*to her*) If this puppy had not intterupted me I was going to say the softest, movingst things, but in the main, I know I meant to say that I roast in Love. When shall I communicate to your heart some of the heat in which I broil?

Lucy

Time may bring about greater wonders.

William

But will time bring it about, my Fair?

Lucy

You are very pressing, I hardly know what to say to you.

William

Madam, 'tis a very pressing busyness to me, upon my Honour.

Lucy

The rules of decency hinder me from explaining my selfe so soon.

William

I'll assure you, madam, all the people of Quality at London step over those rules.

Lucy

What would you have me say?

William

Do but repeat, my little Queen, 'I love you.' Repeat, Goddess, 'I love you.'

Lucy

Ah Insatiable! (*with her Fan before her face*) I love you.

William

I am stiffle'd with happyness. You love me—me! me! you love me!

Lucy

I own these transports are very lively, but will they be lasting when we know one another better?

William

Ah, madam, that refflection makes me tremble. I am afraid you should find me unworthy of your goodness.

Lucy

You think very fine things of me, that perhaps are not true.

William

I ought not speak to you but upon my knees.

Lucy

Pray remember in due time that we are not makers of our own destiny.

William

Fathers impose what they please on their children.

Lucy

For my part, since I have said so much I declare farther, I would have chose you in any rank of Life. Do you feel the same sentiment?

William

Dear Madam, if I had seen you twirling a Mop before the street door you would have appear'd a princesse in my Eyes.

Lucy

Heaven keep you in that mind!

William

To make all sure between us, let us swear to one another eternal fidelity in spite of all Objections whatever.

Lucy

This oath is the most agreable thing in the world to my wishes.

William

'Whatever,' Madam, I stick to 'whatever.'

Lucy

I swear it with all my heart.

William

(*kneeling down*) Let me prostrate my selfe before so much goodness.

Lucy

(*taking him up*) I can't bear to see you in this posture, and you cover me with confusion.

(*Enter Bellinda.*)

What would you have, Lucy?

Bellinda

The Honour to speak to you, Madam, if you please.

William

You may come an hour hence, sweet heart. A London Chamber-maid never comes in without being call'd.

Bellinda

Sir, I have busyness with my Lady.

William

How saucy she is! Send her away, my Goddess. I desire you would let us alone. We have orders to love one another, and we were just about it.

Lucy

Lucy, won't another time do for your busyness?

Bellinda

But—

William

That but is very impertinent.

Bellinda

I'll assure you, Madam, it is busyness of Consequence.

Lucy

You must excuse it then, Sir.

William

I must if I can't help it—what ridiculous servants we have!

(*Exit.*)

Bellinda

It is a strange thing you could not send this Creature away sooner when I wanted to speak with you.

Lucy

By my Faith, Madam, I must either appear the Maid or the mistrisse; I cannot Act both parts at once.

Bellinda

Now he is gone I am mistrisse, I hope. You may see I don't like this man.

Lucy

You have not had time to examine whither you like him or no.

Bellinda

There is no occasion or time for that Examination. I hate the sight of him, but I am afraid My Father does not approve of my Aversion for him, for I see he avoids giving me an Oppertunity of speaking to him; therefore tis your busyness to send Gaymore away by a civil Refusal.

Lucy

But I can't, with your leave.

Bellinda

You can't! Who hinders you?

Lucy

Sir John has order'd me to the contrary.

Bellinda

My Father! This is not of a piece with his usual goodness to me.

Lucy

Positively the contrary.

Bellinda

Well then, I command you to acquaint him with my dislike. Assure him it is what I cannot overcome, and then I am persuaded he will not suffer matters to go farther.

Lucy

But pray Madame, what is the reason of your aversion? I see nothing so disagreable in Mr Gaymore.

Bellinda

In short I don't like him, nor your Questions neither.

Lucy

Take a little time to consider, before you refuse him. This is all my Master asks of you.

Bellinda

I hate him to such a degree, there is no Occasion of hateing him more.

Lucy

I fancy his Beau footman has given you some ill Impression of him.

Bellinda

Impertinence! His Footman? his footman? I trouble my selfe about his footman?

Lucy

I am apt to mistrust him. I see he gives himselfe great airs.

Bellinda

I see you're a fool. Have done with your nonsense. I take care not to discourse with a footman, and the little he has said has been very reasonable.

Lucy

I think tis likely enough he may tell storys of his master for an Oppertunity to display his fine Language.

Bellinda

I see my disguise exposes me to the usage of a real Chambermaid. You fancy your selfe talking to your equal, I suppose. I am sick to hear you. What busyness of yours is it to rail against a poor young

Fellow that has behav'd himselfe very well? I am oblig'd in Honour to justify him.

Lucy

Oh Madam, if you are pleas'd to justify him, I have done. It is indeed nothing to me, and I am sorry I have made you angry.

Bellinda

Angry, Saucy Slut! I am not angry. I don't justify him. What do you mean by justify him? What stuff have you got in your head?

Lucy

I say, madam, I never saw you in such a humour in my Life, and I don't know in what I have offended you. If the Footman has said nothing there is no occasion of any passion about it. I don't doubt what your Ladiship is pleas'd to say. To be sure if you have a good Opinion of him he deserves it, and I have nothing to say against it for my part.

Bellinda

Your part! Your thoughts are very important, truly—what a way of answering she has got! I could cry for rage—

Lucy

What have I said to enrage you so? Is there any Mystery in my words?

Bellinda

Mystery! What Mystery is there in talking of a Footman? I justify him! I have a good opinion of him, a good Opinion! A fine way of talking! What Answer can be made to such impertinencies? You forget entirely who you talk to, and who you talk of. Do you beleive I'll endure this Insolence? or is it fit I should endure it? Begone—out of my sight—I'll assure you I shall take measures to be trouble'd with you no longer.

Lucy

I go in the greatest astonishment I ever was in, in my Life—

(*Exit.*)

Bellinda

(*sola*) I am confounded with her Impudence; what ways of thinking servants have got! I dare hardly recollect the sense of her words.

I am afraid to remember 'em. A footman! Heaven! What a base Idea! I shall not come to my selfe soon after it. (*in a soft tone*) Here he comes, that Object of my rage, of my terror. Poor Fellow, how is he to blame for it? It would be very unjust to quarrel with him for the folly of other people.

(*Enter Gaymore.*)

Gaymore

Lucy, you seem to avoid me, yet I can't help following thee, and I think I have some reason to complain.

Bellinda

I don't desire to hear your complaints, nor indeed to hear you speak at all.

Gaymore

You have so short a time to be trouble'd with my Conversation, I think you may have the Complaisance to suffer it.

Bellinda

Is your Master going away then? The loss will not be great.

Gaymore

Neither of his Company or mine, is not that what you would say?

Bellinda

I don't think of thee at all.

Gaymore

And I think of nothing but you.

Bellinda

Hear me, William, once for all. Go away, stay, return, do what you will: all this ought to be very indifferent to me, and it shall be so. It would be ridiculous in me either to love you or hate you, and I shall never think it worth my while to do either. While I preserve my senses this is the only proper method I can act in, and indeed I should not give my selfe the trouble to explain my thoughts so far to thee.

Gaymore

If you are sincere, which I tremble to imagine, I am miserable for the rest of my Life.

Bellinda

(*aside*) What an unfortunate whim the poor fellow has got in his head! Compassion obliges me to cure it if I can. (*to him*) I don't wish you unhappy. I answer what you say, which is more than I ought, and if you knew all circumstances you would be amaz'd at my good nature. I am amaz'd at it my selfe, and I should perhaps censure it in another, but the knowledge of my own heart supports me. I know I act from a pure motive of Generosity but Generosity may carry people too far, and Generosity does not oblige me to pass whole afternoons with thee. I have been too long here allready. Let the Conversation break off. 'Tis all to no purpose, and the sooner it is broke off the better.

Gaymore

My Lovely Lucy, you thrust a dagger into my heart.

Bellinda

You may tell me thô, before you go, what you had to complain of just now.

Gaymore

Of nothing at all. I wanted a pretext to make you hear me.

Bellinda

(*aside*) What shall I say to him? Poor Man!

Gaymore

Your mistrisse accuses me of speaking ill of my Master.

Bellinda

She is in the wrong. You may deny it boldly, and I'll take care she shan't injure you.

Gaymore

This is not what troubles me.

Bellinda

If this was your busyness, 'tis over. Let us part.

Gaymore

If I must not talk to thee, at least leave me the pleasure of looking at thee—Laugh at me, if you will, I deserve it all. Tis better to part, as you say. Adieu.

(going)

Bellinda

You're in the right, adieu—*(turns back)* I forgot to ask you if your Master is realy going away.

Gaymore

I know I must go away or lose the little reason is left me.

Bellinda

This is no answer to my Question.

Gaymore

The greatest folly I ever committed in my Life was not leaving the house the first moment I saw you.

Bellinda

(aside) I listen. I forget my selfe.

Gaymore

If you could guess, Lucy, the distraction in which I find my selfe.

Bellinda

I have more cause of distraction in my mind.

Gaymore

What is it you complain of? I hope for no return. I dare hardly wish it.

Bellinda

You should not think of it.

Gaymore

Nay, if you did Love me—

Bellinda

(hastily) I love you! Heaven forbid. If I was so wretched, you never should know it, nay, I would no⟨t⟩ know it my selfe. I tremble at the bare mention.

Gaymore

Then I'm quite indifferent to thee.

Bellinda

What should you be else?

Gaymore

What should I be else? I am then very odious to thee?

Bellinda

Pish; no, bless me, that is not the case.

Gaymore

My dear Lucy, repeat again, you can never love me.

Bellinda

I think I have said so allready. You must strive to beleive me.

Gaymore

'Tis true that beleife is necessary to save me from some great
Extravagance. I don't know my selfe what the least hope would
make me capable of. I am sincere with you. I know your Indifference
ought to be more welcome to me than your Love; it is less dangerous,
and I stand in need of every succour against a madness that has
seiz'd me. Say again that you hate me. It is cruel, but it is necessary
for me to beleive it, and I will receive the sentence on my knees as
a favour that you do me.

(*He throws himselfe at her feet, and at that instant Sir John
and his Son come in, and stand conceald by the door.*)

Bellinda

(*aside*) I am undone! My heart melts! I will die rather than suffer
this. Some body will see us. (*to him*) Rise, I beg of thee, William.
Rise. I cannot tell what to say! What is it you ask me? I can't hate
you. I will say any thing to make you rise. I would love you if it was
possible. There is nothing to displease me in your person. Can I
say more?

Gaymore

How, Lucy, is it only the Livery that shocks you? If I was a gentleman would you endure me?

Bellinda

I think I should not hate you.

Gaymore

You would hear me then.

Bellinda

With pleasure hear you.

Gaymore

Your Eyes tell me so, and all my Reason flys before them.

Bellinda

I say any thing to get you off of your knees, and yet you remain in this ridiculous posture.

(Enter Sir John and Ned.)

Sir John

'Tis pity to intterupt you. I see your acquaintance improves very fast, good people.

Bellinda

How can I help the fellow's falling on his knees? I am not of a rank to command him.

Sir John

Nay, you are very well match'd, but I have some orders to give you, Lucy, and then you may renew the Conversation. As for you, William, pray learn to talk better of your Master.

Gaymore

Me, Sir!

Ned

Yes, you. I don't hear you use him with much respect.

Gaymore

I know not what you mean.

Sir John

Wee'l talk of that another time. At present I must speak to Lucy.

(Gaymore goes out.)

What's the matter, Bellinda? Your Eyes fix'd on the ground, and your cheeks all flush'd, you seem in some terrible disorder.

Bellinda

Me disorder'd, Papa! I thank heaven I never was in less disorder in my Life. I am as much compos'd as ever I was. Why should I be in disorder? I beg your pardon, Sir, but I can't help saying this is a very odd fancy. Disorder!

Ned

I see something, my dear Sister, I see something—

Bellinda

Something! What something! Your head has allways something very wrong in it that I am often surpriz'd at and so I am now.

Sir John

I have been persuaded that fellow that has just left you has given you an aversion for his Master.

Bellinda

What, Gaymore's servant?

Ned

Yes, the Galant William.

Bellinda

I did not know his Title before, but the Galant William, since you call him so, never talks of his master.

Sir John

I have been told otherwaies, and I would talk with you about it.

Bellinda

There needs no farther enquiry. I have a natural aversion to Gaymore.

Ned

This aversion is too sudden and too violent to come without having heard something to his disadvantage.

Bellinda

A pretty fancy truly! and who should have told me any thing to his disadvantage? I should be glad to know these secret freinds of mine.

Ned

You are so peevish, Sister, there is no talking with you.

Bellinda

I am weary of the part I act, and I should have discover'd my selfe long since, if I had not been afraid to do it without my father's leave.

Sir John

I desire you would not do it, daughter; and since I have had the Complaisance for you to permit you to wear the disguise, I desire you would have so much for me, to keep it on till you have had time to examine Gaymore's Character, which may have been misrepresented.

Bellinda

You don't hear me, Sir; nobody has misrepresented him to me.

Ned

What! has not that prateing fellow been telling you some storys?

Bellinda

Storys! Storys from a footman! I am very likely to mind his storys! You treat your sister truly in a very becomeing manner! I don't understand this Language. First you see something, then the Galant William, then he tells storys. I must bear this from you, brother, but I own I don't understand the reason of this usage. You grow very incomprehensible.

Ned

Tis your selfe that grows incomprehensible. What is it you quarrel with me about? What suspicion do you think I have in my Head?

Bellinda

This mends things much, Brother, to talk to me of a Suspicion and stuff. I'll swear I won't stay to hear it. I do not find my selfe in a temper to endure it.

Sir John

To say truth, your temper is so chang'd there is no knowing you. I suppose that is [the] reason of what Lucy has been telling us. She said she only hinted that William set you against his Master, and you defended him with so much heat as put her into Astonishment. Both my Son and I chid her for that expression, but those sort of people don't thoroughly understand the words they make use of.

Bellinda

Horrid Creature! She is certainly the most Impertinent hussy upon Earth. I own I justify'd the Fellow because I would be just to every body.

Ned

That is a right principle.

Bellinda

It is very provoking, thô, because I am just, because I would not have an Innocent Servant turn'd away, therefore I astonish people, I am ill temper'd forsooth, and I know not what I say. Then because a Chambermaid talks saucily I must have her odious Expressions repeated to my face. Indeed, Sir, this is not usage for your Daughter, and I declare I can bear it no longer. How have I deserv'd it? What am I accus'd of? This is past a jest. I cannot be easy, and see my nearest Relations treat me in this manner.

Sir John

Keep your temper, Child.

Bellinda

No, Sir, there is no temper in the world that is proofe against such provocations. I hear a style I never heard in my Life. I see this is all from Lucy. She's an Insolent baggage I'll never see again. I know not what fancies she has put into your heads, but I know the footman is innocent of all this, and I desire to hear no more of it. I think I have a great deal of patience.

Sir John

I see indeed that I am much oblig'd to it, for you have a great mind to quarrel with me too. But without any heat, I know no body suspected but this William, and his master has nothing to do but to turn him away.

Bellinda

What a cursed Disguise have I got! How many vexations has follow'd it! I insist on one thing, that Lucy never comes into my sight again.

Sir John

As you will for that, but I beleive I do you a pleasure in sending away the footman. You must needs be weary of his nonsensical Love.

Bellinda

I don't complain of him. He takes me for a Chambermaid and talks to me accordingly, but I take care not to give him the hearing.

Ned

That I question.

Sir John

We saw him on his knees, and heard with what earnestness you persuaded him to rise.

Bellinda

(*aside*) I shall swoon.

Ned

Nay, he seem'd very well satisfy'd with the language of your Eyes and I realy thought the tone of your voice soft enough.

Bellinda

I don't [know] what I said to get rid of him, and I wish, brother, you would spare your Wit for another occasion. The Jest grows very tiresome to me, and I should be glad to see an end of it.

Sir John

All I have to ask of you, daughter, is to stay sometime before you give your final answer in a matter of this Importance, and I beleive I may venture to assure you this delay will be to your satisfaction.

Ned

And I beleive I shall see you marry'd to Gaymore with your own Inclination. In the mean time, Sir, I think William may stay.

Bellinda

Why stay? I would not have him stay. Pray let him begone.

Sir John

Tis his master must determine. Come, Son, let us go to him.

Ned

I hope, sister, to see you in better humour.

(They go out.)

Bellinda

(*sola*) My heart is breaking. I hate every body, I hate my selfe, I could tear the whole world to pieces.

[*Gaymore enters*] (*Gaymore to her*)

Gaymore

I have something to say to you, Lucy.

Bellinda

I will hear nothing from you, William.

Gaymore

But this is a concern of your Master's.

Bellinda

Go tell it him then.

Gaymore

Hear me this once. I have very surprizing things to tell ⟨you⟩.

Bellinda

There is nothing more surprizing than my patience to hear 'em.

Gaymore

Promise me secrecy.

Bellinda

I have never betraid any body.

Gaymore

I am going to prove to you the serious esteem I have for you.

Bellinda

Esteem me if thou wilt, but neither prove it, nor tell me of it.

Gaymore

You shall know my whole heart. You know allready it has not been able to resist your Eyes.

Bellinda

But I shall be able to resist this discourse—adieu for ever.

Gaymore

Stay. It is not William that begs it of you.

Bellinda

Who then?

Gaymore

Ah, Lucy, you shall judge in what distractions I have been.

Bellinda

You distract me.

Gaymore

My Honour obliges me at present to discover the real state of things. It is not Mr Gaymore who is now courting your Lady.

Bellinda

Not Gaymore?

Gaymore

His footman.

Bellinda

Who then am I talking to? Quick.

Gaymore

Himselfe.

Bellinda

(*aside*) My Life is sav'd.

Gaymore

I thought in this disguise to find out the true character of the Woman propos'd to me for a Wife. My father was so good to consent to this stratagem at my earnest request, and the Event has turn'd my head. I dispise the Lady I came to marry, and I adore the Chambermaid that should have been my servant. I am sorry for the sake of Sir John Hearty's family to add, that his daughter has so little taste to grow fond of my footman, and if I don't put a stop to it, is very likely to marry him. What shall I do? You shall advise me, Lucy.

Bellinda

(*aside*) I will have the pleasure of teizing him. (*aloud*) Your affairs are in a very odd situation, but, Sir, in the first place I beg your pardon if I have not behav'd my selfe to you with the respect that I ought.

Gaymore

Dear Lucy, you might have omitted a complement which only serves to put me in mind that we are not so equal as I could wish.

Bellinda

Is your Inclination for me serious enough to make that uneasy to you?

Gaymore

So serious as to make me not able to endure an Engagement with any other Woman. Could you love me, Lucy?

Bellinda

The complement you make me in the condition I am in deserves a better return than the confession of a tenderness that might draw you deeper into a passion not worthy of you.

Gaymore

Are you not charming enough, Lucy, without the addition of so noble a sentiment?

Bellinda

I hear somebody coming. I beg you to retire, Sir, and let me have the honour of talking to you once more before you discover your selfe.

Gaymore

I will be govern'd by you.

(*Exit Gaymore.*)

(*Enter Ned.*)

Ned

I left you in so much vexation, Sister, I realy pity you and come to put you out of it.

Bellinda

Oh, Brother, I shall never be vex'd again as long as I live. I have the prettiest news in the world to tell you. Did not you meet William? not William thô, he told me all. Come along with me to my father. I'll tell him all. Come along. Lord, you are so slow—

(runs out)

Ned

The Girl's mad, I beleive. *(following her)*

Act 3d

(William, Gaymore following him with his Cane up)

William

Master, dear Master, for Heaven's sake—

Gaymore

Scoundrel! *(going to strike)*

William

As many blows as you please but do not ruin my Fortune. I was never near makeing it before.

Gaymore

You Rascal, you deserve to be Cudgell'd 2 hours together.

William

I submit to the Cudgel. You shall break that upon my shoulders, and I'll go fetch another if you please, but suffer me to accept the Good Luck that throws it selfe in my way.

Gaymore

Booby!

William

With all my heart, but Boobys have made their fortunes in all ages.

Gaymore

Son of a Whore!

William

That never was any Objection to a Man's fortune.

Gaymore

Rogue!

William

Then I'm sure I'm in the road to preferment.

Gaymore

Have you the Impudence to suppose I will let you impose on so honest a Gentleman as Sir John Hearty, and that I will be silent while you marry his Daughter in my name? If you dare think of such a project I will first inform this family of what thou art, and then turn you away. Do you hear?

William

I beg you would hear me, Sir. This poor Gentlewoman is in Love with me. I tell you, Sir, her heart is smitten, and I dare swear if I tell the poor thing that I am only your honour's footman she will scorn to forsake me. Only suppose this, and then why should my good fortune make you uneasy?

Gaymore

When I have discover'd your real Quality I care not what you do. If she is so mad to like you she does not deserve a better fate.

William

I will go then and prepare this generous Lady to see me in my own cloaths, and I hope she will like me as well lac'd with silk as with silver, and that I shall sit down at table before I dye, after waiting so long at the sideboard.

(*Exit William.*)

Gaymore

My Head is giddy with all that passes in this House. I guess Lucy has inform'd her mistrisse by this time. I'll see for her and enquire the success.

(*going, meets Ned Hearty*)

Ned

Hearkee, William, a word with you.

Gaymore

Have you any commands for me, Sir?

Ned

You make Love to Lucy.

Gaymore

She is so lovely 'tis hard to do otherwise.

Ned

I see thou'rt a fellow that knows the world. Don't you jest with her?

Gaymore

Sir, if I am serious, and if Lucy should have a taste for my Company why should—

Ned

A taste for thy Company! Ha, ha, ha, tis these pretty fashionable phrases that enchant Mrs Lucy, I suppose.

Gaymore

I only make use of the Phrases that come nearest to express my thoughts, but I presume, Sir, you do not intend to give your selfe the trouble to correct my Language. You were saying something about Mrs Lucy. Are you interested in her Conduct, Sir?

Ned

This is pleasant, 'igad. I think you give your selfe airs of Jealousie. Recollect your selfe a little and know that Lucy is not likely to fall to your Lot. I forbid you to think of her. Not that I am afraid she should Love thee, for I know the baggage has too much pride to condescend to a Livery, but I won't have a Footman for my Rival.

Gaymore

I can easily beleive you are not pleas'd with it, Sir, since as much a footman as I am, I'm not content to have you for mine.

Ned

You are to consider the distance between us.

Gaymore

I know my Duty, Sir—but you are then in earnest with her?

Ned

So much, that I have a design that I don't think fit to declare, but you may guess.

Gaymore

I perceive what you would have me Guess, Sir. No doubt Lucy is very sensible of the Honor you do her.

Ned

What do you think? Am I so ill fashion'd that a Girl can't love me?

Gaymore

Tis a difficult thing to praise a triumphant Rival.

Ned

That expression is a little familiar, but I forgive it to the uneasyness you are in, and to comfort thee must own I can't brag of many favors.

Gaymore

Lucy does not then know the Honor you intend her, Sir?

Ned

Oh yes; I have told her, and she does not seem much touch'd with it, but I don't doubt her good Sense will direct her in an affair so much to her advantage, and thô I had rather gain her by Inclination I love enough to think my selfe happy if I gain her any way. Be silent then, William; for the Future you may very well think, I won't suffer your pretentions where I have fix'd my serious Affection.

(Enter Lucy.)

Here comes the Beauty.

Bellinda

What's the matter, Sir, you seem disturb'd.

Ned

No great matter. I was speaking to William.

Bellinda

He looks melancholy. Did you chide him for any thing?

Gaymore

The Gentleman has declar'd him selfe your Lover, Lucy.

Bellinda

That is no fault of mine.

Gaymore

And forbids me that happyness.

Bellinda

He forbids me then to please you.

Ned

I don't forbid him to be pleas'd with you, my Angel, but I forbid him to tell you any thing about it.

Bellinda

Sir, he has told it me allready.

Ned

Then let him tell you so no more, at least not in my presence. Leave us, William.

Gaymore

Does Mrs Lucy joyn in that command?

Ned

How's that?

Bellinda

Pray Sir—

Gaymore

Is Mr Hearty so happy to please you?

Bellinda

Oh, there is no occasion of any body's forbidding me to like him.

Gaymore

Don't deceive me, dear Lucy.

Ned

I make a pretty figure here, truly! Leave us I say.

Bellinda

Pray, William, oblige the Gentleman.

Gaymore

(*aside to Bellinda going out*) Is [it] not you that I oblige? Ah, Lucy, why did not you tell me of your Lover?

(*manent* [remain] *Bellinda and her Brother.*)

Bellinda

Must not one be very ungratefull to refuse a heart to so sincere a passion?

Ned

(*Laughs*)

(*Enter Sir John.*)

Sir John

You are very merry, Son.

Ned

I am laughing at the rage I have put poor Gaymore into, by my Sister's orders. She has given me the part of her Lover to act, for the dear pleasure of tormenting a man she loves, and I was not very unwilling to be her instrument, on this occasion, because I think he deserves some punishment for his impertinent project, and he has it. I never a saw a poor wretch in more uneasyness in my Life.

Sir John

It will be all made up by the Joy of the discovery we have to make to him, and I think the jest has lasted long enough. You are not displeas'd with his behaviour, Bellinda?

Bellinda

(*sighing*) Indeed, Papa, I don't hate him.

Ned

I beleive not, if one may trust these little airs.

Bellinda

But, my dear Brother, what if I can get him to offer marriage before he knows who I am?

Ned

Why, you vain Devil, how can such a project come into your Head? But I am dear Brother again, heaven be prais'd. You were ready to break my head halfe an hour ago.

Bellinda

Pray, forget that part of the story.

Ned

No, no, I will have the revenge of laughing at the disquiet you were in. You can't imagine the ridiculous figure you made, Ha, ha, ha.

Sir John

Well, daughter, if you can find in your heart to so delay your Lover's happyness, you shall have my leave to divert your selfe your own way.

Bellinda

Oh Sir, tis the highest Obligation you can do me. Tis founding a lasting Happyness between Gaymore and I. I shall remember as long as I live that he would have taken me without either Riches or alliance, and if you knew what a force Gratitude gives to Inclination, and how necessary it is to love with all one's heart a Man one must pass one's Life with, you would forgive me this little tryal of his Love. When we are marry'd the story will divert us for ever. There is something in it so new, so particular, so charming—

Ned

Hey! how her tongue runs. This Love is a great prattler, I find, and I see a Girl will allways serve her own Vanity in the first place.

Sir John

I must own hers will be fully satisfy'd if she can bring this matter about, but do you realy think you can, child?

Bellinda

Halfe a dozen Glances more and 'tis done, Sir.

Ned

Do but observe her Gaity, while I am realy pitying what the Young Man suffers.

Bellinda

He will feel happyness more sensibly. I should despise him if he could think of marrying a Chambermaid without pangs of Reluctance. No, I would have his reason represent to him all the Refflections that are to be made on that Subject. He should know the Injury he is about to do his Fortune, his character, the hazard of disobliging his Father, and yet all these wise considerations be too weak for the power of—

Ned

Your charms, ha, ha, ha. The most insolent plan I ever heard of!

Sir John

'Tis the plan of a handsome wench of 18, Son, but Hist, here's Lucy.

(*Enter Lucy.*)

Lucy

Sir, I hope you han't forgot, I'm sure you was pleas'd to say more than once, that I might do what I would with Mr Gaymore, and realy I can't deny, but with your leave I have taken a little pains. I have no reason to think my Labour in vain. If your honour will discourse with him you'l see a finish'd piece of Work. He is mine from top to toe, and his Estate too into the Bargain, if my Young Lady can yeild it to me.

Sir John

Do you hear, Daughter? What say you to this terrible piece of News?

Bellinda

I won't rob her, Sir, of the fruit of her Labours; and to talk in her style, the man I marry shall be one I have taken pains about my selfe.

Lucy

You are very Generous, Madam. I hope my good Master won't oppose it.

Sir John

Oh, not I, since his Passion is so violent.

Ned

And for me, I promise to rejoyce at it.

Lucy

I give my humble thanks to all the noble Family. (*cursying*)

Sir John

But hearkee, on one condition; you must give him to understand a little who you are.

Lucy

I am afraid he will then soon understand the whole.

Sir John

Sure this finish'd piece of work won't fall to pieces for such a small Rub. I have too good an Opinion of thy Beauty.

Lucy

Lurd! here he comes! for Heaven's sake, leave me with him. I must now display all my Art.

Sir John

That's but reasonable. Come, Children.

(They go out.)

(Enter William.)

William

Bright Lady, I suffer like a Lobster on the Spit in every moment of your Absence. Have you no little impatiencys in mine?

Lucy

Why realy, Sir, I can't help wishing that we were never to part.

William

Madam, I am ready to drop down under the weight of my happyness.

Lucy

I am sure I would not give you a fall for the world.

William

Those words raise me.

Lucy

(with her fan to her Face) My heart is full of kindness for you.

William

Pretty Expression! Let me kiss it while tis warm on your mouth.

(kisses her)

Lucy

(aside) I'll strike while the Iron is hot. *(to him)* Sir, my Father has just now given me leave to tell you that our Nuptials shall be celebrated when you please.

William

I am sensible of my own unworthyness. I have no merit but that of pleasing you, and therefore, can't you give your hand without Sir John Hearty?

Lucy

(*giving her hand*) I give it as the pledge of our union.

William

And I receive it as an Honour I do not deserve.

Lucy

The honour is on my side, Heaven knows.

William

Oh no, I know better things.

Lucy

I look upon your Heart as the greatest Fortune Heaven could bestow on me.

William

We are not yet thoroughly acquainted. I wish you may allways be as well satisfy'd.

Lucy

Your modesty makes me blush. You are not sensible how much I am oblig'd to you.

William

Alas, alas, I am afraid I am too impudent.

Lucy

Tis high time to tell you, Sir, that I can not shew you too much respect.

William

I cannot bear those words from you to me.

Lucy

I know my selfe but too well.

William

But you don't know me, there's the devil on't, and when you do know me I am afraid you won't think me worth knowing. All is not gold that glisters.

Lucy

(*aside*) Here is some mystery in these words. (*to him*) What's the meaning of all this?

William

(*groaning*) The Hare is started.

Lucy

You make me very uneasy. Is it possible, after all, that you are not—?

William

Ah, you discover my nakedness.

Lucy

Pray, explain your selfe.

William

Let me consider how to express it. (*pauses*) Dear Madam, is your Flame very fierce? I shall throw a confounded deal of cold Water upon it!

Lucy

I am impatient.

William

In one word, I am—did you never see a brass shilling? That may give you some Idea of my Circumstances. Thô it looks like Silver yet—

Lucy

Your name, without more ado.

William

(*aside*) My Name! Shall I tell her my name is Will Swing? no! she'll bid me be hang'd. What shall I do? (*to her*) Do you dislike a Soldier?

Lucy
A soldier!

William
Ay, one of those Soldiers that stand Centinel on the stair head.

Lucy
Then you are not Gaymore?

William
He is my commander.

Lucy
Scoundrel!

William
(*aside*) I thought as much.

Lucy
See this puppy here!

William
(*aside*) I am kick'd down 3 pair of stairs.

Lucy
I have been racking my brains for expressions that were respectfull enough, and my knees ake with the humility of the curtsies I have made him.

William
Alas, Madam, if your Ladyship would prefer your pleasure to your pride I should acquit my selfe much better than most Gentlemen in the nation.

Lucy
(*aside Laughs*) I can't help laughing at the fright he is in. (*to him*) I han't so much pride as you think, and I forgive you with all my heart.

William
Your goodness confounds me, but I will do my best to recompence your Ladyship one way or other. You may expect wonders.

Lucy
The Centinel at Mr Gaymore's door deserves the brusher of my Lady's Combs.

William

The brusher of Mrs Bellinda's Combs!

Lucy

She is my Commander.

William

Oh, Pox!

Lucy

Take your revenge.

William

And I have been trembling before this Slut this hour together!

Lucy

Let us come to the point. Do you love me still?

William

Yes, by my Faith; thou hast neither lost thy Eyes or thy Nose, and I remember we swore fidelity in spite of all Objections.

Lucy

Let us comfort one another, then, on the loss of our Quality, and not discover the mistake to our masters. Here comes yours. I'll be gone. (*cursying very low*) Sir, your most Obedient, humble Servant.

William

(*bowing to the Ground*) Madam, your slave to all Eternity. Ha, ha, ha.

(*Enter Gaymore.*)

Gaymore

I see you have been talking with Bellinda. Have you obey'd my Orders?

William

Yes, upon my Life, Sir, and the poor Soul is so mild, and so contented. Oh, my Little William (said she) I love thee and not thy Cloaths, and I dare swear thou lookst as handsome behind the Coach as thy Master that rides in it.

Gaymore

What nonsense is all this?

William

I am in such good earnest, Sir, that I beleive I shall marry her within this two days.

Gaymore

How, marry her!

William

A great piece of busyness, very difficult truly.

Gaymore

Then you have not confess'd the truth.

William

What would you have, Sir? I'll marry her in my Livery Coat, nay in my Frock, if you provoke me. Do you think that a Woman in love with such a shape as this will mind triffles? I have no occasion for your Coat to shine in her Eyes. You make [i.e. may] take it back when you please and give me my own.

Gaymore

You're a Rascal, I see all this is a Trick, and I must desire Sir John Hearty to take care of his Daughter.

William

And do you think the good old man will break his Child's heart for so small a matter? He knows she can't live without me.

Gaymore

Have you seen Lucy?

William

I did not mind her if I did. I have not much regard for chambermaids, and you may do what you please with her.

Gaymore

The fellow's drunk or mad. Begone and sleep.

William

I don't expect you should leave off this way of speaking presently, but when I am marry'd 'tis to be hop'd I shall hear another Tone.

(*Enter Bellinda.*)

Good morrow, Lucy. Be kind to William; the fellow has some good in him.

(*Exit.*)

Bellinda

Sir, I have spoke to Sir John Hearty, but I cannot convince him of the Truth; therefore you must declare your selfe, I think.

Gaymore

(*aside*) How lovely she looks! Why should Young Hearty have been beforehand with me? (*to her*) I'll ride away immediately and take this fellow with me, and leave a note for Sir John that shall let him into the whole Mystery.

Bellinda

(*aside*) Is all his Love come to this? Ride away! my heart sinks!

Gaymore

You don't speak. Won't this method do the busyness?

Bellinda

(*aside*) It won't do mine, I'm sure. (*to him*) Yes, But—

Gaymore

I see nothing else that can be done except I was to go my selfe to him and speak in person, which several reasons hinder me from doing, and hastens my retreat.

Bellinda

As I am ignorant of those reasons, Sir, I can neither approve or blame them.

Gaymore

You may easily guess them, fair Lucy.

Bellinda

Alas, Sir, I am but a chambermaid and I find it in your behaviour but too sensibly. You hate Mrs Bellinda, it may be.

Gaymore

Have I no other reason, think you, to avoid this place?

Bellinda

I don't know. I have not the vanity to think my selfe important enough to engage you any resolution.

Gaymore

Nor you have not curiosity enough to enquire my thoughts of you. Adieu for ever.

Bellinda

You don't understand me, Sir.

Gaymore

—but too well, and I desire you would not explain it to me in a clearer manner.

Bellinda

You are going, then?

Gaymore

You would hasten me.

Bellinda

How well you guess my meaning.

Gaymore

This is too clear indeed—

(going out)

Bellinda

(aside) He goes! I won't love him, I hate him—he stops, he looks back, shall I call him? I can't do it! This is something my Brother has said. What made me employ that Giddy Creature? He never lov'd nothing in his Life, he has no notion—is all my power come to this? I shall dye with confusion—Oh he turns, I revive, but he shall see me going now.

(She makes an offer of going.)

Gaymore

You slipt a word of complaint just now, Lucy, and I won't let you go without showing you that you have no reason to complain of me.

Bellinda

It can be of no consequence to you, Sir, to be justify'd in my Opinion.

Gaymore

That is, you won't talk to me, but why should you, after your Engagement with Mr Hearty?

Bellinda

But what makes you fancy me in any such Engagement?

Gaymore

Did you not send me out of the Way in order to be left alone with him? Could you give me a greater proofe of Indifference or him of Inclination?

Bellinda

(*aside*) He's only Jealous, the dear Creature! (*to him*) You draw strange inferences from triffles.

Gaymore

Teach me to think better, then, charming Lucy. Let me beg you to be sincere. Tell me your real thoughts; you know mine but too well.

Bellinda

What signifys Explanations to one that is going to ride off?

Gaymore

I will not leave you if you wish I should not.

Bellinda

Do not be too inquisitive into my wishes. I may think what is not proper to be told, and why should you be so curious as to what passes in my heart?

Gaymore

Can you be ignorant, that there is nothing so important to me as that?

Bellinda

Why, I own you have taken some pains to make me think so, but If I am so credulous to beleive it, what follows? I will open my breast to you. This Love of yours is a triffling concern to you. There are a thousand ways of putting it out of your head. You will recollect sooner or later the distance between us. You will see variety of new Objects in London, fine Ladys that will endeavor to please you, endless Amusements that present themselves to a Man of your Fortune, alltogether can't fail to make you forget me, or if I am remember'd, you laugh at the time you have thrown away in my Company. But alas, for me the case is very different. If I remember you, as I am afraid I shall, what shall help me against so fatal an Impression? Where shall I pass the uneasy moments of your Absence? All the Splendor of a Court could not please me without you. Imagine to your selfe the pangs I shall feel, and be so generous, not to name Love any more to me. For my part I should scruple to own mine if I felt it, and I would contribute nothing on my side to any projects that are unworthy of your Birth. You see, Sir, I have so much command over my Inclinations not to discover them when they are too presumeing.

Gaymore

My dear Lucy, this innocent description of thy tenderness pierces my very heart. I respect and I adore you. Birth, Fortune, and Reputation are triffles not to be nam'd when they stand in Competition with such a heart. Mine is yours for ever, and my hand shall go along with it.

Bellinda

You deserve I should accept it for daring to throw such a temptation in my way, and am not I very generous to dissemble how I am touch'd? Do you think this Command of my Passions can last for ever?

Gaymore

Then you love me, my charming angel?

Bellinda

No, no, but do not ask that Question over again. I'm afraid I should make another answer.

Gaymore

I am afraid of nothing but loseing thee.

Bellinda

You have forgot Mr Hearty.

Gaymore

No, beautifull Lucy, I am no longer in pain about him. You are too sincere to be capable of a trick. I see it in every lovely line of that dear Face. You are sensible of Tenderness, and I cannot look on you without Transport.

Bellinda

(*sighing*) To what purpose these transports?

Gaymore

Will you refuse me, then?

Bellinda

What, would you realy marry me? Consider who I am, represent to your selfe your Father's anger, all the Consequences—

Gaymore

My Father cannot look on thee without being charm'd. My Estate is large enough without any Addition. You shall dispute no more, for I can never change my Opinion.

Bellinda

You can never change! Ah Gaymore, I am charm'd with that assurance.

Gaymore

Constrain your selfe then no longer. Let me be so happy to hear that you love me—

Bellinda

I can now love you with Honour. I have no more to ask. You will never change?

Gaymore

Never.

(*Enter Sir John, Ned, Will and Lucy.*)

Bellinda

Come, my incredulous Brother, and you, Sir, be Wittness of my Triumph, and see your Daughter the happiest woman upon Earth.

Gaymore

How, Sir John Hearty your Father!

Bellinda

Yes, we have trick'd one another. I have the Joy of being sure of your heart, and you may judge of mine by the pains I have taken to examine into yours.

Sir John

(*giving him a letter*) Do you know this hand? You'll see I was inform'd of your design, which made me disguise my daughter, but she only knew your name from your own mouth.

Gaymore

I am every way happy, and I thank you, Madam, for the Oppertunity you have given me of convinceing ⟨myself⟩ of the truth of your Love.

Ned

(*embraceing him*) Will Gaymore forgive me the disquiet I gave William?

Gaymore

I am oblig'd to you for an uneasyness that adds to my present Felicity.

William

(*to Lucy*) For you, Madam, you have lost your rank, but you have got William by this Frolic.

Lucy

Well; and you've got Lucy.

Sir John

My dear children, I hope these little adventures will prove the Foundation of a lasting happyness, and I have no reason to repent the Indulgence I have shown to your Fancies.

> Would men when to a riper judgment grown
> Kindly Forgive the Follys once their own,
> The Name of Parent children would revere
> And view with kindness when not forc'd by Fear.

APPENDIX I

Text   Bod. MS Eng. misc. b. 169, f. 59 *Written* in December 1736, when LM told Algarotti: 'My picture went last, wrapp'd up in poetry without Fiction.' *Printed* in *Bodleian Library Record*, 1981, p. 240 (see above, p. 287).

This once was me, thus my complexion fair,
My cheek thus blooming, and thus curl'd my Hair,
This picture which with pride I us'd to show
The lost ressemblance but upbraids me now,
Yet all these charms I only would renew   5
To make a mistrisse less unworthy you.

'Tis said, the Gods by ardent Vows are gain'd,
Iphis her wish (however wild) obtain'd,
Pygmalion warm'd to Life his Ivory maid,
Will no kind power restore my charms decaid?   10

With useless Beauty my first Youth was crown'd,
In all my Conquests I no pleasure found,
The croud I shunn'd, nor of Applause was vain
And Felt no pity for a Lover's pain.
The pangs of passion coldly I despise   15
And view'd with scorn the ravage of my Eyes.
Now that contempt too dearly is repaid,
Th'impetuous Fire does my whole Soul invade.
O more than Madness!—with compassion View
A Heart could only be enflam'd by You.   20
In that Lov'd Form there does at once unite
All that can raise Esteem, or give delight,
A Heart like mine is not below your care,
Artless and Honest, tender and sincere,
Where no mean thought has ever found a place   25
Look on my Heart, and you'll forget my Face.

3–4 Quoted from 'Satturday', lines 45–6, p. 202 above.
   8 Iphis, a girl brought up as a boy, had her prayer for manhood granted when she fell in love with another woman (Ovid, *Metamorphoses*, IX. 666–797); LM seems to liken herself to Pygmalion while Algarotti is the female statue.

[Riddle]

Text Bod. MS Eng. misc. b. 169, f. 59 *Written* in company with Hervey, perhaps in 1736. He scribbled a riddle (answer: 'Wortley'): 'The Stuff which we find on beer when tis new / And what all the Wor[l]d say when they [say] what's not true.' LM labelled this 'Hervey' and wrote in her own hand a riddle for 'Montagu'. *Printed* in *Bod. Lib. Record*, 1981, p. 240.

> What Bridgman oft shews as the best of his Works
> And what would make tremble the fiercest of Turks.

  1 Landscape gardener Charles Bridgman (d. 1738) was fond of raising 'mounts'.

Text Bod. MS Eng. misc. b. 169, f. 60 *Written* probably 1736: LM sent Algarotti 'so many verses' (*Letters*, 2. 110). *Printed* in *Bod. Lib. Record*, 1981, p. 243.

> The Gods are not so blest as she
> Whose ravish'd Eyes are fix'd on thee
> Who listens to the soothing sounds
> Of that soft voice which gently wounds
> And sees with more than Human Grace   5
> Sweet smiles adorn thy Angel Face.
>
> But when you tenderly approach
> Panting and breathless at your touch
> I can't support with dazled sight
> Th'impetuous torrent of Delight,   10
> My Heart beats thick, my senses fail,
> Disorder'd, blushing, cold, and pale,
> I sink beneath the powerfull Joy,
> I faint, I tremble and I dye.

  11–14 LM's copy shows that she drafted and re-drafted these lines, whose model is the style of Sappho.

Text Bod. MS Eng. misc. b. 169, f. 60 *Written* probably 1736. *Printed* in *Bod. Lib. Record*, 1981, p. 244.

> Come cool Indifference and calm my Breast,
> Let me forget that I was ever blest.
> If ardent passions are not made to last
> This dear Impression may be soon defaced.

  1 This echoes another of LM's poems (above p. 295); Frances Greville was to write a famous 'Prayer for [or 'Ode to'] Indifference' about twenty years later.
  3–4 These lines echo earlier words but reverse earlier sentiments (above pp. 244, 306).

APPENDIX II

Carabosse

ONCE upon a time there were a Prince and a Princess (for it was thus that my nurse began all the stories with which she rocked me to sleep). The Prince was brave and generous, the Princess beautiful and wise; their virtue and their mutual and constant love were at once the glory and the shame of the century. But as there is no such thing as perfect happiness, they had no children. The temples of all the gods were loaded with their offerings, and all the good fairies of the neighbourhood with their presents, in order to obtain the only thing that they wanted. It is true that the Princess could never be persuaded to inquire after the bad fairies, and it was in vain that the Prince showed her that the wicked could injure as easily as the good could be of service. She always said that to pay court to the vicious was a kind of worship paid to vice and she could not bring herself to it. It is even said that she sometimes allowed herself to blame their conduct in a somewhat foolhardy manner. Finally her wishes were fulfilled: she became pregnant. She did not forget to invite to her lying-in all the good fairies who were her friends, and she prepared presents worthy of being offered to them. To give gems or gold to the mistresses of mines would have insulted them; she knew that they took such little account of it that they often heaped it on the most unworthy mortals the better to show their scorn. She had collected with infinite care beautiful passionate poetry composed by sincere lovers, the portrait of a pretty nun who had never thought about earthly love, a vial (very small to be sure) of tears shed by a young and rich widow alone in her room, and books of theology that had never bored anyone. The fairies were all astonished that she should have been able to find so many rare and precious things; they were eager to show their gratitude by making her child the most accomplished and the happiest person in the world. She brought into the world a little Princess. Scarcely had she seen the light when the fairy Bellinda exclaimed, 'I give her a noble and touching beauty.' She had not finished speaking when a noise was heard like a hundred cannons discharged at once, a hissing like a thousand furious serpents, and they saw coming down the chimney the fairy Carabosse mounted astride an enormous toad. I do not wish to sully my paper with the description of her form, made to inspire disgust and horror. 'I wish' (she cried in a raucous voice) 'that this dear girl lose this admirable beauty by smallpox at the age that she begins to feel its advantages.' The fairy Spirituelle, confident of softening this misfortune, said, 'I give her the finest memory that has ever been, a sound taste, an astonishing vivacity, tempered by a judgement that will measure all her words. She will excel in all kinds of writing: she will be learned without vanity, and lively without giddiness.' 'This wit' (replied Carabosse, with a scornful smile) 'will serve only to attract enemies; she will always be the prey of fools, torn by their malice, persecuted by their attentions.' 'I wish', said the shining Argentine, coming forward, 'that her father be the richest lord of his rank, and that her husband have millions in gold.' 'Yes,' interrupted Carabosse, 'she shall live in the midst of treasures without ever seeing any at her disposal.' 'I endow her', said Hygeia, 'with wholly reliable health, which neither sorrows nor fatigue will be able to diminish.' 'This health', answered Carabosse, 'will inspire in her the rashness to undertake reckless enterprises, and to risk dangers, which will always surround her.' 'She will have', said the lovely Harmonie, 'an exact ear and an exquisite taste in music—' 'I take from her' (cried Carabosse interrupting her) 'the ability to sing, so that she feels all the rage of desire and impotence.' The good fairies, dismayed to see their blessings thus poisoned, spoke to each other quietly, and discussed in what manner this infernal malice could be defeated. Spirituelle believed she had found an infallible cure. 'We must take from her' (said she) 'all the vices, and she will find herself protected from misfortunes which follow them. I take from her' (she added in a loud and firm voice) 'all the seeds of envy and of avarice, which are the sources of mankind's misery; she shall have a sweet and even temper,—' 'and a great fund of tenderness,' cried Carabosse with a peal of laughter which made the palace shake. The good fairies flew away, seeing no remedy for so many evils. The Princess died of sorrow, her child grew more beautiful each day, but . . . [Here the manuscript is defective.]

The Turkey and the Ant

ONE fine autumn day a turkey was marching at the head of his flock with as much pride as a Roman consul at the head of the

Senate. 'My dear brethren' (he said with a Ciceronian eloquence) 'let us take advantage of the delights which nature provides for us. There is certainly no species more favoured under Heaven than ours. We have beauty, and wit into the bargain, and an exquisite taste to know how to enjoy our advantages, but alas! our life is as short as it is beautiful. Man, that cruel tyrant of nature, who is never surfeited with blood, only rarely allows us to reach old age; he pitilessly cuts the thread of our days. I see him already looking at our plumpness with a covetous eye, and in order to satisfy his brutal pleasure, he destines us perhaps (in a few days) some for the spit and the others for the pot. Our feeble innocence cannot resist his strength. Let us content ourselves with following the maxims of true wisdom: let us enjoy the present and submit to the future. I see the ground at the foot of this oak all blackened with a numberless crowd of ants. There is no game more excellent for health, nor more delicious in taste. Let us go, let us enjoy the blessing sent us by the gods.'

An ant replied to him—'And you barbarian, complaining of man! You believe that you are permitted to massacre a whole people for lunch! Know that when we see you plucked we regard that murderous hand as the instrument of just vengeance for the desolation of our race.'

A letter from Lady Wortley Montague, against a maxim of Mons. de la Rochefaucault's, 'that marriages are convenient, but never delightful.'

Text *Annual Register*, 1763, [part 2], pp. 204–9. (Square brackets enclose phrases and sentences omitted by the anonymous translator.) A different translation is in the partially spurious *Additional Volume to the Letters* of LM (1767), pp. 79–108.

IT appears very bold in me to attempt to destroy a maxim established by so celebrated a genius as Mons. de la Rochefaucault, and implicitly received by a nation which calls itself the only perfectly polite in the world, and which has, for so long a time, given laws of gallantry to all Europe.

But, full of the ardour which the truth inspires, I dare to advance the contrary, and to assert, boldly, that it is married love only which can be delightful to a good mind.

Nature sets before us pleasures suited to our species; we have but to follow the instinct infused by taste, and elevated by a lively and agreeable imagination, to find the only felicity mortals are capable of. Ambition, avarice, vanity, can give, in their most perfect enjoyments, but very moderate pleasures, not capable to affect a noble soul. We must regard the gifts of fortune but as so many steps to attain happiness; but we shall never find it, in obtaining her trifling favours, which are no more than the troubles of life, if they are not looked upon as necessary to obtain, or to preserve, a felicity more desirable.

That happiness is to be found only in friendship, founded upon perfect esteem, fixed upon long acquaintance, confirmed by inclination, and enlivened by the tenderness of love; which the ancients have very well described by the figure of a beautiful child: he is pleased with childish games, he is tender and delicate, incapable to hurt, charmed with trifles, all his designs terminate in pleasures; but those pleasures are sweet and innocent. They have represented under a very different figure a passion too gross to be named, but of which the multitude are only capable, I mean that of a satyr, which is more bestial than human; and they have expressed in that equivocal animal, the vice and brutality of the sensual appetite, which is, notwithstanding, the only foundation of all the fine system of polite gallantry.

A passion, that wishes only to content itself with the loss of what it thinks the most amiable in the world; a passion founded on injustice, supported by deceit, and followed by crimes, remorse, shame, and contempt;—can it be delightful to a virtuous heart? Yet this is the amiable equipage of all unlawful engagements; we find ourselves obliged to eradicate from the soul all the sentiments of honour inseparable from a noble education, and to live in an eternal pursuit of that which we condemn; obliged to have our pleasures impoisoned by remorse, and to be reduced to the unhappy state of renouncing virtue, yet not able to content ourselves with vice.

We cannot taste the sweets of perfect love but in a well-suited marriage. Nothing so much distinguishes a little mind as to stop at words. What signifies that custom (for which we see very good reasons) of making the name of husband and wife ridiculous? A husband signifies, in the general interpretation, a jealous mortal, a quarrelsome tyrant, or a good sort of fool, on whom we may impose any thing; a wife is a domestic dæmon, given to this poor man to deceive and torment him. The conduct of the generality of people sufficiently justifies these two characters. But I say, again, What signify words? A well-regulated marriage is not like those of ambition and interest: it is two lovers who live together. Let a priest pronounce certain words, let an attorney sign certain papers; I look upon these preparations as a lover does on a ladder of cords, that he fixes to the window of his mistress. [As long as they live together, what does it matter at what price and by what means?]

It is impossible that a perfect and well-founded love should be happy but in the peaceable possession of the object beloved, and that peace does not take from the sweetness and vivacity of a passion such as I have imagined. If I would amuse myself in writing romances, I should not place the seat of true happiness in Arcadia, or on the borders of Hymen. I am not such a prude as to limit the most delicate tenderness to wishes; I should begin the romance by the marriage of two persons united by their mind, taste, and inclination; can any thing be more happy than to unite their interest and their life? The lover has the pleasure of giving the last mark of his esteem and confidence to his mistress; she, in return, gives him the care of her repose and liberty. Can they give each other more dear or more tender pledges? And is it not natural to wish to give to each other incontestible proofs of that tenderness with which the soul is penetrated?

I know there are some people of false delicacy, who maintain that the pleasures of love are only due to difficulties and dangers. They say, very wittily, the rose would not be the rose without thorns, and a thousand other trifles of that nature, which make so little impression on my mind, that I am persuaded, was I a lover, the fear of hurting her I loved would make me unhappy, if the possession was accompanied with dangers to her. The life of married lovers is very different, they pass it in a chain of mutual obligations and marks of benevolence, and have the pleasure of forming the entire happiness of the object beloved; in which point I place perfect enjoyment.

The most trifling cares of economy become noble and delicate, when they are heightened by sentiments of tenderness. To furnish a room is no longer furnishing a room, it is ornamenting the place where I expect my lover; to order a supper is not simply giving orders to a cook, it is amusing myself in regaling him I love. These necessary occupations, regarded in this light by a lover, are pleasures infinitely more sensible and lively than cards and public places, which makes the happiness of the multitude incapable of true pleasure.—A passion happy and contented, softens every movement of the soul, and gilds each object that we look on.

To a happy lover (I mean one married to his mistress) if he has any employment, the fatigues of the camp, the embarrassments of court, every thing becomes agreeable when he can say to himself, it is to serve her I love. If fortune is favourable, (for that does not depend on merit) and gives success to his undertakings, all the advantages he receives are offerings [that he thankfully places at the feet of his charming friend and that are] due to her charms, and he finds, in the success of his ambition, pleasure much more lively and worthy a noble mind, than that of raising his fortune, or of being applauded by the public. He enjoys his glory, his rank, his riches, but as they regard her he loves; and it is her lover she hears praised, when he gains the approbation of the parliament, the praises of the army, or the favour of his prince. In misfortune, it is his consolation to retire to a person who feels his sorrow, and to say to himself in her arms, 'My happiness does not depend on the caprice of fortune; here is my assured asylum against all grief; your esteem makes me insensible to the injustice of a court, or the ingratitude of a master; I feel a sort of pleasure in the loss of my estate, as that misfortune gives me new proofs of your virtue and tenderness. How little desirable is grandeur to persons already happy? We have no need of flatterers or equipages; I reign in your heart, and I possess in your person all the delights of nature.' In short, there is no situation of which the melancholy may not be softened by the company of the person we love. Even an illness is not without its pleasures, when we are attended by one we love. I should never have done, was I to give you a detail of all the charms of an union in which we find, at once, all that [can satisfy a tender imagination and] flatters the senses in the most delicate and most extended pleasure; but I cannot conclude without mentioning the satisfaction of seeing each day increase the amiable pledges of our tender friendship, and the occupation of improving them according to their different sexes. We abandon ourselves to the tender instinct of nature refined by love. We admire in the daughter the beauty of the mother, and respect in the son the appearances of understanding and natural probity which we esteem in the father. It is a pleasure of which God himself (according to Moses) was sensible, when seeing what he had done, he found it good.

A propos of Moses, the first plan of happiness infinitely surpassed all others; and I cannot form to myself an idea of paradise more delightful than that state in which our first parents were placed: that did not last because they did not know the world; (which is the true reason that there are so few love-matches happy.) Eve may be considered as a foolish child, and Adam a man very little enlightened. When people of that sort meet, they may, perhaps, be amorous at first, but that cannot last. They form to themselves, in the violence of their passions, ideas above nature; a man thinks his mistress an angel because she is handsome; a woman is inchanted with the merit of her lover, because he adores her. The first change of her complexion takes from his adoration, and the husband ceasing to adore her, becomes hateful to her, who had no other foundation for her love; by degrees they are disgusted with one another, and, after the example of our first parents, they throw on each other the crime of their mutual weakness; afterwards coldness and contempt follow a great pace, and they believe they must hate each other because they are married; their smallest faults are magnified in each other's sight, and they are blinded to their mutual perfections [that might touch them in any other person]. A commerce established upon passion can have no other attendants. A man, when he marries his mistress, ought to forget that she then appears adorable to him; to consider that she is but a simple mortal, subject to diseases, caprice, and ill-humour. He must prepare his constancy to support the loss of her beauty, and collect a fund of complacency, which is necessary for the continual conversation of the person who is most agreeable, and the least unequal. The woman, on her side, must not expect a continuance of flatteries and obedience. She must dispose herself to obey agreeably, a science very difficult, and, of consequence, of great merit to a man capable of feeling. She must strive to heighten the charms of a mistress by the good sense and solidity of a friend. When two persons, prepossessed with sentiments so reasonable, are united by eternal ties, all nature smiles upon them, and the common objects become charming.

It appears to me a life infinitely more delightful, more elegant, and more pleasurable, than the best conducted and most happy gallantry. A woman capable of reflection cannot but look upon her lover as her seducer, who would take advantage of her weakness to give himself a momentary pleasure, at the expence of her repose, of her glory, and of her life. A highwayman who claps a pistol to the breast, to take away your purse, appears to me more honest and less guilty; and I have so good an opinion of myself as to think, was I a man, I should be as capable to lay the plan of an assassination as that of debauching an honest woman, respectable in the world, and happy in her marriage. Should I be capable of empoisoning a heart by inspiring it with an unhappy passion, to which she must sacrifice her honour, tranquillity, and virtue! Shall I render a person despicable because she appears amiable to me! Shall I reward her tenderness by rendering her house no longer agreeable, her children indifferent, and her husband hateful! I believe these reflections would appear of the same force, if my sex did render such proceedings excusable; and I hope I should have sense enough not to think vice less vicious because it was in fashion.

I esteem much the morals of the Turks, an ignorant people, but very polite, in my opinion. A gallant convicted of having debauched a married woman, is looked upon by them with the same horror as an abandoned woman by us; he is sure never to make his fortune; and every one would be ashamed to give a considerable employment to a man suspected of being guilty of so enormous a crime.—What would they say in that moral nation, were they to see one of our anti-knight-errants, who are always in pursuit of adventures to put innocent young women in distress, and to ruin the honour of women of fashion; who regard beauty, youth, rank, and virtue, but as so many spurs to incite their desire to ruin, and who place all their glory in appearing artful seducers, forgetting that, with all their care, they can never attain but to the second rank, the devils having been long since in possession of the first!

I own, that our barbarous manners are so well calculated for the establishment of vice and misery (which is inseparable from it) that they must have hearts and heads infinitely above the common, to enjoy the felicity of a marriage such as I have described. Nature is so weak, and so given to change, that it is difficult to support the best-founded constancy, amidst those many dissipations that our ridiculous customs have rendered inevitable. A husband who loves his wife, is in pain to see her take the liberties which fashion allows; it appears hard to refuse them to her, and he finds himself obliged to conform himself to the polite manners of Europe; to see, every

day, her hands a prey to every one who will take them; to hear her
display, to the whole world, the charms of her wit; to shew her neck
in full day; to dress for balls and shows, to attract admirers, and to
listen to the idle flattery of a thousand and a thousand fops. Can any
man support his esteem for a creature so public, or, at least, does
not she lose much of her merit!

I return to the Oriental maxims, where the most beautiful women
content themselves with limiting the power of their charms to him
who has a right to enjoy them; they have too much honour to wish
to make other men miserable, and are too sincere not to own they
think themselves capable of exciting passion.

I remember a conversation I had with a lady of great quality at
Constantinople, the most amiable woman I ever knew in my life,
and for whom I had afterwards the most tender friendship; she
owned, ingenuously, to me, that she was content with her husband.
What libertines you Christian women are! (she said;) it is permitted
you to receive visits from as many men as you please; and your
laws permit you, without limitation, the use of [love and] wine.
I assured her she was very much misinformed; that it was true we
received visits, but those visits were full of form and respect, and
that it was a crime to hear talk of love, or to love any other than our
husbands. Your husbands are very good (said she, laughing) to
content themselves with so limited a fidelity. Your eyes, your hands,
your conversation, are for the public, and what do you pretend to
reserve for them? Pardon me, my beautiful sultana, (added she,
embracing me) I have all possible inclination to believe what you
say, but you would impose upon me impossibilities. I know the
amorous complexion of you infidels, I see you are ashamed of them,
and I will never mention them to you more.

I found so much good sense and truth in all she said, that I could
scarcely contradict her; and I owned at first, that she had reasons
to prefer the morals of the mussulmen to our ridiculous customs
which are surprisingly opposite to the severe maxims of Christianity
[confused with the Libertinage of the Lacedemonians]. And, notwithstanding our foolish manners, I am of opinion, that a woman,
determined to find her happiness in the love of her husband, must
give up the extravagant desire of being admired by the public;
and that a husband who loves his wife, must deprive himself of the
reputation of being a gallant at court. You see that I suppose two
persons very extraordinary; it is not, then, very surprising such

a union should be rare in a country, where it is necessary, in order
to be happy, to despise the established maxims.

I am, &c.

Letter to Mademoiselle

YOU do me great honour (Mademoiselle) to think of me, in a situation as happy as yours, and among illustrious people who should
make you scorn us miserable living ones. I notice that you have
profited infinitely from their company, your style having been
considerably improved during your sojourn in the Elysian Fields.
Your earthly works, although very learned, do not match the beauty
of the letter with which you have honoured me. The pedantry of
your century, which had hardly influenced you, has given way to
French ease and to an agreeable bantering which you have found
(perhaps) in the conversation of Petronius. I congratulate you with
all my heart for these new delights, which I value higher than the
mastery of a hundred different languages. I would willingly exchange six of which I am master for a single ode of Horace or of
Rousseau. I believe that you are now sufficiently free of prejudices
to allow even criticism of your works without impatience, and you
will allow me to say freely that your reasons to prove your thesis

'The study of literature is suitable for a Christian woman'

appear to me sometimes rather weak, and always recited in a dry
and scholastic manner. It is true that you could excuse yourself for
having employed the pedant's expressions for the same reason that
you wore a ruff; it was the fashion of your time to have the mind and
the body stiff, and it is necessary to respect, even to conform to
public foolishness. This century teaches us to view everything from
a political point of view, and it is by this that I should aspire to
prove that learning is very necessary for women. It is certain that
with little knowledge, one begins to doubt, and that doubt naturally
inspires modesty, a virtue which has always been recommended to
the sex, and which they can hardly do without since they are brought
up in such gross ignorance that it is enough for them to mumble
paternosters, in order to believe themselves inspired by Heaven,
and consequently worthy of managing everything at home, scorning
their husbands and maltreating their servants. I dare boldly say

that the behaviour of most women does more harm than good. Imperceptibly they become creatures more harmful than useful. I attribute this corruption to the bad education which stifles the natural wit of some, and increases the foolishness of others. If men would only see us as an element in the state (for I submit to inferiority although I could name a thousand who have written, as you know, to prove the equality of the sexes) they ought to strive to use all talents profitably. Our frailty prevents us from serving in war, but this same frailty gives us great leisure for study. Those who succeed will be able to contribute to the Republic of Letters, and those who do not succeed will at least avoid idleness with all its consequences. We will not be forced to collect a stock of nonsense before daring to speak in elegant conversations, or shine for the moment solely by knowledge of the toilette or of the gaming table. You [?] exactly enough to have given in these [?] which are the shame of humanity.

Pity me, Mademoiselle, there is no such thing here as an academy of gentlemen or of ladies. I don't have a fresh pair of eyes; when they are tired I am forced to listen and talk of losses and gains, which are the only subjects of interest to modern Avignon. If I were honoured with company such as you have, I would renounce with pleasure all my barbarians, and would apply myself to cultivating the goodness which you have shown me with all the gratitude and respect that you deserve from

Mlle
etc.

I am so charmed by your coterie that if you promise to admit me immediately I shall throw myself into the Rhône to seek you, half through desire of seeing you, and half from boredom with all those whom I do see.

To my Reason

I've done with it, I give in, let us submit to fate—
And you, Reason, give up your useless efforts—
In sighs, in regrets, in delusions, in desires,
I let my spirit wander, and I dissolve in pleasure.
This is ludicrous, you say—I admit it, but alas!   5

Isn't human wisdom also ludicrous?
No doubt it's madness, but my madness is dear to me—
Precepts and deliberations, I beg you to be quiet.
These Princes, these Ministers, who are acclaimed for genius,
Who spend their tedious days in vain projects,   10
Are they then wise, and am I mad
When I create in my mind an idol to love?
But I am maddened (I admit it) when my heart tells me softly,
'Think well about it, Manon, he'll not love you;
You can tell from his manner, you can tell from yourself;   15
You understand too much about love when you're in love yourself.'
—This sad truth offends my pride—
I forget him, and Philante remains in my thoughts no more.

Answer to an impromptu Song

Sing, sing of your tenderness,
Steal my heart away by force or by guile,
Try to win it, you may, as far as I'm concerned,
I've made no attempt to defend it so far,
But you've been unable to capture it,   5
And you'll do just as well never to speak of it again.

GENERAL INDEX

INDEX OF FIRST LINES